Empires, Systems and States:
Great Transformations in International Politics

CAMBRIDGE
UNIVERSITY PRESS

PUBLISHED BY THE PRESS SYNDICATE OF THE UNIVERSITY OF CAMBRIDGE
The Pitt Building, Trumpington Street, Cambridge, United Kingdom

CAMBRIDGE UNIVERSITY PRESS
The Edinburgh Building, Cambridge CB2 2RU, UK
40 West 20th Street, New York, NY 10011-4211, USA
477 Williamstown Road, Port Melbourne, VIC 3207, Australia
Ruiz de Alarcón 13, 28104 Madrid, Spain

© British International Studies Association 2001

First published 2001

Printed in the United Kingdom by Henry Ling Ltd at the
Dorset Press, Dorchester, Dorset

A catalogue record for this book is available from the British Library

ISBN 0 521 01686 X Paperback

We Dedicate This Book To

MICHAEL BEVERLY NICHOLSON
1933–2001

In Recognition of His Contribution to the
Study of International Relations,
and as a Founder Member and Supporter of BISA

Empires, Systems and States: Great Transformations in International Politics

CONTENTS

NOTES ON CONTRIBUTORS

Giovanni Arrighi is Professor of Sociology and Director of the Institute for Global Studies in Culture, Power and History at The Johns Hopkins University. His latest books are *The Long Twentieth Century: Money, Power and the Origins of Our Times* (1994) and (with Beverly J. Silver) *Chaos and Governance in the Modern World System* (1999).

Ian Clark is Professor of International Politics at the University of Wales, Aberystwyth. His most recent book is *The Post-Cold War Order: The Spoils of Peace* (Oxford University Press, 2001) and he is now working on a book, also for OUP, entitled *Legitimacy in International Society*.

G. John Ikenberry is Peter F. Krogh Professor of Global Justice at the School of Foreign Service at Georgetown University. He previously taught at Princeton and the University of Pennsylvania. His most recent book is *After Victory: Institutions, Strategic Restraint and the Rebuilding of Order after Major War* (Princeton, 2001). He is the author of the forthcoming books, *State Power and World Markets* (Norton, 2002) co-authored with Joe Grieco, and editor of *American Power and the Future of the Balance of Power* (Cornell, 2002).

Robert Jervis is Adlai E. Stevenson Professor of International Politics at Columbia University. In 2000–2001 he was President of the American Political Science Association. His latest book is *System Effects: Complexity in Political and Social Life* (1997).

Nancy Kokaz is an Assistant Professor in the Political Science Department and Peace and Conflict Studies Program at the University of Toronto. Her research and teaching lie at the intersection of political philosophy and international relations.

Stephen D. Krasner is Graham H. Stuart Professor of International Relations at Stanford University. His recent work includes *Sovereignty: Organized Hypoocrisy* (Princeton University Press: 1999) and *Problematic Sovereignty: Contested Rules and Political Possibilities* (Columbia University Press: 2001).

Hudson Meadwell is an Associate Professor in the Department of Political Science at McGill University and a Research Associate in the Université de Montreal-McGill University Research Group in International Security.

Andreas Osiander studied international relations, history and economics at Tübingen, Paris and Oxford. He has been a junior research fellow at Balliol College, Oxford and held a similar post at the Humboldt University, Berlin. He is currently working on a book on the evolution of social and political macrostructures in the history of Western civilization.

Beverly J. Silver is Associate Professor of Sociology at The Johns Hopkins University. She is co-author of *Chaos and Governance in the Modern World System* (1999) and the author of *Workers of the World in the Twentieth Century* (forthcoming).

James Sofka is Resident Scholar at the Center for Governmental Studies and Teaching Fellow in the Department of Government and Foreign Affairs in the University of Virginia. He is currently completing a manuscript on the theory and practice of eighteenth century international politics.

Carolyn M. Warner is a 2001–02 National Fellow at the Hoover Institution, Stanford University, and an Associate Professor of Political Science at Arizona State University. Her research on imperialism and state destruction in Africa has appeared in the *Review of International Studies*, and the *Review of International Political Economy*. Her book, *Confessions of an Interest Group: the Catholic Church and Political Parties in Europe*, was published by Princeton University Press in 2000. With the aid of funding from the National Science Foundation (SES), the Hoover Institution and the European University Institute, she is conducting research on corruption and fraud in the European Union.

William Wohlforth is Associate Professor of Government at Dartmouth College, author of *Elusive Balance: Power and Perceptions during the Cold War* (Cornell, 1993), and editor of *Witnesses to the End of the Cold War* (Johns Hopkins, 1996) and *Cold War Endgame: Oral History, Analysis and Debates* (Penn State, forthcoming 2002).

Yongjin Zhang is Fellow at the Department of International Relations, Research School of Pacific and Asian Studies in the Australian National University. His main research interest is China and international society. His most recent work is *Power and Responsibility in Chinese Foreign Policy* (co-edited—forthcoming).

ACKNOWLEDGEMENTS

Empires, Systems and States is not only the fourth and final of the Special Issues brought together by the editorial team in the Department of International Politics at Aberystwyth, it is also the very last issue of the Journal that we will be publishing. We would thus like to take this opportunity to warmly thank all those who have supported us over the past few years. We have been fortunate to work with three supportive Chairs of BISA—Chris Brown, Christopher Hill and Richard Little—each of whom have offered valuable advice and encouragement. The same holds for the many members of BISA who have served on the *Review of International Studies* Editorial Committee. Those at Cambridge University Press, including Patrick McCartan, Sue Belo, Gwenda Edwards, Michael Cook and John Haslam, have produced and marketed the Journal with professionalism and enthusiasm. Closer to home, we would like to extend a special thank you to Steve Smith who was Head of Department when we took on the *Review* and provided the necessary resources and leadership at a critical time. And last but by no means least, our two serving editorial assistants—Fiona Stephen and Cindy Germain—whose hard work and dedication over four years has been quite indispensable to the success of the Journal. As this is our swan song, we would like to thank the increasing numbers of scholars from around the world who have submitted to the *Review* and refereed for the *Review*. The latter is time consuming and often goes unnoticed, but the plain fact is without the willingness of referees to pass academic judgement on the work of their colleagues there simply would not be a Journal.

We would also like to extend a word of encouragement and support to the new editorial team based at Exeter. When we took over the Review in 1998 we decided to undertake a number of reforms that we hoped would build on the achievements of our predecessors. We wish the very best to our successors in the expectation that their editorial life turns out to be as intellectually exciting and personally rewarding for them as it has been for the three of us. Finally, we would very much like to dedicate this issue to Michael Nicholson. He was a great friend to many who teach and research in the field of International Relations and a friend more generally to the Association he helped to form and supported unstintingly. His death in October has robbed our community of one of its most intelligent and thoughtful voices. He will be sorely missed by us all.

Michael Cox, Ken Booth and Tim Dunne

FOREWORD

Caught on the hop by both the ending of the Cold War and the demise of the Soviet Union, some specialists in the field of international relations have been endeavouring to make up lost ground by taking the idea of transformations in world history much more seriously than has been done in the past. Throughout the Cold War, there was always considerable scepticism about the so-called 'timeless wisdom of realism' and the associated assumption that the essence of international relations has remained unchanged across time. Nevertheless, during the Cold War, neorealism was extraordinarily successful in setting a research agenda that focused on international anarchy and the premise that system transformation could only be identified in terms of a shift from anarchy to hierarchy. Waltz's theory of international politics was designed to explain why such a transformation has persistently failed to materialize in world history. But there is now a growing recognition, closely associated with the increasing significance attached to constructivist methodologies, that international systems have taken radically different forms across space and time. As a consequence, an emerging research agenda is focusing on major transformations that have taken place in the history of international relations. To make progress, however, an increasingly sophisticated understanding of both the history and theory of international relations is required.

The neorealist assessment of transformation was, of course, challenged from the start. Ruggie famously argued that Waltz's theory was unable to identify feudalism as a distinctive era in the history of international relations. But although Westphalia has conventionally been seen to denote a major turning point, moving from medieval to modern international relations, it was not only Waltz who lacked the theoretical tools to characterize medieval international relations. The inablity of the field to take up Ruggie's challenge perhaps helps to explain why so few specialists questioned Waltz's belief in the enduring 'texture' of international politics. Moreover, no-one seriously denies that down through the ages, international history in all parts of the globe has taken the form of continuous cycles of war and peace. Moreover, the presumption that war is a ubiquitous feature of world history was compounded at the time of the Cold War by the unprecedented dangers associated with another world war. Many specialists in international relations were, not unnaturally, preoccupied by the threat of a global, nuclear holocaust and the urgent need to identify the necessary foundations for an enduring peace in the future. The image of an unchanging international system, therefore, provided a useful spur, driving on theorists in their endeavour to find ways of securing an unprecedented transformation in the historical pattern of international relations. Classical realists, such as Morgenthau, were very much in the vanguard of these attempts to provide a theoretical framework that pointed the way to perpetual peace. The revival of classical diplomacy, Morgenthau hoped, would give us the breathing space within which to create a future world state.

The end of the Cold War, however, put a new complexion on the whole question of system transformation. It led theorists to reassess where we are now positioned in the world history of international relations. There is, perhaps unsurprisingly, little agreement. At one extreme, it is being argued that we are moving into a neo-medieval era with sovereignty becoming increasingly fragmented. At the other extreme, a world state is being forecast. What these disagreements are demonstrating most clearly, is the almost mythical understanding of the past that has often prevailed in the study of international relations, and just how tenuous is our hold on many key theoretical concepts, such as anarchy, society, system, empire, the state, sovereignty, and the balance of power. As attempts are now being made to historicize our understanding of international relations more effectively, so it is becoming necessary to re-theorize some of the most basic concepts used to analyse international relations. The wide-ranging essays in this volume make an important contribution to the current move to historicize the study of international relations. Having read these essays it is very clear that it is essential to reorient our thinking on international relations in Africa and Asia as well as Europe and to reassess the modern world as well as the ancient world. It would be wrong, of course, to suggest that it is only in the wake of the Cold War that there have been attempts to dislodge the image of international relations being played out on a static and unchanging field, but what the essays in this volume do highlight is just how important it is to come to terms with the idea of transformations in international relations.

RICHARD LITTLE
University of Bristol

Empires, systems and states: great transformations in international politics

Introduction

'History is too important to be left to the historians'.[1]

The relationship between history, international history and international relations has never been an easy or a particularly amicable one. To talk of a cold war may be something of an exaggeration, but it does capture something about the way in which the various subjects tended to regard the other for the greater part of the post-war period.[2] Thus practising historians and international historians appeared to have little time for each other,[3] and together had even less for those seeking to establish the new discipline of International Relations. In their eyes 'IR' and its practitioners at best provided an academic gloss on current affairs, or worse still, engaged in an endless series of theoretical speculations about systems in general that told us hardly anything about the real world in particular. Meanwhile, those in International Relations came to look upon their peers in history as producing little more than a series of discrete tales about the past, whose most obvious common features were a failure to provide any serious explanation of why things happened, what generalizations might be drawn from specific events, and how to deduce patterns from a mass of empirical material. There were national variations, of course. In Britain, for example, academic boundaries were never so clearly defined. Indeed, many of the key figures in international relations such as Carr and Toynbee, Butterfield and Wight, were as much historians as they were anything else. Nor did British International Relations undergo the kind of behavioural *perestroika* that was to shape the development of the subject across the Atlantic from the late 1950s and increase the 'great divide' between the social sciences on the one hand—within which International Relations happened to be situated—and the humanities on the other, in which history found itself. The trajectory of International Relations in the United States, however, tended to take it away from history altogether. Hence, having begun life as an historically sensitive project under the watchful eye of Morgenthau in the immediate post-war years, American International Relations slowly but surely metamorphosed into something else, that not only seemed to value measurement and models above knowledge of the past but appeared to have no time for 'real' history' either. Why bother, in fact, if according to Waltz all international systems

---

[1] Quote from Christopher Thorne, 'International Relations and the Prompting of History', *Review of International Studies*, 9 (1983), p. 123.

[2] Caroline Kennedy-Pipe, 'International History and IR: opportunities for dialogue', *International Affairs*, 76: 4 (2000), pp. 741–54.

[3] Gordon Craig, 'The Historian and the Study of International Relations', *American Historical Review*, 88 (1983), p. 2.

were governed by the same law of anarchy? In this way a distance of some proportions opened up that expressed itself in terms of the department one belonged to, the colleagues one spoke to, the journals one wrote for, the conferences one attended, and even the type of books one read.

Fortunately, this estrangement was never total and there were always individuals in the different camps prepared to draw upon the work of those in other disciplines.[4] Even a conservative subject like history was never completely resistant to all forms of theory or intellectual experimentation, and a number of the more innovative scholars made increasing and impressive use of conceptual tools from outside of the subject—so much so that when one leading American historian called in 1980 for greater attention to be paid to what was going on in other fields, he came across as 'someone earnestly advocating the reinvention of the wheel'.[5] Nor, to be fair, were all students of International Relations completely indifferent to history. Indeed, some of IR's more important hypotheses—hegemonic stability theory and the notion of a democratic peace to name but two—could only have been developed in the first place by reference to the past. The past also made its presence felt with the ending of the Cold War: in part because one rather influential commentator at the time argued that it was now coming to an 'end',[6] but more importantly because of what was happening in Central Europe and the Balkans. Here 'history' began to assert itself with a vengeance as nations and peoples began to rediscover or reinvent an identity that had been previously been submerged under the blanket of official communism. In the majority of cases this simply led to the rewriting of school textbooks. Tragically, in the case of the former Yugoslavia, history returned in the form of ethnic cleansing and new (and not-so-new) racist mythologies designed to justify nation-building in states whose individual histories had previously been subsumed under one grand progressive narrative.

The recent 'turn' in International Relations to history in general, and what might be called 'grand history' in particular, was no accident therefore. It might even be argued that International Relations is actually *re*turning to a theoretically sensitive international history that had earlier informed the work of so many of the founding fathers of the discipline. Certainly, there are many trends in the social sciences that point towards a more fruitful dialogue between history, sociology, anthropology and international relations. Most obviously, as demonstrated by the various contributions to this Special Issue, the intellectual *zeitgeist* is one that privileges a cross-fertilization of ideas and approaches. To this, one might add the growing recognition that there are common concerns that require concerted co-operation among intellectuals from different backgrounds.[7] Today, almost no subject is immune from debates about globalization, and the threats (and possibilities) generated by late-modern forces of production and destruction. Closer to home, certain developments

---

[4] Paul W. Schroeder, 'History and International Relations Theory: Not Use or Abuse, but Fit or Misfit', *International Security*, 22:1 (1997), pp. 64–74.

[5] Patrick Finney, 'Still Marking Time? Text, Discourse and Truth in International History', *Review of International Studies*, 27:3, July 2001, pp. 291–308.

[6] On Francis Fukuyama see Chris Brown, 'History Ends, Worlds Collide', in Michael Cox, Ken Booth, and Tim Dunne (eds.), *The Interregnum: Controversies in World Politics, 1989–1999* (Cambridge: Cambridge University Press, 1999), pp. 41–58.

[7] This idea underpinned the previous *Review of International Studies* Special Issue: Ken Booth, Tim Dunne, and Michael Cox (eds.), *How Might We Live? Global Ethics in the New Century* (Cambridge: Cambridge University Press, 2000).

in International Relations hold out the promise of greater engagement with history, sociology, philosophy and comparative politics. The various voices in the Third Debate[8] have brought to the fore the importance of concepts long familiar to other social sciences, such as identity, agency and inter-subjectivity. At the other end of the theoretical spectrum, neo-classical realism is returning to the kind of systematic engagement with history that marked the wave of realist writings in the 1930s and 1940s.

What can International Relations bring to these debates about the formation and transformation of empires, systems and states? Realism has long been out 'on loan' to historical sociologists, many of whom have accepted its key assumptions of the state as actor, the primacy of military security, and the constraints imposed by the structure of self-help generated by the anarchical system.[9] It is this last factor that remains realism's most important contribution to grand history. Irrespective of what goes on inside leaders' minds, or what is held to be right, there are—it is argued— systemic pressures that can and do intervene between intentions and outcomes. Whether these structures are identified with anarchy or modernity, they form part of a 'discourse of eternity'[10] that separates communities into a world of territorial states. Other theoretical approaches also offer significant intellectual resources for understanding patterns of institutional variation in different international systems. The French Annales school, for example, has made one particular kind of contribution through its analysis of the complex ways in which material culture shaped the development of Europe between the fifteenth and eighteenth centuries.[11] Martin Wight's 'embryonic sociology of states systems' is another notion rich in potential too,[12] and though neglected for some time, is beginning to be tapped by modern scholars.[13] Wight is especially useful in bringing to our understanding of grand history a series of conceptual distinctions that enable us to differentiate between suzerainty, hegemony, empire and a 'states system', and whether or not the latter presupposes a common culture and always ends in empire?[14] Then of course there are those two giants of historical sociology—Weber and Marx—who perhaps asked the biggest question of all: under what conditions, and for what reasons, did the structures of economic and political modernity take root in only one part of the world and not others? For this was, as Karl Polanyi observed,[15] the greatest transformation of all, which not only led to the creation of the state as we know it

---

[8] For an elaboration of the different positions in the Third Debate see Steve Smith, 'Positivism and Beyond', in Steve Smith, Ken Booth, and Marysia Zalewski (eds.), *International Theory: Positivism and Beyond* (Cambridge: Cambridge University Press, 1996), pp. 11–44.

[9] This is not to suggest that they have not added to this model, only that they find this a convenient starting point. For a good overview of the relationship between historical sociology and IR, see Stephen Hobden, 'Theorising the International System: Perspectives from Historical Sociology,' *Review of International Studies*, 25:2 (1999), pp. 257–71.

[10] This is R.B.J.Walker's phrase. See his essay 'International Relations and the Concept of the Political', in Ken Booth and Steve Smith (eds.), *International Relations Theory Today* (Cambridge: Polity, 1995).

[11] See Fernand Braudel, *Civilisation matérielle, économie et capitalisme, XVe–XVIIIe siecle*, 3 vols (Paris: Armand Collin, 1979).

[12] An argument made by Andrew Linklater, 'The Sociology of States-Systems', unpublished paper, British International Studies Association Conference, Bradford, 18–20 December, 2000.

[13] Barry Buzan and Richard Little, *International Systems in World History* (Oxford: Oxford University Press, 2000).

[14] See Wight's essay 'De systematibus civitatum' in Andrew Linklater (ed.), *International Relations: Critical Concepts in Political Science*, vol. IV (London: Routledge, 2000), pp. 1253–73.

[15] Karl Polanyi, *The Great Transformation* (Boston, MA: Beacon Press, 1944).

(the most successful unit according to Charles Tilly for waging war against competitors),[16] but propelled Western Europe outwards in a dynamic, and often ruthless, fashion that uprooted other civilizations from the Americas to Asia, and as a result established for the first time in history that which had never existed before: a truly global international system dominated by empires of differing levels of development, varying degrees of influence and complex forms of rule.

Historically, the rise of the modern state has been intimately associated with the concept of sovereignty, and it has been commonplace to date its beginnings to the Peace of Westphalia which ended the Thirty Years' War in 1648. As an influential international lawyer noted three hundred years later, Westphalia was the 'majestic portal' which led 'from the old world into the new world'.[17] Other standard accounts are rarely as absolute in positing a world-historical turning point, but they do, nevertheless, lend support to the view that the Westphalian settlement constituted a defining moment in the history of European international relations. In his influential work, Stephen Krasner has sought to debunk what he sees as this myth of '1648',[18] and in his contribution here continues his assault on a theoretical and historical assumption that has unfortunately become one of those foundational 'truths' of which traditional international relations appears to be especially fond.[19] While his critique is in part aimed at the conventional interpretation of Westphalia, it ranges more widely to include the entire edifice of the 'sovereign state model', by which he means 'a system of authority based on territory, mutual recognition, autonomy, and control'. In practice sovereignty has been compromised in several ways according to Krasner, but primarily through conventions, contract and coercion. Conventions refer to agreements, such as human rights accords that governments sign up to even though this means their policies are subjected to external scrutiny. Contracts are agreements whereby two or more states permit a constraint on their autonomy in return for perceived gains. And coercion includes a range of measures such as economic sanctions, military intervention and settlements imposed on vanquished states after major conflicts. As Krasner observes, 'every major peace settlement from Westphalia to Dayton has involved violations of the Westphalian sovereign state model'.

Krasner's essay convincingly shows how international relations has become a prisoner of its own simplistic understandings of how sovereignty has been exercised in practice. At one level, this is an attack on the common sense of realism; but beneath the surface of his analysis, it is clear that Krasner does not want to jettison realism so much as reconstitute it on the basis of a sophisticated rationalist account of who gets what and how on a global scale. Like Weber he believes that social action is both instrumental and rational. This does not prevent state leaders from acting in accordance with agreed rules or normative expectations, but only providing that these are consistent with their calculation of the national interest. The key point

---

[16] Charles Tilly, *Coercion, Capital and European States, AD 990–1990* (Oxford: Blackwell, 1990).

[17] Leo Gross, 'The Peace of Westphalia 1648–1948', *American Journal of International Law*, 42 (1948), p. 28.

[18] Stephen D. Krasner, 'Westphalia and All That,' in Judith Goldstein and Robert Keohane (eds.), *Ideas and Foreign Policy* (Ithaca, NY: Cornell University Press, 1993).

[19] Daniel Philpott, for example, argues that while 'Westphalia was not a consummate fissure, it was still as clear as historical faults come'. See Daniel Philpott, 'Westphalia, Authority, and International Society', in Robert Jackson (ed.), *Sovereignty at the Millennium* (Oxford: Blackwell, 1999), p. 157.

for realists is that agreed rules and conventions are routinely violated. In other words, international norms have very little constraining effect on the actions of states. Consistent with the tradition of political realism, Krasner believes that 'organised hypocrisy' prevails because of the structure of anarchy. Echoing Waltz's famous aphorism about how anarchy causes war, Krasner argues that 'compromising the sovereign state model is always available as a policy option because there is no authority structure to prevent it'. States, particularly great powers, can violate even the most established rules of international society such as non-use of force and non-intervention in the affairs of another state. The possibilities for hypocrisy in the international sphere are multiplied by the fact that there are many rules and these are often contradictory. State leaders are therefore able to 'pick and choose among different rules'.[20]

More than any other contemporary realist, Krasner has taken on the constructivist argument that rhetoric constrains actions. It is quite possible, he argues, for states to compromise their sovereignty by signing up to international agreements on human rights standards in the knowledge that these will not be implemented in the domestic realm. They can read out a cognitive script at the UN General Assembly proclaiming the importance of universal rights, while allowing officers of their state to routinely torture citizens suspected of ideological or religious 'crimes'. In Krasner's rather damning words, 'actors say one thing and do another'.

Yongjin Zhang's essay on Chinese international relations challenges many of the realist assumptions underpinning Krasner's argument. Consistent with the framing themes of the volume, Zhang maintains that much of what passes for the history of relations between independent communities is highly Eurocentric. Despite fleeting accounts of China's encounter with the West,[21] mainstream international relations has not engaged seriously with ancient and imperial China. This, he argues, is a matter of regret because China represents a fundamental challenge to much of the received wisdom of Anglo-American IR. Most obviously, the Chinese system was especially interesting in that it evolved independently of European influence—or at least did until the nineteenth century. The imprint of modernity in Europe, forged by science, production and trade, left barely a mark on the Sinocentric world until the Opium Wars. This point was cruelly made by the Emperor Ch'ien-lung in 1793 to Lord Macartney who had been dispatched by George III with the aim of expanding trade relations. Such a request was not intelligible to the Chinese Emperor: not only had they no need for British products, the idea of conducting trade relations based on equality with a country ignorant of China's culture and rituals was anathema. The Emperor's advice to the King was that he 'should simply act in perpetual obedience so as to ensure that your country may share the blessings of peace'.[22]

The history of Chinese international relations is also significant because at different times it resembled a multi-states system, an empire, and a sovereign state. Zhang dates the emergence of a multi-state system from 770 BC until the

---

[20] Stephen Krasner, *Sovereignty: Organized Hypocrisy* (Princeton, NJ: Princeton University Press, 1999), p. 6.

[21] Notably the essay by Gerrit Gong on 'China's Entry into International Society', in Hedley Bull and Adam Watson (eds.), *The Expansion of International Society* (Oxford: Clarendon Press, 1984).

[22] Onuma Yasuaki, 'When was the Law of International Society Born? An Inquiry of the History of International Law from an Intercivilizational Perspective', *Journal of the History of International Law*, 2:1 (2000), pp. 1–66, at pp. 28–9.

establishment of 'the first universal empire by the Qin in 221 BC'. During this time 'some of the institutional practices' that characterized the modern European international system 'were already present and functioning in the system of states in Ancient China'. Yet it is the '*Pax Sinica*' that perhaps holds the greatest interest for scholars. This is the label Zhang gives for the imperial Chinese world order that lasted for over two millennia, longer than any other institutional arrangement for organizing international relations.[23] Central to the empire was the 'tribute system' of trade relations which was based on a hierarchy 'with the Chinese emperor sitting at the apex of this order' with a mandate to rule '*Tianzia* (all-under-the heaven)'.[24] Following Reus-Smit's constructivist account of successive European international societies, Zhang claims that we cannot understand Sinocentrism without uncovering its moral purpose and guiding constitutional principles. Tributes thus were not just a form of economic exploitation, but also reflected an elaborate system of obligation informed by Confucian values. But this system could not endure in an age of European expansion, and as Zhang goes on to show, imperial collapse (and with it the disintegration of a distinctly Chinese world order with its own rationale and institutions) quickly followed under the assaults launched by the Europeans. The cherished principles and norms that had hitherto organized their world were rendered irrelevant, and China began another long march which concluded initially in revolution in 1949, and then after decades of Maoist isolation in a tentative—and as yet incomplete—effort to rejoin global international society.

If China offers a stark example of a non-European civilization that successfully resisted the West for several centuries before being ruthlessly 'socialized' by its military and economic superiors in the late nineteenth and early twentieth centuries, Carolyn Warner's essay on the rise of the state system in Africa reminds us of many of the negative consequences that follow from adopting too narrow and singular an understanding of relations between communities. As many contributors to this volume note, there are multiple meanings of what counts as a 'state'. Yet as Warner suggests, it is not uncommon for scholars in international relations to adopt a restrictive model of statehood before searching in vain for evidence of this institutional form outside of Europe. Hence, even if an African state had exclusive authority with territorially delimited borders, it would not have been granted the status of sovereign membership of the international system, not for juridical reasons, but for racial and cultural ones. As a famous English international lawyer wrote at the moment of Europe's greatest power, legal concepts like sovereignty 'cannot be supposed to be understood or recognized by countries differently civilized'.[25]

Early state formation in Africa had very little to do with endogenous factors. This obvious point leads to the observation that the dominant European powers which

---

[23] A claim made by Adda B. Bozeman in *Politics and Culture in International History* (Princeton, NJ: Princeton University Press, 1960), p. 134.

[24] Martin Wight refers to Ancient China as an example of a suzerain state-system (state in the singular) to signify the existence of more or less permanent relations 'while one among them asserts unique claims which the others formally or tacitly accept'. See Wight's essay 'De systematibus civitatum', in Andrew Linklater (ed.), *International Relations: Critical Concepts in Political Science*, vol. IV (London: Routledge, 2000), pp. 1253–73, at p. 1255.

[25] W .E. Hall, quoted in Robert H. Jackson, *Quasi-states: Sovereignty, International Relations and the Third World* (Cambridge: Cambridge University Press, 1990), p. 61.

controlled Africa after the Berlin Conference (1884–5) were empires *as well* as states. In relations with other European powers they recognized an equality of rights and duties, while relations with the non-European world were conducted on the basis of exclusion and dispossession. Colonial rule, Warner reminds us, had the effect of stunting the growth of African economies and enacting closure upon indigenous ideas about community. Why was it that decolonization did not open up new possibilities for an African system that was not based on the separation of peoples into sovereign states? Following Spruyt's analysis of the rise of the territorial state in Europe, Warner offers the explanation that states are more efficient producers of power and wealth. There are strong pressures for socialization in the international system. States would rather deal with quasi-states, those entities that do not possess effective control over their territory, than no state at all.[26] This should not be taken to imply that the sovereign state was the only significant actor in African international relations. Clans, warlords, private economic actors, and transnational institutions and regimes, all possessed interaction capacity on a regional level. This leads Warner to conclude that, just as prior to colonialism 'Africa was host to a wide variety of political forms; in the centuries after, it may continue to do so'.

If the practices of pre-modern China and Africa before colonialism offer us important and fresh ways of thinking of states and state practices in a less Eurocentric fashion, classical Greece still remains the most favoured point of intellectual departure for Western scholars of international relations. Ancient Greece, in effect, has acted as both lesson-provider and teacher for many generations of students; and perhaps nobody has influenced scholars and policymakers more than Thucydides whose *History of the Peloponnesian War* has long served as the bible for modern realism. With its stress on power and the competitive character of international politics, his study (whose influence he predicted would last 'for ever') has clearly had the impact it has not just because it provided a fascinating analysis of the pattern of interaction between the various city-states of Hellas between the eighth and fourth centuries, but because this pattern seemed to resurface again and again in other places at other moments in historical times. This point is made with great force by Nancy Kokaz in her contribution. As she points out, Thucydides' *History* was that quintessential study of the past which always managed to say something relevant about the international condition in general. Indeed, many continue to find the antecedents of the modern states-system in Europe in the pattern of relations so brilliantly dissected by the Greek historian. Robert Gilpin, for example, believes that international politics in the late twentieth century could still be characterized as it was by Thucydides, that is as the struggle for survival conducted and fought by independent political units under conditions where there was no overriding authority.

But as Kokaz reminds us, neither Thucydides, nor the world he tried to describe, can so easily be subsumed within the modern realist canon. Most obviously, the international system he dissected was not composed of independent sovereign states by the time of the Peloponnesian War, but was suffused by formal and informal relations of supremacy and subjugation. In that connection, his volume covered a very interesting period where hegemonic and imperial ties had profusely permeated what used to be an independent states-system. Furthermore, his complex discussion

[26] See Robert Jackson's discussion of the meaning of quasi-states in Jackson, *Quasi-states,* pp. 21–6.

of the city-states and institutions has to be placed within a broader context of 'meaning' that pervaded the ancient Greek international system. This is not to deny the importance of power or suggest that war was not an ever-present possibility. But if the image of the 'state of war' is used to invoke the idea of a world constantly in conflict, then this is a most misleading reading of what was actually going on in Ancient Greece. Force and violence were undoubtedly one part of Greek 'reality'. However, as Kokaz notes, 'security' was not achieved in the Greek international system merely by the accumulation of the weapons of war, but also by (and through) the existence of various normative institutions and practices that helped regulate the pursuit of power. Anarchy in its pure form simply did not exist.[27]

Kokaz's attempt to shift the discussion about Ancient Greece away from a stress on those 'objective' factors favoured by realists towards a more sensitive appreciation of the ways in which norms and informal rules mediated the tendency towards war, is supported in part by Osiander's analysis of 'the minds of the actors' in his reconstruction of medieval Europe.[28] The crux of his argument is that the multitude of diverse actors in *ancien régime* Europe acquired their legitimacy as domains within a single Christian empire. Osiander neatly illustrates this point in his introduction. While life, for the vast majority of peasants, knights and parish priests, carried on independently of the 'semi-mythical figure called the emperor', this did not mean that the discourse of a Christian commonwealth was meaningless. However, to understand the source of this ambiguity we have to immerse ourselves in the legacy of the Roman empire. The emergence of the idea of the *respublica christiana* required a degree of cultural unification produced initially by Hellenization and then Romanization. This, argues Osiander, 'paved the way for the spread of christianity'. By the fourth century, Christianity had become the official and exclusive religion of the Roman empire. Jesus might have intended to give to Caesar what was Caesar's and keep for God what was God's, but in practice this separation became increasingly blurred.[29] The pope was the spiritual head of western christendom and the emperor 'was its highest ranking official'. This presumed unity between pope, emperor and christian rulers was 'an idea that even late medieval thinkers were extremely reluctant to give up' despite the reality of a highly decentralized feudal systems of power relations.

In the second half of his essay, Osiander goes on to consider the intellectual response to the waning power of the Roman emperor. He focuses on a number of writers including the abbot of Admont in Styria, Engelbert and Dante Alighieri. Following Thomas Aquinas, medieval thinkers divided the 'political' into three tiers: households, villages, cities and the '*regnum*' or kingdom, to which Engelbert and Dante added the idea of a 'supreme *communitas,* encompassing the *regna* and coextensive with mankind'. Fourteenth century defenders of the empire saw no contradiction between local princely legitimacy and a universal ideology of Christian

---

[27] For further discussion on Thucydides and international relations see the essays in the section 'Thucydides and Tragedy', *Review of International Studies*, 27: 1 (2001).

[28] In this respect, his essay 'Before Sovereignty' applies the same hermeneutic method that he deployed in his earlier study of the European states system. See Andreas Osiander, *The States System of Europe 1640–1990: Peacemaking and the Conditions of International Stability* (Oxford: Clarendon Press, 1994).

[29] Anthony Pagden, *Peoples and Empires: Europeans and the Rest of the World from Antiquity to the Present* (London: Weidenfield and Nicholson, 2001), p. 71.

unity. A common theme underlying medieval thought was that the empire was needed to maintain a general peace. Kings themselves, such as Edward II of England and Phillip IV of France, were unwilling to take orders from the emperor, but 'they nevertheless readily shared in a political discourse that emphasized their common christianity'. This in itself did not preclude conflict arising about the meaning of Christianity. But even this took place within a system where there existed a common culture and belief system. Of course, *contra* Wight and Bull, this did not mean that the *ancien régime* constituted a 'society of states'. This would have been definitionally impossible in a medieval Europe which was not composed of well-defined sovereign states as such. On the other hand, there was a distinct conception of 'society', one which existed independently of rulers and did not end at the borders of their dominions. To this extent, it was limited not by the boundaries of anybody's power but defined as a common culture and belief system.

One of Osiander's central claims is that the transition from the mediaeval to the modern was a much more gradual process in Europe than some had once presumed. This then raises the intriguing question: how and why did the medieval system based upon feudalism change and with what political consequences? The discussion thus far has been dominated by mainstream historians, often seeking to support or refute the larger Marxist claim that there was a sharp break at some point in the seventeenth society. However, the discussion is now beginning to receive the attention it deserves from students of international relations.[30] And what this work would seem to show is that it was to take some time before something vaguely resembling a modern state system was to emerge. One of the critical moments in this process was the Treaty of Utrecht. Signed in 1713, this not only brought the Wars of the Spanish Succession to an end, but according to most commentary, opened the way for one of those classical long moments in international relations in which the driving purpose of most states was to maintain that larger thing known as 'the balance of power'. This is an idea that James Sofka seeks to challenge. It might well be true that after Utrecht diplomats and policymakers offered what Sofka terms 'obliging references to the balance of power'. Yet at no point did this constrain the different states or stop them seeking to extend their influence by all means at their disposal, including war. Indeed, behind the polite rhetoric of diplomacy and the acceptance of shared norms about international relations, all of the major states were quite ruthless in their pursuit of political power, territorial gain and commercial advantage. The balance of power about which so much was written at the time—and has been talked about since—was not the purpose of international politics but rather the unintended effect of the inability of any one of the dominant powers to establish a clear position of strength over its various rivals. To this extent the notion of a 'balance of power' was less a norm than a rationalization for a situation which none seriously accepted but few had the capacity to undermine. In the end what constrained the hegemonic ambitions of the major powers was not some recognition that the *status quo* was preferable to war, or that law overrode the interests of states, but that war itself was a mightily expensive business that was just

---

[30] For example John Ruggie, 'Continuity and Transformation in the World Polity: Toward a Neorealist Synthesis', in Robert O. Keohane (ed.), *Neorealism and its Critics* (New York: Columbia University Press, 1986), pp. 131–57, Hendrik Spruyt, *The Sovereign State and Its Competitors: An Analysis of Systems Change* (Princeton, NJ: Princeton University Press, 1994).

as likely to bankrupt states as enhance their influence. It was of course the exorbitant costs incurred in fighting the Seven Years War between 1756 and 1763 that prepared the ground for American independence in 1776 and the French revolution a decade later.

The picture that Sofka paints of eighteenth century international relations therefore is one that realists will most readily embrace. Informed by a set of economic ideas in the form of mercantilism which saw trade in zero sum terms—'our trade will only improve by the total extinction of theirs' remarked one British merchant—and driven by a constant fear that at least one of the powers (France) aimed for nothing less than total domination over its rivals, the system was a highly volatile one marked by the periodic bouts of war and punctuated by moments of peace, before further conflict erupted once again.The fact that France did not achieve its hegemonic ambitions did not mean that it had abandoned them. Momentarily contained by a coalition of rivals led by France's main imperial rival, Great Britain, it returned to the international ring after 1789 with capabilities enormously enhanced by the revolution in the shape of an ideological mission, a rationalized administrative structure and a capacity to mobilize the people in a cause that they were now prepared to support. But we should be careful not to confuse things here. The revolution did not lead to the transformation of international relations from a balance of power to a hegemonic model according to Sofka. Instead, it made French primacy feasible for the first time by increasing its ability to wage war successfully, which it did with some élan and success until bitter defeat on the battlefield at Waterloo. Only at this point did the 'world war' between France and Britain finally come to an end leaving the way open for a century-long *Pax Britannica.*[31]

The collapse of Napoleonic ambitions and the creation of an international system whose immediate rationale was to prevent the domination of Europe by any single power is the starting-point of Hudson Meadwell's discussion of the nineteenth century. But it was not just the danger of another hegemon that preoccupied the *status quo* powers after 1815: it was also the fear of revolution itself. Indeed, the whole period thereafter he argues had a definite coherence, a dynamic if you like, that stemmed from the diffusion of political innovations associated with the French revolution whose influence was to shape the ways in which states related to each other at least until 1945—and probably beyond.[32] Moreover, if we are looking for turning-points in international relations, says Meadwell, it did not come with 1815 but 1789, and the challenge which republican ideals posed to the norm of monarchical rule in Europe. As Metternich so aptly observed, Europe was not just geographically defined but constituted an ideological and political space in which an aristocratic order continued to prevail. And if this order came under threat in any one country, this threat had to be met because it constituted a menace to the system as a whole. As was made clear at the Congress of Vienna, 'if kingship was in danger anywhere', then 'all rulers had a duty to intervene to uphold it', another interesting example incidentally of where the sovereignty in theory could be, and frequently was, breached in practice.

---

[31] See Tom Pocock, *Battle For Empire: The Very First World War 1756–1763* (London: Michael O'Mara Books, 1998).

[32] The theme of 'revolution' in international relations is elaborated in detail in Fred Halliday, *Revolution and World Politics: The Rise and Fall of the Sixth Great Power* (Basingstoke: Macmillan, 1999). See the discussion around his book in *Review of International Studies*, 27:4 (2001).

Peace in the nineteenth century therefore did not simply mean the avoidance of war between states, but the regulation of political relations within them spurred on by the fear of radical political and economic change. As Meadwell notes, peace was not 'incidental' but the 'by-product of the desire to avoid revolution'; and in this model where the perceived threat of revolution provoked reaction, and reaction was regarded as the surest way of preventing revolution, democracy was by no means assured. On the contrary, in a Europe where republican democracy was often equated with attacks on the principle of property and the market, democratic forms were far less entrenched by the beginning of the First World War than some later accounts would seem to imply.[33] In fact, before 1914, only three countries in Europe—Switzerland, Portugal and France—were republics, and although this number increased after 1918, many of these collapsed and succumbed to dictatorship in the inter-war period. Ultimately, only one country in the world could claim full republican credentials before the end of World War II: the United States of America. Which raises the obvious question as to whether or not democracy or peace could have ever been established in Europe without American intervention. And if the answer is in the negative, it leads to the interesting (and possibly unpalatable) conclusion that an international system born out of the conflict between revolution and reaction in Europe in one age could only arrive at some form of new equilibrium in another because of the direct support extended to it by the new liberal hegemon rising across the Atlantic.

Logically enough, this leads to the United States and its historic role in international politics, the subject of G. John Ikenberry's article. Blessed by a combination of geography and abundant resources that allowed it full rein to develop more or less unhindered by the threat of other states, by the 1870s the US had already surpassed Britain as the largest and most advanced economy in the world. By the end of the century, of course, it was out-producing nearly all of its main rivals combined as well. Yet whereas the growth of other great powers in history had tended to trigger security dilemma-driven conflict and regional balancing reactions by other states, America's did not. The conundrum is why? Ikenberry offers several explanations: the country's very remoteness, its lack of serious military capacity, its democratic and republican character, and the obvious fact that it had no serious interest in territorial expansion once it had reached the limits of its own frontier by the end of the nineteenth century. The world may have seen many great powers rise up and dominate the international system in the past. But there has only been one great power like America whose power did not seem to threaten others, unless they themselves happened to challenge the power of the United States itself.

According to Ikenberry therefore American power has been different or 'exceptional' in its extent, ideology and purpose. It has also been remarkably successful in managing to achieve and maintain a high level of international legitimacy. This was true during World War II; and but for the historical blip that was Vietnam, it was mainly true during the Cold War as well. Even the way in which the Cold War came to an end—with hardly a shot being fired and largely on American terms—only reinforced its position and a belief in the American way of life. Thereafter, and *contra* the predictions made by writers like Paul Kennedy, the US continued to enjoy

---

[33] On the limits of democracy in Great Britain before 1914, see Michael Bentley, *Politics Without Democracy, 1815–1914* (London: Fontana, 1984).

robust health. Indeed, far from experiencing decline in the 1990s, American power was to undergo what seemed to many to be a major resurgence. Not only that: instead of a multipolar system emerging, an almost unique form of unipolarity was to take shape in which the United States remained by far and away the most dominant player. As the French Foreign Minister conceded (more in sorrow than anger, one suspects) 'the United States' at the end of the millennium was not just more capable than any other country in the world, but was not even 'comparable in terms of power and influence to anything known in modern history'.[34]

Thus by the beginning of the new century, the United States would appear to be more secure than ever in an expanding democratic-capitalist world that was itself the 'dominant reality in world politics'. Naturally, realists would insist that such a condition could not last for ever; that other 'have not' states would rise up to balance and challenge this unprecedented concentration of power in the hands of one state. Ikenberry, however, doubts this, and though recognizing that American power is not viewed as being benign by everybody, points to the remarkable fact that it continues to be welcome by the majority of elites in most countries around the world today. If empires are coercive systems of domination, the American-centred world order is clearly not an empire. However, if we see empires as inclusive systems of order organized around a dominant state whose role is accepted as being quite indispensable to the functioning of the system as a whole, the United States must be seen as having constructed one of the most effective empires in history—against which there now appears to be neither serious political rival nor obvious ideological alternative.

One of the principal reasons for this new-found self-confidence, not surprisingly, was the enormous upheavals that took place in the world after 1989, when first Soviet power retreated from Eastern Europe, then communism collapsed as a serious economic challenge, and finally the USSR fell apart. But according to William Wohlforth, we should be careful not to judge the Soviet empire (and before it the Russian) by what happened to both. As he points out, Russia and its communist successor proved far more durable than the British and Mongol empires. Moreover, Russia and the Soviet Union were hugely successful as great powers playing major roles in European and world politics in the three centuries after 1700. Significantly though, the source of their respective strength—constant expansion—also turned out in the end to be their most obvious weakness, and the enormous costs of maintaining and policing their various possessions brought the different enterprises down, one in 1917, and another nearly three-quarters of a century later.

Yet if traditional Russia and the USSR revealed a self-defeating propensity to expand, how do we explain this and what implications does this have for any credible Waltzian theory of international relations? Wohlforth is well aware of the extent to which the end of the Cold War has been used to refute the basics of realism. However, as he tries to show here (and as he has done in other places) realism should not be so defensive, for not only does it provide an entirely adequate explanation of why the superpower conflict came to an end, but also furnishes us with an equally valid analysis of Russian and Soviet imperialism. In fact, the problem with neorealism when it comes to assessing the dynamics and contradictions of Russian

---

[34] See Michael Cox, 'Whatever Happened to American Decline? International Relations and the New United States Hegemony', *New Political Economy*, 6:3 (2001), pp. 311–40.

expansion, both communist and non-communist, is not that it is wrong but that it is so obviously true. Certainly, the contention that international anarchy generates pervasive insecurity problems that powerfully constrain states and influence their identities and domestic arrangements is a truism for students of Russian and Soviet history. Not only that: Waltz's structural approach to theory, which highlights socialization and selection rather than strict rational choice as the key causal mechanisms, resonates strongly with the empirical literature on Russia. Neorealist theory might not tell us a great deal about the Russian and Soviet past that we did not already know. However, it does provide us with a credible, deductively based explanation of the perennial forces central to an understanding of Russian and Soviet history.

While Wohlforth seeks to understand the demise of the Soviet empire in terms of a more general theory of imperial overstretch, Ian Clark argues in favour of a more norm-based explanation of what happened after 1989. The larger question he addresses, however, is the extent to which the events of that year marked a fundamental 'punctuation point' in world history, and whether future historians of international relations will be adding the date 1989 to the series 1648, 1815, 1919 and 1945. Obviously, just after the Berlin Wall came down, there were few who challenged the idea that the end of the Cold War marked a clear and pronounced break in the history of international relations. But once the dust had settled and analysts had gained some distance from events, it became increasingly evident that much had not changed, and that there remained a number of very familiar landmarks indeed. Thus while the upheavals of 1989 were radical at one level, they were rather conservative at another, leaving much of the post-war order intact. And central to Clark's whole thesis is the argument that far from undermining pre-existing international norms—the three most important being a commitment to market economics, the collectivization of security and a liberal conception of rights—the end of the Cold War only reaffirmed them. These principles had pervaded the post-1945 international order but in the context of the Cold War had operated as principles of exclusion. Now, with 1989, they became agents of admission to international society, justifying the changes that had been made as part of the post-Cold War settlement while legitimizing the reforms to the economic and political structures of the East.

The end of the Cold War therefore changed less than is commonly realized. There is, however, a twist in the tail of Clark's argument: for while the foundations of the Cold War system were constructed upon sovereignty norms such as toleration, non-intervention, and non-use of force, its practices tended to hollow out these normative foundations. This erosion can most obviously be seen in its liberal heartland, where the state no longer enjoys 'exclusive legitimacy' over a range of issues. He links this process to Polanyi's idea of a 'double movement'—the first referring to the completion of the states system through decolonization and the universal extension of sovereign rights and duties to all states, and the second to the process by which the West 'struck back at the very pluralism that the global state system' had 'generated'. And in many ways, the end of the Cold War has been critical to the completion of this transformation, to the degree that we can at last talk, according to Clark, about 'the reinvention of international society'.

Whereas Clark sees the emergence of a more fully developed society of states arising out of the debris left behind by official communism, Arrighi and Silver outline a more disturbing and less benign scenario. Standing apart from the dominant tradition in international relations which has generally said little about material forces, and even less about the relationship between capitalism as a dynamic system and world politics, they see a major sea change taking place in the historical social system leading to a widespread sense of unease about the future. The collapse of communism might have led to a momentary sense of triumph in the West, but as they point out, its demise has also created enormous 'turbulence' in world politics. Outwardly the new world might appear more united around a common set of values than the old one. However, this cannot hide the fact that we are now living through highly disorderly times where the old signposts mean less and less. All that we know—and indeed can know—is that one era of history has ended and that there is little way of predicting what lies ahead, except more uncertainty.

According to Arrighi and Silver, three closely related observations can be made about the present and future that might help us dissipate some of the global fog that currently surrounds discussion about international relations. The first is that at the end of the twentieth century 'finance capital' is dominant, fuelling both the phenomenon of globalization and accelerating rapid change in the world order. The second is that this change knows no bounds, thus its implications are likely to be far-reaching and permanent. And the third that in spite of all the hyperbole surrounding contemporary discussions about US hegemony, American power is far less secure than many would seem to think. Indeed, observers of the American scene are making one of those classic intellectual errors by mistaking 'autumn for spring', and assuming that the recent resurgence of US power represents the beginning of a new robust era. They are making an even bigger one perhaps by overstating the crisis in East Asia and underestimating the capacity of this particularly important area. Much has been written about the end of the short-lived 'Pacific Century'. But as Arrighi and Silver stress, the region remains one of the most dynamic in the world economy today, and the United States (a debtor nation with a huge trade deficit with the countries along the Pacific Rim) will in the end have to make the necessary adjustments to take account of this material power shift. If it does not do so, and refuses to adjust to the 'rising economic power of the East Asia region' then the transition to a new world order will be destabilizing at best, potentially catastrophic at worst.

In a concluding chapter Robert Jervis provides a wide-ranging discussion of the problems and issues involved in thinking about change and transition over the long-term. As he points out, international politics has varied in important dimensions from one geographical area and historical era to another. But this does not mean we cannot detect some discernible patterns in the way in which policymakers behave, even those far removed from each other in terms of ideology, outlook and culture. Without suggesting that international politics has always been determined by an identical set of laws—the thesis usually associated with Waltzian structural realism—it is still worth 'asking whether some key characteristics' can be isolated through time and across space. While not seeking to deny the obvious fact of difference, Jervis suggests that a 'number of processes and characteristics' such as competition and the need to extract and mobilize resources (aspects of international life that have been central to realist discourse) have been fairly common to nearly all known systems. This does not imply that there has been no change over time; but it does point to the fact that there may be more universal patterns at work in international politics than much recent analysis would seem to imply.

That said, we still have to account for change in general and the specific changes that have brought us into the current era. Three developments seem to be crucial to understanding the contours of the modern world according to Jervis: the termination of the bipolar conflict between the USSR and the USA, the end of the Cold War and the dissolution of the Soviet empire. But this is only to identify factors, not to explain them or account for their complex consequences. Nor does it tell us much about either the structure of the contemporary global order and what is novel about it—if indeed there is anything novel at all. However, one change of a quite profound character is bound to impact on the shape of the emerging international system: the unlikelihood of war between the great powers. This will have enormous consequences. After all, throughout history the most powerful states have fought and prepared to fight each other; and if this dynamic were to be removed, it would be as though the law of gravity had been repealed. What consequences this would have on international politics cannot be easily forecast. However, a great many things are going to change as a result, and perhaps the biggest challenge facing students of world politics in the new century will be to explore what an international system without the threat of major war between great powers is actually going to look like. Winston Churchill exaggerated only a little bit when he said that 'people talked a lot of nonsense when they said nothing was ever settled by war. 'Nothing in history', he continued, 'was ever settled except by war'. That this is no longer true, at least in relations among the great powers in the system, possibly provides the single most striking discontinuity in the history of international relations.

Rethinking the sovereign state model

STEPHEN D. KRASNER

The Peace of Westphalia, which ended the Thirty Years' War in 1648, is generally understood as a critical moment in the development of the modern international system composed of sovereign states each with exclusive authority within its own geographic boundaries. The Westphalian sovereign state model, based on the principles of autonomy, territory, mutual recognition and control, offers a simple, arresting, and elegant image. It orders the minds of policymakers. It is an analytic assumption for neo-realism and neo-liberal institutionalism. It is an empirical regularity for various sociological and constructivist theories of international politics. It is a benchmark for observers who claim an erosion of sovereignty in the contemporary world.

This essay demonstrates, however, that the Westphalian sovereign state model has never been an accurate description of many of the entities that have been regarded as states.[1] In fact, the Peace of Westphalia itself had almost nothing to do with what has come to be termed the Westphalian system although I use the term here in deference to common usage. The idea that states ought to be autonomous, free from intervention by external actors was only developed as an explicit principle in the last part of the eighteenth century by the Swiss international jurist Emmerich de Vattel. The assumption that states are independent rational actors can be misleading because it obfuscates the existence of many situations in which rulers have, in fact, not been autonomous. The now almost commonplace view that sovereignty is being eroded is historically myopic. Breaches of the sovereign state model have been an enduring characteristic of the international environment. The principle of autonomy has been violated in the name of other norms including human rights, minority rights, democracy, communism, fiscal responsibility, and international security. Mutual recognition has not always gone to juridically independent territorial entities. There has never been some golden age for sovereignty. The sovereign state model has always been a cognitive script; its basic rules are widely understood but also frequently violated. Normative structures have been decoupled from actual behaviour either because actors embrace inconsistent norms such as human rights and non-intervention, or because logics of consequences driven by power and interest trump logics of appropriateness dictated by norms and principles.[2]

---

[1] This essay develops some of the arguments published earlier as Stephen D. Krasner, 'Compromising Westphalia', *International Security* 20:3 (1995/6). pp. 115–51.

[2] For the distinction between a logic of appropriateness and a logic of consequences see James G. March and Johan Olsen, 'The Institutional Dynamics of International Political Orders', *International Organization*, 52 (1998) and James G. March, with the assistance of C. Heath, *A Primer on Decision Making : How Decisions Happen* (New York: Free Press, 1994).

The sovereign state model is a system of political authority based on territory, mutual recognition, autonomy, and control. Territoriality means that political authority is exercised over a defined geographic space rather than, for instance, over people, as would be the case in a tribal form of political order. Autonomy means that no external actor enjoys authority within the borders of the state. Mutual recognition means that juridically independent territorial entities recognize each other as being competent to enter into contractual arrangements, typically treaties. Control means that there is an expectation not only that sovereign states have the authority to act but also that they can effectively regulate movements across their borders and within them.

Territorial violations of the sovereign state model involve situations in which authority structures are not coterminous with geographic borders. Examples include the European Union with its supranational institutions and qualified majority voting, Andorra, where France and Spain appoint members to the highest court, and the Exclusive Economic Zone (EEZ) for the oceans, within which the coastal state exercises control over commercial activities like seabed exploitation but not shipping.

Violations of the principle of autonomy involving situations in which an external actor is able to exercise some authoritative control within the territory of a state, have been a persistent feature of the Westphalian sovereign state system. Autonomy can be transgressed both if rulers agree to governance structures that are controlled by external actors, or if more powerful actors impose institutions, policies, or personnel on weaker states. Examples of transgressions of autonomy include bondholders' committees that regulated financial activities in some Balkan states and elsewhere in the nineteenth century, International Monetary Fund (IMF) conditionality, protectorates in which major powers control foreign but not domestic policy, provisions for the treatment of minorities imposed on central and eastern European states after the Balkan War of the 1870s and World War I, and the Soviet imposition of communist regimes on its satellite states after the Second World War.

Compromises of Westphalia have occurred in four ways—through conventions, contracting, coercion, and imposition. These four modalities are distinguished by whether the behaviour of one actor depends on that of another and by whether at least one of the actors is better off and none worse off. In conventions, rulers enter into agreements, such as human rights accords, from which they expect some gain, but their behaviour is not contingent on what others do. In contracting, rulers agree to violate the sovereignty of their own state contingent on other signatories honouring their part of the bargain. In coercion, the rulers of stronger states make weaker ones worse off by making credible threats to which the target might or might not acquiesce, or engaging in unilateral moves which undermine the bargaining position of the weaker state. In imposition, the target is so weak that it has no option but to comply with the preferences of the stronger.

Conventions, contracts, coercion, and imposition have all been enduring patterns of behaviour in the international system. Every major peace treaty since 1648— Westphalia, Utrecht, Vienna, Versailles, Helsinki, and Dayton—has violated the sovereign state model in one way or another. Compromising the sovereign state model is always available as a policy option because there is no authority structure to prevent it: nothing can preclude rulers from transgressing against the domestic autonomy of other states or recognizing entities that are not juridically autonomous.

In the international system, institutions are less constraining and more malleable, more subject to challenge than in more settled circumstances. The mechanisms for locking in particular institutional forms, such as socialization, positive reinforcement between structures and agents, or path-dependent processes, are weaker at the international level than in well-established domestic polities. Rulers are more responsive to domestic constituents who might, or might not, embrace the norms of the Westphalian sovereign state system. Power is asymmetrical making coercion and imposition available options.

The sovereign state model is a cognitive script characterized by organized hypocrisy. Organized hypocrisy occurs when norms are decoupled from actions. Actors say one thing and do another. In the international environment this occurs both because actors endorse norms that can be mutually inconsistent, such as universal human rights and non-intervention, and because logics of consequences usually trump logics of appropriateness. Organized hypocrisy is characteristic of any political organization whose leaders must appeal to different constituencies.[3] The problem of uniting principles and actions is more acute in international environments than domestic ones because the norms embraced by local and foreign actors will not always coincide and because the opportunities for action based on coercion and the use of force are greater. All international systems, whether the Westphalian sovereign state system or the Sinocentric tributary state system or the medieval European world of overlapping authority, have been characterized by organized hypocrisy.[4]

Defining sovereignty

In practice the term sovereignty has been used in many different ways. In contemporary usage four different meanings of sovereignty can be distinguished: interdependence sovereignty, domestic sovereignty, Vattelian sovereignty, and international legal sovereignty.

Interdependence sovereignty refers to the ability of states to control movement across their borders. Many observers have argued that sovereignty is being eroded by globalization resulting from technological changes that have dramatically reduced the costs of communication and transportation. States cannot regulate transborder movements of goods, capital, people, ideas, or disease vectors. Governments can no longer engage in activities that have traditionally been understood to be part of their regulatory portfolio: they cannot conduct effective monetary policy because of

---

[3] The idea of organized hypocrisy is developed in Nils Brunsson, *The Organization of Hypocrisy: Talk, Decisions and Actions in Organizations*, trans. Nancy Adler (Chichester, UK and New York: Wiley, 1991). For a discussion of political organizations see especially pp. 27–31. For a discussion of decoupling see W. Richard Scott, *Institutions and Organizations* (Thousand Oaks, CA: Sage, 1995), and John W. Meyer, John Boli, George M. Thomas, and Francisco O. Ramirez, 'World Society and the Nation-State', *American Journal of Sociology*, 103 (1997).

[4] For the Sinocentric system see Stephen D. Krasner, 'Organized Hypocrisy in 19th Century East Asia', *International Relations of the Asia Pacific*, 1 (2001). For the medieval system see Marcus Fischer, 'Feudal Europe, 800–1300: Communal Discourse and Conflictual Practices', *International Organization*, 46 (1992).

international capital flows; they cannot control knowledge because of the Internet; they cannot guarantee public health because individuals can move so quickly across the globe. The issue here is not one of authority but rather of control. The right of states to manage their borders is not challenged, but globalization, it is asserted, has eroded their ability to actually do so.

Domestic sovereignty refers to authority structures within states and the ability of these structures to effectively regulate behaviour. The classic theorists of sovereignty, Bodin and Hobbes, were concerned primarily with domestic sovereignty. Both wrote in the context of religious wars in Europe that were destroying the stability of their own polities; Bodin himself was almost killed in religious riots in Paris in 1572. They wanted above all to establish a stable system of authority, one that would be acknowledged as legitimate by all members of the polity regardless of their religious affiliation. Both endorsed a highly centralized authority structure and rejected any right of revolt.[5] In practice, the vision of Bodin and Hobbes has never been implemented. Authority structures have taken many different forms including monarchies, republics, democracies, unified systems, and federal systems. High levels of centralization have not been associated with the order and stability that Bodin and Hobbes were trying to guarantee.

The acceptance or recognition of a given authority structure is one aspect of domestic sovereignty; the other is the level of control that officials can actually exercise. This has varied dramatically. Well ordered domestic polities have both legitimate and effective authority structures. Failed states have neither. The loss of interdependence sovereignty, which is purely a matter of control, would also imply some loss of domestic sovereignty, at least domestic sovereignty understood as control, since if a state cannot regulate movements across its borders, such as the flow of illegal drugs, it is not likely to be able to control activities within its borders, such as the use of these drugs.

Vattelian sovereignty refers to the exclusion of external sources of authority both *de juri* and *de facto*. Many analysts, including myself, who have argued that the principle of autonomy did not have much to do with 1648 have in the past used the term Westphalian sovereignty. The notion that states could do as they pleased within their own borders had almost nothing to do with the Peace of Westphalia. The principle that rulers should not intervene in or judge domestic affairs in other states was actually introduced by two international legal theorists in the latter part of the eighteenth century, Emmerich de Vattel and Christian Wolff. Wolff wrote in the 1760s that 'To interfere in the government of another, in whatever way indeed that may be done is opposed to the natural liberty of nations, by virtue of which one is altogether independent of the will of other nations in its action'.[6] During the nineteenth century the principle of non-intervention was championed by the Latin

---

[5] Jean Bodin, *On Sovereignty: Four Chapters from The Six Books of the Commonwealth*, ed. and trans. Julian H. Franklin (Cambridge: Cambridge University Press, 1992), pp. 13–14; Quentin Skinner, *The Foundations of Modern Political Thought*, volume 2: *The Age of Reformation* (Cambridge, UK: Cambridge University Press, 1978), pp. 284–87.

[6] Quoted in Aaron J. Thomas and Ann Van Wynen Thomas, *Non Intervention; The Law and Its Import in the Americas* (Dallas, TX: Southern Methodist University Press, 1956), p. 5. See also Emmerich de Vattel, *The Law of Nations; or, Principles of the Law of Nature, Applied to the Conduct and Affairs of Nations and Sovereigns*. From the new edition trans. Joseph Chitty (Philadelphia: T. & J. W. Johnson, Law Booksellers, 1852), p. 155.

American states, the weaker entities in the international system. It was not formally accepted by the United States until the 1930s.

International legal sovereignty refers to mutual recognition. The basic rule of international legal sovereignty is that recognition is accorded to juridically independent territorial entities which are capable of entering into voluntary contractual agreements. States in the international system, like individuals in domestic polities, are free and equal. International legal sovereignty is consistent with any agreement provided that the state is not coerced.[7]

The rules, institutions, and practices that are associated with these four meanings of sovereignty are neither logically nor empirically linked in some organic whole. Sovereignty refers to both practices, such as the ability to control transborder movements or activities within a state's boundaries, and to rules or principles, such as the recognition of juridically independent territorial entities and non-intervention in the internal affairs of other states. A state might have little interdependence sovereignty, be unable to regulate its own borders, but its Vattelian sovereignty could remain intact so long as no external actor attempted to influence its domestic authority structures. A failed state like Somalia in the late 1990s offers one example. States can enjoy international legal sovereignty, mutual recognition, without having Vattelian sovereignty; the eastern European states during the Cold War whose domestic structures were deeply penetrated by the Soviet Union offer one example. States can voluntarily compromise their Vattelian sovereignty through the exercise of their international legal sovereignty: the member states of the European Union have entered into a set of voluntary agreements, treaties, that have created supranational authority structures such as the European Court of Justice and the European Monetary Authority. States can lack effective domestic sovereignty understood either as control or authority and still have international legal sovereignty— Zaire/Congo during the 1990s is an example. Sovereignty is a basket of goods that do not necessarily go together.[8]

Sovereignty and international relations theory

The sovereign state model is a basic concept for the major theoretical approaches to international relations, including neorealism and neoliberal institutionalism, for both of which it is an analytic assumption, as well as international society perspectives, for which it is a constitutive norm. For neorealism, the ontological givens in the international system are Westphalian sovereign states, understood as unitary rational actors operating in an anarchic setting and striving to enhance their well-being and security. These states are constrained only by the external environment, that is, by the power of other states. Realism does not suppose that all states can guarantee their autonomy. If, however, a state loses its autonomy—if, for instance,

---

[7] Lassa Oppenheim, *Oppenheim's International Law*, 9th edn. Edited by Sir Robert Jennings and Sir Arthur Watts (Harlow, Essex: Longman, 1992), pp. 365–7.
[8] Michael Ross Fowler and Julie Marie Bunck, *Law, Power, and the Sovereign State: The Evolution and Application of the Concept of Sovereignty* (University Park, PA: The Pennsylvania State University Press, 1995), pp. 116–117.

its political structures and personnel are chosen by others—then neorealism has nothing to say about how such penetrated states which do not have Vattelian sovereignty might act. The relations between Czechoslovakia and the Soviet Union after the Prague Spring of 1968, for instance, are not amenable to realist analysis. Czechoslovakia was not responding to external constraints, as an autonomous or Vattelian state might. Its policies were dictated by externally imposed constitutional structures and personnel.

Similarly, the sovereign state model is an analytic assumption for neoliberal institutionalism.[9] The actors are assumed to be Westphalian sovereign states, unified rational autonomous entities striving to maximize their utility in the face of constraints that emanate from an anarchic although interdependent international environment. What distinguishes neoliberalism from neorealism is its different understanding of the characteristic problem for these states: for neoliberal institutionalism, the problem is the resolution of market failures, whereas for neorealism it is security and distributional conflicts.

The sovereign state model is also a core concept for international society approaches, most notably the English School and various constructivist approaches.[10] Here the sovereign state model is understood as a constitutive norm which generates actors and defines their competencies. All participants in international society—public officials, diplomats, statesmen, political leaders—hold the same fundamental views about the nature of the system, the actors, and how they can behave. Modern international society is composed of territorial units within which public institutions exercise exclusive authority. Actions follow particular patterns not because they are dictated by some higher authority, or coerced by the threat of force, or constrained by the power of other states, but because players have a shared intersubjective understanding. The role of sovereign states permits some kinds of activities but not others.

The sovereign state model is an excellent starting point for analysing (neorealism or neoliberal institutionalism) or understanding (international society perspectives) much of what goes on in the international environment. A great deal of what takes place is completely consistent with the sovereign state model, whether it is treated as an analytic assumption or behavioural regularity generated by intersubjective shared understanding: the claims of external actors are rebuffed; authoritative decision-makers declare war, form alliances, enter into trade agreements, and regulate migration.

As this article demonstrates, however, there have been many other situations in which the principles associated with mutual recognition and state autonomy has

---

[9] Robert O. Keohane, *After Hegemony: Cooperation and Discord in the World Political Economy* (Princeton, NJ: Princeton University Press, 1984) is the seminal exposition of this perspective.

[10] Hedley Bull, *The Anarchical Society* (London: Macmillan, 1977); John G. Ruggie, 'Territoriality and Beyond: Problematizing Modernity in International Relations', *International Organization*, 47 (1993), pp. 139–74; Alexander Wendt, *Social Theory of International Politics* (Cambridge: Cambridge University Press, 1999). J. Samuel Barkin and Bruce Cronin, 'The State and the Nation: Changing Norms and the Rules of Sovereignty in International Relations', *International Organization*, 48 (1994), pp. 107–30. See Barry Buzan, 'From International Realism to International Society: Structural Realism and Regime Theory Meet the English School', *International Organization*, 47 (1993), pp. 327–52, for a comparison of US and British approaches to international relations. For a recent debate on the English school, see the Forum in *Review of International Studies*, 27 (July 2001), pp. 465–509.

been violated. Some are the result of an inability to control either transborder flows or domestic behaviour, leading rulers to conclude contractual arrangements that are consistent with international legal sovereignty, but which compromise domestic autonomy or establish new institutional arrangements that transcend territoriality. Some are the result of major powers imposing personnel, policies, or institutions on weaker states, a situation that violates both Vattelian and international legal sovereignty.

Violations of the principles of non-intervention and recognition based on territoriality and juridical autonomy have been an enduring characteristic of the international system, both before and after the Peace of Westphalia. The Westphalian sovereign state system, like other international systems, is characterized by competing norms, an absence of universal authority structures, and power asymmetries. For political leaders operating in an extremely complex environment and responsive to multiple constituencies, organized hypocrisy is irresistible.

Modalities of compromise

The principles of autonomy and recognition based on territoriality and juridical autonomy can be breached through conventions, contracts, coercion, or imposition. The four modalities through which autonomy and territoriality can be compromised are distinguished by whether they are pareto-improving or not, and contingent or not. Conventions and contracts are pareto-improving, that is, they make at least one party better off without making anyone worse off. Rulers are not forced into such arrangements. They enter them voluntarily because compromising the principles of the sovereign state model is more attractive than honouring them. Coercion and imposition leave at least one of the actors worse off; they are not pareto-improving. Contracts and coercion involve contingent behaviour; the actions of one ruler depend upon what the other does. Conventions and imposition do not involve contingent behaviour.

Conventions

Conventions are agreements in which rulers make commitments that expose their own policies to some kind of external scrutiny by agreeing to follow certain domestic practices.[11] Signatories might, for instance, endorse liberal conceptions of human rights, or agree to hold regular elections, or stipulate that religious or ethnic identity would not affect the franchise or opportunities for employment, or that refugees would be entitled to specific social security benefits and educational opportunities.

Conventions are voluntary and they make at least one actor better off without making any worse off. If they did not, rulers would not sign them. The signatories do not usually secure any direct gain except the pledge from other parties to the

---

[11] I am indebted to James McCall Smith for suggesting the term conventions.

agreement that they will behave in the same way. The willingness of a particular state to abide by a convention is not contingent on the behaviour of others. Some rulers can violate a convention without prompting any change in the domestic policies or institutions of others.

In the contemporary world, the most obvious class of conventions is human rights accords. Human rights agreements cover relations between rulers and ruled, including both citizens and non-citizens. They involve pledges by national authorities to treat individuals within their territory in a certain way. By the last decade of the twentieth century there were around 50 such agreements, both universal and regional.[12]

These conventions cover a wide range of issues including genocide, torture, slavery, refugees, stateless persons, women's rights, racial discrimination, children's rights, forced labour, and the right of labour to organize. In some instances, human rights agreements specify only relatively broad principles, but in others they are very precise. For instance, the 1953 Convention on the Political Rights of Women, which has been ratified by more than 100 countries, provides for equal voting rights for women and equal rights to hold office. The 1979 Convention on the Elimination of all Forms of Discrimination Against Women, which has been ratified by more than 120 states, obligates parties to take all legal measures necessary to assure the equality of men and women, to 'modify the social and cultural patterns of conduct of men and women', to provide equal access to education, to take measures to assure 'the same opportunities to participate actively in sports and physical education', to assure equal work opportunities including promotion and job security, to introduce paid maternity leave, and to offer adequate prenatal and postnatal care including 'free services where necessary'.[13]

The enforcement and monitoring mechanisms for these agreements vary enormously. Some, such as the Universal Declaration of Human Rights, do not have the status of a formal treaty and are devoid of monitoring provisions. Other conventions (for example those on slavery, the status of refugees, and political rights of women) provide that disputes can be referred to the International Court of Justice. No human rights cases have, however, been referred to this Court. A number of conventions (such as those on racial discrimination, apartheid, and the rights of the child) provide for the creation of committees that receive information and can, with the approval of the concerned states, investigate alleged violations.

The European Convention on Human Rights, which entered into force in 1953, and subsequent protocols, offers, along with other European institutions, the most far-reaching example of infringements on Vattelian sovereignty. The European human rights regime has elaborate monitoring and enforcement procedures. The European Commission on Human Rights can receive complaints from individuals, nongovernmental organizations (NGOs), and states; it receives about 4,000 communications a year. The European Court of Human Rights can make decisions that are binding on national jurisdictions. The jurisdiction of the Commission

---

[12] United Nations, *Human Rights: International Instruments: Chart of Ratifications as of 31 December 1993*, ST/HR/4/Rev.9 (New York, 1994); Ian Brownlie, *Basic Documents on Human Rights*, 3rd edn. (Oxford: Clarendon Press, 1992).
[13] Convention on the Elimination of all Forms of Discrimination Against Women, in Brownlie, *Basic Documents*, pp. 106–8, Art 5a.; Art. 10f; Art. 13.2.

(composed of independent experts) and of the Court have been recognized by the signatories to the Convention. Decisions of the Commission and the Court have led to changes in detention practices in Belgium and Germany, alien law in Switzerland, and trial procedures in Sweden. Greece, confronted with expulsion, withdrew from the Council of Europe after an investigation by the European Human Rights Commission found that the military regime had violated human rights.[14]

There is no single explanation for why countries sign conventions. The European Convention, with its significant enforcement and monitoring capabilities, could be concluded and strengthened over time because the signatories were committed to the principles and rules specified in the agreement. States in which democratic commitments had been shaky, most importantly Germany, were the strongest supporters of the agreement.[15]

Conventions with no monitoring or enforcement provisions, such as the Universal Declaration of Human Rights, or with only limited provisions for national reporting, have been signed even by countries with abysmal human rights records. When enforcement and monitoring mechanisms are weak, and where there is, in fact, limited domestic support for human rights, signing may have no consequences for states engaging in repressive domestic policies. Such situations would be consistent with the sovereign state model. The Soviet bloc countries routinely ratified human rights agreements. As of 1 September 1987, the Soviet Union, Bulgaria, Czechoslovakia, and Romania had all ratified 14 out of the 22 extant UN human rights instruments, East Germany 16, and Poland 13. For the industrialized democratic countries there was wide variation. The United States had ratified six conventions, Switzerland eight, Italy and the United Kingdom 15 each, France and West Germany 16 each, Sweden 18, and Norway 18.[16]

Why would rulers bother to join agreements with no intention of honouring them, even if monitoring and enforcement provisions are weak? The policies of the Soviet bloc could be written off as either pure cynicism or an effort to convince third parties. States may also sign because participation is understood as something that a modern state does. For many Third World states, clues to appropriate behaviour are signalled by the international environment, especially international organizations and more powerful states.[17]

---

[14] Jack Donnelly, *International Human Rights* (Boulder, CO: Westview, 1992), pp. 82–3; David P. Forsythe, *Human Rights and World Politics* (Lincoln: University of Nebraska Press, 1989), p. 19; Andrew Moravcsik, 'Lessons from the European Human Rights Regime', in Inter-American Dialogue, *Advancing Democracy and Human Rights in the Americas: What Role for the OAS?* (Washington, DC: Inter-American Dialogue, 1994), p. 47.

[15] Andrew Moravcsik, 'The Origins of Human Rights Regimes: Democratic Delegation in Postwar Europe', *International Organization*, 54 (2000), p. 217. Moravcsik, 'Lessons', pp. 54–5.

[16] Derived from information in United Nations, *Human Rights Status of International Instruments as at 1 September 1987*, n.d.

[17] John Meyer and others have argued that many of the formal stances of rulers (not necessarily their actual behaviour) are dictated not by internal characteristics, such as the level of socioeconomic development, but rather by expectations that are generated in the international system. See J.W. Meyer, *et al.*, 'World Society and the Nation-State'. For example, states create science agencies, even if they have no scientists. See Martha Finnemore, 'International Organizations as Teachers of Norms: The United Nations Educational, Scientific, and Cultural Organization and Science Policy', *International Organization*, 47 (1993).

Contracts

A contract is an agreement between the legitimate authorities in two or more states or state authorities and another international actor, such as an international financial institution, that is mutually acceptable, pareto-improving, and contingent. A contract can violate the sovereign state model if it subjects domestic institutions and personnel to external influence, or creates institutional arrangements that transcend national boundaries. Obviously, many contracts between states do not transgress the sovereign state model. An international agreement that obligates a state only to change some specific aspect of its foreign policy would not be a violation of autonomy, nor would a treaty that involved only a change in domestic policy but had no other consequences.

Rulers must believe that a contract makes them better off. Otherwise they would not enter into it in the first place, since the *status quo* remains available unless more powerful states can change the 'best alternative to no agreement' (BATNA) in ways that make the target state worse off than in the *status quo ante*, but better off if its leaders sign a new agreement than if they do not.[18] The behaviour of one of the actors is contingent on the behaviour of the others. In contractual arrangements, rulers would not compromise the autonomy of their state unless the behaviour of others also changed: if one actor abrogates the contract the other would prefer to do so as well.

Historically, sovereign lending, especially to weaker states, has frequently involved contractual arrangements that compromise the autonomy of the borrower. Borrowers have not simply agreed to repay their obligations, an arrangement that would have no impact on autonomy. Rather they have agreed to dedicate specific revenues, or to accept oversight of domestic policies, or to permit revenues to be collected by foreign entities, or to change their domestic institutional structures.

Sovereign lending poses unique problems. In lending between private parties, it is possible to appeal to a court system if the borrower fails to repay; lenders can also seek collateral that can be seized if the borrower defaults. However, loans to sovereigns preclude review by any authoritative judicial system and collateral is hard to come by. Withholding future funds may be the only sanction available to lenders. There have been many defaults.[19]

One approach is to charge high interest rates to compensate for the risks inherent in extending credit to sovereigns, but not to compromise the domestic autonomy of the borrower. This was the typical practice during the Renaissance: private inter-

---

[18] Lloyd Gruber has called this 'go it alone' power. See Lloyd Gruber, *Ruling the World: Power Politics and the Rise of Supranational Institutions* (Princeton, NJ: Princeton University Press, 2000), pp. 7–12.

[19] For a review of defaults in the nineteenth and twentieth centuries, see Peter H. Lindert and Peter J. Morton, 'How Sovereign Lending Has Worked', in Jeffrey D. Sachs (ed.), *Developing Country Debt and Economic Performance* (Chicago, IL: University of Chicago Press, 1989), pp. 41–3. For a review of experiences in Latin America, see Carlos Marichal, *A Century of Debt Crises in Latin America: From Independence to the Great Depression 1820–1930* (Princeton, NJ: Princeton University Press, 1989). Lending to the sovereign can also be a problem domestically, not just internationally. Efficient domestic financial institutions required the creation of an institutional structure that provided lenders with the confidence that they would be repaid if they lent money to their own sovereigns. See Douglass North and Barry Weingast, 'Constitution and Commitment: The Evolution of Institutions Governing Public Choice in Seventeenth Century England', *Journal of Economic History*, 49: 4 (September 1989), pp. 803–33.

national bankers did charge high interest rates, and sovereigns did default. This regime for sovereign lending was, paradoxically, more consistent with the sovereign state model than more recent practices, because it did not involve violations of Vattelian sovereignty.[20]

High interest rates and frequent defaults, however, may not be the best solution for either borrowers or lenders. Sovereign borrowers would prefer lower interest rates, but they can only secure such terms if they can in some way tie their own hands, that is, limit their discretion so that potential providers of capital have more confidence of being repaid. One strategy is for borrowers to violate their own domestic autonomy by giving lenders some authority over fiscal, and sometimes other, activities within their own borders. International sovereign lending in the nineteenth and twentieth centuries, especially to weaker states, has been character-ized by contracts in which borrowers secure funds by reassuring lenders that obligations will be honoured because Vattelian sovereignty is violated: lenders part with their funds at lower interest rates because they are given some control over the domestic activities and institutional arrangements of the borrower.

During the nineteenth century, contractual arrangements involving sovereign loans frequently violated autonomy, sometimes in the initial contract, more fre-quently *ex post* if the sovereign threatened to default. Greece, the first state to become independent from the Ottoman Empire, offers examples of several con-tractual arrangements that involved compromising autonomy to secure foreign funds. When Greece was recognized as an independent state in 1832, it received a 60 m franc loan from Britain, France, and Russia, but only by signing an agreement pledging that the 'actual receipts of the Greek treasury shall be devoted, first of all, to the payment of the said interest and sinking fund, and shall not be employed for any other purpose, until those payments on account of the installments of the loan raised under the guarantee of the three Courts, shall have been completely secured for the current year'.[21] In 1838 the entire finances of Greece were placed under a French administrator.[22]

Greece could not secure new loans during the middle of the nineteenth century in part because it was in default on its 1832 obligations. After 1878 its borrowing increased substantially, but to secure these funds Greece committed specific revenues, including the customs at Athens, Piraeus, Patras, and Zante and the revenues from the state monopolies on salt, petroleum, matches, playing cards, and cigarette paper. The loan of 1887 gave the lenders the right to organize a company that would supervise the revenues that were assigned for the loan.[23]

In 1897, after a disastrous war with Turkey over Crete, Greece's finances col-lapsed. It was unable to service its foreign debt or to pay the war indemnity that was demanded by Turkey. Germany and France, along with private debtors, pressed for

---

[20] Garrett Mattingly, *Renaissance Diplomacy* (Boston, MA: Houghton-Mifflin, 1955), p. 59; Edward W. Fox, *History in Geographic Perspective: The Other France* (New York: Norton, 1971), pp. 60–1; Benjamin J. Cohen, *In Whose Interest? International Banking and American Foreign Policy* (New Haven, CT.: Yale University Press, 1986), pp. 84–90.

[21] Quoted in John A. Levandis, *The Greek Foreign Debt and the Great Powers, 1821–1898* (New York: Columbia University Press, 1944), p. 36.

[22] Charles Jelavich and Barbara Jelavich, *The Establishment of the Balkan National States* (Seattle, WA: University of Washington Press, 1977), p. 75.

[23] Levandis, *The Greek Foreign Debt*, p. 67.

an international commission of control. Greece acceded when it became clear that this was the only way to secure new funding, and Britain, which had been more sympathetic to preserving Greek autonomy, then accepted the Control Commission. The Commission, which consisted of one representative appointed by each major power, had absolute control over the sources of revenue needed to fund the war indemnity and foreign debt. The Commission chose the revenue sources that it would control. They included state monopolies on salt, petroleum, matches, playing cards, cigarette paper, tobacco duties, and the customs-revenues of Piraeus. Disputes that might arise between the Commission and agencies of the Greek government were to be settled by binding arbitration. The members of the Commission were given the same standing as diplomats. One member of the Greek parliament argued that the establishment of the Control Commission suspended the independence of Greece.[24]

Greece's experience with foreign lending is not unique. During the nineteenth century, the domestic autonomy of all of the successor states to the Ottoman Empire as well as many Latin American countries was compromised through contractual arrangements involving international loans. When countries went into default, lenders set up control committees to oversee restructuring of the government's finances and other activities. Such committees were established for Bulgaria, Greece, Serbia, the Ottoman Empire, and Argentina.[25] Confronted with imminent default, the Ottoman Empire agreed in 1881 to put some of its revenues under the control of creditors. These included the salt and tobacco monopolies; stamp, spirit, and fishing taxes; and the annual tribute from Bulgaria (which was never paid). A separate administration controlled by the bondholders was created to collect revenues. By 1912 it had over eight thousand employees.[26]

In return for a loan consolidation in 1895, Serbia created a monopolies commission that was charged with overseeing the revenue from the state monopolies on tobacco, salt, and petroleum; liquor taxes; some stamp taxes; and some railway and customs revenues. Revenues from these monopolies were committed to paying off foreign loans and did not flow into the Serbian treasury. The Monopolies Commission was composed of four Serbians and one German and one French representative of foreign bondholders.[27]

Since World War II, contractual arrangements that violate autonomy have become routine for international financial institutions (IFIs). The conditionality requirements of these organizations can violate Vattelian sovereignty, although they are consistent with international legal sovereignty. IFI conditionality can specify changes in domestic policy, modify domestic conceptions of legitimate practices, and influence institutional structures.

Conditionality was not part of the Bretton Woods agreements. During the negotiations that created the International Monetary Fund and the World Bank, the

---

[24] Ibid., pp. 97–112.

[25] Cohen, *In Whose Interest?*, p. 103.

[26] Herbert Feis, Europe, *The World's Banker 1870–1914: An Account of European Foreign Investment and the Connection of World Finance with Diplomacy Before World War I* (New York: W.W. Norton, 1965), pp. 332–4; Donald C. Blaisdell, *European Financial Control in the Ottoman Empire: A Study of the Establishment, Activities, and Significance of the Administration of the Ottoman Public Debt* (New York: Columbia University Press, 1929).

[27] Feis, *The World's Banker*, pp. 266–8.

European representatives successfully resisted US efforts to give the new institutions significant supervisory powers. Potential debtor countries, the Europeans, wanted to defend their autonomy, whereas the major world creditor, the United States, was perfectly willing to violate the sovereign state model. The United States, however, had the money and ultimately the United States prevailed. In 1950, conditionality was accepted in principle by the executive directors of the IMF because it was the only way to induce US policymakers, who had blocked virtually all activities for several years, to allow operations to resume. Conditionality formally became part of the IMF Articles of Agreement by amendment in 1969.[28]

The conditions attached to IMF lending have covered a wide range of domestic activities including aggregate credit expansion; subsidies for state-owned enterprises; the number of government employees; the indexation of salaries; subsidies on food, petroleum, and fertilizers; government investment; personal, payroll, and corporate taxes; excise taxes on beer and cigarettes; and energy prices; they have also touched on issues that are explicitly concerned with international transactions including exchange rate and trade policies. Structural adjustment programmes introduced by the World Bank in the 1970s involved general economic reforms, such as changing taxes, tariffs, subsidies, and interest rates; budgetary reforms; and institution building, rather than just funding specific projects like roads or dams. International financial institutions have tried to alter domestic institutional structures, not just policies. They have supported particular actors and agencies in borrowing countries. They have placed their own personnel in key bureaux.[29] At their annual meeting in 1996 the president of the World Bank and the managing director of the International Monetary Fund committed themselves to a more aggressive attack on corruption in Third World states. The Bank official co-ordinating these new policies stated that 'You will see us giving a much higher profile to governance and corruption concerns in a selective way, delaying disbursements until we are satisfied, or suspending it altogether'.[30] In 1997 the theme of the World Bank's *World Development Report* was the state and the report was sub-titled *The State in a Changing World*. The report stated that the 'clamor for greater government effectiveness has reached crisis proportions in many developing countries where the state has failed to deliver even such fundamental public goods as property rights, roads, and basic health and education'.[31] It describes the situation in Sub-Saharan Africa as one in which there is an urgent priority to 'rebuild state effectiveness through an overhaul of public institutions, reasserting the rule of law, and credible checks on abuse of state power'.[32] These very same governments are, of course, some of the Bank's major clients. The reports goes on to specify fundamental tasks for the state

---

[28] Sidney Dell, *On Being Grandmotherly: The Evolution of IMF Conditionality*, Essays in International Finance no. 144 (Princeton, NJ: International Finance Section, Department of Economics, Princeton University, October 1981), pp. 8–10; Robin Broad, *Unequal Alliance: The World Bank, The International Monetary Fund, and the Philippines* (Berkeley, CA: University of California Press, 1988), pp. 24–25.

[29] International Monetary Fund, Fiscal Affairs Department, *Fund-Supported Programs, Fiscal Policy, and Income Distribution*, Occasional Paper no. 46 (Washington, DC: International Monetary Fund, 1986), p. 40, and Table 12. Broad, *Unequal Alliance*, pp. 51–3.

[30] *New York Times* 11 August, 1997; 31 July 1998.

[31] World Bank, *World Development Report, 1997 The State in a Changing World* (Washington: World Bank, 1997), p. 2.

[32] World Bank , *The State*, p. 14.

including establishing a foundation of law, protecting the environment, and shielding the vulnerable, to chastise governments for spending too much on rich and middle class students in universities while neglecting primary education, and to admonish them to manage ethnic and social differences.[33] Executives are urged to limited their discretionary authority in order to contain opportunities for corruption.[34] Finally, and most ambitiously, the European Bank for Reconstruction and Development is the first IFI to explicitly include political conditionality. The first paragraph of the *Agreement Establishing the European Bank for Reconstruction and Development* states that contracting parties should be 'Committed to the fundamental principles of multiparty democracy, the rule of law, respect for human rights and market economics'.[35]

In sum, sovereign lending has, since the nineteenth century, been characterized by contractual arrangements that have compromised the domestic autonomy of borrowers. The motivations of lenders have varied. In the nineteenth century lenders frequently acted simply to enhance the probability that they would be repaid, although in both the Balkans and Latin America security considerations (balancing against other great powers) were also involved. In more recent years lenders have been concerned not simply with repayment but also with economic reform for humanitarian, ideological, or security reasons. Regardless of motivation, violations of the sovereign state model have been the norm for sovereign lending to weak states since the Napoleonic wars. Conditionality and Vattelian sovereignty, mutually contradictory principles, have operated alongside each other for two centuries. The greater saliency of conditionality, especially since the end of the Cold War, is consistent with the analysis offered here: in a world with mutually inconsistent norms, outcomes depend on power and interests, and the collapse of the Soviet Union has left the industrialized market economy countries freer to pursue more intrusive conditionality. Recent developments in international financial institutions are also, however, compatible with those who contend that the conventional sovereign state model is eroding. The evidence is inconclusive.

Coercion and imposition

Coercion and imposition exist along a continuum determined by the costs of refusal for the target state. Coercion occurs when rulers in one state threaten to impose sanctions unless their counterparts in another compromise their domestic autonomy. The target can acquiesce or resist. Imposition occurs when the rulers or would-be rulers of a target state have no choice; they are so weak that they must accept domestic structures, policies, or personnel preferred by more powerful actors or else be eliminated. When applied against already established states, coercion and imposition are violations of international legal as well as the Vattelian sovereignty. When applied against the would-be rulers of not yet created states, coercion and

---

[33] Ibid., p. 4.
[34] Ibid., p. 8.
[35] *Agreement Establishing the European Bank for Reconstruction and Development*, Paris, 1990.

imposition are violations of the sovereign state model because the autonomy of any state that does emerge has been constrained by external actors, but are not violations of international legal sovereignty, which only applies once a state has secured international recognition allowing it to enter into agreements with other states.

Unlike either conventions or contracts, coercion and imposition leave at least one actor worse off. The *status quo ante*, which the target prefers, is eliminated as an option by the initiating actor. If one state successfully coerces or imposes on another changes in the latter's institutions, policies, or personnel, then the target is no longer a Vattelian sovereign: its policy is constrained not simply by the external power of other states, but also by the ability of others to change the nature of the target's internal politics. Political leaders in the target state are not free to consider all possible policies because some options are precluded by externally imposed domestic structures, policies, or personnel. Indeed the rulers themselves might simply be the quislings of the dominant state.

Coercion and imposition, unlike conventions and contracts, always involve power asymmetry. Imposition entails forcing the target to do something that it would not otherwise do. Physical force, or the threat thereof, matters. Coercion involves asymmetrical bargaining power in which the initiator can make a credible threat, or use 'go it alone' power to create a situation in which the target is better off signing than not, but worse off than in the *status quo ante*, which is no longer an available option. If an actor has 'go it alone' power then the BATNA (best alternative to no agreement) is not the *status quo*.[36]

Economic sanctions aimed at domestic institutions, policies, or personnel are an example of coercion. Out of the 106 specific cases of economic sanctions during the twentieth century presented by Hufbauer, Schott, and Elliot, seventeen involved efforts to protect human rights, and sixteen were attempts to change the character of the domestic regime of the target by either removing the ruler or changing the institutional structure. For example, the United Kingdom used economic pressure to try to remove the Bolshevik regime in the Soviet Union after World War I. The United States attempted to eliminate Juan Peron in Argentina during and after World War II. Collective sanctions against South Africa with the aim of ending apartheid were authorized by the United Nations from 1962 until 1994. The United Kingdom enacted sanctions against Uganda from 1972 to 1979 to force out Idi Amin. The European Community used economic pressure against Turkey in 1981–82 to encourage the restoration of democracy. Between 1970 and 1990 the United States imposed sanctions against more than a dozen countries for human rights violations.[37] In all of these cases the target, even if it did not comply with the sanctions, was worse off than it had been because it could not, at the same time, both avoid sanctions and maintain its *ex ante* policies. Either it suffered sanctions, at least for some period of time, or it had to change its policies.

Imposition is the logical extreme of coercion. It is a situation where the target is so weak that it has no choice but to accept the demands of the more powerful state. Force is the most obvious instrument of imposition. Great powers, however, have

---

[36] For an excellent discussion of bargaining power, although not imposition, see John S. Odell, *Negotiating the World Economy* (Ithaca, NY: Cornell University Press, 2000). For 'go it alone' power see Gruber, *Ruling the World*.

[37] Gary C. Hufbauer, Jeffrey J. Schott, and Kimberly A. Elliot, *Economic Sanctions Reconsidered: History and Current Policy*, 2nd edn. (Washington, DC: Institute for International Economics, 1990).

been cautious about attempting to impose violations of the sovereign state model when such policies have been opposed by their major rivals. If the major powers pursue opposing policies then imposition is very unlikely, if not impossible, because even a weak target can get external support. Imposition has occurred when there has been either a condominium among the major powers or the acceptance of spheres of influence.

Examples of imposition within spheres of influence include the US military occupation of a number of Caribbean and Central American states. The United States has sent troops to Cuba, the Dominican Republic, Nicaragua, Haiti (nine times), Panama, and Grenada in response to civil unrest, loan defaults, or threats of foreign intervention and has imposed constitutions, customs receiverships, and judicial control. South Africa used military pressure to secure compliant regimes in Lesotho both before and after the end of apartheid. During the Cold War, the Soviet Union dictated the domestic institutional structure and the policies of its east European satellites: Poland, Hungary, Romania, Czechoslovakia, and Bulgaria did not have Vattelian sovereignty even though they did have international legal sovereignty. For a time Poland's minister of defence was a marshal in the Soviet army. The militaries of the eastern European states were penetrated by the Soviet military and by their own communist parties, which were themselves penetrated by the Communist Party of the Soviet Union.[38] The foreign policy of Poland in 1958, or Cuba in 1908, could hardly be analysed from any perspective that used the sovereign state model as a starting point.

One of the more enduring examples of coercion and sometimes imposition under great power condominium has involved efforts to secure minority rights in eastern and central Europe. All of the states that emerged from the Ottoman and Habsburg empires were compelled to accept provisions for minority protection as a condition of international recognition. In 1832, the British, French, and Russians imposed on Greece its constitutional structure (monarchy), its monarch (Otto, the under-age second son of the King of Bavaria), and specific policies including protection for religious minorities. Greece had no bargaining leverage because its resources were so limited, not least because of dissension among the Greek revolutionaries themselves. In the Treaty of Berlin of 1878, the following language was applied to Montenegro, Serbia, and Bulgaria:

The difference of religious creeds and confessions shall not be alleged against any person as a ground for exclusion or incapacity in matters relating to the enjoyment of civil and political rights, admission to public employments, functions, and honours, or the exercise of the various professions and industries in any locality whatsoever. The freedom and outward exercise of all forms of worship shall be assured to all persons belonging to [Montenegro, Serbia, and Bulgaria], as well as to foreigners, and no hindrance shall be offered either to the hierarchical organization of the different communions, or to their relations with their spiritual chiefs.[39]

---

[38] Condoleezza Rice, *The Soviet Union and the Czechoslovak Army* (Princeton, NJ: Princeton University Press, 1984), ch. 1; Christopher D. Jones, 'National Armies and National Sovereignty', in *The Warsaw Pact: Alliance in Transition?* Edited by David Holloway and Jane M.O. Sharp (Ithaca, NY: Cornell University Press, 1984).

[39] Treaty of Berlin, 13 July, 1878, in Fred L. Israel (ed.), *Major Peace Treaties of Modern History, 1648–1967*, vol. I (New York: McGraw-Hill, 1967), Articles V, XXVII, XLIV. See also Jelavich and Jelavich, *Balkan National States*, pp. 50–2, 68–72, 156; and A.C. Macartney, *National States and National Minorities* (London: Oxford University Press, 1934), pp. 166, 168.

The Treaty also included provisions for the protection of minority rights in Romania and in the Ottoman Empire itself.[40]

The 1878 Berlin Treaty settlements were examples of coercion rather than imposition. The would-be rulers of the target states did not want to grant minority rights, and they did have some leverage. Their first-best outcome would have been recognition and no constraints on their domestic autonomy. They acquiesced, however, to European demands because international recognition with minority rights provisions, which might be evaded, was better than no recognition at all.

The would-be leaders of all of the states that were created after World War I (or were successors to the defeated empires) had to accept extensive provisions for the protection of minorities. As in Greece in 1832, these would-be rulers had limited bargaining leverage. Austria, Hungary, Bulgaria, and Turkey were defeated states, and minority protections were written into their peace treaties. Poland, Czechoslovakia, Yugoslavia, Romania, and Greece were new or enlarged states. They signed minority rights treaties with the Allied and Associated Powers. Albania, Lithuania, Latvia, Estonia, and Iraq made declarations as a result of pressure from the victorious powers when they applied to join the League of Nations.[41]

The protections accorded to minorities were detailed and extensive. The Polish Minority Treaty, for instance, provided that 'Poland undertakes to assure full and complete protection of life and liberty to all inhabitants of Poland without distinction of birth, nationality, language, race or religion'. Religious differences were not to affect public or professional employment. Where there were a considerable number of non-Polish speakers, they would be educated in their own language in primary school, although the state could mandate the teaching of Polish. Jews would not be obligated to perform any act that violated the Jewish Sabbath and therefore elections would not be held on Saturday.[42] The Treaty was made part of the fundamental law of Poland.

With the exception of Hungary, which wanted protection for the many Hungarians in neighbouring countries, and Czechoslovakia, which wanted to reassure its large German minority, the minorities rights treaties of Versailles are examples of imposition.[43] For the rulers or would-be rulers of these states, the *status quo* was non-existence. They would not have states to rule unless they accepted the conditions imposed by the victors in World War I. They lacked material, military, and diplomatic resources to bargain or resist.

The Balkan crises of the 1990s evoked a response from the major powers reminiscent of nineteenth century efforts to establish stability. Minority rights were explicitly included in the conditions for European Community recognition of the successor states of Yugoslavia. On 16 December, 1991, the foreign ministers of the European Community made acceptance of the Carrington Plan, formally the Treaty Provisions

---

[40] Treaty of Berlin, Articles LXIV and LXII.

[41] Inis L. Claude, Jr., *National Minorities: An International Problem* (Cambridge, MA: Harvard University Press, 1955), p. 16; and Dorothy V. Jones, *Code of Peace: Ethics and Security in the World of the Warlord States* (Chicago, IL: University of Chicago Press, 1991), p. 45.

[42] Polish Minorities Treaty, Articles 2, 7, 8; and 11. The text of the Treaty is reprinted in Macartney, *Minorities*, pp. 502–6.

[43] For discussions of attitudes toward the minority treaties in different states see Sebastian Bartsch, *Minderheitenschutz in der internationalen Politik : Völkerbund und KSZE/OSZE in neuer Perspektive* (Oplanden, Germany: Westdeutscher Verlag, 1995).

for the Convention (with the former republics of Yugoslavia), the prerequisite for recognition. Chapter 2 of the Carrington Plan stipulated that the Republics would guarantee the right to life, to be free of torture, to liberty, to public hearings by an impartial tribunal, to freedom of thought, to peaceful assembly, and to marry and form a family. These rights were to apply to all regardless of sex, race, colour, language, religion, or minority status. The Republics were to respect the rights of national and ethnic minorities elaborated in conventions adopted by the United Nations and the CSCE, including the then proposed United Nations Declaration on the Rights of Persons belonging to National or Ethnic, Religious, and Linguistic Minorities, and the proposed Convention for the Protection of Minorities of the European Commission. The republics were to protect the cultural rights of minorities, guarantee equal participation in public affairs, and assure that each individual could choose his or her ethnic identity. Members of minority groups were to be given the right to participate in the 'government of the Republics concerning their affairs'.[44] In local areas where members of a minority formed a majority of the population they were to be given special status including a national emblem, an educational system 'which respects the values and needs of that group',[45] a legislative body, a regional police force, and a judiciary that reflects the composition of the population. Such special areas were to be permanently demilitarized unless they were on an international border. The rights established in the convention were to be assured through national legislation.[46]

The implications that can be drawn from the data presented thus far about the empirical validity of the sovereign state model are modest because I have selected on the dependent variable. Nevertheless, several inferences are reasonable. The sovereign state model has never been taken for granted; rulers have explored institutional alternatives. In some areas of the world, notably central and eastern Europe, there have never been any smaller states that enjoyed full Vattelian sovereignty. Many developing countries that have signed stand-by agreements with international financial institutions have had to agree to changes and ongoing supervision of their domestic institutions and policies. In one way or another—as a result of conventions, contracts, coercion, or imposition—most of the states in the contemporary international system do not fully conform with the sovereign state model.

Peace settlements

The major peace settlements from Westphalia to the present offer another body of data, one not selected on the dependent variable, with which to examine the actual functioning, or lack thereof, of the sovereign state model. Major peace treaties embody the shared understanding of rulers, or at least the deals that they have found mutually acceptable. All of the major treaties, beginning with the Peace of

---

[44] European Community, Treaty Provisions for the Convention (with the former republics of Yugoslavia) 1991, ch. 2. 4.

[45] European Community, Treaty Provisions for the Convention, ch. 2.5c.

[46] Beverley Crawford, 'Explaining Defection from International Cooperation: Germany's Unilateral Recognition of Croatia', *World Politics*, 48 (1996), p. 497.

Westphalia in 1648, have included violations of the 'Westphalian' model, specifically the principle of autonomy. Infractions against the sovereign state model, whether in the form of conventions, contracts, coercion, or imposition, have been justified by alternative principles that are inconsistent with autonomy, such as human rights, minority rights, fiscal responsibility, domestic stability, or external balance.

The Peace of Westphalia of 1648 (comprising the two separate treaties of Münster and Osnabrück), has generally been understood as a critical event in the development of the modern sovereign state system characterized by juridically independent, territorial, and autonomous political entities. In a widely cited article published in 1948 Leo Gross argued that to the Peace of Westphalia is 'traditionally attributed the importance and dignity of being the first of several attempts to establish something resembling world unity on the basis of states exercising untrammeled sovereignty over certain territories and subordinated to no earthly authority'.[47] For Gross the central importance of Westphalia is that it established an international system based on the equality of states whether Catholic or Protestant, republican or monarchical, and undermined the hierarchy of the medieval world. More recently Daniel Philpott has affirmed the central importance of Westphalia, arguing that 'in the wake of Westphalia states became the chief form of polity in Europe' and that 'following Westphalia, states became virtually uninhibited in their internal authority'.[48]

The treaties concluded at Westphalia do not provide much evidence for the assertion that the Peace itself was any kind of decisive transition point. The Peace brought to an end the Thirty Years War which had devastated the centre of Europe, especially the Germanic lands. It was a complicated document with provisions about various dynastic claims, division of territory, the practice of religion, and the constitution of the Holy Roman Empire. The Treaty of Osnabrück was concluded between the Habsburg monarch who was the Holy Roman Emperor and the Protestant ruler of Sweden; the Treaty of Münster was concluded between the Emperor and the Catholic king of France. In many ways it is easier to regard the peace as a new constitution for the Holy Roman Empire than to see it as a confirmation of what came to be termed the Westphalian system.[49]

The specific issue at Westphalia was how the Empire, which had lost the war, would satisfy France and Sweden which had won.[50] The more general problem was to find some way of dealing with the religious disorders that were tearing Europe apart and threatening to undermine regime stability across the continent. The Thirty

---

[47] Leo Gross, 'The Peace of Westphalia 1648–1948', *American Journal of International Law*, 42 (1948), p. 20.

[48] Daniel Philpott, 'The Religious Roots of Modern International Relations', *World Politics*, 52 (2000), pp. 211 and 212.

[49] For a excellent critiques of the Westphalian myth see Andreas Osiander, 'Sovereignty, International Relations, and the Westphalian Myth', *International Organization*, 55 (2001), pp. 251–87; Stéphane Beaulac, 'The Westphalian Legal Orthodoxy—Myth or Reality', *Journal of the History of International Law*, 2 (2000), pp 148–77; John G. Gagliardo, *Reich and Nation, The Holy Roman Empire as Idea and Reality, 1763–1806* (Bloomington, IN: University of Indiana Press, 1980), pp. 44–6, and Derek Croxton, 'The Peace of Westphalia of 1648 and the Origins of Sovereignty', *The International History Review*, 21 (1999). Croxton is particularly compelling in demonstrating that the individuals involved in the Westphalian negotiations did not hold modern conceptualizations of sovereignty. See especially pp. 579–89.

[50] A. W. Ward, 'The Peace of Westphalia', in *The Cambridge Modern History*, vol IV: *The Thirty Years War* (Cambridge: Cambridge University Press, 1907), pp. 400–5.

Years War, fuelled in part by religious antipathies, resulted in more than two million battle deaths, a larger carnage than any conflict except for the First and Second World Wars.[51] It had been preceded by the religious wars in France during the latter part of the sixteenth century. The Civil Wars in England rent the English monarchy through the middle part of the seventeenth century.

The Peace imposed a territorial settlement that was advantageous to the victors, France and Sweden. France was granted control over the bishoprics of Metz, Toul, and Verdun which had been under *de facto* French control for a century. Alsace was granted to France by Austria, even though the Austrian claim to Alsace was questionable. One provision of the treaty states that the ancient privileges which these local nobles had enjoyed with regard to the Empire should be retained with respect to France, but another provision of the treaty granted France 'all manner of Jurisdiction and Sovereignty'.[52]

Sweden's fundamental territorial objective, to secure a position on the southern shore of the Baltic, was satisfied in a completely medieval way. The King of Sweden received eastern Pomerania, the islands of Rugen, Usedom and Willin, the bishoprics of Bremen and Verden and the port of Weismar. These were granted to Sweden not in full sovereignty, but as fiefs of the Holy Roman Empire.[53] The rulers of Sweden were given a place in the Imperial Diet under the titles of the Dukes of Bremen, Verden, and Pomerania, the Princes of Rugen and the Lords of Wismar. The prerogatives of the ruler of Sweden were specified with regard to appeal to either of the imperial courts—the Aulic Court or the Imperial Chamber. Sweden was given the right to erect a university and to collect certain tolls. The Hanseatic towns in the areas ruled by Sweden were, however, to maintain their traditional rights of liberty and freedom of navigation.[54]

While rhetorically endorsing the Augsburg principle that the prince could set the religion of his subjects (*cuius regio, eius religio*), the actual provisions of the Peace constrained sovereign prerogatives in Germany in favour of some forms of religious toleration. Those Catholics who lived in Lutheran states or Lutherans who lived in Catholic states were given the right to practice in the privacy of their homes, and to educate their children at home or to send them to foreign schools. Five cities with mixed Lutheran and Catholic populations were to have freedom of religious practice for both groups. In four of these cities, offices were to be divided equally between Catholics and Lutherans. The Treaty of Osnabrück provided that Catholics and Lutherans should be equally represented in the assemblies of the Empire. Religious issues were to be decided by a consensus that included both Catholics and Protestants. Representatives to the imperial courts were also to include members of

---

[51] Charles Tilly, *Coercion, Capital and European States, AD 990–1990* (Cambridge, MA: Basil Blackwell, 1990), pp. 165–6.

[52] Treaty of Münster, reprinted in Fred Israel (ed.), *Major Peace Treaties* (New York: McGraw Hill, 1967), art. LXXVI, for quote, art. LXXI, art. LXXIV; Ward, 'Westphalia', pp. 404–6; E. A. Beller, 'The Thirty Years War', in *The New Cambridge Modern History*, vol. IV: *The Decline of Spain and the Thirty Years War 1609–1648/59*, edited by J.P. Cooper (Cambridge: Cambridge University Press, 1970), p. 353.

[53] Treaty of Osnabrück, reprinted in Clive Parry (ed.), *The Consolidated Treaty Series*, vol I: *1648–1649* (Dobbs Ferry, NY: Oceana, 1969), Article X, pp. 244ff; Ward, 'Westphalia', pp. 403–4; Beller, 'Thirty Years War', p. 354.

[54] Treaty of Osnabrück, art. X.4.

both religions. If the judges divided along religious lines, then the case could be appealed to the Diet of the Holy Roman Empire, where a decision also required a consensus of Protestants (only Lutherans and Calvinists were included) and Catholics.[55]

The Peace of Westphalia also dealt with a number of issues related to the constitutional arrangements of the Empire. The Emperor was elected by a group of religious and secular nobles called the electors. The Peace increased the number of electors from seven to eight by restoring an Electorship to the Duke Palatine. The rights of succession for the ruling house of Bavaria were spelled out, including a provision that the Electoral seat held by Bavaria would disappear were there to be no male heir because Bavaria and the Palatinate would then be ruled by the same family.[56]

This effort to dictate the internal organizational arrangements of the Holy Roman Empire in an international treaty are hardly consistent with conventional notions of sovereignty. Westphalia did not abolish the Empire, which might have been consistent with a new world of sovereign states, nor did Westphalia treat the Empire as if it were a sovereign state with the right to determine its own constitutional structure. Instead, the treaties involved external actors, who guaranteed the provisions of the treaties, in the internal affairs of Germany.

For the conventional interpretation of the Peace of Westphalia, which underscores 1648 as a break with the past, the most important provisions of the Treaties are the ones that recognize the prerogatives of the princes within their own territory and give them the right to make alliances with other states. The established view is that this is a confirmation of a fundamental attribute of sovereignty, the right of every state to carry out its own foreign policy. With this right the principalities of the Holy Roman Empire could be understood as autonomous states rather than as parts of some larger corporate body. The section of the Treaty of Münster that recognizes the right to make treaties states that:

> Above all, it shall be free perpetually to each of the States of the Empire, to make Alliances with Strangers for their Preservation and Safety; provided, nevertheless, such Alliances be not against the Emperor, and the Empire, nor against the Publick Peace, and this Treaty, and without prejudice to the Oath by which every one is bound to the Emperor and the Empire.[57]

The Treaty of Münster is 42 pages long. It contains 128 provisions. The right to make treaties is given in one sentence in a section of the Treaty that spells out the rights of states within the Holy Roman Empire to participate in the deliberations of the Empire and which concludes with an admonition that no Treaty should be directed against the Emperor and the Empire. Only after the fact can this be read as an endorsement of the principle of sovereignty which rejects any external restraint on the way in which states might conduct their foreign policies.

Moreover, the treaty-making power recognized at Westphalia simply reaffirmed an already existing right. The more powerful German states had conducted inde-

---

[55] Treaty of Osnabrück, Articles V and VII.
[56] Treaty of Osnabrück, Article IV; Treaty of Münster, XIV.
[57] Treaty of Münster, Article LXV; a similar provision is found in the Treaty of Osnabrück, Article VIII.1.

pendent foreign policies before the conclusion of the Peace. The Schmalkalden League formed by six Protestant princes and ten cities in 1531 was in continuous contact with Denmark, England and France. The Protestant princes signed a treaty of alliance with Henry II, the King of France, in 1552. Both the Palatinate and Brandenburg concluded alliances with the Dutch Republic around 1605. A new Protestant alliance, the Union, was formed in 1608. The Union made concrete agreements with England, France, and the Netherlands.[58]

The Peace of Westphalia did not affirm Vattelian sovereignty. The principalities of the Empire did not become autonomous states. The settlement of 1648 did, however, undermine the position of the Papacy and erode the already weakening notion of a Christendom. It reflected and promoted foreign policy based on the principle of balance of power. The balance of power, however, does not preclude efforts by powerful states to influence the domestic authority structures of weaker ones. In an anarchic system balancing may be internal or external, and external balancing can involve efforts to alter regime types or authority structures in other states, not just alliances. The Peace reflected the short term interests of the victorious powers, France and Sweden, rather than some overarching conceptualization of how the international system should be ordered. It used medieval structures and concepts, altering the electoral system of the empire, satisfying Sweden by awarding fiefdoms, as much as modern ones. The Peace of Westphalia was not Westphalian.

The Treaties of Münster and Osnabrück did not sanction the right of German princes to do whatever they pleased with regard to the practice of religion within their own territories. The Peace dictated a set of internal practices for much of the Holy Roman Empire. The Treaties were guaranteed by France and Sweden, providing legitimation for challenges to German autonomy. In the area of religion, the central political question of the seventeenth century, the Peace of Westphalia was less consistent with the sovereign state model than was the Peace of Augsburg, concluded almost a century earlier.[59]

The Peace of Westphalia is an example of contract. The Habsburg monarch did not want to sanction Protestantism. He refused to accept toleration in the areas that he ruled directly but that were outside the Holy Roman Empire. Ending the Thirty Years War with provisions for religious toleration was, however, preferable to more fighting.

The Peace of Utrecht was signed in 1713. It brought an end to war between France, the major power in Europe, and an alliance that included England, Holland, Sweden, the Austrian Habsburgs, the Holy Roman Empire, Savoy, and many German principalities. The war had been precipitated by Louis XIV's efforts to extend his control to Spain and even Austria. The Peace provided that Philip V, a Bourbon, would be recognized as the King of Spain, but only if the Bourbon family agreed that France and Spain would never be united under a single ruler. Utrecht was a contract between Britain and France in which, in exchange for peace and

---

[58] Geoffrey Parker, *The Thirty Years' War* (London: Routledge and Kegan Paul, 1984), p. 2. John G. Gagliardo, *Germany Under the Old Regime, 1600–1790* (London: Longman, 1991), pp. 23–25; Gagliardo, *Reich and Nation*, p. viii.

[59] Even the Peace of Augsburg provided for religious toleration in several German cities that had mixed Catholic and Lutheran populations. See Gagliardo, *Germany*, pp. 16–21.

some territorial aggrandizement, Louis XIV accepted constraints on the domestic political arrangements and personnel that could govern France and Spain.[60]

One outcome of the peace settlements reached at the conclusion of the Napoleonic wars, although not the only one, was the creation of the Holy Alliance. The aim of the Holy Alliance, established by Prussia, Austria, and Russia, was to prevent the rise of republican governments. The members of the Alliance pledged to resist such developments domestically and to repress them internationally. A protocol signed at the Conference of Troppau in 1820 stated:

States which have undergone a change of government due to revolution, the results of which threaten other states, ipso facto cease to be members of the European Alliance, and remain excluded from it until their situation gives guarantees for legal order and stability. If, owing to such alterations, immediate danger threatens other states, the parties bind themselves, by peaceful means, or if need be by arms, to bring back the guilty state into the bosom of the Great Alliance.[61]

The rulers of the powerful conservative states of Europe had no compunction about using coercion or imposition to violate the sovereign state model in the name of an alternative principle, the preservation of peace through the repression of republican governments, although the Holy Alliance had only limited success partly because of British resistance. Austria received international approval for the repression of republican governments in some German states and in Naples. At the Congress of Verona in 1822, France secured the support of Russia, Prussia, and Austria to intervene in support of the monarchy in Spain, which it did in 1823. The Alliance functioned until 1825, when it broke up over the question of whether to intervene to aid the rebellion in Greece.[62] The Holy Alliance was not only an instrument of coercion and imposition *vis-à-vis* potential republican governments, but also a convention among the signatories who committed themselves to maintain their own conservative regimes.

Provisions of the Treaty of Versailles and other agreements reached at the end of World War I were explicitly designed to alter the domestic political arrangements of the new states that emerged after the conflict. The treaties and the League of Nations embodied Wilsonian conceptions of the relationship among the rights of minorities, national self-determination, democracy, and international peace. Collective security could only work with democratic states. Democratic states had to respect national self-determination. National self-determination, however, could not resolve the problem of minorities. Therefore, the rights of minorities had to be

---

[60] Mark Trachtenberg, 'Intervention in Historical Perspective', in Laura W. Reed and Carl Kaysen (eds.), *Emerging Norms of Justified Intervention: A Collection of Essays from a Project of the American Academy of Arts and Sciences* (Cambridge, MA: American Academy of Arts and Sciences, 1993), p. 17; W.E. Lingelbach, 'The Doctrine and Practice of Intervention in Europe', *Annals of the American Academy of Political and Social Science*, 16 (1900), p. 5; Andreas Osiander, *The States System of Europe 1640–1990: Peacemaking and the Conditions of International Stability* (Oxford: Oxford University Press, 1994), pp. 123–33.

[61] Quoted in Thomas and. Thomas, Jr., *Non-Intervention*, p. 8.

[62] Goronwy J. Jones, *The United Nations and the Domestic Jurisdiction of States: Interpretations and Applications of the Non-Intervention Principle* (Cardiff: University of Wales Press, 1979), pp. 3–4; R.J. Vincent, *Nonintervention and International Order* (Princeton, NJ: Princeton University Press, 1974), pp. 77–79, 86–7; Stanley Hoffman, 'The Problem of Intervention', in Hedley Bull (ed.), *Intervention in World Politics* (Oxford: Clarendon Press, 1984), p. 12.

protected so that they would accept and support the democratic polities within which they resided. The minorities treaties associated with the Versailles settlement violated the sovereign state model. They were imposed on the would-be rulers of new and powerless states, and were repudiated when it later became apparent that neither the Great Powers nor the League of Nations could or would enforce them. Symmetrical conditions concerning the treatment of minorities were never accepted by the victorious powers. There were no international agreements about the treatment of the Irish by the British government, or of Asians and blacks by federal or state authorities in the United States.[63]

There was no general peace settlement after World War II; rather, the United States and the Soviet Union coerced or contracted to encourage political regimes that were consonant with their own preferences. In 1975, however, the major powers did conclude the Final Act of the Helsinki Conference on Security and Cooperation in Europe (CSCE). The CSCE was a contract between the Soviets and the West in which the Soviets nominally accepted some human rights principles and the West recognized existing borders and regimes in Europe. The CSCE reflected the Soviet effort to secure legitimation of their dominance of eastern Europe, and the desire of the West to get the Soviets to accept some liberal precepts. Principle VI of the 'Declaration on Principles Guiding Relations between Participating States' endorsed non-intervention, while Principle VII endorsed human rights including freedom of thought, conscience, and religion. The West used the Helsinki accord to pressure the Soviet Union on human rights, rejecting the charge that this amounted to inter-ference in internal affairs by claiming that human rights were universally recognized and that non-interference referred only to efforts to dictate to other countries.[64]

Most recently the Dayton Accords designed to establish a stable and tolerant political system for Bosnia included extensive violations of Vattelian sovereignty. Annex 6 committed the signatories—The Republic of Bosnia and Herzegovina, the Federation of Bosnia and Herzegovina and the Republika Srpska—to honour the provisions of 15 international and European human rights accords. It provided for the creation of an Ombudsman for human rights who would have diplomatic immunity, would not be a citizen of any parts of the former Yugoslavia, and would initially be appointed to a five-year term by the Organization for Cooperation and Security in Europe; as well as a 14 member Chamber of Human Rights, four of whose members would be appointed by Bosnia and Herzegovina, two by the Republic of Srpska, and the other eight, none of whom would be citizens of the states that had been part of Yugoslavia, by the Committee of Ministers of the Council of Europe. Individuals could bring complaints to the Chamber whose decisions, taken by a majority vote, would be binding on the signatories. Non-governmental organizations and international organizations were to be invited to Bosnia to monitor the implementation of the terms of the Annex. After five years the Chamber and the office of the Ombudsman would pass to the control of Bosnia and Herzegovina, if all of the parties agreed. The goal of the Dayton accords was to make Bosnia a conventional state that would conform with the sovereign state model, but the leaders of the major powers believed that they could only accomplish

---

[63] Jones, Code of Peace, p. 45.
[64] R. J. Vincent, *Human Rights and International Relations* (Cambridge: Cambridge University Press, 1986), pp. 66–70.

this goal by compromising Bosnia's Vattelian sovereignty at least in the short and medium term.[65] Hardly a new story for the Balkans.

Hence, every major peace settlement from Westphalia to Dayton has involved violations of the sovereign state model. At Utrecht and Helsinki, rulers entered into contracts that compromised, either immediately or potentially, the domestic autonomy of some states. In the Holy Alliance and at Versailles and Dayton, rulers in the most powerful states imposed their preferences regarding specific domestic policies and sometimes even constitutional structures. There was always some competing principle—the need for religious peace at Westphalia, for balance of power at Utrecht, for international peace at Vienna and Versailles (assumed to emerge from completely different kinds of domestic regimes), for stability at Helsinki and Dayton—that was invoked to justify compromising the sovereign state model.

Conclusions

The sovereign state model has persisted for a long period of time but its defining principles—non-intervention and mutual recognition of juridically independent territorial entities—have often been ignored. It has been both enduring and flimsy. The sovereign state model is not a stable equilibrium: actors have frequently had both the incentive and power to deviate from it. It is not a generative grammar, producing individual entities (states) that replicate and reinforce the general model: states have acted in ways that are inconsistent with the model either by voluntarily accepting constraints on their own autonomy or by imposing authority structures on others. The sovereign state model is not a set of constitutive rules the violation of which means that some other game is being played (as would be the case if a bishop were moved in a straight line in chess instead of along a diagonal): if a ruler agrees that domestic ethnic minorities will be given specific rights and that behaviour will be monitored by external actors, or that financial affairs will be managed by a committee appointed by foreign bondholders, he is not understood to have done something incomprehensible nor will he or others necessarily claim that his state is no longer sovereign. Whether or not a ruler's opponents chastize him for adopting policies inconsistent with Vattelian sovereignty will depend upon their assessment of the political benefits of invoking such norms.

Norms associated with the sovereign state model are a widely available cognitive script. They can be more easily invoked than historical structures that have become obsolescent, such as the tributary state model which has been mostly forgotten even in East Asia (although the Chinese treatment of Hong Kong can be seen as a manifestation of traditional Sinocentric practices), or institutional forms whose underlying principles have not been explicitly formulated and labelled, such as the European Union, for which contemporary observers are still seeking an appropriate

---

[65] United States, Department of State, *The Bosnia Agreement*, 1995. Susan L. Woodward, 'Compromised Sovereignty to Create Sovereignty: Is Dayton Bosnia a Futile Exercise or an Emerging Model?', in Stephen D. Krasner (ed.), *Problematic Sovereignty: Contested Rules and Political Possibilities* (New York: Columbia University Press, 2001).

appellation (although European forms, including the insistence on political democracy not just economic openness, have been copied in other areas of the world such as the Mercosul agreement in South America). Given how complicated and multi-faceted most international environments are, political actors will try to maintain a repertoire of available normative options. No principle or norm will be taken for granted. Intellectual constructs will be debated over extended periods of time and only sometimes codified in unambiguous ways, and even then subject to challenge by potentially contradictory ideas. Political leaders must struggle with concrete problems that may, or may not, be best resolved by invoking the most widely available norms. How should Sweden's territorial ambitions be satisfied in 1648? How should a fifteenth century Chinese emperor, operating in a system in which he and only he is regarded as having the Mandate of Heaven, interact with powerful and rich Moslem rulers from central Asia whose own belief systems preclude acknowledging the emperor's supremacy? Given the Islamic division between the House of God and the House of Infidels, how should the Ottoman sultan treat his European counterparts as they became more powerful during the seventeenth century? How should national self determination and minority rights be resolved after the First World War? How can all attributes of the European Union including open labour markets be expanded to eastern Europe without undermining support for integration in western Europe? No single set of coherent principles, whether those of the sovereign state model, or the Sinocentric tributary system, or medieval Europe, or the Islamic world, will provide optimal outcomes for rulers in all of the situations which they confront in the international environment. Regardless of what cognitive scripts are most available, actions will be decoupled from norms.

Rather than being treated as a set of constitutive rules or as an analytic assumption, the sovereign state model is better understood as an example of organized hypocrisy. Political leaders are inevitably faced with situations in which the actions that they take and the norms that they have endorsed will not be mutually consistent. Organized hypocrisy is characteristic of international environments because: (1) actors, whether they be states, city states, empires, trading leagues, or tributary states have different levels of power; (2) rulers in different political entities will be responsive to different domestic norms which may, or may not, be fully compatible with international norms; (3) situations arise in which it is unclear what rule should apply, and there is no authority structure that can resolve these ambiguities. In any international system logics of consequences will dominate logics of appropriateness.

System, empire and state in Chinese international relations

YONGJIN ZHANG[1]

Two criticisms have long been directed at the theorization of international relations (IR): ahistoricism and Eurocentrism. Westphalia, it is argued, has been so stigmatized that it has become synonymous with the beginning as well as the end of what we understand as international relations. Rationalist theorizing in general, of both the neorealist and neoliberal persuasions, has produced a set of deductive theories that aim and claim to transcend history. Neorealism of the Waltzian brand in particular is 'cleansed' of history.[2] Such concepts as state, system and sovereignty, so central to the theorizing enterprise, have rarely been historicized in their proper context.[3] Although such indictment is not new and the problematic of the discipline has been long recognized, challenges have not been adequately taken up even when the end of the Cold War shattered the disciplinary complacency and exposed its inability to explain and understand, let alone to predict, the fundamental transformation in contemporary international relations. The remedies are, nevertheless, slow in coming. The English School, it is true, has managed to eschew ahistoricism through their concerted efforts to 'invent international society'.[4] Historical narratives of the evolution and expansion of international society by members of the English School, from Herbert Butterfield, Hedley Bull and Martin Wight to Adam Watson and Robert Jackson, constitute an indispensable part of their theorizing.[5] It is also true that the recent intervention of historical sociology and the constructive turn in

[1] Part of this article was presented at a round-table discussion at the Department of International Relations, Research School of Pacific and Asian Studies at the Australian National University in June 2001. I would like to thank the round-table participants for their valuable comments and suggestions. I would also like to thank the editors of the *Review*, particularly Tim Dunne, for their helpful comments on an earlier version of this article.
[2] Benno Teschke, 'Geopolitical Relations in the European Middle Ages: History and Theory', *International Organization*, 52:2 (1998), p. 328.
[3] For a good summary of such criticisms, see Barry Buzan and Richard Little, *International Systems in World History—Remaking the Study of International Relations* (Oxford: Oxford University Press, 2000). See also Christian Reus-Smit, 'The Idea of History and History with Ideas: Toward a Constructivist Historical Sociology of International Relations', in John M. Hobson and Steve Hobden (eds.), *Bringing Historical Sociologies into International Relations* (forthcoming).
[4] See Tim Dunne, *Inventing International Society: A History of the English School* (New York: St. Martin's Press, 1998).
[5] See in particular, Herbert Butterfield and Martin Wight (eds.), *Diplomatic Investigations: Essays in the Theory of International Politics* (London: Allen and Unwin, 1966), Martin Wight, *Systems of States*, edited with an introduction by Hedley Bull (Leicester: Leicester University Press, 1977), Hedley Bull and Adam Watson (eds.), *The Expansion of International Society* (Oxford: Clarendon Press, 1984), Adam Watson, *The Evolution of International Society: A Comparative Historical Analysis* (London: Routledge, 1992), and Robert H. Jackson, *The Global Covenant: Human Conduct in a World of States* (Oxford: Oxford University Press, 2000).

theorizing about IR have led us into deeper and broader sweeps of world history in the search for historicized conceptions of state and for the institutional rationality of international relations. Ironically, such greater historical sensitivity may have reinforced rather than mediated existing Eurocentrism. Ancient Greece—the Hellas, the Roman Empire, and medieval European history have been either rediscovered or reaffirmed as the most favoured, if not the only, pre-Westphalian 'testing ground' for existing IR theories. The nature of political orders beyond European history and their historical transformations still remain largely outside the empirical purview of much recent theorizing of IR.[6]

It is therefore not surprising that though fleeting and flirting references to fragments of the history of Chinese international relations, particularly the Warring States period, have often been made in theoretical works of IR, Ancient and Imperial China has not been taken very seriously.[7] Adda Bozeman's work published more than forty years ago still stands as a rare exception in this regard.[8] To the extent that the system of states in Ancient China and the so-called Chinese world order have been looked at, the subjects remain the privileged preserve of Sinologists and Chinese historians.[9] Yet, the Chinese experience is uniquely challenging, as it evolved entirely independently of European influence until modern times. Ancient China produced one of the earliest systems of states in the world, which initially paralleled and later survived the existence of the Ancient Greek city-states system. Imperial China, in addition, presided over a long-lasting social order in East Asia, an international system of a sort nestled in a distinct civilization and with its own structuring and organizing principles. Until the second half of the nineteenth century, Chinese international relations were subject to their own distinctive rules, norms, discourses and institutions. Epic transformations, too, have taken place in Chinese international relations. How the system of states emerged from the collapse of the central authority of the Zhou Dynasty in the eighth century BC and why a universal empire was reduced to a civilizational state in the twentieth century presents both challenges and implications for a historically informed IR theorization. If a truly world historical perspective is imperative in remaking the studies of international relations, as Barry Buzan and Richard Little have advocated,[10] it is time to bring China in.

[6] See for example John M. Hobson, 'The Historical Sociology of the State and the State of Historical Sociology in International Relations', *Review of International Political Economy*, 5:2 (1998), pp. 284–320; Stuart J. Kaufman, 'The Fragmentation and Consolidation of International Systems', *International Organization*, 51:2 (Spring 1997), pp. 173–208; Steve Hobden, 'Theorising the International System: Perspectives from Historical Sociology', *Review of International Studies*, 25:2 (1999), pp. 257–71. Teschke, '*Geopolitical Relations*', pp. 325–58, and Christian Reus-Smit, *The Moral Purpose of the State: Culture, Social Identity, and Institutional Rationality in International Relations* (Princeton, NJ: Princeton University Press, 1999). Kaufman, though, has tentatively looked at the history of ancient Middle East as a testing case.

[7] Watson's *The Evolution of International Society* does contain a brief chapter on the Ancient Chinese system of states. See pp. 85–93.

[8] Adda B. Bozeman, *Politics and Culture in International History* (Princeton, NJ: Princeton University Press, 1960). Bozeman devoted a whole chapter in this book (Chapter 4) to studying international relations in Chinese history. What also makes Bozeman's book different is that she weaves this into a truly international history, which she views indivisible as a universally shared fund of human experience.

[9] See for example John K. Fairbank (ed.), *The Chinese World Order: Traditional China's Foreign Relations* (Cambridge, MA: Harvard University Press, 1968), and Richard Louis Walker, *The Multi-State System of Ancient China* (Westport, CT: Greenwood Press, 1971).

[10] Buzan and Little, 2000.

In this essay, I provide a broad analytical canvas of three historically varying forms of international order that China has experienced: the onset and endurance of a multi-state system in Ancient China, the triumph and vicissitudes of a unified and universalist empire and a world order associated with it, and its eventual encountering with the European international society and the metamorphosis of the Chinese empire into a state among states in the Westphalian order. My main purpose in providing the analytical discussions that follow is threefold. First, it is to look at how states and political entities are bound together in their interactions not just beyond the misty horizon of the European experience but also before the rise of European civilization. How earlier human enterprises (from Sumerian to Persian and from Ancient Greek to Ancient Chinese) function in organizing and regulating their mutual relations clearly forms and frames the deep historical context from which the modern international system emerges. Second, it is to subject what Northedge once called 'ancestors of the modern system'[11] in Chinese history to an institutional analysis. Ideas and practices and institutional achievements and failures of the multi-state system in Ancient China and the enduring Chinese world order, I believe, still raise questions of broad intellectual concerns that continue to resonate in contemporary international relations. Finally, an equally important purpose that I hope this analytical essay will serve is to foster an appreciation from a deeper historical perspective of the discomfort and unease that China has experienced in its relations with contemporary international society.

This is an ambitious task and as a consequence my efforts are exploratory and suggestive. The main body of the first section provides a concise discussion of institutional features of the system of states in Ancient China to see how some basic ideas and institutions in the modern European international system are already working there, albeit conceptualized differently. I also investigate in this section how and why philosophical discourse during this period frames the *raison d'être* for the emerging *Pax Sinica*. The second section studies puzzles surrounding *Pax Sinica*—the Imperial Chinese world order. It explores the tribute system as a system of thought and institutions regulating Imperial China's international relations. The puzzle of the longevity and resilience of *Pax Sinica*, which prevailed in the Chinese world for more than two millenniums, opens up my discussions of institutional rationality of the Chinese world order in this section. In the third section, I offer an analytical account of how the third great transformation of Chinese international relations not only 'squeeze[d] a civilization into the arbitrary, constraining framework of the modern state'[12] but also brings China into the emerging global international society. My reflections are offered in the conclusion.

The system of states in Ancient China: institutional features and intellectual legacies

The emergence of a multi-state system in Ancient China is commonly attributed to the decline and eventual collapse of the central public authority of the Zhou

---

[11] F. S. Northedge, *The International Political System* (London: Faber & Faber, 1976), pp. 34–52.
[12] Lucian Pye, 'China: Erratic State, Frustrated Society', *Foreign Affairs*, 69:4 (Fall 1990), p. 58.

Dynasty. Although the systemic power configurations in the Spring and Autumn period (770 BC to 476 BC) and the Warring States period (475 BC to 221 BC) varied radically,[13] this system of states sustained 'international' relations of Ancient China for over five centuries, only to be replaced by the establishment of the first universal Chinese empire by the Qin in 221 BC. Ancient Chinese states, then, faced the classical dilemma of any decentralized international system, that of anarchy. What were the innovative extra-territorial institutions and practices that were designed to mediate anarchy and solve the problem of co-operation and conflict? In other words, what were the basic institutional features of the Ancient Chinese states-system? I argue that elements of constitutional principles and some basic institutional practices that are said to have characterized the modern European international system were already present and functioning in the system of states in Ancient China. They were nevertheless conceptualized differently. Further, such institutional arrangements and practices were underscored and sustained by the existence of a common culture.

Common culture

A system of states, in Wight's words, 'presupposes a common culture'.[14] Unlike the Greek city-states system, which grew out of barbarism, the multi-state system in Ancient China emerged in the heartland of the Chinese civilization. Moreover, in the five centuries of its existence, it never expanded beyond the Chinese cultural area.[15] Cultural commonality was further underscored by a shared recent past and shared legends, which bound these states together.[16] One could also talk about a common descent, as the rulers of these nascent states were all from the aristocracies of the Zhou Dynasty. That reinforced their common identity, and even common morality. *Zhou Li* (the rites of the Zhou), for example, informed extensively various institutions that played the most important role in regulating relations among Ancient Chinese states.[17] Finally, the common language of the Chinese performed

[13] The differences have been captured nicely by a Chinese historian when argued that 'Whereas wars during the Spring and Autumn period were waged mainly to contend for hegemonic leadership (Ba), wars waged during the Warring States period aimed at annexation'. Yang Kuan, *Zhan Guo Shi* (A History of the Warring States Period) (Shanghai: Shanghai People's Press, 1998), p. 2.

[14] Wight, *Systems of States*, p. 46.

[15] The Chinese cultural area was, it should be noted, an ever-expanding one. Cultural commonality in the Ancient Chinese world refers to an existing state of affairs as much as a creative process. The sinicization of barbarians (*yi xia bian yi*) was already in dynamic full swing in the Spring and Autumn period. The states of Chu and Yue, which were regarded as 'non-Chinese', were fully assimilated through participating in the rivalry for Ba (hegemony/leadership) and in the political order. Both indeed won leadership contests at various times during the Spring and Autumn period. The state of Qin, which eventually unified China at the end of the Warring States period, was once regarded as 'semi-barbarian', as it was situated at the periphery of the Chinese cultural world.

[16] All these states, estimated at between 148 and 170 at the beginning of the Spring and Autumn period, had previously been principalities of the Zhou Dynasty. They emerged as states with independent claims only when the authorities of the Zhou Court slowly but inexorably dissolved. Many of them however retained a semblance of allegiance to the Zhou Court until as late as the end of the fifth century BC.

[17] Hong Junpei, *Chunqiu Guoji Gongfa* (International Law in the Spring and Autumn Period) (Taipei: Literature, History and Philosophy Publishing House, 1975), pp. 58–62.

dual functions in enhancing the cultural basis of the Ancient Chinese states-system. The common identity of the states against the non-Chinese speaking 'barbarians' was enhanced, and the bilateral and multilateral state-to-state communication and diplomacy, and mutual understanding among peoples, was facilitated.[18] Such a high degree of commonality in terms of culture, history and language among members of the Ancient Chinese world went a long way towards accounting for the homogeneity of members in terms of the structure both of the state and of government that characterized the Ancient Chinese states-system.[19]

Extra-territorial institutions and practices

If the assumption of the existence of a states-system accepts the presence of a common culture, it must be safely assumed that a common culture among members facilitated the emergence and operation of extra-territorial institutions that operated to regulate interstate relations and sustain the system *per se*. Given frequent occurrences of wars and the intensity of conflicts, it is hard to imagine that such intensive and comprehensive intercourse—political, military, economic and cultural —among states in Ancient China was possible without some sort of *jus gentium*. What were then important extra-territorial institutions and practices that prevailed in Ancient China? In other words, what norms were endorsed, exemplified and codified, and what codes were sanctioned, honoured and observed by members of the Ancient Chinese states-system in peace as well as in war? Ample evidence suggests that as a response to challenges encountered in solving problems of co-operation, conflict, and co-existence, an elaborate culturally informed web of codes was formulated and followed by member states in their mutual relations within the Chinese system.[20] Among the most important are sovereignty, diplomacy, the balance of power and rituals (dealt with in turn below).

By the term external sovereignty I mean 'the exclusive capacity to conclude international treaties, declare war, and have diplomatic representation'.[21] There was certainly no formal legal expression of external sovereignty as a constitutional principle in the Ancient Chinese states-system. However, one does not need to dig deep to locate its firm institutional ground.[22] Ancient Chinese states, for example,

---

[18] It is not uncommon, for example, for diplomats and scholarly advisers to serve several courts in their lifetime and even at the same time. Confucius was one such ineffective adviser to a number of courts other than his native one. See Joseph R. Levenson and Franz Schurmann, *China: An Interpretive History from the Beginnings to the Fall of Han* (Berkeley, CA: University of California Press, 1969), p. 46.

[19] This is of course not to deny the existence of localism as seen in broad differences in dialect, customs, religion, legends and cults, which existed among the various regions prior to the Spring and Autumn period.

[20] The American sinologist William A. P. Martin is probably the first Western scholar to compare rules and norms of Ancient Chinese international relations to modern international law. At the International Conference of Orientalists in Berlin in 1881, Martin presented a paper entitled 'Traces of International Law in Ancient China'. A revised version of this paper is included in William A. P. Martin, *The Lore of Cathay* (London: Oliphant, Anderson & Ferrier, 1901), pp. 427–49. Martin was also responsible for translating Henry Wheaton's *Elements of International Law* into Chinese in 1864, the first of its kind, which was published by the government of the Qing Dynasty.

[21] Teschke, 'Geopolitical Relations', p. 350.

[22] This is also the case with the ancient Greek and Renaissance Italian states-systems. Christian Reus-Smit, *The Moral Purpose of the State*, p. 6.

monopolized the right to declare war against each other. Thus in a bilateral treaty between the state of Qin and the state of Chu in 579 BC, it was stipulated that 'Chu and Chin [Qin] shall not go to war with each other'.[23] Those states also frequently changed their allies and made treaties among themselves, as discussed below. To the extent that these states were territorialized, sovereignty informs territoriality, too. It was not uncommon practice for a state to cede part of its territory either as a condition for peace, or as an exchange for a favour, or as an expression of gratitude.[24] States also controlled the right of passage through their territory by foreign diplomatic envoys.[25] More interestingly, states acknowledged mutually their right to offer political asylum, particularly to the nobility of other states. Some states also agreed on the rule related to the extradition of criminals and traitors, which were in some cases explicitly written into treaties. [26]

A wide range of diplomatic practices was conducted among members of the Ancient Chinese states-system, ranging from frequent diplomatic messengers, regular court visits and conferences of princes as 'moments of maximum communication'.[27] It was customary that the rulers themselves attended and signed bilateral and multilateral treaties committing their states. It is claimed that the head of the Qi state called for and attended personally twenty-four bilateral and multilateral 'summit meetings' between 681 and 644 BC.[28] What is sometimes claimed to be the world's first multilateral disarmament conference was held in 546 BC.[29] Spies and hostages were well-established institutions in the diplomatic system, too.[30] Although permanent resident diplomatic missions were not maintained, frequent diplomatic contact and communication was ensured by the fact that all important occasions in the life of a ruling prince/king, including his birth, death, marriage, burial and assumption of throne, all obliged friendly states to send diplomatic envoys to deliver congratulations or convey condolences.[31] After dispensing with proper ceremonies, these occasions became regular diplomatic channels to discuss interstate affairs. Diplomacy encompassed so wide a range of activities that a rich vocabulary had to be developed to record them and to

---

[23] Walker, *Multi-State System of Ancient China*, p. 83. It has also been noted that states in Ancient China agreed that a state should not be invaded in the year in which its ruler has died, or in which there has been an insurrection within the state. Hong Junpei, *International Law*, pp. 266–8. A number of culturally informed rules amounting to the laws of war were also practised. For more details, see William A. P. Martin, *The Lore of Cathay*, pp. 443–8.

[24] Sun Yurong, *Gudai Zhongguo Guojifa Yanjiu* (A Study of International Law in Ancient China) (Beijing: Chinese University of Politics and Law Press, 1999), pp. 80–81.

[25] In Walker's words, 'It was customary for envoys to obtain permission for passage through the states which lay in the path of their missions. Envoys who attempted to pass without permission were seized and some were put to death'. Walker, *Multi-State System of Ancient China*, p. 24. See also Sun Yurong, *International Law in Ancient China*, p. 86.

[26] Roswell Britton, 'Chinese Interstate Intercourse before 700 BC', *American Journal of International Law,* 29 (1935), pp. 630–2. See also Walker, *Multi-State System of Ancient China*, p. 90.

[27] Wight, *Systems of States*, p. 32.

[28] Walker, *Multi-State System of Ancient China*, p. 79.

[29] Ibid, pp. 56–8. See also Hsu Chao-yun, 'The Spring and Autumn Period', in Michael Loewe and Edward L. Shaughnessy (eds.), *The Cambridge History of Ancient China: From the Origins of Civilization to 221 BC* (Cambridge: Cambridge University Press, 1999), p. 562.

[30] It was not an uncommon practice, for example, for the two states that were party to a bilateral treaty to exchange hostages as a guarantee for the enforcement of the treaty signed. On such occasions, hostages were often sons of the rulers.

[31] Hong Junpei, *International Law*, pp. 164–212.

distinguish one from another.[32] Not surprisingly, a disproportionately large body of the state administration grew and functioned to deal with external affairs. Diplomatic reciprocity and diplomatic immunity were norms recognized and granted. [33]

The balance of power was the most vital institution that sustained the existence of the Ancient Chinese system of states. It is in fact difficult to contest the argument that it is the collapse of the balance of power that led to the establishment of the first Chinese empire in 221 BC by the Qin state. Two important Chinese classics, *Chunqiu* (The Annals of Spring and Autumn) and *Zuozhuan* (Zuo's Tradition) record chronologically the rise and fall of states and are rich in stories of how states played the balance of power game for survival, protection, conservation and expansion. The idea and practice of balance of power can be found in the rich vocabulary about Ba (leadership/hegemony), Meng (covenant/alliance), and Hui (convention/conference). The best part of the Warring States period saw the unravelling of the balance of power among seven contending states. To the strategy of *lianheng* (forming vertical alliances) initiated by the other six states to contain the Qin, the Qin state responded innovatively with a counter strategy of *hezong* (forming horizontal alliances), which sought to strike alliance relationships with any one or more of the other six states. Combined with its strategy of *yuanjiao jingong* (making alliance with distant states, while attacking the ones that are nearby), the Qin emerged victoriously as the unifier of China. *Hezong lianheng* and *yuanjiao jingong* are now two important legacies in Chinese strategic thinking.

In a broad sense, the rules, norms and accepted behaviours and the institutional practices discussed above, with the exception of balance of power, were conceptualized in Ancient China as *li*, meaning rituals. They were thought to be morally and not legally binding codes. Conceptualized as a totality, it was arguably fundamental to the operation of the Ancient Chinese states-system. Such a different conceptualization informs us of a uniquely Chinese view of how human life, including 'international' life, should be organized. As an ancient institution, *li* predated the emergence of the Chinese states-system. It derived from the Chinese belief in a hierarchical cosmic order within which every being was assigned a proper place. Harmonious co-operation and co-existence could only be achieved by close observation of propriety. *Li* therefore governed not only the conduct of individuals, but also that of states. Serious violation or even incompetent observation of *li* in interstate relations could have put the moral authority and legitimacy of a ruler into question, and may even have brought collective condemnation of, or war against, the perpetrator state. Some twentieth century Chinese scholars argue that rules and norms embodied in *li* were comparable to international law.[34] In a narrower sense,

---

[32] Walker noted this with clarity. 'The free Chinese sources record the various diplomatic activities under such terms as Chao, a court visit paid by one ruler to another; *hui*, meetings of officials or nobles of different states, *pin*, missions of friendly inquiries sent by the ruler of one state to another; *shi*, emissaries sent from one state to another; *shou*, hunting parties where the representatives of different states combined business with pleasure'. Walker, *Multi-State System of Ancient China*, p. 75.

[33] See Xu Chuanbao, *Xianqin Guojifa zhi Yiji* (Traces of International Law in Ancient China) (Shanghai: Commercial Press, 1931), pp. 127–50 and Sun Yurong, *International Law*, pp. 93–118.

[34] Fung Yu-lan explicitly argued, for example, that 'These peacetime and wartime *li*, as observed by one state in its relations to another, were equivalent to what we now call international law'. Fung Yu-lan, *A Short History of Chinese Philosophy* (New York: Macmillan, 1953), p. 178.

rituals refer to ceremonies and ceremonial behaviour. Even in such a narrow conceptualization, strict observation was required. A large number of diplomatic representations were obliged and reciprocated among states simply for the purpose of observing rituals, for example, of the assumption of the throne and the death of a ruler.

Intellectual legacies

Ancient China was, however, not just a period of warring states. Like the contemporaneous ancient Greece, it was also the age of philosophers when a 'hundred schools of thought' flourished. All major Chinese philosophical traditions trace their origins to the period.[35] Philosophical discourses in this period were to leave two important intellectual legacies on conception, design and operation of the social order in the Chinese world. The discourse on human nature exposed conflicting views between two dominant schools of thought, Confucianism and Legalism. While Confucians, particularly Mencius, regarded human nature as fundamentally good or at least perfectible through education, Legalists held that human nature was inherently evil and aggressive, and if unrestrained, always led to conflict.[36] For Confucians, therefore, benevolent government or rule by virtue (*de zhi*) offered the best chance for peace and avoidance of conflict, as it brought out the best in humans. For Legalists, on the other hand, only stringent measures and harsh control in the form of an authoritarian and even totalitarian government could prevent conflict. Whereas the Legalists resorted to a rigid system of laws as governing institutions, Confucians advocated rule by moral examples. They therefore advanced contradictory propositions of the causes of war, the purpose and function of government and institutions and systems that best served to promote harmonious co-existence of social groups and political communities. They promoted different visions of the moral and social order both within and beyond the state.

The Confucian discourse also sought to perpetuate an idealization of Ancient China's unity under the Zhou Dynasty. A moral conviction that the universe is one peaceful and harmonious whole prevailed in Ancient China. It long predated Confucius and his contemporaries. It assumed a natural harmony between heavenly and earthly forces and projected an image of the entire universe as a world-embracing community. Such universalist thought was, in Bozeman's words, 'restated and amplified' by Confucians.[37] For Confucians, the preordained order of natural harmony in such cosmic unity could only be achieved when man's conduct correlated to it by observing strictly five important human relationships: those between husband and wife, father and son, older and younger brother, friend and friend, and sovereign and minister. All kinds of political conduct must conform to these norms, beyond family, within state and in the sphere of humanity at large.

---

[35] Levenson and Schurmann, *China: An Interpretive History*, pp. 56–61. See also Fung Yu-lan, *A Short History*.

[36] A number of short excepts from classical Chinese philosophical writings on opposing views of human nature can be found in Evan Luard (ed.), *Basic Texts in International Relations: The Evolution of Ideas about International Society* (New York: St. Martin's Press, 1991), pp. 5–17.

[37] Bozeman, *Politics and Culture*, p. 134.

The idealization of the feudal ideal of the political unity of Ancient China attributed mainly to Confucians was arguably one of the most important philosophical legacies that had a lasting impact on the Chinese view of the world. It was claimed that China, or the civilization known to Confucians, had always been ruled by a single monarch in antiquity. It fostered a longing for the golden age of antiquity when harmony and peace were said to prevail. For Confucians in the Warring States period, political unity became a perennial ideal. Mencius is reputed to have advised a prince that 'Where there is unity, there is peace'. Such a concept of political unity associated with harmony and peace has, ever since, exercised a greater hold on the Chinese imagination than the actual record of belligerency, discord and enforced unification which are characteristic of many periods of Chinese history.

Confucius and Confucians represented one school of thought in the Warring States period. They were important, not only because they turned out to be harbingers of a future age, but also because Confucian ideas, 'amorphous, adaptable and various' as they are,[38] were used for the design of imperial institutions and systems of government and governance, particularly in the Han Dynasty, as the Confucian-legalist amalgam (the so-called Imperial Confucianism) became the prevailing ideology in the imperial bureaucracy. The common notion of universal kingship became inextricably associated with the peculiarly Confucian mystique of rule by virtue and with 'absolutization of the Confucian moral order'.[39] The *raison d'être* for the emerging *Pax Sinica* after the Han Dynasty was naturally underlined by the rise of Confucianism during the Han, which ensured that the cosmic and social universe was reimagined and the universal kingship was reinvented to invest the Chinese emperor, the Son of Heaven, with mediating moral power between heaven and earth, for achieving harmony and order in social as well as cosmic space.

Pax Sinica and the tribute system: institutional resilience and rationality

The transformation of the Ancient Chinese interstate system into a universal empire was accomplished when six other contending states were vanquished by the Qin one by one in quick succession in the short period between 230 and 221 BC. The establishment of the first unified empire in China was however historically contingent, particularly on the military power of the Qin state and the operation of a set of institutions introduced by Lord Shang. It was also contingent on the dominance of Legalist thought in the Qin statecraft that worshipped despotic power and rule by law and force. The Confucian discourse that promoted the myth of China's political unity in antiquity may have also helped legitimize the replacement of the anarchic system of multiple states by a universal empire.[40] Over the next two millenniums,

---

[38] Martin Wight, *International Theory: The Three Traditions* (edited by Gabriele Wight and Brian Porter), (London: Leicester University Press, 1991), p. 66.

[39] Benjamin Schwartz, 'Perception of World Order, Past and Present', in John K. Fairbank (ed.), *The Chinese World Order*, p. 278.

[40] This probably explains why Ancient Greeks 'unaccountably missed a manifest destiny' of turning the states system of Hellas into a union of federation or an empire, though the ancient Greeks, too, entertained a strong idea of great political unity. Kaufman recently argued that strong principles of city-state identity held by both the Sumerian cities and the Greek cities also acted to resist unification and withheld the legitimacy of established empires. Kaufman, 'Fragmentation and Consolidation', pp. 193–4.

Imperial China created and sustained an international system that 'proved to be more enduring and successful than the comparable order of any other historical nation'.[41] *Pax Sinica*, frequently labelled as the Chinese world order, took centuries to take its definitive shape amidst the vicissitudes of the Chinese empire. It is, however, the only 'sub-global international system', in Buzan and Little's words, that survived the ancient and classical period and flourished in the better part of modern world history. It co-existed with the European society of states until the second half of the nineteenth century when it was incorporated into the Westphalian order. As such, it can be counted as one of the greatest institutional innovations and achievements of traditional China. One of the remarkable feats of *Pax Sinica*, which is also an enduring puzzle, is the longevity and flexibility of its fundamental institution, the tribute system.

The tribute system in theory and practice

The origin of the tribute system (*chao gong ti xi*) as special trading arrangements can be traced back at least to the Han Dynasty, the 'formative years' of such institutions in Chinese international relations.[42] Early records of China's tributary relations included various missions from the ancient Roman and Persian empires.[43] However, the tribute system that evolved throughout centuries was much more than a trading network, or even an international economic system. Already during the Han Dynasty, tributes played important political functions in keeping peace with, as well as in winning, allies against the aggressive Xiongnu, the principal threat to the Chinese empire.[44] Understandably, it was during the Tang Dynasty (618–907), after imperial unity was re-established, that the tribute system witnessed its most aggressive and rapid expansion and institutionalization. It extended to see the participation of many non-Chinese states and polities from Central, South and Southeast Asia.[45] Some Tang records claim that China had as many as seventy-two tributaries.[46]

The physical expansion of the tribute system paled into insignificance when compared with the maturation of the tribute system as the institutional expression of *Pax Sinica*. The existence and expansion of the tribute system was underlined by basic assumptions of the superiority of Chinese civilization. Increasingly during the Tang Dynasty, they became mutually constitutive. While the tribute system was seen as embodying the political submission of barbarians, this perceived political sub-

[41] Bozeman, *Politics and Culture*, p. 143.
[42] He Fangchuan, *Huayi Zhixu Lun* (A Study of Pax Sinica), *Journal of Peking University* (Philosophy and Social Sciences edn.), 6 (1998), p. 32.
[43] Geoffrey Hudson, *Europe and China: A Survey of Their Relations from the Earliest Times to 1800* (Edward Arnold, 1961) and Yu Yingshih, *Trade and Expansion in Han China: A Study in the Structure of Sino-Barbarian Economic Relations* (Berkeley, CA: University of California Press, 1967).
[44] Yu Yingshih, *Trade and Expansion*, pp. 48–54.
[45] He Fangchuan, *A Study of Pax Sinica*, pp. 32–35. He also noted that during the Song Dynasty, the 'Silk Road on the sea' brought more Southeast Asian countries into closer relations with China in the tribute system.
[46] Fang Yaguang, *Tangdai Duiwai Kaifang Chutan* (Preliminary Studies of Tang's Opening to the Outside World) (Hefei: Huangshan Books Publisher, 1998), p. 14.

mission reinforced Imperial China's sense of superiority. Such tributary relationships that matured during the Tang thus became the only normative order that did not contradict the Chinese worldview. The central assumption of such a worldview was that China was *the* civilization. The Chinese emperor, as the Son of Heaven, had the mandate of Heaven to rule *Tianxia* (all-under-heaven). The natural extension of this logic had two important implications, at least in theory. One was that the institutional structure of the Chinese world order had to be hierarchical, with the Chinese emperor sitting at the apex of this order with a heavenly mandate. The other was that China, as the superior moral power, was responsible for maintaining and harmonizing this order with the moral examples it set, with institutional innovations and with force if necessary. The tribute system became in this light an institutional arrangement through which the moral authority of the Chinese empire could be translated into 'normative pacification' in Chinese international relations.[47]

At a more practical level, the tribute system was an institutional complex to ensure co-existence among the entities of the Chinese empire: barbarian tribes, kingdoms, peripheral political communities and eventually even the European states. Over time it became the institutional solution to co-operation problems among polities interacting with Imperial China in the Chinese world. Three observations must be made with regard to such interactions. First, participants in the Chinese international system interacted with Imperial China in decisively different fashions, contingent upon their geopolitical locations, cultural and historical linkages and commercial interests. Whereas Inner and Central Asian nomadic and barbarian tribes participated in the Chinese world order mostly through war and conquest,[48] the participation of European empires and states was almost exclusively through trade until the mid-nineteenth century. Second, whereas the intensity of interactions between Imperial China and other participants varied individually and temporally, in general, those participants did not interact with each other in any meaningful manner. European states certainly did not enter into any meaningful relationship with any Inner and Central Asian barbarian tribes through their participation in the Chinese world order. Even Annam and Korea, two core members of the Chinese tribute system, did not have regular and sustained contact with each other. One possible exception was between Korea and Japan.[49] Third, it follows that the pattern of interactions in the Chinese international system was radically different from the two models that Buzan and Little have suggested. It conforms neither to the more primitive linear pattern nor to the multiordinate pattern that is largely based on the European experience.[50] The interactions within the Chinese international system are still better captured by a radiational pattern with Imperial China at the centre.

---

[47] The term is from Michael Mann. For more discussions on transnational moral authority in international relations, see Rodney Bruce Hall, 'Moral Authority as a Power Source', *International Organization*, 51:4 (Autumn 1997), pp. 591–622.

[48] Sechin Jagchid and Van Jay Symons, *Peace, War and Trade Along the Great Wall: Nomadic-Chinese Interaction Through Two Millennia* (Bloomington, IN: Indiana University Press, 1989), and Thomas Barfield, *The Perilous Frontier: Nomadic Empires and China* (Cambridge, MA: B. Blackwell, 1989).

[49] Two points must be made here. First, such relations were not regarded as interacting within the Chinese world order. Second, the Koreans viewed the interactions with China and Japan differently. In the first instance, it was *shida*, a small country serving a large one, and in the second, *jiaolin*, intercourse with a neighbouring kingdom. The other interesting case was Liuqiu, which was a tributary to both China and Japan from the seventeenth century onwards.

[50] For the description and diagrams of these two patterns, see Buzan and Little, *International Systems*, pp. 96–8.

Acute contradictions have been noted between the normative claims embodied in the tribute system that perpetuated the myth of Chinese moral and cultural superiority and the actual behaviour of Chinese rulers in dealing with other members within the Chinese world order. Chinese assumptions about super- and subordination between China and all other tributary countries were not necessarily accepted by others.[51] There are many examples, too, where Chinese emperors explicitly acknowledged the equality of 'barbarians' with the Chinese and even acquiesced in the Chinese inferiority.[52] The *Heqin* (peace and friendship) policy implemented during the Han Dynasty, when it paid tribute to Xiongnu and even married one princess to pacify the barbarian Shanyu, are examples.[53] The Northern Song emperors were known to have concluded treaties with the Qidan ruler of the Liao (916–1125) in 1005 and 1042 respectively, accepting inferior status and agreeing to pay annual tribute. In 1142, the Southern Song did the same with the Jin (1115–1234) now replacing the Liao.[54] Even the powerful and ambitious Yongle Emperor (1402–24) of the Ming was believed to have addressed Central Asian monarchs on equal terms.[55] Conventional wisdom finds it difficult to square such tensions. 'The chief problem of China's foreign relations', Fairbank asserted more than thirty years ago, 'was how to square theory with fact, the ideological claim with actual practice'.[56]

Does this disjuncture between theory and practice add weight to Krasner's argument that 'organized hypocrisy'[57] is 'the normal state of affairs'? The hypocrisy embodied in the organizing principles, norms and practices of the Chinese world order is embedded as an intended institutional feature. It may be indeed argued that it is precisely such purposive institutional ambiguities in the actual operation of the tribute system that made it a flexible system for the conduct of Imperial China's foreign relations.[58] The myth of Chinese superiority had to be maintained, however, for domestic purposes. As Joseph Fletcher concluded in his study of Sino-Central Asian tributary relations:

Within the empire, the myth of world suzerainty was a useful ideological instrument for ruling China, and as Shahrukh's ambassadors and the khojas found, it was not to be compromised. But in foreign affairs the myth often proved a hindrance. Then quietly, the emperor practised what he pleased, not what he preached. Relations on an equal basis with

---

[51] See Lien-sheng Yang, 'Historical Notes on the Chinese World Order', and Mark Mancall, 'The Ch'ing Tributary System: An Interpretive Essay', both in John K. Fairbank (ed.), *The Chinese World Order*, pp. 20–33, and pp. 63–89.

[52] See for example, Morris Rossabi (ed.), *China Among Equals: The Middle Kingdom and Its Neighbors, 10th–14th Centuries* (Berkeley, CA: University of California Press, 1983).

[53] Yu Ying-shih, *Trade and Expansion*, p. 41. See also Li Dingyi, *Zhonghua Shigang* (A Brief History of China) (Beijing: Peking University Press, 1997), pp. 103–4.

[54] John K. Fairbank *China: A New History* (Cambridge, MA: Belknap Press of Harvard University Press, 1992), p. 114.

[55] Joseph F. Fletcher, 'China and Central Asia, 1368–1884', in Fairbank (ed.), *The Chinese World Order*, pp. 209–216.

[56] John K. Fairbank, 'A Preliminary Framework', in Fairbank (ed.), *The Chinese World Order*, pp. 2–3.

[57] This is borrowed from Krasner. In Krasner's conceptualization, the discrepancy between the professed ideals embodied in the notion of sovereignty and the actual behaviour of its adherents is considered organized hypocrisy. Stephen D. Krasner, *Sovereignty: Organized Hypocrisy* (Princeton, NJ: Princeton University Press, 1999).

[58] For more arguments about for the flexibility of China's tributary system, see Mark Mancall, 'The Ch'ing Tribute System'.

Herat, Lhasa, Kokand, or Moscow were not exceptions to Chinese practices at all. They were customary dealings on the unseen side of a long-established tradition.[59]

The Chinese, barbarians and the world

The formation, evolution and operation of the tribute system, and by the same token its ambiguities and resilience, were underlined by a perennial discourse on the distinction and relationship between the Chinese and barbarians. The discourse was about cultural unity of the Chinese world as much as about how civilization and barbarism define each other. 'China is the centre and is meant to exercise control over barbarians, whereas barbarians are outsiders who should submit themselves to China'.[60] Such was the moral conviction and cultural assumption in the discourse. The Chinese assumption of cultural superiority was further reinforced by its contact with barbarians along its borders. A rigid dichotomy became embedded in Imperial China's conceptualization of its relationship with other peoples and political entities. A relationship of superordination and subordination so conceived as a system of co-existence between the Chinese and barbarians also complied with the Confucian assumptions about cosmic harmony.

Yet, Chinese is more a culturally than racially defined concept. As discussed above, to sinicize the barbarians (*yi xia bian yi*) was one main thrust of imperial expansion. Non-Chinese ethnic groups could become Chinese and be brought into the embrace of the Empire when they had accepted Chinese customs, Confucian ideology and when they performed proper rituals. As noted by Fairbank, the idea of *laihua* (come and be transformed) implied an acculturation process and reflected the Chinese conviction that barbarians could be transformed, that is, sinicized, by simple exposure to Confucianism and to the Chinese culture.[61] Distinctions were thus maintained between inner barbarians (more sinicized) and outer barbarians (less sinicized). All 'uncivilized barbarians' could become 'civilized' barbarians'.[62] There was, therefore, only a thin line between the Chinese and barbarians. Equally, there was the barbarism of the Chinese to consider, though the Chinese were mostly silent about it. Such dialectic interpretation of Chinese *vis-à-vis* barbarians leaves a large room for manoeuvring but also creates a great ambiguity. As a tenth century Chinese philosopher, Han Yu, noted, 'when Confucius composed the Spring and Autumn [Annals], if the leaders of the land adopted alien modes of behaviour he treated them as aliens; but once they had advanced into the countries of the centre, he treated them as he did the inhabitants of the centre.'[63] In the twentieth century, such ambiguity and ambivalence continued to be used to circumvent an acute problem presented to Chinese political theory by Imperial China's conquest and prolonged rule by cultural aliens. In a discourse with Derk Bodde about foreign domination of the Chinese empire, Fung Yu-lan argued that when the Mongols and

---

[59] Fletcher, 'China and Central Asia', p. 224.
[60] He Fangchuan, *A Study of Pax Sinica*, p. 37.
[61] Fairbank, 'A Preliminary Framework', pp. 8–9.
[62] Lien-sheng Yang, 'Historical Notes', p. 21.
[63] Michael Loewe, 'The Heritage Left to the Empires', in Michael Loewe and Edward L. Shaughnessy (eds.), *The Cambridge History of Ancient China*, p. 993.

Manchus conquered China, 'they had already to a considerable extent adopted the culture of the Chinese. They dominated the Chinese politically, but the Chinese dominated them culturally. They therefore did not create a marked break or change in the continuity and unity of Chinese culture and civilization'.[64]

Towards an institutional rationality

Some fundamental questions remain. Why should the Chinese international order have been organized differently, for example, from both the ancient Greek city-states system and the modern international society that developed in northern Europe from around 1500? What made it so different? Why did rival institutional alternatives fail to replace it even when foreign domination of Imperial China prevailed as during the Yuan Dynasty with *Pax Tartarica* and the Qing Dynasty with the Manchu rule? Why did the tribute system persist and even expand when the Chinese empire was extremely weak (during the Song Dynasty, for example)? In the final analysis, what accounted for the institutional rationality of the tribute system?

Unravelling these puzzles entails an investigation into what Reus-Smit calls the 'deep constitutional structure' of *Pax Sinica*. Constitutional structures of any international society, in Reus-Smit's conceptualization, are complexes of metavalues that 'define the social identity of the state, and the broad parameters of legitimate state action'.[65] Three components of these complexes of metavalues are hegemonic beliefs in the moral purpose of the state, the organizing principle of sovereignty, and norms of pure procedural justice. Most importantly, constitutional structures are historically contingent as they are informed by their own historical and cultural contexts. Reus-Smit further contends that it is the variation in the ideas about the moral purpose of the state that explains the divergent institutional designs and practices of historical societies of states.[66] If we follow this argument to its logical conclusion, the endurance of a particular world order can therefore be attributed to the persistence of a dominant idea about the moral purpose of the state.

How much can this insight help? Adopting Reus-Smit's analytical template in explaining institutional variations of historical societies of states takes us a step further. In Chinese international society, the hegemonic belief in the moral purpose of the state, and indeed of all political and social communities from family, tribe to empire, is embodied in Confucianism. It is to promote social and cosmic order and harmony.[67] This provides the 'justificatory foundations' for the constitutive principle of the Chinese world order and informs systemic norms of procedural justice. As the Confucian conception of the world is civilizational, the organizing principle of

---

[64] Fung, 'A Short History', p. 188.

[65] Reus-Smit, *Moral Purpose of the State*, p. 39.

[66] This is understandably a rather crude summary of Reus-Smit's central arguments about the constitutional structures of international society. For more details, see Reus-Smit, *Moral Purpose of the State*, pp. 26–39.

[67] 'The orthodox line of Confucianism', Schwartz observed, 'considered the main purpose of the state to be the support and maintenance of the moral, social, and cultural order of social peace and harmony'. Benjamin Schwartz, *In Search of Wealth and Power: Yen Fu and the West* (Cambridge, MA: Belknap Press of Harvard University Press, 1964), p. 10.

sovereignty[68] is concentrically hierarchical, with China sitting at the core and others assigned a place according to how 'civilized' they are. An elaborate set of rituals (*li*) are designed and evolved as an ancient standard of 'civilization', which define the norms of procedural justice and the observance of which decides the places of others in the hierarchy of the Chinese world order. It also enables others to participate in this order. Seen in such a light, the tribute system is the fundamental institution that embodies both philosophical assumptions and institutional practices within the Chinese world order and that structures relations and ensures co-operation between China and other participants in *Pax Sinica*. It is also through the tribute system that peacetime diplomacy is carried out. For the purpose of comparison, the following table is illustrative.[69]

An analysis of institutional rationality provides suggestive answers to the questions of the distinctiveness as well as the longevity of the Chinese world order. So long as the hegemonic belief in the moral purpose of the state and more broadly, of the political community incarnated in Confucianism, prevails, the tribute system as a basic institutional practices in the Chinese world order is likely to stay. At the same time, it suggests an alternative and tentative solution to two important puzzles at which historians have long marvelled. First, the Chinese world order prevails in

Table 1. *Constitutional structures and fundamental institutions of international societies: a comparison.*

Societies of states	Ancient Greece	Imperial China[70]	Modern society of states
Constitutional structures			
1. Moral purpose of state	Cultivation of *bios politikos*	Promoting cosmic and social harmony	Augmentation of individuals' purposes and potentialities
2. Organizing principle of sovereignty	Democratic sovereignty	Sovereign hierarchy (civilizational)	Liberal sovereignty
3. Systemic norm of procedural justice	Discursive justice	Ritual justice	Legislative justice
Fundamental institutions	Interstate arbitration	Tribute system	Contractual international law multilateralism

[68] For want of a better word, I use it here guardedly and with reservation.
[69] This table is adapted from Reus-Smit, *The Moral Purpose of the State*, p. 7.
[70] I use this here to refer mostly to what can be regarded as the inner circle of the Chinese world order.

times of Imperial China's military weakness precisely because military strength on its own is neither a necessary nor a sufficient condition for the maintenance of this order. Second, as long as non-Chinese ruling elites accept, as the Chinese do, those assumptions underlining the prevailing belief in the moral purpose of the state, no alternative institutional designs seem to serve the purpose better. These tentative answers raise an important question. Is the clash between the European international society and the Chinese world order in the second half of the nineteenth century attributable primarily to the conflict between the two different conceptions of the moral purpose of the state?

China as a state among states: the Imperial collapse and intellectual contest

Even when we could not provide definitive answers to the question raised above, it is indisputable that the collapse of the Chinese world order in the second half of the nineteenth century was accompanied by the demise of the Chinese belief in the moral purpose of the state. More fundamentally, Imperial China, as an empire and a civilization, was to be transformed into a nation-state within a short span of seventy years after the first violent arrival of the European international society in East Asia as seen in the armed conflicts during the Opium War (1839–42). In that time, Chinese images of the world and of international order were shaken distressingly in the first instance before being rejected forever. While political economy may explain the cyclic dynastic rise and fall in Chinese history, it was the encountering of the two international orders, European and Chinese, that is mostly responsible for the imperial collapse that brought to an end the history of all dynastic cycles in China. The third great transformation in Chinese international relations not only brought China into the emerging global international society, but also made expanding European international society global.

The arrival of the European international society

The first extensive and substantive intellectual and cultural contact between China and Europe was initiated by Jesuit missionaries towards the end of the sixteenth century. As is well known, the Jesuits diffused the European ideas of science in China, including elements of mathematics, astronomy, geography and medicine, thus making the Chinese aware of the existence of an admirable, though not necessarily equal, civilization other than the Chinese. They also introduced the Chinese civilization to Europe. Matteo Ricci, for example, was believed to be the first to present a map of the world to the Chinese Emperor in 1601. The Jesuits also helped draft in Latin Imperial China's peace treaty with Russia in 1689—the Treaty of Nerchinsk, thus involving themselves in China's diplomacy with a European power.[71] This process differed from the encounter with European international society two hundred years later in several important aspects. First and foremost, the agents were

[71] Hudson, *Europe and China*, pp. 291–329.

missionaries of a religious faith, not diplomats or soldiers acting on behalf of a state. There was neither political power nor economic force behind them. Second, it followed that cultural exchange and the spread of religious beliefs were sought in this contact, not political gains nor economic benefits. Third, by the same token, this contact did not challenge or threaten either the dominant view of the world held by the Confucians or the existing political and moral order prevailing in Imperial China.[72] It is also worth remembering that this had happened before the onset of the Westphalian order and the formation of a European society of states in the mid-seventeenth century. Many ideas associated with modern international society, such as independent states, equal sovereignty, and exclusive territoriality, were still to be firmly embedded in the practice of European international relations. Moreover, confidence in the superiority of the European civilization was yet to be established.

The first arrival of European international society to China predated the Opium War (1839–42)—the date that is conventionally regarded as the arrival of Western powers—by almost fifty years. In 1793, the first British diplomatic mission to China led by Lord Macartney secured an audience with Emperor Qianlong on 14 September. This unprecedented initiative failed, apparently because Macartney had refused to kowtow to Emperor Qianlong. Behind Macartney's refusal, however, lay a fundamental constitutive principle of European international society: sovereign equality.[73] Underlining King George III's request presented to Qianlong by Lord Macartney were a number of assumed norms in European diplomatic practices, such as resident diplomacy and reciprocity.[74] Macartney's refusal and King George III's request therefore amounted to an initial European assault on the fundamental institutions of the Chinese world order. As Macartney observed at the conclusion of his ill-fated mission, 'Nothing is more fallacious than to judge of China by any European standard'.[75] Small wonder that the second British embassy led by Lord Amherst in 1816 was rejected for similar reasons. Where diplomats failed, soldiers soon took over. The year 1840 then marked the violent arrival of the European society of states followed by a series of bloody encounters.

The European expansion into China, however, introduced not a set of norms and principles prevailing in the European society of states but instituted a roll of different rules and institutions designed in particular to govern relations between China and Europe and more broadly, the West. These rules, institutions and practices were embodied in the so-called treaty system. As Watson noted, 'the rules and institutions which the Europeans spread out to Persia and China in the nineteenth century were those which they had evolved with the Ottomans (for example, capitulations, consulates with jurisdiction over their nationals) rather than those in use within Europe itself (for example, free movement and residence virtually

---

[72] The persecutions of Christianity during the seventeenth and eighteenth century owes much to the official intolerance for domestic political reasons rather than outright challenge posed by Christianity to the Confucian ethics and social order.

[73] In one conversation with Chinese mandarins prior to his audience with Emperor Qianlong, Macartney claimed that King George III was the 'greatest sovereign of the West' and Qianlong, 'the greatest sovereign of the East'. Alain Peyrefitte, *The Collision of Two Civilizations: The British Expedition to China in 1792–1794*, trans. Jon Rothschild (London: Harvill, 1993), p. 211.

[74] For a brief version of King George III's letter to Qianglong, see ibid, pp. 195–7.

[75] J. L. Cranmer-Byng (ed.), *An Embassy to China: Lord Macartney's Journal* (London: Longman, 1962), p. 219.

without passports)'.[76] The treaty system in China, which was not totally abolished until 1943, became both the inspiration and the target of Chinese nationalism at the turn of the century. Towards the end of the nineteenth century, as imperial institutions were crumbling one after another, the accommodation of Imperial China into the emerging global international society, like many other non-European countries, was subjected to China fulfilling the standard of (European) 'civilization', which by then had become part of customary international law.[77]

The imperial collapse

The imperial collapse here refers not to the disintegration of the Qing Dynasty brought about by fatal imperial decay and violent internal convulsion, particularly in the second half of the nineteenth century. It refers to two processes that deprived the Chinese world order of its rationale and institutional foundation. From this perspective, it is no coincidence that it is exactly during what Hobsbawm identified as the age of empire (1875–1914) that the Imperial Chinese world order collapsed under the assaults of the European society of states.[78] Analytically, the collapse of this universal empire underwent two processes. One was China's loss of tributary states along the periphery of the Empire. The expansion of Europe in the form of British, French and Russian imperialism, and later the Japanese imperial expansion, reached the peripheral areas of the Middle Kingdom from the 1870s onwards. Of all the tributary states listed in the 1818 edition of the *Collected Statutes of the Qing Dynasty*,[79] Liuqiu was annexed by Japan in the 1870s; Britain took Burma after the third Anglo-Burmese War in 1885 and made it a province of British India in 1886; France colonized Annam twenty-five years after its first invasion in 1858; Laos became first a province of Siam and, in 1893, a French protectorate; and Korea was lost to Japan in 1895 after the Sino-Japanese War.[80] This painful process totally destroyed any *raison d'etre* for the tribute system.

It was nevertheless the second process, that is, the crumbling of the entire pack of imperial institutions and the final collapse of the imperial polity *per se*, that rendered the Imperial collapse irrevocable. It was more than symbolically important that in 1861, Emperor Xianfeng grudgingly conceded that Imperial China had to deal with Europe on the basis of sovereign equality[81] and that in 1873, kowtow was officially abolished in Sino-foreign relations. Acknowledging sovereignty and equality as the most fundamental principle in China's international relations amounted to admitting the irrelevance of basic assumptions of the Sino-centric view of the world. The establishment of the *Zongli Yamen* in 1861 as Imperial China's first prototype Foreign

---

[76] Adam Watson, 'Hedley Bull, States Systems and International Society', *Review of International Studies*, 13:2 (1987), p. 151.

[77] Gerrit Gong, *The Standard of 'Civilization' in International Society* (Oxford: Clarendon Press, 1984).

[78] E. J. Hobsbawm, *The Age of Empire, 1875–1914* (New York: Pantheon Books, 1987).

[79] Fairbank, 'A Preliminary Framework', p. 11.

[80] Only Siam escaped the European imperialist colonization of Southeast Asia, becoming a buffer zone between the British and French colonies in the area.

[81] In an edict sanctioning the signing of the Treaty of Tianjin, the Emperor reluctantly decreed, 'England is an independent sovereign state, let it have equal status [with China]'. Yongjin Zhang, *China in the International System, 1918–1920: The Middle Kingdom at the Periphery* (Basingstoke: Macmillan, 1991), p. 17.

Office was the first important institutional change of China's conduct of international affairs. It was followed by China's hesitant adoption of a host of basic European institutions and practices in international relations from resident diplomacy to international law.[82] In the end, however, nothing short of a total transformation of the imperial polity would do. The Imperial Qing government's attempts at constitutional monarchy after the Boxers fiasco were no other than an acquiescence in the total collapse of the universal kingship. The abolition of the Imperial examination system in 1905 removed, once and for all, Confucianism as the moral and intellectual foundation for the imperial order.[83] In this sense, the reform in the final decade of the Qing Dynasty constituted an integral part of the Imperial retreat. The Republican revolution became but a logical conclusion of such a collapse.

These dual processes of Imperial collapse marked the agonizing transition of China from a universal empire to a 'civilized' state. They were also processes through which Imperial China was gradually and forcibly accommodated into the emerging global international society. At the root of the fierce contest between Imperial China and the European society of states was mutual rejection of each other's institutional arrangements and underlying assumptions about how a world order should be organized. In this violent contest, the metavalue complex that informed the constitutional structure of the Chinese world order disintegrated. Imperial China was thus confronted by a dual challenge at the turn of the twentieth century. One was how to build down the empire into a state. And the other was how to build up China (from its largely local and provincial basis) into a nation and a state as conceptualized by the invading Europeans so as to prevent China from becoming 'a mere geographic expression' (Metternich).[84]

Intellectual contest

The arrival of the European international society, with its ideas about the 'international' and what world politics was all about, induced a greater intellectual challenge than the eventual collapse of the Chinese world order. For those professed Confucian cosmopolitans who were living in the nineteenth century, their one-time 'universal empire' suddenly became provincial. The cherished principles, ideas, norms and institutions that had hitherto organized their world were promptly rendered irrelevant. When *Tianxia* (all-under-heaven) shrank to *guojia* (state), *the* Chinese world became *a* China in *the* world. Confucian cosmopolitans, erstwhile institutional innovators and designers, had to accept alien institutions as indispensably instrumental in China's handling of its relationship with the wider world. Confucian China, however, did not concede without putting up an obstinate intellectual contest. Such a contest constituted an integral process through which the Chinese came to terms with radical changes in their world.

---

[82] Immanuel Hsu, *China's Entrance into the Family of Nations—The Diplomatic Phase, 1860–1880* (Cambridge, MA: Harvard University Press, 1960), and Gerrit Gong, 'China's Entry into International Society', in Bull and Watson (eds.), *The Expansion of International Society*, pp. 171–84.
[83] Yongjin Zhang, 'China's Entry into International Society: Beyond the Standard of "Civilization"', *Review of International Studies*, 17:1 (1991), pp. 3–17.
[84] Quoted in Jerome Ch'en, *China and the West: Society and Culture, 1815–1937* (London: Hutchinson, 1979), p. 42.

For orthodox Confucianists, the problems of the day and particularities of China's social and political situation in the second half of the nineteenth century could only be understood in terms of the past. The European expansion was therefore identified with traditional 'barbarian' invasions in earlier times. The new world that China experienced was in this sense comparable to the Warring States period in Chinese history. It was only natural that 'China's response to the West' was initially sought through the reinterpretation of the Chinese heritage and timeless wisdom, rather than through denial and rejection. The grudging and limited endorsement of European institutions mentioned above in dealing with China's foreign relations during the Tongzhi Restoration period (1862–74) did not reflect deep normative changes so much as the application of 'practical statesmanship' within the limits of Confucian assumptions about eternal normative values and immutable principles of statecraft.[85]

Such an intellectual contest shifted ground radically when China's plight was turned into an acute crisis by Imperial China's defeat in the Sino-Japanese War of 1894–95. The question now was not whether European institutions were alien or even possibly adaptable to the Chinese tradition, but whether eternal Confucian values and institutions had become obstacles to the preservation of China as a state in the face of relentless Western intrusion. Almost overnight, Confucianism lost its initiative and force. Confucianism, in order to be retained, had now to be reinterpreted in terms of the Western tradition.[86] Crudely but subtly, the crisis turned two previously compatible goals into an antithetical choice: the survival of China as a state *vis-à-vis* the preservation of Confucian values and institutions. Loyalty to China as a state and a nation took priority over the commitment to traditional Confucian ethics and values: this led to the alienation of Chinese elites from authentic Chinese traditions and contributed to the awakening of Chinese nationalism. From Yan Fu's attempts to transvaluate traditional values by introducing Herbert Spencer and social Darwinism[87] to Liang Qichao's cry for the birth of a 'new people' as an earlier effort to construct an 'imagined community' of the Chinese nation, one can see that the contest between China and the West created what Bozeman calls 'a state of sociological neurosis' in Chinese society.[88] Political nationalism and cultural iconoclasm associated symbolically with the May Fourth movement was no more than a radical continuation of such an intellectual contest. The introduction of Marxism and the establishment of the Chinese Communist Party in 1921 should be seen as a revolt against the West, not only in terms of confronting its political and military dominance but also in terms of challenging its intellectual and cultural domination.

---

[85] Teng, Ssu-yu and John K. Fairbank (eds.), *China's Response to the West: A Documentary Survey, 1839–1923* (Cambridge, MA: Harvard University Press, 1954).

[86] Joseph R. Levenson, *Confucian China and Its Modern Fate: A Trilogy* (Berkeley, CA: University of California Press, 1972), vol. 1, p. ix. Levenson made a revealing comparison between two encounters of Confucianism and Western thought. In his words, 'In the first case, the Chinese tradition was standing firm, and Western intruders sought admission by cloaking themselves in the trappings of that tradition; in the second case, the Chinese tradition was disintegrating, and its heirs, to save the fragments, had to interpret them in the spirit of the Western intrusion'.

[87] See Benjamin Schwartz, *In Search of Wealth and Power*.

[88] Bozeman, *Politics and Culture*, p. 8.

Conclusion

In the twentieth century, war, revolution and reform are social processes that have ravaged as well as rescued China, as its social and political order has been reshaped and reconstructed time and again. In the same period, China's socialization within the Westphalian order has been anything but easy. Symbolically, the century opened with the Boxer Rebellion and the subsequent Allied military intervention. It closed with China being a permanent member of the UN Security Council and becoming a member of the World Trade Organization. Yet, even at the dawn of the new millennium, China's full membership in the global international society continues to be contested, as many question China's sincerity and willingness to accept the responsibilities that are associated with Great Power status. As a rising power, China, for its own part, has fiercely contested the normative changes in post-Cold War international society that have seen human rights and democratization become part of the daily round of political practice. As the world seems to be moving beyond Westphalia, China stands as a staunch defender of the Westphalian order.

Why then does the accommodation of China into the evolving global international society prove to be such an difficult task? What answers are suggested by this investigation into the *longue durée* of Chinese history? Lucian Pye recently remarked that '[T]he starting point for understanding the problem is to recognize that China is not just another nation-state in the family of nations. China is a civilization pretending to be a state'.[89] This proposition suggests an alternative way to appreciate the difficulties in understanding contemporary China in global international society. From the long historical perspective provided in this essay, China is still in the throes of the third great transformation of its international relations. Further, for the Chinese, this transformation differs from the previous two in that conflicts and contestations now are inter-civilizational, rather than intra-civilizational. The 'clash' of civilizations which Samuel Huntington famously celebrated, is not just a scenario for the future of international relations but should also be seen as an intimate part of its history.

The institutional analysis of the first two historically varying forms of international order in Chinese history poses important questions about the relationship between the past and the present. It illuminates the diversity and richness of international life in world history, in terms of institutional arrangements, traditional conceptualizations of order, and political thought and behaviour. Such diversity and richness is unfortunately what is sorely missing in IR theorizing. No credible IR theory, however, can be built only upon the narrow confines of the European historical experience. The empirical universe that IR theory needs to address must expand decisively into the non-European world and beyond Westphalia. China's rich and deep history is an important avenue for exploring other world orders. In the analysis above, I have provided a starting point for thinking about how China conceptualized relations among political communities, designed appropriate institutions to resolve problems of conflict and co-existence, and operated successfully in an international system of its own making over millenniums.

---

[89] Lucian Pye, 'China: Erratic State, Frustrated Society', p. 58.

The rise of the state system in Africa

CAROLYN M. WARNER[1]

Africa's relation to the concept and practice of 'state' and 'states system' has been problematic since its first encounters with those who were armed with the concept. In observing the collapse of authority and governance in a number of African states, some scholars have suggested that Africa presented the states system with alternative political organizations. Others argue that so long as there is a kernel of armed authority in territorially demarcated areas, a state exists. Africa's polities have often responded unconventionally, yet strategically, to interaction with the sovereign state system first elaborated by the Europeans. To comprehend the novelty, or lack of it, in the 'state system' of contemporary Africa, we need to know something about its pre-colonial political structures and organizations and about the imprint of empires (the construct which effectively limited the 'international' system of sovereign states to the West) on Africa. Did colonialism and the Western system of sovereign states rule out alternative structures for the newly independent African states? What might alternative structures have looked like? What impact did colonial rule have on the development of states in Africa? Does contemporary Africa have a 'state system'? This article addresses these questions in the context of the Special Issue's concern with both the structure of the international system and developments among and between the units.

It begins by considering alternative, abstract conceptions of the political communities which constitute states. Attempting to use these definitions in the African context illustrates the difficulties of formulating a workable definition of the state, and also highlights the differences among various scholars about what constitutes a suitable definition. Realist, Institutionalist, Constructivist, and Comparativist criteria face a terminological jungle as well as incredible empirical diversity when studying African polities over the last 500 years.

Defining the state

In an essay titled 'The Character of a Modern European State', Michael Oakeshott writes that in the sixteenth century the word 'state' 'stood for a somewhat new kind of human association which had been emerging, more rapidly and more clearly in some parts of Europe than in others, for over a century'. He adds that the word

---

[1] The author would like to thank Manfred Wenner for his helpful editorial comments, and especially for his contribution to her understanding of Islam. She is very grateful to Robert Warner and Elaine Jordan for technical assistance.

'provided little to identify, and much less to specify, the character of the association thus named'.[2] Four hundred years later, and with an added concern to understand the development of 'state systems' in non-European parts of the world, the problem is still with us.

To the question, 'what is a state?', numerous definitions have been offered by scholars from different subfields of political science. Most definitions convey the notion that the state is an entity which controls conflict between individuals within a bounded territory, or, conversely, calls upon individuals to participate in conflicts with other bounded territories.[3] Another view is that the state is the allocative mechanism within a political system.[4] Such a system is one in which humans continuously interact with one another as they seek to satisfy their individual desires.[5] In a political system, there is some general agreement on the 'rules of the game', and support for the government in its role as the mediator of competing claims. A third view is of the state as a symbolic system, in which ritual and culture create and bind a political community.[6]

The Realists present a forceful rebuttal to these views. Perhaps the most well-known challenge to the view of the state as an authoritative allocator of values is that of Carl Schmitt.[7] He points out that humans may be organized into communities, but each community inhabits an anarchic international system. Therefore, the essence of the political is making a distinction between 'friend and enemy'. What matters is not the character of the state, but whether there exists a community willing and able to define itself against a 'non-self'. This is strictly a public act. The political entity understands itself as such only because of 'the real existence of an enemy'.[8] Only after this political entity is protected can other values and projects be pursued. The state is that entity which is capable of imposing 'its own unqualified right to existence in the face of all other vital forces'.[9] The definition of a political entity is one-dimensional: 'that grouping is always political which orients itself toward this most extreme possibility', that is, making and acting upon a friend-enemy distinction. The locus of sovereignty is in that which makes the decision for the group, and the state is that which holds power over the physical lives of men.[10]

Other theorists have argued that, fundamentally, the state is 'organized violence'. Alexandro Passerin D'Entreves makes the argument that the development of the notion of the state as a sovereign, legal entity grew out of the historical necessities confronting medieval political theory. There was a need to characterize the 'greater

---

[2] Michael Oakeshott, *On Human Conduct* (Oxford: Oxford University Press, 1975), p. 196.

[3] For example, J.P. Nettl, 'The State as a Conceptual Variable', *World Politics*, 20 (1968), pp. 559–92; for a critique, see Peter Gourevitch, 'The Second Image Reversed: the International Sources of Domestic Politics', *International Organization*, 32:4 (1978), pp. 881–911.

[4] David Easton, *A Framework for Political Analysis* (Englewood Cliffs, NJ: Prentice-Hall, 1965).

[5] See also Oakeshott, *On Human Conduct*, p. 261.

[6] Two striking examples are in Clifford Geertz, *Negara: The Theatre State in Nineteenth-Century Bali* (Princeton, NJ: Princeton University Press, 1980); Mabel Berezin, *Making the Fascist Self: The Political Culture of Interwar Italy* (Ithaca, NY: Cornell University Press, 1997).

[7] Schmitt specified Harold J. Laski, *Studies in the Problem of Sovereignty* (New Haven, CT: Yale University Press, 1917) as his main target.

[8] Carl Schmitt, *The Concept of the Political*, trans. George Schwab (New Brunswick: Rutgers University Press, 1976), pp. 49, 19, 28, 53.

[9] F. Meinecke quoted in Crawford Young, *The African Colonial State in Comparative Perspective* (New Haven, CT: Yale University Press, 1994), p. 9.

[10] Schmitt, *The Concept*, p. 38, 37, 47.

complexity of human intercourse', and a need to 'assess the proper seat of power' in such a way as 'to differentiate the State from other social institutions'.[11] D'Entreves notes that the concept is indebted to Roman law, for it is Roman law which posits that 'there is somewhere in the community ... a *summa potestas*, a power which is the very essence of the State'.[12]

By restricting the 'political' to the capacity of a community to make and act on such a distinction, Schmitt misses the politics and process inhering in the act of constituting the collectivity.[13] How do members of what appears to be a political community come to recognize themselves as being a community, distinct from other individuals and other entities, and as being a community worthy of self-defence? Is the threat of elimination *the* one element which 'forges' the 'decisive entity which transcends the mere societal-associational groupings'?[14] Africa provides some interesting perspectives on this view.

The state, then, is the supreme political entity; it represents the '*institutionalization of power*'[15] the nature of which is nevertheless dependent upon the manner in which people order their self-interested interactions with one another (as David Easton would assert).[16] This concentration of power, this bid for state sovereignty, whether by an individual or group, entails a struggle not just over power but over the rules which are to control its legitimate expression. The state's recognition of itself as a distinct entity is dependent upon the outcome of internal allocative struggles and upon the generation of values held in common. The values and culture can transform the very nature of the actors within the state, leading to a transformation in the character of that state. Implicit in this is the notion that the character of a state is being perpetually redefined. As Kenneth Dyson has put it, 'Being in part constitutive of political activity and of the state itself, the idea of the state is connected in an intimate, complex and internal way with that conduct, shaped by and shaping it, manipulated by and imprisoning the political actor whose political world is defined in its terms'.[17] How it comes into being, even whether it will, can never be taken for granted.

Territoriality has come to be a key feature in several definitions of the state. In Weber's famous formulation, '[t]he term "political community" shall apply to a community whose social action is aimed at subordinating to orderly domination by the participants a "territory" and the conduct of the persons within it, through readiness to resort to physical force, including normally force of arms'.[18] For scholars and the international legal community, sovereign control over a specific territorially-bounded population has continued to be a defining feature of a state.

[11] D'Entreves, *The Notion of the State: An Introduction to Political Theory* (London: Oxford University Press, 1967), p. 89. See also Charles Tilly, *Coercion, Capital, and European States, AD 990–1990* (Oxford: Oxford University Press, 1990); Margaret Levi, *Of Rule and Revenue* (Berkeley, CA: University of California Press, 1988).

[12] D'Entreves, *The Notion*, pp. 92, 93. Emphasis in original.

[13] Gianfranco Poggi, *The Development of the Modern State: A Sociological Introduction* (Stanford, CA: Stanford University Press, 1978), pp. 11–12.

[14] Schmitt, *The Concept*, p. 45.

[15] J. P. Nettl, 'The State', p. 563.

[16] Easton, *A Framework*.

[17] Kenneth Dyson, *The State Tradition in Western Europe* (Oxford: Oxford University Press, 1980), p. 3.

[18] Guenther Roth and Claus Wittich (eds.), *Economy and Society*, vol. 2 (Berkeley, CA: University of California Press, 1978), ch. IX, p. 901.

When pressing beyond the realist assumption that takes the existence of states for granted, to ask why states and not some other type of entity are the main units in the international arena, some scholars of IR have distilled the state's features to three key institutions: (1) a hierarchical authority structure which accepts no extra-territorial jurisdiction, that is, it has sovereign authority; (2) territorial demarcation with formal boundaries; and (3) a public judicial authority with codified laws.[19] The latter criterion implies that there is a division between public office and the person who occupies the office. The argument is that, given extant political and economic conditions during a particular era of European history, these traits proved themselves to be more functional, in an evolutionary sense, than those of the state's rivals (city-states and city-leagues). These traits are in line with a definition generally accepted by Comparativists: 'We consider the state to be a set of organizations invested with the authority to make binding decisions for people and organizations juridically located in a particular territory and to implement these decisions using, if necessary, force'.[20]

Constructivists and some legal scholars argue that this is a thin definition of a state. It ignores the community which constitutes the state, and since not all entities called or recognized as being 'states' meet those criteria, it is a deceptive definition. Statehood, according to Christopher Clapham, had as its central concept a *'public character'*, in which states claim 'to act collectively on behalf of their citizens'.[21] Presumably, those political communities which did or do not do so are not states. Yet the extent to which any sovereign state acts for the common good of its citizens and not the private interests of certain powerful groups and individuals is a much debated topic, and leads us back to Schmitt's analysis. Further, as Robert Jackson has argued, numerous political communities which do not meet Clapham's criterion are now accorded sovereign status, and others, which would seem to meet it, are not.[22] The response of the Constructivist school (see below) is that states exist because we say that they do.

While Weber is most remembered for defining the state as 'a human community that (successfully) claims the monopoly of the legitimate use of physical force within a given territory', it is worth noting, as Constructivists have, that Weber suggested that a state exists when 'the action of various individuals is oriented to the belief that it exists or should exist'. That the state is territorial and sovereign over a territory depends on us defining it as such, and on others acting as if it were. This gives entry to the Constructivist definition of a state, that it is a 'corporate agency', which is also more than the sum of its individual parts; it is a set of rules and an organization that acts (or claims to act) on behalf of a collectivity—a community.[23]

[19] Hendrik Spruyt, *The Sovereign State and Its Competitors* (Princeton, NJ: Princeton University Press, 1994), p. 39.
[20] Peter B. Evans, Dietrich Rueschemeyer and Theda Skocpol (eds.), *Bringing the State Back In* (Cambridge: Cambridge University Press, 1985), pp. 47–8.
[21] 'Degrees of Statehood', *Review of International Studies*, 24 (1998), pp. 143–57, here at p. 154. Italics in original.
[22] Robert H. Jackson, *Quasi-States: Sovereignty, International Relations and the Third World.* (Cambridge: Cambridge University Press, 1990).
[23] Max Weber, *From Max Weber: Essays in Sociology* (New York: Oxford University Press, 1958), p. 78; Alexander Wendt, *Social Theory of International Politics* (New York: Cambridge University Press, 1999), p. 219; see also Cynthia Weber, *Simulating Sovereignty: Intervention, the State and Symbolic Exchange* (Cambridge: Cambridge University Press, 1995).

It also depends on a 'story of origins' which sees the Peace of Westphalia as having instituted the sovereign territoriality of state-like polities, inaugurating the international system of states.[24] The Constructivist view implies that the development of the state system in Africa has been dependent on 'actors' defining, while using the terms and concepts of sovereign statehood, 'who they are and what they want'.[25] Ironically, this view contains the essence of Schmitt's identity politics and Easton's allocation politics.

In practice, scholars of different traditions, such as the Institutionalists and Constructivists, borrow from each other. One noted Institutionalist stipulates that the spread of sovereign territorial states partly depended upon states recognizing, anointing, certain other political entities as being like them.[26] Constructivists stress that the state has bureaucratic (and not just symbolic, discursive) structures of control and of collective decision-making.

While mainstream IR and its critics have been preoccupied by the idea that, as of about 1600, the international system became one of sovereign territorial states—the 'Westphalian' system,[27]—other political forms simultaneously existed in the world, and other political forms with considerable international reach and influence were developed by the same 'sovereign, territorial' states, namely, empires. Krasner (in his contribution to this issue) suggests that the Westphalian model is violated by states when they, by contract or convention, surrender some of their sovereignty, or when other states compromise that sovereignty through coercion or imposition. Yet the point of departure is still the existence of some semblance of a sovereign territorial state—a state which decides to act towards, or which is acted upon by, other states.

The pre-colonial system of political entities in Africa

This does not adequately capture much of Africa's political history. In the pre-colonial era, some political entities began to approximate the Westphalian state, others had different organization structures and operating principles. In the post-colonial era, the Westphalian model is violated as much by the states' failure to generate an authority which could, by contract or convention, alienate its own sovereignty, as by coercion or imposition of a rival power base *from within*. This section surveys the varieties of polities present in Africa at the time that states were consolidating in Europe. The differences are quite enlightening. In fact, the various types of political communities which existed in Africa before colonialism present problems for our use of the term state. The easiest solution is to assign them other labels, reserving 'state' for those entities which are sovereign, territorial, and bureaucratized, with a legal system separate from any specific rulers. There is an

---

[24] A. Claire Cutler, 'Critical Reflections on the Westphalian Assumptions of International Law and Organization: A Crisis of Legitimacy' *Review of International Studies*, 27 (2001), pp. 133–50, here at 134–5. More generally, Roxanne Doty, *Imperial Encounters: The Politics of Representation in North-South Relations* (Minneapolis, MN: University of Minnesota Press, 1996).

[25] Wendt, *Social Theory*, pp. 336–7.

[26] Spruyt, *The Sovereign State*.

[27] Ibid.; John Gerard Ruggie, *Constructing the World Polity* (New York: Routledge, 1998); Wendt, *Social Theory*.

inevitable Western bias in doing so: states as so defined first emerged in the West. The purpose of the following section is to review some of the pre-colonial African polities, their authority structures, and to discuss the problem of the definition of the state through an analysis of Islam-based polities.

To read the history of fifteenth to nineteenth century Africa is to be struck by the wealth of organizational forms taken by its polities, not to mention the plethora of terminology which European scholars have applied to them. It is hard to know whether the variety of fifteenth–nineteenth century political entities named by scholars really were distinctly different categories, or whether scholars are merely trying to vary their vocabulary. In one region, Senegambia, the same scholar discusses 'states', 'kingdoms', 'autocracies', 'vice-royalties', 'confederations', coastal and island 'peoples', and 'theocracies'.[28] Another scholar refers to 'city states', 'empires', 'sultanates', 'states', 'dynasties', and 'nomadic confederations' in North Africa and Central Sudan.[29] Others note 'pastoral societies', 'clans', 'tribes', 'war lords' and 'semi-autonomous vassal states', and still others, 'cities' and 'houses'.[30] East Africa was apparently populated by 'dynasties', 'tribes', 'states', 'kingdoms', 'tributary states', 'sub-dynasties', 'clans' and 'sub-kingdoms'.[31] A state might encompass several kingdoms.[32] More recently, the terms 'decentralized' or 'stateless' societies have been used to refer to very small polities with personalized rule, in which no one had the power or authority to coerce anyone else.[33]

How were these polities structured? In the area now known as Uganda, some polities were based on the 'free association of men in clientelist relations'.[34] The fifteenth and sixteenth centuries saw the formation of 'confederacies' of small communities based on 'kinship or clan ties'.[35] Other structures were more complicated. The 'Houses' of polities in the Eastern Niger Delta were structured much like small city-states of medieval and early modern Europe. Based on wealth acquired through trade, entrepreneurs 'began to build up their personal households'. Marriages also enabled an entrepreneur to increase his personal control over individuals, and thus increase his power in the community. When he had acquired a certain level of wealth, 'he equipped a war canoe and showed himself to the

[28] B. Barry, 'Senegambia From the Sixteenth to the Eighteenth Century: Evolution of the Wolof, Sereer and Tukuloor', in Ogot (ed.), *General History of Africa*, pp. 262–99; see also Christophe Wondji, *La côte ouest africaine* (Paris: Éditions L'Harmattan, 1985).

[29] J.O. Hunwick, 'Songhay, Borno and Hausaland in the Sixteenth Century', in J.F. Ade Ajayi and Michael Crowder (eds.), *History of West Africa*, vol. I, 2nd edn., pp. 264–301.

[30] Murray Last, 'Reform in West Africa: the Jihād Movements of the Nineteenth Century' in J.F.A. Ajayi and Michael Crowder (eds.), *History of West Africa*, vol. II (London: Longman Group, 1974), pp. 1–29, here at pp. 10–13; S.F. Nadel, 'The Kede: A Riverain State in Northern Nigeria', in Fortes and Evans-Pritchard (eds.), *African Political Systems*, pp. 165–96, here at p. 166; E.J. Alagoa, 'The Niger Delta States and Their Neighbours to 1800', in Ajayi and Crowder (eds.), *History of West Africa*, vol. I, pp. 331–73, here at p. 341.

[31] Roland Oliver, 'Discernible Developments in the Interior *c.* 1500–1840', in Roland Oliver and Gervase Mathew (eds.), *History of East Africa*, vol. I (London: Oxford University Press, 1963), pp. 169–211.

[32] Ndaywel Nziem, 'The Political System of the Luba and Lunda: Its Emergence and Expansion', in Ogot (ed.), *General History of Africa*, vol. 5, pp. 588–607, here at pp. 593–4.

[33] Martin Klein, 'The Slave Trade and Decentralized Societies', *Journal of African History*, 42 (2001), pp. 49–65, here at p. 52.

[34] K. Oberg, 'The Kingdom of Ankole in Uganda', in M. Fortes and E.E. Evans-Pritchard (eds.), *African Political Systems* (London: Oxford University Press, 1970), pp. 121–64, here at p. 135.

[35] A.A. Boahen, 'The States and Cultures of the Lower Guinean Coast' in Ogot (ed.), *General History*, pp. 399–433, here at p. 412.

amanyanabo [leader] and community as a political leader, ... and became a member of the King's council', which decided foreign and domestic policy. Given that there was constant competition between Houses for increased wealth and a larger network of individuals obligated to a House, the community's leader 'had to cope with these inter-House conflicts as well as to protect his position against the ambition of the House heads'.[36] Stripped of its cultural and ethnic content, this could describe a form of political organization in medieval Europe. Polities sometimes consolidated for protection against pirates, head hunters, slave raiders or other attackers, or were linked in vertical ties to one authority when one, in taking over a trade route, obtained *de facto* control over the villages along the route.[37]

Scholars who have developed classification schemes for pre-colonial African polities have noted extensive diversity within very broad categories. Peter Lloyd found numerous kingdoms grouped in 'recognizable clusters' such as 'the Western Sudan, Ghana and Dahomey'. They had in common an acceptance of the idea of divine kingship, and each cluster may have shared some other cultural traits, but 'the political structure of neighbouring kingdoms' often was 'markedly different'.[38] There is extensive debate about the extent to which sovereign state concepts of public authority, that were distinct from the specific individual who held authority, existed, but it would be a mistake to adopt Van Creveld's position, that 'not one African or Asian society seems to have developed the concept of the abstract state as containing both rulers and ruled but identical with neither'.[39] As with the formative years of the European sovereign territorial states, the physical boundaries of these kingdoms are not clear to scholars and seem not to have been always clear to the populations concerned.[40]

Islamic states / polities

In fact, for Islamic-based polities, territoriality was a secondary consideration. Membership in the polity (and community) was tied to allegiance to a belief and not to a clan, class or territory. Because Islam had a substantial impact on the shape and destiny of many African polities, and because of the challenges which Islamic-based polities pose for definitions of the state, it is instructive to consider how Islamic polities were governed.

Although the rise and spread of Islam out of the Arabian Peninsula in the seventh century was, in one sense, quite clearly 'territorial', that is, it conquered territory

---

[36] E.J. Alagoa, 'The Niger Delta States and Their Neighbours, to 1800', in Ajayi and Crowder, *History*, vol. I, pp. 331–73, here at pp. 341, 343, 344.

[37] Oliver, 'Discernible Developments', p. 210; Klein, 'The Slave Trade', p. 60; Alagoa, 'The Niger Delta States', pp. 345–6, 352.

[38] Peter C. Lloyd, 'The Political Structure of African Kingdoms: An Exploratory Model', in Michael Banton (ed.), *Political Systems and the Distribution of Power* (London: Tavistock, 1965), pp. 63–112, here at p. 69.

[39] Martin Van Creveld, *The Rise and Decline of the State* (Cambridge: Cambridge University Press, 1999), p. 315. For an exploration of African concepts of rule, see 'Issues in Divine Kingship'.

[40] Thomas Ertman, *Birth of the Leviathan: Building States and Regimes in Medieval and Early Modern Europe* (Cambridge: Cambridge University Press, 1997); Jeffrey Herbst, 'The Creation and Maintenance of National Boundaries in Africa', *International Organization*, 43:4 (Autumn 1989).

which was until that time under the control of the Eastern Roman Empire, the Persian Empire, and so on, one could argue that the primary motivation was not the conquest of territory for its own sake. It was, rather, to spread the message of Muhammad and Islam. There are two pieces of evidence for this, which, regardless of the motivation for territorial conquest, highlight key features of Islamic polities.

The first is the mechanism by which (non-Islamic, religiously-identified) groups were governed: in essence they were allowed to become (remain) self-governing entities under their own system of laws (the system which the Ottoman Empire institutionalized under the term '*millet*' [nation]) as long as they recognized the suzerainty of the Islamic Empire, and paid their taxes (the '*jizya*').

The second requires that we confront the thorny question of whether there is a distinction between 'state' and 'religion' in the Islamic context. Most introductory works on Islamic 'political' thought make the point that, in theory, there is no distinction in Islam between these two realms. As in other complex political questions, there is here a 'level of analysis' issue.

In the basic formulation of Islam, there is indeed no distinction between 'the state' and 'religion'. The clearest evidence for the validity of this claim is that the life and career of Muhammad are the ideal, the perfect model of politico-religious leadership for Muslims. (And, in fact, that is what Muhammad's life after the Hijra personifies: leadership of the Islamic community at the same time as he carried out what we would today call 'administrative' and 'political' functions in Madina after 622 AD).

However, after Muhammad's death (and the resulting conflict over leadership of the Islamic community—the *ummah*), and the responsibilities associated with governing the vast expanses of territory and the array of peoples which had come under the Islamic empire's sway, a very clear distinction between the two realms emerges, best illustrated by the two 'offices' which develop:

1. The '*caliph*' (from the Arabic '*khalifah*', the 'successor'), who is the 'successor' of Muhammad as the leader of the *ummah*; and
2. The '*sultan*' (from the Arabic '*salata*', which means 'power', 'might', 'strength', and most importantly, 'authority'), who is the individual who exercises power and authority—in other words, what Western political thought would recognize as the 'head of government', that is, the individual who controls the administrative machinery and personnel of the 'state' and is the primary policymaker in temporal affairs.

This distinction enables us to say that, indeed, a state exists (since there is a separation of functions). Note that the distinction of 'state' which is being used here is that there is a piece of territory under the exclusive domain of the ruler, there is a population which recognizes and/or accepts the individual as ruler, and there is a bureaucracy which administers the law, collects taxes, and so on. While that conclusion may therefore be warranted, there are additional considerations.

First, nearly every ruler of an Islamic polity (whether Sunni or Shi'a) was inclined to term himself 'amir al-mu'minin' ('commander of the faithful'), the *political equivalent* of 'caliph'. In other words, he lay claim to being Muhammad's successor as the head of the 'true' community of Islam, the real ummah. The rather clear implication is that there is no distinction between the 'state' and the 'religion' at this level of analysis.

Second, all such rulers essentially carried out the secular function of 'kingship', that is, they were the primary policymaker within their polity; they controlled the machinery of the 'state' (such as it was), the military, were recognized by others in their leadership position, and also carried out the 'religious function' of being the leader of an, if not the only, Islamic community.

Third, after the fall of Baghdad to the Mongols and the 'death' of the Abbasid 'state' (1258 AD), no Muslim ruler was willing to arrogate to himself the title of caliph; the term went into desuetude (which is not to say, as indicated above, that some Muslim rulers did not think of themselves as legitimate successors to leadership of an Islamic community).

Fourth, not one of these rulers ever arrogated to himself the right to make laws or policy for the non-Muslim inhabitants; indeed, in modern terminology, they were autonomous entities within the confines of the Islamic polity. (The leaders of these communities had independent access to the sultan, set their own tax rates among their members, set education policy, determined personal status, and so on). In that sense, it is important to remember that the Islamic polity did not see itself as a territorial enterprise. (More on this below.)

Fifth, these rulers typically made no distinction between a 'public' and a 'private' sphere of activities, policies, and spheres of control. In fact, traditional Islam provides no basis for making a distinction between these two spheres, and in reality the vast majority of Islamic rulers made no such distinction.

This characteristic continues into modern times: the Islamic rulers of polities in various places throughout the Islamic world had no reason to implement any such distinction: the private 'purse' of the ruler is the same thing as the 'public purse'.

Perhaps the continued relevance of many of these points into the twentieth (and twenty-first) centuries is best provided by a short look at some Arab/Muslim monarchs of this period: King Hasan of Morocco, King Husayn of Jordan, King Ahmad of Yemen, and King Abd al-Aziz al-Sa'ud of Saudi Arabia. All of these monarchs lay claim to some form of religious rationalization for their leadership function: in the case of the rulers of Morocco and Jordan, the claim was based upon their descent from the prophet Muhammad; in the case of Abd al-Aziz, the claim was based on his leadership of the Wahhabi Movement of Islam; in the case of King Ahmad, who actually lay claim to the title 'amir al-mu'minin', he believed himself to be the legitimate successor/leader of the entire Islamic *ummah*. However, it is in the characteristics of the Saudi monarchy that one most clearly sees the continued lack of clear separation of public and private spheres. Although Abd al-Aziz, like the rulers of Kuwait, Bahrain, and elsewhere, eventually divided his income into thirds (one-third for his personal use, one-third for the administration of the realm [primarily for the military], and one-third invested in financial instruments in the West), there was (and remains) no legal provision or requirement for such a division to exist.

In other words, at the next level of analysis, once again we are faced with the lack of any clear distinction between the state and religion, between public and private spheres—they are all part of a seamless web of relationships and responsibilities.

Modern Islamic reformers have sought, and generally found, citations in Islamic texts, including the Quran, which can be used to support their call for reform and modernization of these traditional institutions and practices; but it is important to remember that the average Muslim finds nothing particularly offensive or unusual when a Muslim ruler makes no distinctions between his religious function/leadership, his political, economic and social responsibilities, and his private life.

In those West African polities which came under the influence of Islam prior to their confrontations with the West and its (nation-)states, a number of these ideas and conceptions were an integral part of their views of the nature of government, politics and religion. It would appear that among these were (in no particular order):

(1) The view that a leader who carries out what we might term 'secular' functions, such as controlling the military, ineluctably also carries out religious functions (consider, again, that Muhammad was a military leader, as well as an administrator, as well as a prophet), and *vice-versa*.

(2) The community, the *ummah*, consists of individuals (and groups) who have accepted membership and the responsibilities and rights associated with such membership; those who have not elected to join are not considered 'citizens' or subject to the decisions (military, political, social, economic, and so on) made by the *ummah* (however broadly or narrowly that may be defined in different areas).

(3) Legal requirements, that is, the Law (the *Shari'ah*), applies only to members of the community; non-members are not bound by its moral, ethical, economic and social prescriptions and rules. Non-Muslims may live under their own code of laws (as long as they do not try to impose them on Muslims, seek to convert Muslims, behave in a manner offensive to Muslims, or make alliances with other non-Muslims that threaten the safety and well-being of the *ummah*).

(4) Muslims are bound by the requirements of their legal and religious systems even if living under the temporal control of non-Muslims. Although Muhammad recognized that some of the prescriptions and requirements of the faith might be difficult to implement in a non-Muslim environment, and allowed for temporary suspension thereof, it was always believed that Muslims should attempt to bring non-Muslim areas into the Dar al-Islam (the House of Islam, that is, where Islam is numerically and politically dominant).[41]

(5) The 'realm' of the ruler (no matter the indigenous term used, such as caliph or Amir) extends to all of the adherents of the faith, no matter where they may be at any given time; it is *not* territorially bound, defined or delimited.

It should not, therefore, be terribly surprising that the political interaction between the very differing conceptions of community, the 'state', and the role of religion held by Catholic and Protestant Europeans and Muslim Africans, would lead to friction, misunderstandings, and conflicting claims in the realm of economics, politics, and social *mores*. It was probably inevitable that without any structural mechanism to facilitate compromise, much less any organized effort to reconcile differing views on

---

[41] It is interesting to note in this regard that Muslims in contemporary Europe have asked that the traditional right of autonomy in matters of education, personal status, family law, dress, etc., which were granted to European Christians in the Middle East in the Umayyad and Abbasid Caliphates and then more formally in the Ottoman Empire (and which continue in certain areas to the present day) should be extended to them while they reside in Europe. This claim, and the logic upon which it rests, has been a rather regular 'bargaining position' of Muslims since the mid-1970s, when the Egyptian Imam of the Regent's Park Mosque in London made the case to British authorities. (S.A. Pasha, 'Muslim Family Law in Britain'. Unpublished paper presented to the House of Commons, 1977; cited in: Joergen S. Nielsen, *Towards a European Islam* (London: Macmillan Press for the University of Warwick, 1999), ch. 7.

such matters, who emerged as the 'victor' would be the result of conflicts carried out using economic and military measures. With fewer resources, a far less centralized administration, and a decentralized relationship between the pieces of the realm, the Islamic states of West Africa stood very little chance against the economic and military might of the European empires.

One such case is the Sokoto Caliphate. While often referred to by Africanists as a 'state', the Sokoto Caliphate was a congeries of 'emirates', or local governments, which were united 'by common membership of one Umma [community of believers] dedicated to the upholding of Islam and of Dār-al-Islām',[42] who agreed that the Caliph was the supreme temporal and spiritual authority. It was not a set of people brought into a contiguous territory with a marked separation of private from public power.[43] This was also the case for the nascent states/large kingdoms of West Africa in their dealings with the Europeans. Islam-based polities also signed treaties with other states or polities (an accepted practice, even with non-Muslim polities), and attempted to enforce their control over territories. When Umar Tal, the prominent leader of what most historians refer to as the *jihad* in West Africa which formed the basis of the Tukulor empire, entered a rival polity's vassal city, the latter's leader wrote to Umar, saying 'It has come to our attention that you entered Sinsani without our knowledge or permission'.[44] Even if the polity's territory was non-contiguous, it would claim its treaties were binding on those who were members of the *ummah*.

Even though the Caliph was considered sovereign for those communities which swore allegiance to him, and though he claimed the right to establish treaties, the leaders (emirs) of those communities often had separate enemies. The Caliph became involved in trying to co-ordinate defence efforts. Such a system makes a hash of Schmitt's view that the central criterion of a political community or state is that which distinguishes itself from all the enemies—all in the community have the same enemy. It also contravenes the accepted social science view of a state as being that which represents all its inhabitants uniformly in dealings with an identifiable 'external' realm—that is, with other states and international actors.

The structure of the African Islamic polities also poses a problem for our idea of a state to the extent that each emirate was composed of multiple villages, and while the emirate claimed a central authority structure, most of what passed for politics occurred at the village level as a result of decisions and actions taken at the local level. Lloyd comments that the villager lived 'subject to both forms of government' and that 'two different sets of political norms' were involved. Johnston refers to the duality of a 'feudal structure' in which 'authority was first centralized and then extensively delegated'.[45]

---

[42] R.A. Adeleye, 'The Sokoto Caliphate in the Nineteenth Century' in Ajayi and Crowder (eds.), *History of West Africa*, vol. II, pp. 57–92, here at 75; see also H.A.S. Johnston, *The Fulani Empire of Sokoto* (London: Oxford University Press, 1967); Murray Last, *The Sokoto Caliphate* (London: Longmans, 1967), pp. 46–60, 145–9.

[43] One of the signs of a sovereign territorial state is that it recognizes other, like entities as being sovereign in their own territory. European trades and colonial officials observed that some African polities signed treaties between themselves, which would imply a recognition of exclusive spheres of authority. John D. Hargreaves (ed.), *France and West Africa: An Anthology of Historical Documents* (London: Macmillan, 1969), p. 113.

[44] David Robinson, *The Holy War of Umar Tal* (Oxford: Clarendon Press, 1985), p. 263.

[45] Lloyd, *The Political Structure*, p. 71; Johnston, *The Fulani Empire*, p. 170.

If we choose not to call the Sokoto Caliphate a state, and instead call it an empire, we must be careful to recognize that it had structures of governance which succeeded in making the 'authoritative allocations of values' which are held to be a key activity of a state. (The concatenation of multiple, non-contiguous and enclave entities into a larger polity has led some scholars to coin the term 'segmentary state'.)[46] In addition, the Sokoto Caliphate rulers used patronage to secure their support bases; disputes between sub-units (the emirates) were mediated by the Caliph who also chose, from a list of suggested 'candidates', the emirs, and 'had a coherent machinery of government'.[47] That said, social scientists might be more comfortable calling the Caliphate an empire—an entity claiming 'military and spiritual' sovereignty without territorial limits. The Sokoto Caliphate was not the only type of Islamic polity in Africa. Others, such as the Tukulor Empire, known for its 'national unity and political centralization',[48] appear to have more closely approximated a 'traditional' state structure. Its authority structures evolved over time: the Islamic-based Tukulor empire at first was heterocephalous, with multiple authorities laying claim to the population.[49] These Islamic polities point to the insufficiency of the term 'state' in describing many pre-colonial African societies (and contemporary political systems). This descriptive inadequacy is not due to the fact that their sovereignty as states was breached but that they do not meet the basic criteria set for them by the Western sovereign state model.

Pre-colonial Africa in the international political economy

If, in the West, trade was a major factor in the development of sovereign territorial states, what was its impact in Africa? In particular, what effects did the international political economy have on emerging African political structures? Were there patterns to its effects? A study aimed at answering these questions has yet to be written, perhaps because it appears there was no consistent pattern.

It has generally been thought that the slave trade, and then other forms of trade, began to favour the coastal polities. Several of the polities that were slave hunters or producers of gold became powerful kingdoms.[50] This thesis, as summarized by Martin Klein, 'links the formation of highly militarized states in West Africa to the increase in demand for slaves after the development of sugar plantations in the West Indies and sees slave production and the slave trade as crucial to the functioning and reproduction of such states as Oyo, Asante, Futa Jallon and Segu'.[51] Recently, several

---

[46] Aidan Southall, 'State Formation in Africa', *Annual Review of Anthropology*, 3 (1974), pp. 153–65, here at p. 156.

[47] Adeleye, *The Sokoto Caliphate*, p. 83.

[48] Y.F. Hasan and B.A. Ogot, 'The Sudan, 1500–1800' in B. A. Ogot (ed.), *General History of Africa*, vol. V (Berkeley, CA: Heinemann, 1992), pp. 170–99, here at pp. 172 and 196–7.

[49] Robinson, *The Holy War of Umar Tal*, p. 79.

[50] A.A. Boahen, 'The States and Cultures of the Lower Guinean Coast', in Ogot (ed.), *General History*, pp. 399–433, here at 412–15; Robin Law, 'The Politics of Commercial Transition: Factional Conflict in Dahomey in the Context of the Ending of the Atlantic Slave Trade', *Journal of African History*, 38 (1997), pp. 213–33.

[51] Martin A. Klein, 'The Slave Trade and Decentralized Societies', *Journal of African History*, 42 (2001), pp. 49–65, here at p. 49.

historians have convincingly argued that 'slave production and trade' could flourish even in the absence of militarized kingdoms such as Asante. 'Where warfare and raiding had increasingly limited results, commercial and client linkages became effective mechanisms for extracting slaves from decentralized societies because they mobilized agents within the targeted societies'. Collaborators were easy to find, and communities discovered that '[t]he slave trade became a way of getting rid of enemies and unwanted people'. Slave traders were not restricted to suppliers from the large militarized states such as Asante, but were also able to create networks which took advantage of inter- and intra-village disputes to generate a supply of slaves.[52] While the market may have prompted notable adjustments in social and political structures within and across African polities, it did not inexorably distil African polities into two types: powerful, militarized states and weak, defenseless, acephalous societies.

Scholars disagree on whether Islam provided the impetus or the excuse for political organization in parts of Africa, but it is clear that Islam conditioned large parts of Africa's pre-colonial politics. The Arab historian of the fourteenth century, Ibn Khaldūn, wrote of the Islamic conquest in the Sudan that the Muslims 'triumphed over the Sudanese, destroyed their dwellings and country, levied tribute, forced many of them to join Islam, and subjugated them'.[53] That Islam had a role in the destruction and subjugation may be irrelevant: humans always find ways to dominate and kill each other. What is more important was the influence Islam had on the type of political structures put in place after conquest.[54] The reforming zeal of a certain leader 'can be seen, on the one hand, as having led to the creation of the Sokoto Caliphate, with the captives and the slave trade as a side effect, or, on the other, as the political reorganization of a society that was becoming increasingly dependent on slave labor for production'. Manning gives an economic interpretation to an apparently religious movement, the Mahdist of the [Nilotic] Sudan, noting it coincided with an 'anti-slave-trade' agreement between the ruler of the Sudan and the British: 'Those who then joined with the Mahdi to proclaim a rightly guided, theocratic state included slave merchants and planters, whose slave villages produced grains and manufactures for domestic sale and export'.[55] The Sokoto Caliphate had no scruples about slavery or about providing male slaves with female slaves in order to make control easier, yet treated slaves according to Islamic principles.[56]

Changes in the slave trade (with demand from Europe and the Americas having fallen) ended the population drain, (the demographics are themselves a heavily disputed subject), and also prompted some traders to invest in (local slave) plantations. This, in turn, led to 'rapid population growth and disputes over land ownership'.[57]

[52] Klein, 'The Slave Trade', pp. 58, 59, 62.
[53] Nehemia Levtzion, 'The Early States of the Western Sudan to 1500', in Ajayi and Crowder (eds.), *History*, vol. I, pp. 114–151, here at p. 124.
[54] Timothy Cleaveland, 'Islam and the Construction of Social Identity in the Nineteenth-Century Sahara', *Journal of African History*, 39 (1998), pp. 365–88.
[55] Patrick Manning, 'Contours of Slavery and Social Change in Africa', *The American Historical Review* 88:4 (1983), pp. 835–57, here at pp. 852, 855.
[56] Paul E. Lovejoy, 'The Characteristics of Plantations in the Nineteenth-Century Sokoto Caliphate', *The American Historical Review*, 84:5 (1979), pp. 1267–92; Manning, 'Contours', p. 855. Likewise Christianity left an imprint, albeit of a different sort, on African polities and post-colonial states. On the latter, see Ronald Kassimir, 'Uganda: the Catholic Church and State Reconstruction', in Leonardo A. Villalón and Phillip A. Huxtable (eds.), *The African State at a Critical Juncture* (Boulder, CO: Lynne Rienner, 1998), pp. 233–53.
[57] Manning, 'Contours', p. 854.

This could have been expected to have led to a demand, on the part of quarrelling land owners, for a sovereign authority to adjudicate conflicts and to guarantee contracts—in other words, a state. Instead, as Europeans became involved in disputes, sometimes deliberately exacerbating them and thus artificially heightening the 'demand' for authority, their actions and the European political responses prevented a local, autonomous 'supply' of authority from reorganizing and emerging.

In West Africa, several powerful kingdoms emerged with the slave trade and Africa's incorporation into the international economy: Asante, Fante, Denkyira, Akwamu, Dahomey. At the same time, several Islamic empires established them-selves. Both political forms, kingdoms and empires, appear to have profited from the slave trade and other kinds of business, rendering it difficult to argue that, in Africa, trade was a force for establishing the Westphalian style of sovereign state. Non-contiguous, and hence non-territorially fixed, organizations (such as Tukulor, Sokoto) seem to have been able to profit from international trade, and, after the British banned slavery, to have been able to shift to other forms of commerce.[58] Co-existing with, at times conquered by, these powerful polities were a variety of other types of polities. Some scholars argue that, at least for the slave trade, effects 'varied sharply from polity to polity'.[59] By the mid-nineteenth century, after 250 years of international trade, largely in primary products[60] (if one can also call a human being such), the natural selection effects expected by the IR Institutionalists appear not to have occurred. Trade in Africa appeared to have allowed a variety of forms to flourish.

The European powers preferred this multiplicity of political communities, as it prevented any one or two powerful African states from emerging and dominating international trade, setting mercantilist prices and terms of trade. The alleged advant-ages of sovereign statehood were not recognized by the Europeans: any efficiencies the Europeans would have derived from one African sovereign representing and guaranteeing the behaviour of a set of people within a specific territory were, apparently, considered negligible in comparison to the profits to be had by preventing African trade monopolies.

To the extent that mutual recognition of state sovereignty was necessary to grant African polities statehood, it is clear that the Europeans were unwilling, perhaps unable, to recognize 'stateness' or similarities in the organizational structure of various African polities. As Tarikhu Farrar has noted, there was a change over the centuries in the labels given to African rulers. Those offices which had previously been called 'kingships' were later labelled 'chieftancies'.[61] Racism may have been a factor,[62] so too

---

[58] Paul E. Lovejoy, 'The Characteristics of Plantations in the Nineteenth-Century Sokoto Caliphate', *The American Historical Review*, 85:5 (1979), pp. 1267–92.

[59] Patrick Manning, 'Contours of Slavery and Social Change in Africa', *The American Historical Review*, 88:4 (1983), pp. 835–57, here at p. 849.

[60] David Eltis and Lawrence C. Jennings, 'Trade Between Western Africa and the Atlantic World in the Pre-Colonial Era', *The American Historical Review*, 93:4 (1988), pp. 936–59.

[61] 'When African Kings Became "Chiefs": Some Transformations in European Perceptions of West African Civilization, c. 1450–1800', *Journal of Black Studies*, 23:2 (December 1992), pp. 258–78.

[62] It is evident in many statements by British and French explorers. F.J. McLynn, *Hearts of Darkness: The European Exploration of Africa* (London: Hutchinson), pp. 308–311; Le Capitaine Binger [Louis Gustave], *Du Niger Golfe de Guinée par le pays de Kong et le Mossi*, vols. I & II (Paris: Hachette, 1892). Yet Europeans also laboured to develop an appropriate, respectful terminology for African political/social structures and offices. See, for instance, Ray A. Kea, *Settlements, Trade, and Polities in the Seventeenth-Century Gold Coast* (Baltimore, MD: Johns Hopkins University Press, 1982), pp. 98–101, 104–5, 113–4.

the European perception of great contrasts in infrastructures, population, military power, influence over the hinterland, and so on: Kumasi was not London, and Masina was not Paris.

The Europeans sought to thoroughly dominate the area and monopolize its trade; their method was, at first, to prevent further consolidation of African kingdoms, then, second, to colonize them. The Realist response, logically enough, would be that this was the inevitable result of an extraordinary imbalance of power between industrializing European states and agricultural African polities.

The broad outlines of sixteenth–nineteenth century African history should be familiar to scholars of European state-formation.[63] In Africa as in Europe, political entities engaged in warfare, kings and similar titular 'sovereigns' struggled to estab-lish their authority over sets of groups and individuals, in the process producing various authority structures. Some of these demonstrated temporal and spatial overlaps, some managed to wield political authority over expressly demarcated borders, many relied upon religious rationalizations, and dynastic conflicts were quite common. Traders and merchants wanted independence from the restrictions imposed on their activities by aristocratic families, not to mention the monarch. Economic entrepreneurs sought alliances with partners in other systems (including European ones!). Social groupings engaged in conflicts over *mores*, influence, and power, with the political authorities (whether termed caliph, amir, and so forth) attempting to maintain a coherent socio-political system (if for no other reason than to maintain their position and power).

Amidst this patchwork quilt of political entities, several were apparently moving in the direction of sovereign statehood, consolidating rule with territorial boundaries, developing notions of a supreme authority, and of at least some public law not dependent on the persona of the ruler (but see the above discussion of Islamic entities). Whether they would have become what Western scholars recognize as modern sovereign states is not knowable. We can only conjecture that since a number seemed to be developing the requisite attributes prior to colonization, they may have.

I have argued in this Journal that the failure of African polities to become what Westerners recognize as sovereign territorial states was not due to an incapacity to participate in international trade, or withstand the changes in social structure brought by changes in trade commodities. Rival arguments suggest the opposite.[64] No matter how one constructs the argument, and what evidence one brings to bear on the hypotheses, it is clear that the myriad historical structures of pre-colonial Africa were eclipsed by the Westphalian state model. Yet that political structure was not imposed on the African polities *until decolonization*. If, following the logic of the political economists, sovereign territorial statehood met the material interests of European traders and monarchs in Europe, it appears that empire met their interests elsewhere. Alternatively, one would have to postulate the argument that empire, rather than sovereign territorial statehood, was a more 'efficient' form in general, for the international system.

---

[63] Carolyn M. Warner, 'The Political Economy of "Quasi-Statehood"and the Demise of 19th Century African Politics', *Review of International Studies*, 25 (1999), pp. 233–55.

[64] A.G. Hopkins, 'Asante and the Victorians: Transition and Partition on the Gold Coast', in Roy Bridges (ed.), *Imperialism, Decolonization and Africa* (London: Macmillan, 2000), pp. 25–64.

Spruyt's argument, and that of Institutionalists in general, requires us to consider why, if sovereign territorial states were the efficient solution for Europe, that form did not and was not allowed to spread to other parts of the world. While Britain and France may have become 'classic' sovereign territorial states, they both also had the word 'empire' attached to their systems, and, after decolonization, they have existed in the international system both as sovereign states and as the 'British Commonwealth' and the 'French Union'. In addition, they are members of the 'European Union'. If evolutionary theory is applicable to international relations in the way advocated by many political economists, international politics appears to allow more diversity of form than expected by these scholars. This is the area where Constructivists are persuasive: states are states only when others recognize them as such, and what may have been states instead become colonial fodder when more powerful states say so.[65]

Decolonization also depended upon the will of the more powerful states, and it is to the post-colonial era that I now turn.

What impact did the empires have on the current African state system?

The imprint of empire on the African state system was undoubtedly substantial. I will not try to evaluate the extent of it, but rather raise points about several major effects. At one extreme is the argument that colonial rule had an enormous, deleterious and completely transformative effect on Africa. Young puts it most forcefully: 'one consequential factor in the crisis faced by most African states by the late 1970s—and intensifying since—was the singularly difficult legacy bequeathed by the institutions of rule devised to establish and maintain alien hegemony'. Africa faced the brunt of the developed sovereign territorial state competing not with one or two other powers, but with several all at once: 'The forces of conquest were under a pressure unusual in imperial annals to give muscular effect to the doctrine of effective occupation, exhumed and sanctified at the Berlin Congress'. In addition, the imperial powers insisted that the colonies pay for themselves and pay immediately. According to Young, this led to repressive and brutal extractive mechanisms.[66] These imperatives were backed by an ideology of racism which was at its 'historical zenith', and by advanced military technologies.[67]

Colonial rule infantilized African politics, stunting its growth such that after forty years of indirect rule, British officials noted 'one always had a feeling of despair reading [provincial reports from the Gold Coast]. The unending … palavers, apathy, lack of real interest, lack of policy, lack of coordination, lack of vision characterized the whole administration of the Gold Coast and the sooner it [was] given a real jolt the better for all concerned'. As Gocking notes, '[t]he competition for office that indirect rule unleashed did much to undermine what officials hoped

---

[65] The problem is that Constructivists have difficulty accounting for which political organizations can force their definitions on others.

[66] Herbst gives the Berlin Conference a different interpretation: these were not states on steroids rolling over Africa, but states seeking to minimize expenditures and conflicts with each other in Africa ('Boundaries', pp. 683–5, 688).

[67] Young, *The African Colonial State*, pp. 244, 278, 280.

would be a smooth-functioning native order'.[68] Imposing colonial authority over local authority inevitably undermined the latter. The French were particularly insistent that 'the native chief must be our instrument', and 'The native chief never speaks or acts in his own name, but always in the name of the *commandant de cercle*'.[69] One could argue that had colonial rulers established complete hegemony and totally reorganized African society in the manner which they desired, it is quite possible that the African states would have started with a much more stable and extensive political and economic infrastructure, and that these states would be better able to cope in the modern world.

There is a revisionist current which argues that African polities only partly absorbed European notions of 'stateness' and political behaviours. Just as a number of scholars have argued that the sources of pre-colonial demise were largely rooted in the African polities themselves, recent works take issue with Young's claim that the colonial state 'totally reordered political space, societal hierarchies and cleavages, and modes of economic production'. These revisionists emphasize continuities in structures and practices, adaptations but not submission to European concepts of politics and state.[70] For instance, in Buganda, the English only grafted their ideas and practices of individual land ownership onto pre-colonial practices, turning peasants and chiefs into tenants and landlords, thus continuing the original hierarchies. McKnight paints an image of Bugandan social groups strategically using new colonial institutions to further their own interests.

Yet the revisionists, to make their point, must downplay the extent to which the interests of the colonized were shaped by the new colonial structures. For instance, private property created a new set of interests and strategies for attaining them. Goals changed, self-definitions altered, and the colonized Africans incorporated new concepts into their politics. As A.F. Robertson's work on the deposition of Asante chiefs shows, British 'over-rule added a further level of authority to the Ashanti chiefly hierarchy'. Those 'tacticians' interested in over-throwing or in promoting a chief saw in British rule a new resource, not merely a new external authority. And when actors obtain new resources, and also when conflicts which were previously adjudicated internally have an external judge, actor strategy changes even if the goal remains the same. With the arrival of the British, the English language was used in filing and pursuing a deposition claim against an Asante chief (a local political structure left intact by the British), and rulings were now written.[71] These changes gave an edge to those educated in English, and lent an air of finality to the decisions.

The colonial powers' efforts to dramatically alter African societies also have their source in the ideology of scientific planning which became prevalent in the West

[68] Roger Gocking, 'A Chieftaincy Dispute and Ritual Murder in Elmina, Ghana, 1945–6', *Journal of African History*, 41 (2000), pp. 197–219, here at p. 217.

[69] In Hargreaves, *France and West Africa*, p. 213, 212. See also Mahmood Mamdani, *Citizen and Subject: Contemporary Africa and the Legacy of Late Colonialism* (Princeton, NJ: Princeton University Press, 1996).

[70] Young, *The African Colonial State*, 9; Apter, 'The Subvention of Tradition'; Glenn H. McKnight, 'Land, Politics, and Buganda's 'Indigenous' Colonial State' *The Journal of Imperial and Commonwealth History*, 28:1 (January 2000), pp. 65–89; A.F. Robertson, 'Ousting the Chief: Deposition Charges in Ashanti', *Man*, 11:3 (September 1976), pp. 410–27; Frederick Cooper, *Decolonization and African Society* (Cambridge: Cambridge University Press, 1996).

[71] A. F. Robertson, 'Ousting the Chief: Deposition Charges in Ashanti', *Man* New Series 11:3 (1976), pp. 410–27, here at pp. 416, 417. The British, recognizing the significance of the throne for the Asante king, banished it until they realized that doing so made indirect rule more difficult.

(and the Soviet Union) in the 1920s and 1930s and lasted through the 1950s.[72] With domination as the effective result, the British undertook large scale agricultural transformations, all of which failed (for example, Shire Valley in Malawi, groundnut production in Tanganyika). As James C. Scott says, '[t]he point of departure for colonial policy was a complete faith in what officials took for "scientific agriculture" on the one hand and a nearly total scepticism about the actual agricultural practices of Africans on the other'. British experts were brought in to plan the colonies' agricultural development. They 'were inclined to propose elaborate projects—"a total development scheme", a "comprehensive land usage scheme"'. The planners dismissed the local knowledge of the peasants, since it hadn't been arrived at by 'scientific' analysis.[73]

Oddly, the failures of these large-scale planned 'rural settlement and production schemes' did not dissuade post-colonial states from attempting some of their own. It is not clear that this was, as Young might expect, because the colonial states had inculcated the new elite with the colonials' way of thinking and governing, or whether it was because the new leaders were attracted by the communist ideology, which was inherently optimistic about the possibilities (and exigent about the need) for large scale planning involving extensive resettlement and massive agricultural production. It's also plausible that the new elites, bequeathed political structures, societies and economies woefully behind the Western world and needing development in order to profit from international trade, saw large scale transformations as the only means of catching up to the West.

In Tanzania, Julius Nyerere tried a version of collectivization, with rural populations forced to move into government built, standardized villages, and to work on large, single crop farms. His justification: 'if you ask me why the government wants us to live in villages, the answer is just as simple: unless we do we shall not be able to provide ourselves with the things we need to develop our land and to raise our standard of living'. While state involvement in development may have been the solution, the specific strategy, given the conditions, doomed the project to failure. But the concern here is what connection the strategy had with the imprint of empire. While the idea of massive development and transformation may have been internalized and used by the new elite, Nyerere did try to give his strategy a non-Western stamp: 'we should gradually become a nation of *ujamaa* villages where the people co-operate directly in small groups and where these small groups co-operate together for joint enterprises'.[74] To the extent one can say that empires bequeathed underdeveloped state institutions and a faith in planning to the independent African rulers, the empires had a definite long term impact on the character of states in Africa, and on their *non*-development.

The impact is also seen in the state-building efforts of early post-independence leaders, and here, it seems, colonial rule was not the juggernaut Young depicts it as: if it had been, the African elite would not have needed to build up their bureaucracies.

---

[72] James Fairhead and Melissa Leach, 'Desiccation and Domination: Science and Struggles over Environment and Development in Colonial Guinea', *Journal of African History*, 41 (2000), pp. 35–54; Monica M. Van Beusekom, 'Disjunctures in Theory and Practice: Making Sense of Change in Agricultural Development at the Office du Niger, 1920–60', *Journal of African History*, 41 (2000), pp. 79–99.

[73] James C. Scott, *Seeing Like a State* (New Haven, CT: Yale University Press, 1998), p. 226.

[74] Scott, *Seeing*, p. 230.

The colonial state apparatus had, if at all, built only weak administrative and infrastructure links to much of the state's territory. As in Tanzania, '[t]he vast majority of the Tanzanian rural population [11–12 million people] was, in terms of legibility [infrastructure, information] and appropriation [taxation, citizenship], outside the reach of the state'. Independence leaders had to build the state and establish an administrative presence in areas the colonial powers had left untouched. 'Modernization required, above all, physical concentration into standardized units that the state might service and administer'. Unfortunately, they replicated both the colonial states' use of large-scale planning and homogenized housing and agriculture, and their use of force when incentives did not work.[75]

An additional effect is conceptual: the impact came from the beliefs, or, as Benedict Anderson put it, the 'imaginings', of Europeans. Indigenous political thought, concepts of authority and government, and so on, of African polities were largely superceded by or subordinated to European versions. If one accepts the constitutive force of ideas, this is of no small consequence.[76] Young argues that the newly independent states were 'successors to the colonial regime, inheriting its structures, its quotidian routines and practices, and its more hidden normative theories of governance. Thus, everyday reason of state, as it imposed its logic on the new rulers, incorporated subliminal codes of operation bearing the imprint of their colonial predecessors' (and, of course, most of the post-colonial elites were Western-educated).[77]

One might also consider that the new African political elite may have chosen to adopt the programmes and policies which were associated with, and promoted by, the clearest, most obvious, most powerful opponent of the former colonial powers in the international arena, that is, the Soviet Union. Precisely because the USSR was the public opponent of their former colonial masters in the international arena, its policies, programmes, mechanisms, and so on, for 'development' were automatically worth considering (and even slavishly copied). Clearly, at least in the view of the leaders of most of these states, the programmes and policies of the former colonial states had not accomplished the 'development' and 'modernization' which would give these states international status and recognition, much less domestic prosperity. In many quarters, there was the widespread view of the USSR of a state and government which, through massive programmes of industrialization had succeeded in moving from being a third-rate agricultural state into the status of a world power, challenging the United States and its (former colonialist) allies for control, leadership, and power in the modern world, and even beating the US in the 'space race'.

The fact that Ethiopia, which was never colonized, also, but later (in the 1970s and 1980s) tried forced resettlement and large scale agricultural production suggests that the colonial state had less to do with these post-colonial states' activities than did elites' interests in making their entities into Western-style sovereign states and in 'modernizing' the economy. Mengistu 'decried Ethiopia's reputation as "a symbol of backwardness and a valley of ignorance"'.[78] In the end, the dislocations, the starva-

---

[75] Ibid., pp. 229, 231, 232–7; also Herbst, 'Boundaries'.
[76] Vesna Goldsworthy, *Inventing Ruritania: The Imperialism of the Imagination* (New Haven, CT: Yale University Press, 1998); Edward W. Said, *Culture and Imperialism* (London: Chatto & Windus, 1993).
[77] Young, *The African Colonial State*, p. 283.
[78] Scott, *Seeing*, p. 248.

tion, and brutality which the forced resettlements and new agricultural techniques produced in turn contributed to political instability and to the growing economic problems. Farmers went from producing surpluses on their own plots, thanks to their intimate knowledge of local conditions and their initiative, to being unskilled workers on 'foreign' terrain. Efforts to achieve rapid development, which were simultaneously efforts to seem like a state, had devastating results.

Pan Africanism

Upon gaining independence, was it inevitable that the former colonies would become sovereign states? Why did the Pan African movement not provide an alternative conception and structure for political organization and authority in Africa? To answer these questions we must first address the questions of what was the Pan African movement and what would a Pan African polity have looked like?

The history of the Pan African movement has been well-documented, as has the fact that it took a variety of forms: in addition to being a political movement (promoting 'the intellectual understanding and cooperation among all groups of African descent in order to bring about the emancipation of black peoples'),[79] it was also a literary and cultural movement. Yet to speak of 'it' in the singular implies unity in a movement that was characterized by myriad interpretations of 'Pan Africanism' and its goals, and promoted by multiple and diverse organizations and leaders. Contemporary observers used the plural when writing of the unity movements,[80] and there, perhaps, lies the crux of 'its' downfall: a multiplicity of material interests, some with significant structural bases, and of ideological leanings and goals. At the broadest level, there were disagreements within the so-called 'Black Triangle' of the United States, the West Indies, and Black Africa, and there were divisions within each of these. A case in point is the fact that the man whose name is most closely linked with the movement, W.E.B. Du Bois, thought continental Africans needed civilizing, and were not ready for self-governance. That view was rebuked by the continental Africans.[81] (Though some did express concern that they needed more time before independence).

The death-knell to the cross-continents and regions movement was sounded in 1958 by Kwame Nkrumah, with his call for an 'All Independent African States Conference' and an 'All African Peoples' Conference'.[82] Concerns in Africa had, logically, turned towards a specific goal which set continental Africans apart from those in the US and the West Indies: that of attaining independence from colonial rule.

Following the Pan African movement was the Organization of African Unity (OAU), which was 'a compromise between radically differing views of African unity,

---

[79] Nagueyalti Warren, 'Pan-African Cultural Movements: From Baraka to Karenga', *Journal of Negro History,* 75:1–2 (1990), pp. 16–28, here at p. 16.

[80] Erasmus H. Kloman, Jr., 'African Unification Movements', *International Organization,* 16:2 (1962), pp. 387–404.

[81] Alexandre Mboukou, 'The Pan African Movement, 1900–1945: A Study in Leadership Conflicts Among the Disciples of Pan Africanism', *Journal of Black Studies,* 13:3 (1983), pp. 275–88; 277, 280.

[82] Mboukou, *The Pan African Movement,* p. 281.

between those who thought of African unity as a symbolic and tactical aspect of a revolutionary movement and those who thought of it as an alliance between sovereign states to protect their newly acquired status in the world community'.[83] The OAU, however, had entered a world already peppered with a plethora of regional and rival 'unity' groups. Like the Pan African movement, the OAU found-ered on the incentives political leaders had to promote the specific interests of their states and themselves, and on competing definitions of goals.

What would a Pan African polity have looked like? Again, starting with the broadest level, it presumably would have accorded some legal, authoritative and redistributive powers to a community of individuals dispersed across the US, the West Indies and Africa. One's legal status would not be based on the state within which one resided, that is, it would be non-territorial. This community would have had to negotiate with each of the states in the relevant regions for its individual political status, or perhaps within the framework of the United Nations, with the necessary bilateral agreements made afterward. It is important to note that the idea of non-territorial communities continues to have meaning in the contemporary world (see also n. 41, above): a contemporary example of such a community with non-territorial legal status is the language communities of Belgium. Rights and duties are based on membership in a group, not on presence in a territory. Or, perhaps it would have been limited to Pan Africanism in Africa. Here one might have a large state, with near-continent wide spread (as, say, the United States).

The failure of Pan Africanism

As with the failure of the Pan European movement after World War II, the failure of the Pan-African movement may have been over-determined. Constructivists would emphasize the hegemony of the idea of the sovereign state: the international system would not have recognized any political structure other than a sovereign state as the basis for political organization in Africa; Institutionalists would emphasize the incentives which borders and existing political structures created. The quasi-state-hood school, incorporating aspects of both perspectives, would note that Pan Africanism was not an alternative because independence leaders got sovereignty 'on the cheap'.[84] To have superseded the sovereign state structure, they would have had to expend enormous resources. With ordinary state sovereignty, politicians did not even have to demonstrate that they had the full institutional structures of modern states, nor demonstrate that they had full authority. According to Robert Jackson, sovereign statehood was seen as 'egalitarian' and arguments for it being 'granted categorically even if the territory in question was extremely marginal became morally impregnable'.[85] Institutionalists note that sovereign territorial statehood is convenient as an information economizer. As Herbst suggests, recognizing boundaries and control of the capital city obviates other states' needs to see if a

---

[83] Immanuel Wallerstein, 'The Early Years of the OAU: The Search for Organizational Pre-Eminence', *International Organization*, 20:4 (1966), pp. 774–87, here at p. 774.
[84] Mayall in Young, *The African Colonial State*, p. 29.
[85] Jackson, *Quasi-States*, p. 104.

'state' really has effective control of a territory, really does act for the collectivity, really has a public administrative and judicial system, and so on.

The Institutionalist arguments take two forms. One argues largely from the basis of colonial institutions, the other on the logic of boundaries. I turn first to the imprint of colonial institutions as an obstacle to post-independence unity, and unity on some other basis besides that of the sovereign territorial state. There is extensive debate about the extent to which colonial institutions 'froze' pre-existing political arrangements. If the 'freezing' argument is correct, then pan-Africanism was doomed to failure because it had neither the material resources nor the ideological means to bring together in a coherent governing structure the myriad polities and ethnicities that marked the colonial states. If colonial rule did not 'freeze' pre-colonial structures and alignments, it nevertheless deliberately discouraged unity within each colonial state in order to reduce the likelihood of successful challenges to colonial rule. An alternative argument would say that pre-colonial polities were not frozen in place under colonial rule; rather, the colonial states did not implement any significant changes for the simple reason of cost considerations. Thus, the colonial powers only discouraged unity as a side-effect of trying to rule on the cheap—trying to rearrange African political structures, and trying to bring some uniformity to the societies within the territorial boundaries, would have been an enormously expensive undertaking for which the colonial governors had not the resources. Ruling through local political structures was the rational response to the conditions (though France and the Great Britain clearly differed on how direct/indirect their rule was). Whatever the exact character of transformation effected by the colonial powers on the pre-existing African polities, the pan-African movement faced enormous obstacles to unity.

Jeffrey Herbst's boundaries argument, while more directed at accounting for why, despite their lack of correspondence to ethnic, national, and political organizations, the sovereign state boundaries drawn up at the partition of Africa have remained largely unchallenged, provides a concise answer to the question of why the Pan-African movement failed. Herbst reasons that Africa poses particular problems to creating a boundary system, and that once any boundaries are in place, the risks of disaster to each state in trying to alter them are far greater than any problems created (for the actors in control) by the boundaries themselves. First, '[t]he continent cannot be divided into natural frontiers, and there is really no way to divide people because loyalties are diffuse and quite capable of changing, depending on the specific politics of the nation-state'. Second, 'once African boundaries begin to change there would be an indefinite period of chaos (given that there is no set of universally recognized natural frontiers to revert to), the grave danger of not cooperating [to maintain boundaries] is clear to all'.[86] Applied to the failure of Pan-Africanism, Herbst's view would say that African elites had a very strong incentive to adhere to their states' status as sovereign territorial entities, rather than to renounce territoriality as a key organizing principle.

Spruyt's Rationalist argument views boundaries and sovereignty from a different angle, which suggests a slightly different account of why Pan Africanism failed. This

---

[86] Herbst, 'Boundaries', p. 688, 689. For a different argument, but which leads to a similar expectation, see Ravi L. Kapil, 'On the Conflict Potential of Inherited Boundaries in Africa', *World Politics*, 18:4 (1966), pp. 656–73.

argument stresses that sovereign territoriality reduced 'transaction and information costs' between economic actors. States became the dominant 'unit' in the international system because, first, they were more effective at mobilizing their societies' resources, were able to make credible commitments about future actions between their populations and other international actors, and because states had 'spatial limits to authority' thus avoiding confusing and costly jurisdictional overlap.[87] As Spruyt notes, this type of unit, the sovereign territorial state, arose at a particular time and in response to a convergence of socioeconomic and political developments, and so we might expect that at some time in the future, the state will give way to something else.

To substantiate his argument, Spruyt notes that the Italian and German city-states were accorded sovereign status, even though 'this was not a reflection of their material power or geographic size. Instead, this was the result of their empowerment as equivalent actors on the international scene, because of their external similarity to sovereign, territorial states'. They were considered 'organizationally compatible with sovereign states'.[88] In the context of the contemporary African system of states, what is striking about Spruyt's analysis is the fact that many African states are not similar to sovereign territorial states, yet they remain considered so. The fact that they are may lend further support to the claim in Spruyt's argument that sovereign states prefer, as a matter of efficiency and reduced transaction costs, dealing with what they are willing to consider sovereign states, so will continue to act as if such entities exist even where they do not (Zaire/the Congo, Rwanda, Sierra Leone).[89] As William Reno states, 'Stronger state reluctance to permit disorder ensures nominal support for territorial integrity'.[90] We might recall that Catholicism's status in the international system was only 'solved' when Mussolini granted the Church the status of a sovereign, *territorial* state. It is of note that Catholicism is the only religion which has observer status at the United Nations, and to which other states send diplomatic missions. Thus, Pan Africanism failed because the other units in the international system valued sovereign states.

Some reflections on the contemporary African state system

According to international law, and as recognized by other states, Africa is home to a multitude of sovereign states. While for the most part current boundaries are accepted as legitimate, many states themselves may lack a central locus of authority, and there are significant areas where boundaries are in dispute. In numerous places states do not seem to be 'sovereign' even if they are territorial. Crawford Young bluntly notes that African states are characterized by '[f]ragments of state authority [which have] become instruments of predation among dispersed structural segments

[87] Spruyt, *The Sovereign State*, pp. 88, 185–6.
[88] Ibid., pp. 176, 179.
[89] David Williams, 'Aid and Sovereignty: Quasi-States and the International Financial Institutions'. *Review of International Studies*, 26 (2000), pp. 557–73.
[90] 'Sierra Leone: Weak States and the New Sovereignty Game', in Villalón and Huxtable (eds.), *The African State*, pp. 93–108, here at p. 108.

and individual actors'.[91] Robert Jackson and Carl Rosberg have called these 'quasi-states'—states with the internationally recognized juridical trappings of sovereign statehood, but which lack the features expected elsewhere in a state.[92] As Joshua Bernard Forrest notes, 'a greater proportion [than in the past] of Africans are now experiencing political life with no minimally viable state presence'.[93]

Some observers are not so pessimistic, but they seem contradicted by the perspective and evidence to which they point, in this case the opinion and evidence provided by Forrest: Huxtable notes that 'Even the countries in which state collapse is most severe, discussed here by Joshua Forrest in Chapter 3, contain some entity that is generally regarded as "the state". The state as an institution for organizing politics certainly appears robust, despite predictions of its imminent demise'.[94] Catherine Boone suggests that Africa does have cases of relatively successful state-building efforts, and that these have usually occurred 'in the Africa of peasant commodity production' rather than 'in the extractive and plantation enclaves'.[95]

Huxtable goes on to suggest that, 'The African state may disintegrate, not because of the failure of Africans to adapt to the world system, but because the state itself has become inadequate for the realities of the current world system'.[96] The sovereign territorial state may retort that 'reports of my death have been premature'. State collapse in Africa has been fuelled by the efforts of competing elites to control the state or to create one of their own. The internal conflicts are still over issues which seem to be core questions of state: who controls what territory and which institutions for the benefit of whom, who has the authority to make friend/enemy distinctions, and what is the political community's identity and what are its constitutive elements? Yet Huxtable's statement contains an important truth: the modern state is not adequate to meeting the demands placed on it. What is striking is that even when the state was apparently at its zenith, it constructed other organizational forms: the empire, and, after two world wars raised questions about the severe costs of the world being defined by sovereign territorial states, the regional economic or political union. Ruggie notes that 'the first specifically modern invention of diplomacy was the principle of extraterritoriality: having so profoundly redefined and reorganized political space, the possessive individualist states "found that they could only communicate with one another by tolerating within themselves little islands of alien sovereignty"'.[97] And as African states began to attain independence, they immediately created numerous cross-national organizations.[98] Their behaviour is in line with Stephen Krasner's statement that '[t]he basic organizing principle of

---

[91] Young, *The African Colonial State*, p. 23.

[92] *Personal Rule in Black Africa* (Berkeley, CA: University of California Press, 1982).

[93] 'State Inversion and Nonstate Politics', in Villalón and Huxtable (eds.), *The African State*, pp. 45–56, here at p. 45.

[94] Phillip A. Huxtable, 'The African State Toward the Twenty-first Century: Legacies of the Critical Juncture', in Villalón and Huxtable (eds.), *The African State*, pp. 279–94, here at p. 279.

[95] Catherine Boone, 'Empirical Statehood and Reconfigurations of Political Order', in Villalòn and Huxtable (eds), *The African State*, pp. 129–142, here at p. 131.

[96] Phillip A. Huxtable, 'The African State Toward the Twenty-First Century: Legacies of the Critical Juncture', in Villalòn and Huxtable (eds.), *The African State*, pp. 279–93, here at pp. 292. See also Martin van Creveld, *The Rise and Decline of the State* (Cambridge: Cambridge University Press, 1999).

[97] Ruggie, *Constructing*, p. 149.

[98] As contemporary observers noted: Erasmus H. Kloman, Jr., 'African Unification Movements', *International Organization*, 16:2 (1962), pp. 387–404.

sovereignty—exclusive control over territory—has been persistently challenged by the creation of new institutional forms that better meet specific material needs'.[99]

The current 'state system' in Africa is marked by numerous 'states' in which 'rule based upon violent accumulation creates archipelagos of control rather than hegemony over a contiguous territory'. As the warlord polities of Zaire/the Congo, and of Liberia show, new political organizations have emerged in Africa 'that are not states, yet are capable of "sovereign" diplomacy in the international state system'.[100] A number of militarized elites have violated sovereign state boundaries, have engaged in deliberate state destruction, and otherwise appear to be ignoring the alleged advantages of boundaries and sovereign statehood. They have been able to control the distribution of resources, and have appropriated for themselves the right to identify enemies. This, unfortunately, is the world as Schmitt saw it: raw force defining 'international' relations and relations between 'communities'. There is no agreement on the 'authoritative allocation of values', on the rules governing resource access and distribution. What matters is not the character or structure of the state, but whether there exists a community willing and able to define itself against a 'non-self'. The political entity is a political entity only because of 'the real existence of an enemy'. The essence of a political community is its willingness and ability to differentiate itself, to assert its existence.[101] Applied to the African context, whether warlords and rebel groups, or the existing 'state', can succeed may not depend so much on their attaining the structure of a sovereign territorial state but on their ability to crush rivals. Their capacity to do so may, in turn, depend on their control of resources valued in the international economy, and on their links to public and private international economic actors. Perhaps the problem for Africa is that, given international norms and the current structure of the international system of states, it is constrained to force its politics into the 'state' format, even while it seems unable to do so. As William Reno notes, the '[r]ulers that survive develop alternative, rational forms of political organization suited to Africa's marginal position in the changing global economy'.[102] In the centuries prior to colonialism, Africa was host to a wide variety of political forms; in the centuries after, it may continue to be so.

---

[99] 'Westphalia and All That', in Judith Goldstein and Robert O. Keohane (eds.), *Ideas and Foreign Policy* (Ithaca, NY: Cornell University Press, 1993), p. 235.

[100] Reno, 'Sierra Leone', p. 106; William Reno, *Warlord Politics and African States* (Boulder, CO: Lynne Rienner,1998); Boone, 'Empirical Statehood', p. 141.

[101] Schmitt, *The Concept*, pp. 19, 53.

[102] 'War, Markets, and the Reconfiguration of West Africa's Weak States', *Comparative Politics*, 29:4 (1997), pp. 493–510, here at p. 493.

Between anarchy and tyranny: excellence and the pursuit of power and peace in ancient Greece

NANCY KOKAZ*

Ancient Greece is not unfamiliar to International Relations scholars. Thucydides' *History of the Peloponnesian War* has been especially influential in shaping our understanding of the ancient Greek international system, not only because it is the best historical source available, but also in light of the status it has achieved as the foremost classic of International Relations.[1] Of particular interest to International Relations have been questions concerning the character of the system and the units within it, and how these have affected the dynamics of conflict and co-operation in the international arena. Many find the antecedents of the modern European states-system in the pattern of relations that emerged between the independent city-states of Hellas roughly between the eighth and fourth centuries BC. Like our contemporary international system, the ancient Greek international system was anarchic in the sense that it lacked an overarching common government.[2] The primary unit of the system was the *polis*, or independent city-state. The polis bore some resemblance to the sovereign state of today in the sense that each *polis* constituted a political authority that recognized no superior, and demanded and accorded recognition internationally on that basis. As Wight puts it, such reciprocity is the defining feature of a states-system: 'not only must each [state] claim independence of any political superior for itself, but each must recognize the validity of the same claim by all the others'.[3] This conception of the units and the system relies heavily on the dominant contemporary formulation of sovereignty as 'the idea that there is a final and absolute authority in the political community' and its international corollary

---

* I wish to thank Tim Dunne for valuable comments on an earlier draft, and Stanley Hoffmann and Jill Frank for encouragement in the initial stages of writing. Stanley Hoffmann also deserves special mention for being an excellent mentor and a source of endless inspiration at all times.

    Notes on citations: All emphases in citations are original, unless otherwise indicated. All square brackets in citations are my own and have been added for the sake of stylistic and contextual clarity. The only exception concerns the square brackets in citations from Aristotle's *Nicomachean Ethics*, which have been added by Terence Irwin, the translator of the text I have used, to 'denote insertion of words not found in the manuscripts'. See translator's note in Aristotle, *Nicomachean Ethics* (Indianapolis: Hackett, 1985), p. xxv.

[1] Martin Wight goes even farther in suggesting that Thucydides' *History* is the only counterpart of the acknowledged classics of political study in International Relations. Martin Wight, 'Why is There No International Theory?', in James Der Derian (ed.), *International Theory: Critical Investigations* (New York: New York University Press, 1995), p. 31.

[2] Martin Wight, *Power Politics* (Leicester: Leicester University Press, 1978), p. 105. For Wight, as for most International Relations scholars, anarchy refers not to a chaotic lack of order, but rather to the absence of a common government at the global level.

[3] Martin Wight, *Systems of States* (Leicester: Leicester University Press, 1977), p. 23.

'that no final and absolute authority exists elsewhere than in the community'.[4] Despite these initial similarities, however, the unity of the *polis* in ancient Greece was based on radically different moral foundations. It shall be my central claim that these differences, more so than the similarities, are crucial for grasping the dynamics of the exercise of power in ancient Greece in domestic and international politics alike.

The ancient Greek international system is typically treated as a clear example of the international (or independent) states-system, because of the type of systematic relationships its constituent units found themselves in—namely that of independence and sovereign equality *vis à vis* each other.[5] By contrast, in a suzerain states-system, one unit asserts supremacy over the others, as in the cases of the Roman Empire or the Abbasid Caliphate.[6] While it is true that the initial centuries of the ancient Greek international system probably constituted a clear case of an international states-system composed of independent sovereign units, by the time of the Peloponnesian War, the system was suffused by formal and informal relations of supremacy and subjugation, as well. In that connection, Thucydides' *History* covers a very interesting period where hegemonic and imperial ties had profusely permeated what used to be an independent states-system. In light of these complex relationships, I suggest that the question of classification is peripheral, even though it has aroused a significant degree of interest in International Relations.[7] Much more productive is the investigation of the main dynamics of conflict and co-operation in the system, without too much regard for how the system is classified. Doyle's work is groundbreaking in this respect in its exploration of the sources of different forms of power in ancient Greece. His analysis emphasizes the explanatory role of political unity in determining whether a *polis* was able and willing to exercise imperial power, ended up being subjugated in the periphery, or managed to attain independent resister status in transnational society.[8] Lebow's distinction between hegemony and empire in terms of the legitimacy of the exercise of power is also very helpful here. Lebow shows how fifth century BC Greek understandings of hegemonic and imperial power framed the message of the *History*. Hegemony was associated with honour, while empire signified sheer control.[9] Based on this difference, Lebow

---

[4] F. H. Hinsley, *Sovereignty* (New York: Basic Books, 1966), pp. 1, 158.

[5] Thus, Wight writes that 'if we were to define the kind of states-system we are concerned with by enumeration, we have perhaps three clear examples: the Western, the Hellenic-Hellenistic or Graeco-Roman, and the Chinese between the collapse of the Chou empire in 771 BC and the establishment of the Ts'in Empire in 221 AD'. Wight, *Systems of States*, p. 21.

[6] Ibid., p. 22.

[7] My concern echoes and takes further worries that have been expressed about the use of rigid classificatory schemes. As Watson puts it: 'I have become increasingly doubtful about sharp distinctions between systems of independent states, suzerain systems and empires. I now prefer to define the wider subject by saying that, when a number of diverse communities of people, or political entities, are sufficiently involved with one another for us to describe them as forming a system of some kind (whether independent, suzerain, imperial or whatever), the organization of the system will fall somewhere along a notional spectrum between absolute independence and absolute empire.' Adam Watson, *The Evolution of International Society* (New York: Routledge, 1992), p. 13. I take Watson's claim further and suggest that even classification along a spectrum obscures more than it reveals, as it does not address the fundamental dynamics of interaction that remain constant no matter where the system may be on the classificatory scheme. This is especially true given that multiple types of relationships often coexist at the same time in the same system.

[8] Michael Doyle, *Empires* (Ithaca, NY: Cornell University Press, 1986), ch. 3.

[9] Richard Ned Lebow, 'Thucydides the Constructivist', *American Political Science Review* (forthcoming, September 2001), p. 550.

maintains that empire without hegemony, or sheer power without legitimacy, is not sustainable in Thucydides' narrative.[10] Taken together, Doyle and Lebow's findings reveal the causal significance of legitimately constituted political unity in ancient Greece. I take these observations a step further and suggest that the issues of political unity and the legitimate exercise of power can only be understood in light of the moral ideals upon which political institutions rested.

In a nutshell, I argue that it is crucial to place Thucydides' discussion of power and institutions in the broader context of meaning that pervaded the ancient Greek international system to fully understand the operation of that system. This leads to a rediscovery of the links between the practice of excellence and the quest for political unity—a link which sheds light on the pursuit of power in domestic and international politics. Most importantly, it focuses our attention on political unity as the main source of power and highlights the significance of the connection between the institutional sources and moral foundations of such unity, with significant repercussions for contemporary theorizing in International Relations concerning international systems. At the very least, if power and institutions are closely tied to excellence in securing a form of political unity conducive to the good life, then available treatments of the ancient Greek international system remain incomplete. As a remedy, I attempt to develop a more comprehensive account of the moral foundations of conflict and co-operation in Thucydides' work. The development of such an account is especially important in light of the contemporary tendency to derive lessons concerning the eternal wisdom of Realism in international affairs from the *History*. To illustrate, it is to timeless lessons about the centrality of power that Gilpin points to when he argues for the contemporary relevance of Thucydides. 'Ultimately', Gilpin writes, 'international politics can still be characterized as it was by Thucydides'.[11] I wholeheartedly agree, but for very different reasons. The careful study of the ancient Greek international system, and especially Thucydides, offers valuable insights into the workings of international systems in general and remains highly relevant to understanding international politics today. The only way to attain these insights, however, is through a thorough analysis of the broader cultural and political challenges that marked the era under investigation and determined how power was to be pursued and used. The same is true of institutions and practices that facilitated co-operation in the system. Thucydides has a lot to say on both questions and strives to reach lasting scientific generalizations, but his aspiration to build a science of international relations can only be realized by placing these law-like generalizations in the context of meaning that informed them in the first place. In the absence of such contextualization, contemporary appropriations can only yield partial and misleading accounts.

Ancient Greece and International Relations: Realists and their critics

A theme which has proved to be of lasting interest to International Relations scholars concerns whether the ancient Greek international system is best understood as a

---

[10] Ibid., p. 13.
[11] Robert Gilpin, *War and Change in World Politics* (Cambridge: Cambridge University Press, 1981), p. 228.

state of war. 'For Thucydides, war—' writes Russett, 'or at best the condition we moderns would call deterrence—was the necessary consequence of such competitive relations in an anarchic interstate system without superordinate authority to impose some kind of peace and order'.[12] To make matters worse, Russett adds, this state of war was not mitigated by common institutions and practices as '[t]he world of Thucydides had no effective interstate organization that encompassed Greek civilization'.[13] Similarly, Doyle, who otherwise provides a much more nuanced picture of the historian's Realism, suggests that 'Thucydides is essentially a Realist, who believed that none of the traditional moral norms linking individuals across state boundaries have reliable effect'.[14] 'Interstate relations in his view exist in a condition where war is always possible', Doyle continues, since 'international anarchy precludes the effective escape from the dreary history of war and conflict that are the consequences of competition under anarchy'.[15] Not surprisingly, these theoretical presuppositions about the consequences of anarchy have led to an almost single-minded effort to understand the causes of war in ancient Greece, with very limited attention being devoted to understanding the moral and institutional underpinnings of peace.[16] The assumption of a state of war is so common that even a study of fairness and kindness in Thucydides begins by noting the irony involved in exploring such a theme, based on the initial belief that '[t]he world and the war which Thucydides describes are commanded by force and violence. The Athenian

---

[12] Bruce Russett, 'A Post-Thucydides, Post-Cold War World', *Mediterranean Quarterly*, 4:1 (Winter 1993), p. 46.

[13] Ibid., p. 50.

[14] Michael Doyle, *Ways of War and Peace: Realism, Liberalism, and Socialism* (New York: W. W. Norton, 1997), p. 51. To support the view that moral norms are ineffective (and even irrelevant) in international relations, most Realists rely on the infamous Melian dialogue, where the stronger Athenians demand that the weaker Melians join their empire and reject the Melians' objection concerning the unfairness of this demand, stressing, instead, expediency based on a comparative analysis of power in their response: 'Instead we recommend that you try to get what it is possible for you to get, taking into consideration what we both really do think; since you know as well as we do that when these matters are discussed by practical people, the standard of justice depends on the equality of power to compel and that in fact the strong do what they have the power to do and the weak accept what they have to accept'.[14] Thucydides, *History of the Peloponnesian War* (New York: Penguin, 1972), V.89. This is a notoriously complex passage, however, and its message is heavily contested. While the Melian dialogue clearly points to the importance of power in politics, it is far from clear that it asserts the irrelevance of justice and fairness. I will not discuss this issue any further here.

[15] Doyle, *Ways of War and Peace*, p. 51. For Doyle, the central strand that unifies all realists despite their other differences is 'a distinctive view of what constitutes international politics (their "dependent variable"). They are theorists of the "state of war". They discount any claims to system-wide international order other than that based ultimately on power or force, finding instead that among independent states, or other international actors, international society is best described as a condition of international anarchy. This is a condition that places all states in a warlike situation of reciprocal insecurity in which every alliance is temporary and every other state is a possible enemy, which makes, Hobbes argued, the possibility of war continuous.' Ibid., p. 43.

[16] As Reus-Smit astutely observes: 'International Relations scholars have focused almost exclusively on the nature and causes of conflict between the city-states, with most energies devoted to explaining the Peloponnesian War. While this is a worthy focus, patterns of cooperation between the city-states have received very little attention. In fact, one could easily conclude from the existing literature that the city-states of ancient Greece existed in a constant state of war, that cooperation was negligible or nonexistent, or that the city-states created little in the way of institutions to facilitate coexistence.' Christian Reus-Smit, *The Moral Purpose of the State: Culture, Social Identity, and Institutional Rationality in International Relations* (Princeton, NJ: Princeton University Press, 1999), p. 40.

empire is founded on fear and gathers only hatred.'[17] Thus, it comes as a surprise to de Romilly that one can also find hints of the political importance of goodwill based on fairness and kindness in the text.

The depiction of the ancient Greek international system as a state of war is largely misleading. If by the state of war is meant simply the possibility for war to break out at any moment because of the lack of a single political authority common to all of Hellas, then the ancient Greek international system was indeed a state of war. But that does not tell us anything about the dynamics of ancient Greek international politics as it amounts no more than a reassertion of the formal definition of anarchy.[18] If, however, the function of the image of the state of war is to invoke the idea of a world constantly at war—where force and violence reign supreme, where no norms or institutions exist to provide effective restraints, where self-help is the only way to attain security—as is more often the case than not with Realist accounts, then it yields an inaccurate description of the ancient Greek international system, which also embodied various normative institutions and practices to regulate the pursuit of power. Wight's work does an excellent job of documenting the existence of rudimentary forms of diplomacy and international law in ancient Greece alongside various pan-Hellenic institutions as well as what can be termed Hellenic public opinion.[19] Inter-*polis* communications were carried out by travelling ambassadors and resident *proxenos*—citizens of one *polis* who represented the interests of another *polis* towards which they were known to have a friendly disposition. International obligations based on inter-*polis* treaties, sworn alliance commitments, or various customary practices of proper behaviour were largely upheld. With regard to international law, I take issue with Wight's claim that 'the Hellenic system had no notion of international law'.[20] The *History* is full of observations that prove otherwise, such as the tremendous importance accorded to international treaties, the observance of certain rules of warfare for the most part, and the complex judicial system through which the Athenians governed their empire, to give just a few examples.[21] I suspect Wight's view resulted from his equation of international law with formally enacted rules, of which the ancient Greeks did not

[17] Jacqueline de Romilly, 'Fairness and Kindness in Thucydides', *Phoenix*, XXVIII:1 (Spring 1974), p. 95. The claim that the Athenian empire was based on fear and gathered only hatred is not uncontroversial. The Athenians themselves believed that they were worthy of their power because of the superiority of their institutions. Thus, when Pericles declares Athens 'an education to Greece', he appeals to the power Athens possesses abroad which has been won by the superior virtue of the Athenians in order to substantiate his view. Pericles adds that in the case of Athens and Athens alone, 'no invading enemy is ashamed at being defeated, and no subject can complain of being governed by people unfit for their responsibilities'. Thucydides, II.41. The Athenians in Sparta at the outbreak of the war also emphasize the excellence of the legal institutions through which they exercise their imperial power. Thucydides, I.77. Furthermore, many in the empire welcomed the opportunity to row in the Athenian navy, to employ Athenian currency, and to make use of the Athenian legal system. For a helpful discussion of the popularity of the Athenian empire, see Adda Bozeman, *Politics and Culture in International History* (Princeton, NJ: Princeton University Press, 1960).

[18] Against one of the founding theoretical presuppositions of International Relations, one could also add here that the presence of a single political authority is never in itself a guarantee against the eruption of a state of war, but that is a different matter.

[19] Wight, *Systems of States*, ch. 2.

[20] Ibid., p. 50.

[21] For a brief overview and helpful references, see K. J. Holsti, *International Politics: A Framework For Analysis*, (Englewood Cliffs, NJ: Prentice Hall, 1992). For more detailed discussions, see Coleman Phillipson, *The International Law and Custom of Ancient Greece and Rome* (London: Macmillan, 1911); Arthur Nussbaum, *A Concise History of the Law of Nations* (New York: Macmillan, 1961).

have very many, and his general frustration with the lack of guarantees for the enforcement of the informal rules that did exist, which is a problem that is not unique to ancient Greece but plagues international law in general.

Pan-Hellenic institutions and practices—and some add, a common Greek identity —also shaped the complex web of meaning within which co-operation took place in inter-*polis* relations in ancient Greece.[22] The two most important pan-Hellenic institutions, the Olympic games and the Oracle at Delphi, both of religious origin, injected a certain degree of order into international interactions and came close to constituting an early variant of international public opinion. Interstate procedures for peaceful conflict resolution, such as third party arbitration, were commonly resorted to, and on the whole, proved to be very effective.[23] Perhaps most effective of all in regulating wartime conduct were the informal and 'unwritten conventions governing inter-state conflict' deriving from common practice. These unwritten conventions were a varied bunch, ranging 'from what might be called neoformal rules to practices conditioned largely by practicality'.[24] Drawing on a wide array of sources, Ober summarizes the most important ancient Greek rules of warfare as follows:

1. The state of war should be officially declared before commencing hostilities against an appropriate foe; sworn treaties and alliances should be regarded as binding.
2. Hostilities are sometimes inappropriate: sacred truces, especially those declared for the celebration of the Olympic games, should be observed.
3. Hostilities against certain persons and in certain places are inappropriate: the inviolability of sacred places and persons under protection of the gods, especially heralds and suppliants, should be respected.
4. Erecting a battlefield trophy indicates victory; such trophies should be respected.
5. After a battle, it is right to return enemy dead when asked; to request the return of one's dead is tantamount to admitting defeat.
6. A battle is properly prefaced by a ritual challenge and acceptance of the challenge.
7. Prisoners of war should be offered for ransom, not summarily executed or mutilated.
8. Punishment of surrendered opponents should be restrained.
9. War is an affair of warriors, thus noncombatants should not be primary targets of attack.
10. Battles should be fought during the usual (summer) campaigning season.
11. Use of nonhoplite arms should be limited.
12. Pursuit of defeated and retreating opponents should be limited in duration.[25]

---

[22] For an argument on the presence of a common Greek identity, see Robert Connor, 'Polarization in Thucydides' in Richard Ned Lebow and Barry Strauss (eds.), *Hegemonic Rivalry: From Thucydides to the Nuclear Age* (Boulder, CO: Westview Press, 1991), pp. 65–6.

[23] Reus-Smit, *The Moral Purpose of the State*, ch. 3. See also Marcus Tod, *International Arbitration Amongst the Greeks* (Oxford: Clarendon Press, 1913).

[24] Josiah Ober, *The Athenian Revolution: Essays on Ancient Greek Democracy and Political Theory* (Princeton, NJ: Princeton University Press, 1996), p. 56.

[25] Ibid.

Ober goes on to suggest that 'most of these informal rules were followed most of the time, in intra-Greek warfare of about 700 to 450 BC'.[26] I want to add the additional claim that these rules defined what the practice of war was and how it was understood in the ancient Greek context. As such, the state of war that characterized the system, if there was such a state, cannot be understood without reference to them. Violations of these rules have to be read as just another illustration of the tragic descent of Greece below the confines of civilized behaviour.[27]

A further area of interest to International Relations scholars has concerned the structure of the ancient Greek international system and its causal role in determining (or influencing) the direction of events. For Realists, the particular distribution of power in the system and the consequences of changes in that distribution are deemed to be crucial for understanding the causes of the Peloponnesian War. This focus on the structural distribution of power can take two forms, each emphasizing a slightly different aspect of power relations. The first is manifested in an interest in studying the polarity of the system and its implications for international stability. 'The World of Thucydides was bipolar', maintains Russett, 'with two great states arrayed against each other, each leading a vast alliance of roughly equal power. That bipolarity seemed to make inevitable each side's fear of any increment to the power of the other, resulting in whatever protective military action each side thought necessary'.[28] The second emphasizes the important role of variations in the distribution of power in bringing about instability and war. A Thucydidean observation that is dear to the hearts of many Realists in this regard concerns the historian's location of the main cause of the Peloponnesian war in power shifts in the structure of the system. 'What made war inevitable' writes Thucydides, 'was the growth of Athenian power and the fear which this caused in Sparta'.[29] Gilpin draws on this observation in support of his power transition theory, whereby the uneven growth of power and the mutual fears and clashes of interest it engenders produces a situation ripe for conflict, where the resulting systemic disequilibrium is likely to be resolved by war.[30] Both of these positions have been challenged. To give some examples, Connor shows that Thucydides subverts the notion of bipolarity by underscoring how Corcyra, Thebes, and the Greek city-states of Sicily—all potentially critical players in the Peloponnesian war—held back from committing themselves to either side so as to try to further their own interests.[31] Kauppi suggests that the system was multipolar in light of the critical role played by Persia in the last stages of the war. He adds that changes in the distribution of power need not lead to war and have not done so historically.[32] Lebow highlights the domestic factors and the leadership blunders that played a crucial part in bringing about the war.[33] Kagan

---

[26] Ibid.

[27] In a similar vein, Lebow also stresses the importance of conventions for the preservation of civilization and the sense of tragedy that pervades the *History* upon the violation of such conventions. Lebow, 'Thucydides the Constructivist', pp. 551–3.

[28] Russett, 'A Post-Thucydides, Post-Cold War World', p. 48.

[29] Thucydides, I.23.

[30] Gilpin, *War and Change in World Politics*.

[31] Connor, 'Polarization in Thucydides', pp. 54–60.

[32] Mark Kauppi, 'Contemporary International Relations Theory and the Peloponnesian War' in Lebow and Strauss (eds.), *Hegemonic Rivalry*, pp. 108–11.

[33] Richard Ned Lebow, 'Thucydides, Power Transition Theory, and the Causes of War' in Lebow and Strauss (eds.), *Hegemonic Rivalry*, pp. 125–65.

demonstrates that Athens' power was not rising in the years that preceded the outbreak of the war.[34] These criticisms, taken together, reveal the inadequacy of a simplistic systemic explanation of the Peloponnesian war that focuses on bipolar distributions and power transitions at the expense of other causal variables.

The debate about ancient Greece in International Relations has largely taken place between Realists and their critics. Structural Realist readings, with their emphasis on polarity, power transitions, and the systemic causes of the war, are important, not only because they set the terms for subsequent discussions in the field, but also because they point to the central importance of power in politics, domestic and international. Critical scholarship is equally valuable for providing a more nuanced and accurate understanding of the realities of ancient Greek politics, through the extension of causal analysis, beyond the system to uncover factors that operated at various levels of analysis and the study of the institutions and practices that constrained power politics and made co-operation possible. I want to go a step further to explore the moral underpinnings of conflict and co-operation in ancient Greece, by probing the context of meaning that shaped the pursuit of power, as well as the operation of basic co-operative institutions and practices. I argue that it is important to try to decipher how Thucydides conceptualized power and institutions against the background of the most important political challenges that marked the ancient Greek international system, as they were perceived at the time he wrote his *History*. Such an investigation indicates that the primary driving mechanism of ancient Greek politics was the quest for political unity, an enterprise that, in its turn, was closely tied to an ideal of the good life. Not any form of unity was welcomed; tyranny was held in as much contempt as anarchy. Avoiding these two extremes necessitated the proper use of power within proper institutional frameworks in a way that furthered the practice of excellence. It is only in light of these links between political unity and the good life that a robust understanding of the dynamics of the ancient Greek international system can be attained.

Bringing the quest for political unity back into the centre of political analysis offers an invitation to explore the continuities between domestic and international politics. Unity is a source of power in domestic and international politics alike. Furthermore, the principal question of securing political unity turns domestic and international politics into two sides of the same coin. The struggle for power is pervasive in all politics; it has the potential to promote or undermine political unity whether it takes place in a domestic or international forum. Similarly, the institutions and practices upon which political unity rests operate inside as well as outside, even if they do so in slightly different ways. In light of these important continuities, I try to weave the lessons from domestic and international episodes in Thucydides' work into a single narrative in my investigation of the sources of unity. The continuity thesis has a certain degree of affinity with critical arguments that have urged the importance of integrating insights from multiple levels of analysis for understanding the determinants of international interactions. I want to stress, however, that this is not an attempt to label Thucydides, as it cuts across the divide between Realists and their critics. Early Realists were well attuned to the continuities between domestic and international politics, while many critics of Realism uphold the opposition between

---

[34] Donald Kagan, *On the Origins of War and the Preservation of Peace* (New York: Doubleday, 1995), ch. 2.

the two realms.[35] Labelling tends to be a deceptive exercise in the first place as it obscures more than it reveals about the thinker or period under scrutiny. My goal here is not to take sides in the debate between Realists and their critics, but rather to attend to a dimension of ancient Greek politics that has been neglected in this debate, in the hope that the analysis will move the discussion further.[36]

The fundamental challenge: securing political unity

The main unit in the ancient Greek international system was the *polis* and the most pressing political challenge was the preservation of its independence. Political unity was critical for achieving and safeguarding the independence of the *polis*.[37] The type of unity that was called for varied according to particular circumstances. Internal unity was the most important requirement of independence. It was only after its internal unity was compromised that Melos submitted to Athens, despite the initial inequalities of power that the Melian dialogue emphasizes. Incidentally, neutral Melos had been able to successfully resist a previous Athenian siege that took place in 426 BC, 10 years before its final conquest by Athens. When the Athenians decided to try again in 416 BC, 'there was some treachery from inside, [and] the Melians surrendered unconditionally to the Athenians', Thucydides tells us.[38] As important as internal unity was, however, some occasions required external unity as well for successful resistance to an external threat to independence. Thus, Hermocrates appeals to Sicilian unity to end the war between the Greek city-states of Sicily in the face of an impending Athenian intervention:

[T]aken all together, we are all of us neighbours, living together in the same country in the midst of the sea, all called by the same name of Sicilians. There will be occasions, no doubt, when we shall go to war again and also when we shall meet together among ourselves and make peace again. But when we are faced with a foreign invasion, we shall always, if we are wise, unite to resist it, since here the injury of any one state endangers all the rest of us.[39]

---

[35] For very good examples of early Realists who endorse the continuity thesis, see Max Weber, 'Politics as a Vocation' in H. Gerth and C. Wright Mills (eds.), *From Max Weber: Essays in Sociology* (New York: Oxford University Press, 1972); Hans Morgenthau, *Politics Among Nations: The Struggle For Power and Peace*, 5th edn. revised (New York: Alfred A. Knopf, 1978).

[36] Reus-Smit's work is a noteworthy exception. Reus-Smit argues that conceptions of the moral purpose of the state exert a significant influence on the choice of international institutions because such conceptions make part of the constitutional structure of international society that defines the social identity of the state and shape the nature of international co-operation. See Reus-Smit, *The Moral Purpose of the State*. While I have my doubts about the 'social identity' part, I am on the whole persuaded by this argument. I am concerned about the social identity thesis because it is not clear to me that the moral purpose of the state defined its social identity, and that the identity of the state in turn shaped the nature of international co-operation in ancient Greece. It seems to me that the identity of the state was determined not by a common conception of the moral purpose of the state, but rather by its internal organization, and this led not to co-operation but to constant interventions in other city-states to bring like-minded governments to power. Thus oligarchic Sparta intervened to assist oligarchs and democratic Athens intervened to assist democrats throughout Hellas. Furthermore, there was no clear preference for one form of government over the other, as Plato and Aristotle's discussions illustrate well. What is right on, however, is Reus-Smit's emphasis on the moral purpose of the state. The link between the state and the good life shaped the conception of all institutions and conventions, and hence affected the nature of international co-operation dramatically.

[37] Doyle, *Empires*, ch. 3, 6.

[38] Thucydides, V.116.

[39] Ibid., IV.64.

Earlier in the same speech, Hermocrates applies the model of unity to Sicily as a whole when he warns that 'internal strife is the main reason for the decline of cities, and will be so for Sicily, too, if we the inhabitants, who are all threatened together, will stand apart from each other, city against city'.[40] As these passages make obvious, political unity was seen as the best remedy for external encroachments on independence. It is important to remember here that the independence of the *polis* could be undermined both internally and externally. Internal disintegration was a great danger; the anarchy that civil war brought about set the stage for many calamities.[41] But if anarchy was to be avoided, so was tyranny, whether it was internally or externally imposed. In fact, very often, the two threats reinforced each other, with anarchy facilitating tyrannical rule and tyranny generating internal disorder. How, then, could the vicious cycle of anarchy and tyranny be broken? Through the establishment of a well-ordered *polis* whose stability was supported by the right institutions. As such, the question of which institutions were best suited to securing the unity of the *polis*, and under what conditions, emerged as the fundamental question, one that coloured every aspect of ancient Greek international interactions.

It is in this light that Thucydides' emphasis on power should be understood. Power and political unity, both crucial for the independence of the *polis*, went hand in hand for the historian. Political unity was an important—if not the most important—source of power, and power, in its turn, made political unity sustainable over time. Thus, in the examples of Melos and Sicily discussed above, it was the power that stemmed from unity that made the Melian and Sicilian resistance to Athens successful. Similarly, in the Athenian case, Thucydides notes that Athens remained strong as long as she was united, even in the face of all the misfortunes that befell her. As Thucydides puts it, despite all the difficulties they encountered in the last stages of the war, the Athenians 'none the less held out for eight years against their original enemies, who were now reinforced by the Sicilians, against their own allies, most of which had revolted, and against Cyrus, son of the King of Persia, who later joined the other side and provided the Peloponnesians with money for their fleet. And in the end it was only because they had destroyed themselves by their own internal strife that finally they were forced to surrender'.[42] It was neither the Sicilian disaster nor the abandonment of her allies nor the Persian support of Sparta that finally brought Athens down, but her loss of political unity. The causal link between power and unity is relatively uncontroversial here.

Perhaps even more importantly, both power and unity were also closely connected to an ideal of the good life in the ancient Greek context—a connection that was crucial for comprehending the causal link between unity and power itself. The connection is distinctly present in the works of the philosophers. Aristotle expresses it most forcefully in stating that 'the state comes into existence, originating in the

---

[40] Ibid., IV.61.
[41] Thucydides' account of the civil war in Corcyra is the ultimate illustration of the utter devastation internal disintegration entails. It is very likely that Thucydides' description of Corcyra informed Hobbes' conception of the state of nature as a condition of total warfare where life was nasty, brutish, and short. Hobbes was an attentive student and great admirer of Thucydides, who also produced an eloquent translation of the *History*. See David Grene (ed.), *The Peloponnesian War: The Complete Hobbes Translation* (Chicago, IL: The University of Chicago Press, 1958).
[42] Thucydides, II.65.

bare needs of life, and continuing in existence *for the sake of the good life*.[43] The good life entails the practice of excellence in the lives of individuals as well as political communities. Thus, not only the power and unity of the *polis*, but also the very goal of political independence, is irrevocably tied to the practice of excellence. It is only when this link is brought to the fore that a meaningful understanding of the foundations of political power and unity can be attained. Tying unity and power to a moral ideal of living well was not merely a philosopher's dream, either. A similar, if less systematic, connection between politics and the good life can be discerned in work of Thucydides.[44] In that respect, Thucydides and Aristotle have a lot in common. Contrary to received wisdom, I argue that it is more accurate to read Thucydides as a forerunner of Aristotle rather than a follower of the sophists for a full appreciation of the subtlety of his thought.[45] Such a repositioning places the notion of proper use in the practice of excellence at the centre of the historian's analysis of political unity, with significant ramifications for his treatment of power and institutions in international affairs.

As already stated, a central aim of my exploration is to enrich the analysis of conflict and co-operation by paying close attention to the context of meaning within which the pursuit of power and peace takes place. Such attention reveals that a sound understanding of the dynamics of the ancient Greek international system can only be attained in light of the links between power, political unity, and the practice of excellence that predominantly shaped its context of meaning. Accordingly, not all forms of political unity are conducive to human flourishing. As pernicious as anarchy may be, its exact opposite, tyranny, is equally dangerous. Both threaten the good life, and the good life is what the *polis* seeks to bring about. As Aristotle puts it in the opening passage of the *Politics*:

Every state is a community of some kind, and every community is established with a view to some good; for everyone always acts in order to obtain that which they think good. But, if all communities aim at some good, the state or political community, which is the highest of all, and which embraces all the rest, aims at good in a greater degree than any other, and at the highest good.[46]

This passage makes it very clear that political unity is valuable in light of its connection to the good life. It is for this reason that Aristotle thinks of political science as the ruling science. Political science has this character because it aims at knowledge of the highest good. In other words, political science, which aims to discover the good of the *polis*, has a controlling position over all other sciences, even those aiming at the good of the individual, because 'though admittedly the good is the same for a city as for an individual, still the good of the city is apparently a greater and more complete good to acquire and preserve. For while it is satisfactory to acquire and preserve the good even for an individual, it is finer and more divine to acquire and

---

[43] Aristotle, *Politics* (Cambridge: Cambridge University Press, 1988), 1252b29. Emphasis mine.

[44] Aristotle's method would rule out such dreaming in the first place, as he believed in the importance of starting from received wisdom and existing conventions in his search for the elements of the good life.

[45] For instance, there are striking similarities between the Thucydidean and Aristotelian conceptions of the nature-convention distinction. I have explored in more detail the similarities in the two thinkers' treatments of nature and power as well as their implications for our understanding of International Relations elsewhere. Nancy Kokaz, 'Moderating Power: A Thucydidean Perspective', *Review of International Studies* (27:1, 2001).

[46] Aristotle, *Politics*, 1252a1.

preserve it for a people and for cities.'[47] Since the good life for humans is understood in terms of activity expressing excellence, the acquisition and preservation of the good of the political community must also be understood in terms of the practice of excellence.[48] These links should be taken to heart in exploring the dynamics of the ancient Greek international system, as they capture crucial features of the context of meaning that shaped how political analysis was undertaken at the time.

Once the connection between politics and excellence is recognized, the question of how to think about the moral foundations of political unity acquires a special urgency. Proper use emerges as a central category in the practice of excellence. As neither anarchy nor tyranny contribute to the good life, the challenge becomes articulating a form (or various forms) of political unity that make(s) the proper use of political power possible. What, then, can the basis of such unity be? The distinction between nature and convention is highly relevant here since it played a prominent role in ancient Greek discussions of excellence and the good.[49] This had ramifications for political analysis, as the question of whether political unity was grounded in nature or convention was highly contested. Complex articulations of the respective roles of nature and convention can be found in the thought of individual thinkers. Aristotle, for example, famously asserted that 'it is evident that the state is a creation of nature, and that man is by nature a political animal'.[50] And yet, at the same time, Aristotle recognized the possibility of multiple routes to political unity, as given by the constitutions of different well-ordered states, and these constitutions were in place by convention. The basis of unity could change, as the conventions changed. 'For since the state is a partnership, and is a partnership of citizens in a constitution, when the form of the government changes and becomes different, then it may be supposed that the state is no longer the same', Aristotle wrote.[51] These passages suggest that the links between nature, convention, and excellence were complex, and that both nature and convention had a role to play in establishing forms of political unity conducive to the good life.

I examine the convention part of the picture here. More broadly, I am interested in investigating how political unity was understood in the ancient Greek context in light of its vital connection to the good life. I address this question by offering a close reading of how Thucydides conceived of the role of convention in the practice of excellence. My goal is to explore the types of conventions upon which political unity could be based in ancient Greece to avoid the twin pitfalls of anarchy and tyranny. Could divine law offer a stable solution? If the laws of the city were tied to the divine, could there be any place for human law? If, by contrast, the laws of the city were not tied to the divine, what were the foundations upon which human law rested? What role did unwritten laws and cultural practices, such as friendship, have to play? Did Thucydides have a clear preference among the multiplicity of conventional possibilities that the ancient Greek context of meaning made available? Did he unequivocally reject or endorse a particular source of unity? What does that

---

[47] Aristotle, *Nicomachean Ethics* (Indianapolis, IN: Hackett, 1985), 1094b5–1094b10.
[48] In Aristotle's words, 'the human good turns out to be the soul's activity that expresses virtue'. Ibid., 1089a20.
[49] The nature-convention distinction was first articulated by the sophists in terms of a stark opposition. Subsequent thinkers tried to bring the two sides of the opposition together in more complex ways.
[50] Aristotle, *Politics*, 1253a1.
[51] Ibid., 1276b1.

imply for how he conceptualized the relationship between political unity and the good life? It is crucial to try to answer these questions in order to grasp the full significance of Thucydides' analysis of the pursuit of power and peace and develop a richer understanding of the structure and dynamics of the ancient Greek international system. My analysis reveals that, for Thucydides, political unity could rest on a wide range of conventional foundations as long as these were properly used to promote the practice of excellence. Thus, institutions and practices of co-operation had to be evaluated not only in terms of the constraints they placed on the exercise of power, but also in light of how they were used. Finally, excellent conventional foundations that were conducive to the good life were also a source of power in international affairs.

Embarking on the quest for unity: the role of divine law

'We must assume that a states-system will not come into being', writes Wight, 'without a degree of cultural unity among its members. The three states-systems that we have taken as paradigms, the Greek, the Western, and the early Chinese, each arose within a single culture.'[52] Religious institutions and practices were a funda-mental source of cultural unity in ancient Greece, not only in the system but also for the *polis*. Just as the religiously based institutions and practices common to all Hellas that have already been discussed provided the means of cultural unity in the system, the religious institutions and practices specific to each city-state had the potential for being the fountain of unity for the *polis*. Impiety was considered to be a direct threat to internal political unity, as the trial and execution of Socrates amply illustrate.[53] Religious conventions often guided political behaviour as well, both in internal and external affairs. Finally, ideas about divine justice were invoked to explain the eventual downfall of Athens. The question, then, becomes whether such religious conventions can form the basis for the right kind of political unity—a kind of unity conducive to the good life—and what sorts of beliefs about divine interven-tion in human affairs such unity requires. I suggest that Thucydides' treatment of the divine shows that religiosity did have a part to play in the practice of excellence when properly used, without necessitating a belief in divine justice.

Divine law occupies a peculiar place between nature and convention. Although my focus is on the conventional sources of unity here, this does not mean that nature is irrelevant to the discussion. The interrelationships between nature, convention, and excellence are complex, and this is nowhere more evident than in the analysis of the religious foundations of political unity. If divine law constituted a plausible basis for political unity, was that by nature or by convention? On the one hand, divine law was tied to the conventions of each *polis*. Ancient Greek religion was not a religion of salvation but was oriented toward civic rituals, with different cities having their own Gods and exclusive festivals. Yet, the divine was also invoked in the name of natural justice, as when Antigone appealed to something higher than the laws of the

[52] Wight, *Systems of States*, p. 33.
[53] Plato, 'Apology of Socrates' in Thomas West and Grace Starry West (eds.), *Four Texts on Socrates* (Ithaca, NY: Cornell University Press, 1995), pp. 63–98.

city.[54] It is not possible to uncover a consensus as to whether divine law was given by nature or by convention. This, however, is not the question that I am interested in pursuing here. Instead, I emphasize how religion was used as a conventional foundation for political unity, whether the divine is ultimately understood to originate in nature or convention. Thucydides' analysis is instructive here, as it brackets questions about the nature and origins of the divine, and focuses instead on its political functions. Accordingly, the historian offers neither an outright rejection nor an uncritical endorsement of divine law, but instead emphasizes the importance of its proper use in the practice of excellence.

At first glance, it is easy to read Thucydides as a harsh critic of religion, to suppose that 'his *History* unfolds without gods or oracles or omens'.[55] There are numerous instances in the *History* where Thucydides finds fault with religiosity, divine prophecies, and oracles, and favours rational scientific explanations of the causes of events. To give a few well-known examples, Thucydides is quite critical of how people adapted 'their memories to fit their sufferings' in their interpretation of oracles during the plague.[56] He cynically asserts that there was one, and only one instance of an oracle being proved accurate, the prediction that 'the war would last for thrice nine years'.[57] He implies that the Melian trust in divine assistance, prophecies, and oracles in the face of overwhelming power was foolish, as signalled by the remarks of the Athenian envoys and the eventual fate of Melos.[58] He condemns the religious frenzy that surrounded the disfiguration of the Hermae leading to savagery in Athens and the eventual recall of Alcibiades.[59] He gives a moving description of how the Athenian expedition to Sicily, the greatest action ever to be undertaken in Hellenic history, ended with 'the most calamitous of defeats' because the general Nicias delayed withdrawal due to an eclipse of the moon, an unfavourable omen.[60] Based on these remarks and many more, it might seem reasonable to conclude that Thucydides had no taste for religion.

As important as the above references are, however, they reveal only one side of the story. Alongside the disdain of religious injunctions, oracles, and omens can be found the horrific accounts of the plague and civil war in Corcyra. During the plague at Athens, Thucydides tells us, people 'became indifferent to every rule of religion and

---

[54] Antigone defied the laws of the city to bury her brother in accordance with divine law, which she understood to be natural and eternal. She proudly declared that the lawmaker's orders have to give way before divine law in her response to Creon: 'Nor did I think that your orders were so strong that you, a mortal man, could over-run the gods' unwritten and unfailing laws. Not now, nor yesterday's, they always live, and no one knows their origin in time.' Sophocles, 'Antigone' in David Grene and Richmond Lattimore (eds.), *Sophocles I* (Chicago, IL: The University of Chicago Press, 1954), p. 174.

[55] M. I. Finley, 'Introduction' in Thucydides, *History of the Peloponnesian War*, p. 20.

[56] Thucydides, II.54.

[57] Ibid., V.26.

[58] Ibid., V.103. Melos refused the Athenian injunction to join the Athenian empire, and was conquered as a result, upon which the Athenians 'put to death all the men of military age whom they took, and sold the women and children as slaves'. Ibid., V. 116. I will not discuss the case of Melos any further here, as I do not think that it is necessary to judge the question concerning divine justice to see what the political functions of religion could be. Let me just note in passing that I find the theme of misuse of tendencies in nature (i.e. the misuse of hope on behalf of the Melians and the misuse of power on behalf of the Athenians) more intriguing and more important than the matter of divine intervention for understanding the message of the Melian dialogue.

[59] Ibid., VI.27–VI.29 and VI.60–VI.61.

[60] Ibid., VII.50 and VII.87.

law'.[61] Traditional burial ceremonies were disrupted, the usual laments for the dead were given up, a 'state of unprecedented lawlessness' ensued as '[n]o fear of god or law of man had a restraining influence'.[62] Similarly, in Corcyra, the sanctity of sacred places was violated as suppliants from the temple of Hera who agreed to a trial were condemned to death, the remaining suppliants committed suicide in the temple, and 'men were dragged from the temples or butchered on the very altars'.[63] In both situations, the dissolution of religious restraints led to tremendous human suffering. Indeed, after witnessing the horrors of the collapse of religion, it is difficult not to agree with Marinatos that 'Thucydides supported religion because he saw that it helped preserve the norms and morals of society'.[64] Similarly, religion provided important restraints in international affairs. As already noted, religious rites about the exchange of the dead were strictly followed in the conduct of war; sacred truces were generally observed; and the inviolability of sacred places was ordinarily upheld. There was one significant exception, when the Athenian fortification of the temple of Apollo at Delium was reciprocated by a Boeotian refusal to return the Athenian dead. The Athenians defended the fortification of the temple and violation of the sacred water on grounds of necessity. Yet, the Athenian argument that 'even the god would look indulgently on any action done under the stress of war and danger' was not very convincing to the Boeotians.[65] The matter was finally resolved when the defeated Athenians withdrew from the temple, upon which the Boeotians returned the Athenian dead.[66] The Delium incident is no doubt a case of religious offence, but even so, it simultaneously demonstrates the power of religiosity for introducing a modicum of restraint and order to warfare.

Not surprisingly, what ties the praise and criticism of religion together for Thucydides is its use. As Marinatos notes, the Athenian position at Delium represented a misuse of religion.[67] She goes on to suggest that Thucydides was very upset by the 'demagoguery of the seers and oracle-mongers'[68] and the superstitious acceptance of such demagoguery by the public that generally resulted in destructive courses of policy. 'For Thucydides,' writes Marinatos, 'superstition is not erroneous belief only, but misuse of religion'.[69] The problem is not with oracles, then, which are generally ambiguous and indicate the truth for those who can understand it, but with those who exploit religiosity for their own purposes, such as the chresmologues. Also to blame are the public and the individuals who are gullible enough to believe the chresmologues or who do not succeed in interpreting genuine Delphic oracles correctly.[70] Oost also emphasizes how Thucydides was not necessarily critical of oracles *per se*, but of their reception, and especially of the 'too ready credulity of people in general'.[71] What really disturbed Thucydides, Marinatos suggests, and I

---

[61] Ibid., II.52.
[62] Ibid., II.51–II.53.
[63] Ibid., III.81.
[64] Nanno Marinatos, *Thucydides and Religion* (Konigstein: Verlag Anton Hain, 1981), p. 56.
[65] Thucydides, IV.98.
[66] Ibid., IV.97–IV.101.
[67] Marinatos, *Thucydides and Religion*, p. 39.
[68] Ibid., p. 63.
[69] Ibid., p. 62.
[70] Nanno Marinatos, 'Thucydides and Oracles', *The Journal of Hellenic Studies*, CI (1981), pp. 138, 140. See also Marinatos, *Thucydides and Religion*, pp. 56, 64.
[71] Stewart Irvin Oost, 'Thucydides and the Irrational: Sundry Passages', *Classical Philology*, LXX:3 (July 1975), p. 194.

believe she is correct, was that the misuse of religion very often resulted in social disaster, whether it be in the form of savage disorder or erroneous policy decisions.[72] The recall of Alcibiades was once such instance of the misuse of religiosity, since Alcibiades had conducted himself perfectly in his public capacity whatever his personal faults may have been.[73] The case of Nicias and the eclipse of the moon which delayed the Athenian withdrawal from Sicily and ended in the utter destruction of the expedition is another instance. Thucydides notes that Nicias was 'rather over-inclined to divination and such things'.[74] As Oost points out, Thucydides here criticizes the excessive devotion of Nicias to religion, which implies that the historian 'had a conception of a degree of religiosity which is *not* excessive'.[75]

In a nutshell, proper use is vital for religion to assume a positive function in the quest for political unity. If Nicias and the chresmologues represent the drawbacks of excess religiosity, the plague and Corcyra warn about the dangers of deficiency. Strauss is right on target, when he notes that 'Thucydides' theology—if it is permitted to use this expression—is located in the mean (in the Aristotelian sense)' between excess and deficiency.[76] Proper use requires moderation. Proper use also requires practical wisdom in determining what moderation demands, as evidenced by the emphasis on correct interpretations that avoid excess. As Oost notes, Thucydides constantly submits religiosity to rational testing in trying to determine its proper use.[77] Moderation and practical wisdom go together in the proper use of religion in the practice of excellence. Acknowledging the importance of the proper use of religion in terms of its contribution to the practice of excellence does not require one to be pious or to believe in divine retribution, even though that may help. Hence, a central question that has puzzled many analysts of the role of the divine in the *History*—that of whether Thucydides provides evidence for divine justice when he recounts the disaster that befell the Athenians in the Sicilian expedition after their misdemeanour in Melos—does not need to be settled. One does not need to hold, with Marinatos, that 'the pattern of Athens' downfall illustrates divine justice'[78] on my account of the role of religion in Thucydides' work. All it takes to accord religion its proper place in the practice of excellence is to recognize the importance of its proper use in human terms.

Grounding human law: consent, coercion, and respect

Human law, written and unwritten, plays a similar function for grounding political unity in the practice of excellence. The already cited passages from Corcyra and the plague highlight the crucial importance of not only divine, but also human law. Just like religion, human law has a vital role to play in injecting moderation and practical

---

[72] Marinatos, *Thucydides and Religion*, pp. 62–3.
[73] Thucydides, VI.15.
[74] Ibid., VII.50.
[75] Oost, 'Thucydides and the Irrational', p. 192.
[76] Leo Strauss, 'Preliminary Observations on the Gods in Thucydides' Work', *Interpretation*, 4:1 (1974), p. 12.
[77] Oost, 'Thucydides and the Irrational', p. 195.
[78] Marinatos, *Thucydides and Religion*, p. 58.

wisdom into domestic and international politics, and it is upon these foundations that co-operative practices regulated by law must rest. The final part of the Athenian dictum at Melos, that of treating the weak, the suffering, the oppressed, or more generally those in an inferior position, with moderation, presupposes the special significance of the proper use of law in this respect. Textual evidence for this claim is abundant. In his discussion of Corcyra, Thucydides notes with regret the disastrous consequences of the repeal of 'those general laws of humanity which are there to give a hope of salvation to all who are in distress'.[79] Pericles underscores the importance of obedience to the laws, 'especially those which are for the protection of the oppressed, and those unwritten laws which it is an acknowledged shame to break'.[80] The Melians reiterate the importance of laws and principles which tend 'to the general good of all men: namely, that in the case of all who fall into danger there should be such a thing as fair play and just dealing'.[81] *Contra* Saxonhouse's suspicious remarks, it is no coincidence that 'the speeches, especially those of men who speak from positions of weakness, are replete with reference to the laws of the Hellenes'.[82] It is natural for a writer who was as concerned with human suffering as Thucydides that laws should play a part in alleviating those sufferings by offering protection and hope to the downtrodden.

How were the laws to perform that function? A simple answer would look at consent or coercion or a combination thereof.[83] Surely, agreement and consent did have an important role in generating moderation. The best example from international affairs is the observance of international treaties. In fact, before the outbreak of war, both sides take extreme care not to violate the agreement of the peace treaty that concluded the first Peloponnesian War. Corcyra appeals in part to the treaty to legitimize its alliance request from Athens after the controversy with Corinth over Epidamnus. Thus, the Corcyraean representatives tell the Athenians: 'It is not a breach of your treaty with Sparta if you receive us into your alliance. We are neutrals, and it is expressly written down in your treaty that any Hellenic state which is in this condition is free to ally itself with whichever side it chooses'.[84] The Athenians decide to make a limited defensive alliance with Corcyra as opposed to a full alliance in recognition of the fact that a full alliance which could require them to join in an attack on Corinth 'would constitute a breach of their treaty with the Peloponnese'.[85] Finally, the Spartan declaration of war is based on a vote that concludes that the Athenians had broken the treaty.[86] Furthermore, treaties with arbitration clauses for the peaceful resolution of disputes were quite effective in the avoidance of hostilities when they were observed. Clearly, agreement, as enshrined in international law based on treaty, was crucial for the promotion of moderation in international politics.

---

[79] Thucydides, III.84.
[80] Ibid., II.37.
[81] Ibid., V.90.
[82] Arlene Saxonhouse, 'Nature and Convention in Thucydides' *History*', *Polity*, 10:4 (Summer 1978), p. 475, fn. 27.
[83] Consent and coercion represent typical justifications for the authority of the political community in 'domestic' political theory. In defiance of the distinction between domestic and international politics, Thucydides offers examples from both realms in his discussion of the proper use of institutions.
[84] Thucydides, I.35.
[85] Ibid., I.44.
[86] Ibid., I.87–I.88.

Unfortunately, agreement, as such, is not enough. For Thucydides, equally important was how agreement was used. The most striking illustration of the abuse of
agreement in international affairs comes in the actions of the Athenian general
Paches in Notium in his interactions with the rival general Hippias at the time of the
Athenian intervention on behalf of the Colophonian side during party strife there:

> Paches invited Hippias, the general of the Arcadian mercenaries, inside the fortification for a
> discussion, promising that, if no agreement was reached, he would see that he got back again
> safe and sound to the fortification. Hippias therefore came out to meet Paches who put him
> under arrest, though not in chains. He then made a sudden attack and took the fortification
> by surprise. He put to death all the Arcadian and foreign troops who were inside, and later, as
> he had promised, he brought Hippias back there, and as soon as he was inside, he had him
> seized and shot down with arrows.[87]

Paches kept his promise: as he had agreed, he returned Hippias to the Arcadian
fortification safe and sound. However, the particular use of agreement in this
instance is absolutely outrageous and does not contribute one inch to the practice of
excellence. The example shows how agreement, misused, can be utterly destructive
for moderation and practical wisdom. Practical wisdom here is to be distinguished
from what Aristotle called cleverness or what we call prudence or instrumental
rationality today. 'There is a capacity, called cleverness, which is such as to be able to
do the actions that tend to promote whatever goal is assumed and to achieve it'
wrote Aristotle. Practical wisdom 'is not the same as this capacity [of cleverness],
though it requires it'.[88] Practical wisdom cannot be the same as sheer calculativeness
(cleverness), because practical wisdom is understood in terms of the goals that are
chosen as well as the actions undertaken to achieve them. Instrumental rationality is
only a part of this account, it needs to be accompanied by the right ends in order to
make a positive contribution to the practice of excellence.

A more familiar problem lies in the hazards of disregarding agreements. This is a
problem that has forever haunted proponents of international law: a treaty may be
agreed upon, but in the absence of enforcement power, how can it be ensured that it
will be abided by? In the example just discussed, Paches could have easily broken his
word as opposed to keeping it in a perverse way as he did. A more typical example
comes during the Peace of Nicias. As Thucydides notes, this peace was no peace in
reality:

> [I]t would certainly be an error of judgement to consider the interval of the agreement as
> anything else except a period of war. One has only to look at the facts to see that it is hardly
> possible to use the word 'peace' of a situation in which neither side gave back or received what
> had been promised; and apart from this there were breaches of the treaty on both sides.[89]

Agreements are great, but if they are not upheld, they don't amount to much. It is
only in their proper use, that is in their observation in accordance with the spirit of
the agreement in a way that is conducive to moderation, that agreements can
promote the practice of excellence.

Is it through coercion, then, that human law operates in the practice of excellence?
Fear of punishment is cited as an important factor in producing obedience to the law

---

[87] Ibid., III.34.
[88] Aristotle, *Nicomachean Ethics*, 1144b20–1144b35.
[89] Thucydides, I.26.

in various instances in the *History*. Most notably, with respect to the lawlessness of the revolution in Corcyra, Thucydides refers to erosion of the *fear* of law. 'As for the offences against human law,' he writes, 'no one expected to live long enough to be brought to trial and punished'. As a result, '[n]o fear of god or law had a restraining influence'.[90] Similarly, in the debate about the proper punishment to be accorded to Mytilene after her unsuccessful revolt, both speakers concentrate on the power to coerce. Cleon reminds the Athenians that their 'leadership depends on superior strength and not on any goodwill' of the allies,[91] while Diodotus cynically ties obedience to the law to the fear of punishment:

Cities and individuals alike, all are by nature disposed to do wrong, and there is no law that will prevent it, as is shown by the fact that men have tried every kind of punishment, constantly adding to the list, in the attempt to find greater security from criminals. It is likely that in early times the punishments even for the greatest crimes were not as severe as they are now, but the laws were still broken, and in the course of time, the death penalty became generally introduced. Yet even with this, the laws are still broken. Either, therefore, we must discover some fear more potent than the fear of death, or we must admit that here certainly we have not got an adequate deterrent. . . . In a word, it is impossible (and only the most simple-minded will deny this) for human nature, when once seriously set upon a certain course, to be prevented from following that course by the force of law or by any other means of intimidation whatever.[92]

Compliance with the law originates from intimidation on this line of reasoning, as obedience is procured by deterring potential violators from crime through the utilization of the fear of punishment.

Does Diodotus give us an adequate account of the role of law in the practice of excellence? I would suggest not. Aristotle expressed the crux of my disagreement when he distinguished between the just person and just actions. For Aristotle, 'the just and temperate person is not the one who [merely] does these actions, but the one who also does them in the way in which just and temperate people do them'.[93] In order to be excellent, the agent must first 'know [that he is doing virtuous actions]; second, he must decide on them, and decide on them for themselves; and third, he must also do them from a firm and unchanging state'.[94] The last two conditions are 'all-important' and can be 'achieved by the frequent doing of just and temperate actions'.[95] In that sense, fear of punishment may be an important tool in providing the proper habituation which Aristotle greatly cared about, but it cannot in any way be a replacement for the practice of excellence itself—namely, for the doing of right actions for the right reasons. A person who does excellent actions because of nothing else but fear cannot be excellent. Thucydides would have agreed, as evidenced by his juxtaposition of Diodotus' account of law with the loftier Periclean vision. '[W]e keep to the law' Pericles tells the Athenians, '[t]his is because it commands our deep respect'.[96] Obedience here rests not on fear but on respect, respect based on the greatness and excellence of Athens. The importance of the

[90] Ibid., III.53.
[91] Ibid., III.37.
[92] Ibid., III.45.
[93] Aristotle, *Nicomachean Ethics*, 1105b5.
[94] Ibid., 1105a30.
[95] Ibid., 1105b1.
[96] Thucydides, II.37.

Athenian constitution and laws for her excellence are duly recognized.[97] The principle of fear whose role in domestic and international affairs is expounded by Cleon and Diodotus cannot be for people who care about the practice of excellence, it is fit only for tyrants or criminals. No wonder then, that Cleon calls the Athenian empire a tyranny, or that Diodotus equates human nature with the propensity to criminality.[98] I am tempted to suggest that Thucydides agreed with Diodotus' conclusion that punishment ought to be employed with moderation and put to proper use, understood as the advantage of Athens in this particular instance, while he disagreed with Diodotus' analysis.

If it cannot be maintained that law based on pure fear and coercion contributes to the practice of excellence, can it at least be held that it serves the cause of a less noble, but maybe more immediately urgent cause, that of stability? Sometimes, but not always. A law which does not command the goodwill and respect of those to whom it applies, whether it be in domestic or international politics, cannot be very stable. Even Pericles recognized that coercive power cannot last forever. In domestic affairs, as soon as the coercive capacity of the law is weakened, the result would be complete anarchy. Thucydides discusses the drastic consequences of the dissolution of goodwill, friendship, and trust among the citizens in Corcyra at some length for good reason. In noting the important links between friendship and civil peace and unity, the historian comes close to Aristotle who also emphasized that since 'friendship would seem to hold cities together' it was a matter of great concern to legislators.[99] 'For concord would seem to be similar to friendship' wrote Aristotle, and legislators 'aim at concord above all, while they try above all to expel civil conflict, which is enmity'.[100] Aristotle could have easily been writing about Corcyra! Similarly, in foreign affairs, associations built on fear and force as opposed to goodwill cannot in any way be lasting, as the examples of Corcyra–Corinth and Mytilene–Athens amply illustrate. In explaining their grievances about Corinth to the Athenians in their request for alliance, the Corcyraeans assert that even colonial relations based on force cannot be lasting since 'every colony, if it is treated properly, honours its mother city, and only becomes estranged if it has been treated badly. Colonists are not sent abroad to be the slaves of those who remain behind, but to be their equals'.[101] It should be understandable, then, that Corcyra, as a maltreated colony, turns elsewhere for assistance. Similarly, in trying to secure Spartan help for their rebellion from Athens, the Mytilenians emphasize that their rebellion should not be condemned as a betrayal since their alliance with Athens was based on fear, and alliances based on fear are not long-lived:

> In most cases goodwill is the basis of loyalty, but in our case, fear was the bond, and it was more through terror than through friendship that we were held together in alliance. And the alliance was certain to be broken at any moment by the first side that felt confident that this would be a safe move to make.

Fear and terror cannot be the basis of lasting communities and stable laws, domestic or international, since the bonds forged by fear are dissolved as soon as the balance

---

[97] Ibid., II.36.
[98] Ibid., III.37.
[99] Aristotle, *Nicomachean Ethics*, 1155a20.
[100] Ibid., 1155a25.
[101] Thucydides, I.34.

of forces changes. Something more than fear, namely, goodwill, friendship, and trust are also required if we are to obey the laws because of the deep respect they command.

Unwritten law: the place of friendship and expediency

All the examples discussed so far in the exploration of the proper conventional sources of political unity point to the importance of goodwill, friendship, and trust in making law in general, and human law in particular, an effective part of the practice of excellence. Goodwill, friendship, and trust are not enacted into law in the same way that treaties, constitutions, or legal decrees are; yet they perform a vital function in politics nevertheless. This is precisely what Pericles must have had in mind when he referred to the importance of obeying 'those unwritten laws which it is an acknowledged shame to break'.[102] *Contra* Connor, it is neither surprising nor a mere rhetorical device, that the Spartan peace offer that came after the defeat at Pylos was couched in the language of friendship: 'Sparta calls upon you to make a treaty and to end the war. She offers you peace, alliance, friendly and neighbourly relations'.[103] Friendly relations and lasting peace were closely tied to moderation in the Spartan proposal:

[N]o lasting settlement can be made in a spirit of revenge, when one side gets the better of things in war and forces its opponent to swear to carry out the terms of an unequal treaty; what will make the settlement lasting is when the party that has it in his power to act like this takes instead a more reasonable point of view, overcomes his adversary in generosity, and makes peace on more moderate terms than his enemy expected.[104]

A peace concluded in the spirit of friendship requires the exercise of moderation. Similarly, as Pearson notes, Thucydides relays the pre-war diplomacy between Corcyra, Corinth, and Athens 'as though it were a matter of meeting obligations' of friendship and justice. 'It is significant that Thucydides should present the story in this manner,' Pearson concludes, 'because it shows his belief that Greece still thought of international relations in terms of justice and friendship, not exclusively in terms of self-interest'.[105] Clearly, friendship is linked to justice and moderation in this account.

What exactly does the ideal of friendship entail? The traditional definition of friendship in popular ethics in ancient Greece is 'helping one's friends and harming one's enemies' Pearson suggests, based on a review of the literary and philosophical sources of the period.[106] This definition provides the justification for certain uses of force in intercity politics. Based on the traditional definition, offensive attacks can be

---

[102] Ibid., II.37.
[103] Ibid., IV.19.
[104] Ibid., IV.19.
[105] Lionel Pearson, 'Popular Ethics in the World of Thucydides', *Classical Philology*, LII:4 (October 1957), p. 232.
[106] Lionel Pearson, *Popular Ethics in Ancient Greece*, (Stanford, CA: Stanford University Press, 1962), pp. 16–18. See also book I of Plato's *Republic* for an interesting discussion of the traditional conception of friendship.

defended on the grounds that they are 'taken in return for an injury or in gratitude for some favour from another source. If no such explanation can be given, the aggressor is guilty of a blatant act of hybris'.[107] The multiple appeals in the *History* to gratitude—gratitude for favours received in the past, or gratitude for requested benefits in return for which favours can be offered in the future—become intelligible in light of this conventional definition. Friendship, understood as such, interjects some degree of moderation into international politics since '[u]nprovoked attack, according to the conventional view, is the clearest type of injustice'.[108] To illustrate, the traditional definition of friendship deems the unprovoked Athenian attack on Melos to be an outrageous act of injustice. The traditional code thus condemns unprovoked aggression in international affairs, and effectively promotes moderation. Furthermore, as Pericles observes, the bestowing of favours in relationships of friendship involves 'free liberality' which is another dimension of the practice of excellence, even if Thucydides does not emphasize this dimension as much as Aristotle does.[109]

Unfortunately, as important as the popular definition of friendship may be in some instances, it is not always conducive to the practice of excellence if not properly used. The most striking example, as Pearson points out, comes in the case of Plataea. The Thebans and Spartans lay siege to the city of Plataea after the Plataeans refuse the Spartan offer of neutrality because of their loyalty to Athens. The city voluntarily comes over when defeat is imminent on the promise of a fair trial by the Spartans. The Spartan judges ask the Plataeans one question: 'Have you done anything to help the Spartans and their allies in the present war?'[110] Even though this may not seem like a fair question to us (after all, how could an Athenian ally be reasonably expected to help the Spartan side in the war?!!), Pearson notes how the Spartan action can be technically justified in terms of pre-existing bonds of friendship between Sparta and Plataea that the Plataeans themselves appealed to in their supplication for mercy. On this line of reasoning, the Plataeans can be held accountable for not having done anything to help their friends—i.e. the Spartans—in the war, and 'they are treated accordingly not as brave and stubborn enemies, but as false friends who fail in an important obligation'.[111] Furthermore, the Spartans had obligations of friendship towards their allies, the Thebans, who were the bitterest enemies of the Plataeans. 'It was largely, or entirely, because of Thebes that the Spartans acted so mercilessly towards the Plataeans', Thucydides tells us.[112] What does the historian think of this usage of the traditional code? As Pearson notes, 'Thucydides withholds comment. It is left for the reader to consider if the old code of behaviour is a sound guide when it leads to this brutal treatment of a defeated enemy'.[113]

The general direction of the *History* is such that Thucydides could not have approved of such brutal treatment, I would suggest. The appropriate analogy here is with the case of Mytilene, whose account directly precedes the narrative of the end

---

[107] Ibid., p. 142.
[108] Ibid.
[109] Thucydides, II.40.
[110] Ibid., III.52.
[111] Pearson, 'Popular Ethics in the World of Thucydides', p. 234.
[112] Thucydides, III.68.
[113] Pearson, 'Popular Ethics in the World of Thucydides', p. 234.

of Plataea in the structure of the work. In a way, Cleon's demand for inflicting the death penalty on Mytilene can be justified in terms of the traditional code of friendship as it relates to punitive justice. As Cleon forcefully asserts, Mytilene injures Athens by rebelling, and as such deserves punishment as retribution for the harm she inflicts. The injury is especially grave because of the supposed bonds of friendship between Athens and Mytilene as represented by Mytilene's privileged status in the empire, and the voluntary and calculated nature of her rebellion which counts as a terrible breach of that friendship.[114] The guilt of Mytilene is never in question in the Mytilenian debate. Yet, Thucydides is shocked by the severity of the chosen penalty, even if it is deserved. He welcomes the reversal of the decision in favour of adopting a more moderate form of punishment and he celebrates the narrow escape of Mytilene from massacre.[115] The use of the traditional code of friendship in a way that would create uncalled-for suffering cannot contribute to the practice of excellence. In that sense, an Aristotelian conception of friendship probably comes closer to Thucydides' understanding of how friendship is to be used in politics.

An Aristotelian conception of friendship is superior to the traditional code for three reasons. First, Aristotle defines friendship as 'reciprocated goodwill' that is undertaken willingly, for 'we should never make a friend of someone who is unwilling'.[116] This precludes the possibility of calling relationships based on sheer force by the name of friendship, and expecting what is proper among friends to hold in such situations. Second, Aristotle distinguishes between different kinds of friendship and insists that justice in different friendships 'is not the same in each case but corresponds to worth; for so does the friendship'.[117] Hence, we are not expected to return favours to friends in the same way in every case, as friendship is directly connected to worth understood in terms of excellence. Third, Aristotle recognizes that 'generally speaking, we should return what we owe'.[118] However, if in the particular circumstances that we face, not returning what we owe is more excellent, we should choose this option, because 'sometimes even the return of a previous favour is not fair [but an excessive demand.]'[119] Instead, 'we should accord to each what is proper and suitable'.[120] The Plataean response to the Spartan accusation of false friendship becomes intelligible in these terms. As paraphrased by Pearson, the Plataeans claim that '[n]ot only are the Spartans asking too much in expecting to be valued above the Athenians as friends, but they are themselves in the wrong for valuing Theban friendship above friendship with the Plataeans'.[121] Thucydides, too, seems to be suggesting that friendship corresponds to worth here, and consequently that it may not always be proper to return favours, depending on the situation. In that sense, the traditional code is appropriate in so far as it contributes to the practice of excellence, this is what constitutes its proper use. Thucydides would have agreed, I think, as his quiet disapproval of the use of the code in Plataea and Mytilene suggests.

---

[114] Thucydides, III.39–III.40.
[115] Ibid., III.49.
[116] Aristotle, *Nicomachean Ethics*, 1155b30, 1163a1.
[117] Ibid., 1161a20.
[118] Ibid., 1165a1.
[119] Ibid., 1165a5.
[120] Ibid., 1165a15.
[121] Pearson, *Popular Ethics in Ancient Greece*, p. 155.

The case of Mytilene is also interesting in another respect, as it points to how even arguments from expediency have a contribution to make to the practice of excellence when properly used. Diodotus is able to convince the Athenians to reverse the original decision of putting to death the entire male population and enslaving the women and children of Mytilene on the grounds that it is more useful for Athens to inflict a more moderate punishment.[122] Diodotus is explicitly hostile to 'being swayed too much by pity or by ordinary decent feelings' and asks Athenians to be guided strictly by their self-interest.[123] Of course, it might be that Diodotus felt the need to lie in order for his advice to be heeded, a quandary which he himself identified to be a problem for democratic deliberation in his speech. It is a sad predicament of democratic assemblies, Diodotus maintains, that 'just as the speaker who advocates some monstrous measure has to win over the people by deceiving them, so also a man with good advice to give has to tell lies if he expects to be believed'.[124] Putting aside the issue of whether Diodotus was lying or not when he invited the Athenians to consider solely their own self-interest, Thucydides does not seem to be too disturbed by the use of the argument from self-interest and expediency here even if Diodotus was not lying. The narrative makes it clear that he considered Diodotus to be the speaker with the good advice. In that sense, expediency and moderation may come together in the practice of excellence.[125]

However, just like laws based on pure coercive power, rule based on sheer expediency at all times is for tyrants. It is not surprising then, that Euphemus equates expediency with tyranny in the debate at Camarina in his efforts to explain to the Sicilian Greeks why it is in the Athenian self-interest that they be free and strong while their kinsmen in Greece are enslaved. 'When a man or a city exercises absolute power the logical course is the course of self-interest', Euphemus claims.[126] Absolute power is exercised as such here and not necessarily in accordance with excellence, as perhaps better rendered in the Hobbes translation, which uses the word 'tyrant' to describe the man who exercises absolute power.[127] Similarly, the Athenian actions in Melos, as opposed to the Athenian words, represent a tyrannical exercise of power. It is precisely this transformation into tyranny that leads Connor to conclude that '[w]hatever our reactions to what happens to the Melians, it is hard to escape a feeling of horror at what is happening to the Athenians'.[128] Furthermore, not only is the principle of pure expediency in opposition to virtue, but just like the principle of fear, it can be self-defeating. The Athenians claimed that subduing Melos was in their self-interest, and Athens surely prevailed in the short run. However, as de Romilly notes, it is not so clear that the Melian decision was in the

---

[122]   Thucydides, III.46–47.
[123]   Ibid., III.48.
[124]   Ibid., III.43.
[125]   Classical Realists have a point when they argue that policies based on self-interest often lead to more moderate results. See Morgenthau, *Politics Among Nations*; Stanley Hoffmann, *Duties Beyond Borders: On the Limits and Possibilities of Ethical International Politics*, (Syracuse, NY: Syracuse University Press, 1981); Arnold Wolfers, *Discord and Collaboration: Essays on International Politics*, (Baltimore, MD: Johns Hopkins Press, 1962); E. H. Carr, *The Twenty Years' Crisis, 1919–1939: An Introduction to the Study of International Relations*, (New York: Harper & Row, 1964); George Kennan, *American Diplomacy*, expanded edn. (Chicago, IL: The University of Chicago Press, 1984).
[126]   Thucydides, VI.85.
[127]   Thucydides, VI.85 in Grene (ed.), *The Complete Hobbes Translation*.
[128]   Robert Connor, *Thucydides*, (Princeton, NJ: Princeton University Press, 1984), p. 154.

Athenian self-interest in the long run as it promoted a general atmosphere of ill-feeling which encouraged her imperial allies to rebel.[129] The ambiguity should not come as a surprise in the work of someone as attentive as Thucydides was to the role of the unpredictable in an uncertain future. Thus, expediency becomes an appropriate guide to conduct only in its proper use.

Excellence and the foundations of power and peace

What emerges from the above discussion is that when properly used, religiosity, consent, coercion, friendship, and even expediency have an important role to play in establishing how laws operate in the practice of excellence. Reminiscent of Aristotle, the right institutions become a crucial part of this account for Thucydides in nurturing the right habits for excellence. But what does the practice of excellence entail for politics? How can we judge whether conventions are put to proper use? The probe into the moral foundations of political unity reveals that Thucydides seemed to understand the practice of excellence specifically as the promotion of moderation and practical wisdom in politics. Thus, I agree with Strauss, that for Thucydides, 'a sound regime is a moderate regime dedicated to moderation'.[130] Thucydides' dislike of the extreme uses of conventions comes in every shape and form. From contempt for the excessive religiosity of Nicias to disdain for the excessive enthusiasm for the Sicilian expedition fuelled by the chresmologues, from regret about the deficiency of conventional values experienced in the plague in Athens and civil war in Corcyra to disapproval of the newly minted excesses of these events, the language of multiple passages clearly reveals where the historian's sympathies lie. 'And as usually happens in such situations', Thucydides sadly notes in his account of Corcyra, 'people went to every extreme and beyond it'.[131] In the terrible course of events, party membership surmounted family relations and religious fellowships, 'since party members were more ready to go to any extreme for any reason whatever'. Even though both parties 'had programmes which appeared admirable—on one side political equality for the masses, on the other the safe and sound government of the aristocracy', these programmes were professed with 'violent fanaticism' in practice. 'As for the citizens who held moderate views, they were destroyed by both the extreme parties, either for not taking part in the struggle or in envy at the possibility that they might survive'.[132] Corcyra is the ultimate case of the collapse of moderation as it illustrates the consequences of both deficiency in old established conventions and excess in new ways. Once again, Thucydides' language is very suggestive of Aristotle, who defined excellence as 'a mean between two vices, one of excess and one of deficiency'.[133]

The discussion of the sources of political unity also makes clear that moderation is closely tied to practical wisdom in the *History*. Extremes are avoided by the proper

---

[129] de Romilly, 'Fairness and Kindness in Thucydides', p. 99. For textual references, see also Thucydides, IV.81.
[130] Leo Strauss, *The City and Man* (Chicago, IL: The University of Chicago Press, 1964), p. 153.
[131] Thucydides, III.81.
[132] Ibid., III.82.
[133] Aristotle, *Nicomachean Ethics*, 1107a1.

use of conventions in particular situations, and this requires practical wisdom. A good example comes in the context of the emphasis placed on the proper interpretation of oracles, but the same holds true of all forms of conventions. Proper use entails both moderation and practical wisdom. Hence moderation and practical wisdom are intimately connected in the practice of excellence for Thucydides. Aristotle would have wholeheartedly agreed. Practical wisdom, for Aristotle, is not 'about universals only. It must also come to know particulars, since it is concerned with action and action is about particulars.'[134] As MacIntyre brilliantly discusses, Aristotle also recognized that practical wisdom and moderation were intimately connected.[135] Accordingly, moderation preserves practical wisdom and practical wisdom is that which is preserved by moderation.[136] Furthermore, moderation requires practical wisdom, because excellence expresses correct reason, and 'correct reason is reason that expresses intelligence'; it follows that all excellence requires practical wisdom.[137] Thus, practical wisdom and moderation are inseparably bound together for Aristotle, and maybe not as systematically, but nevertheless still obviously, for Thucydides, as well.

The implications of this account of political excellence for conceptualizing political unity are significant. First, the conventional foundations of political unity have a proper use in the practice of excellence, understood above all as moderation and practical wisdom by Thucydides. It is only through the linking of conventions to excellence in light of an ideal of the good life that forms of political unity that lie between anarchy and tyranny can become possible. In this account, no single source of unity is rejected outright, or endorsed uncritically. Instead, all depends on the proper use of institutions and practices of co-operation. Second, the right sort of political unity is a fundamental source of power, at home as well as abroad. Doyle documents this empirical link well when he puts forward legitimately constituted political unity as a crucial variable in his historical sociology of empires.[138] Doyle's argument is that such political unity is a major determinant of why some city-states became imperial metropoles, while others succumbed to imperial rule and were turned into subordinate peripheries, and still others were successfully able to resist imperial encroachment. The hypothesis holds up well in the context of ancient Greek imperial interactions, with the lack of political unity being the main factor that differentiated subordinate peripheries from both imperial metropoles and independent resisters. To support his view, Doyle invokes the examples of Melos, Syracuse, and Athens.[139] As already discussed, Melos was only finally conquered after some internal treachery undermined its unity, Syracuse was successfully able to stage and lead a resistance to the Athenian expedition by uniting the city-states of Sicily, and Athens ultimately lost its empire and the war primarily as a result of internal strife. It seems that political unity was a tremendous power resource in

---

[134] Ibid., 1141b15.
[135] Alasdair MacIntyre, '*Sophrosune*: How a Virtue Can Become Socially Disruptive', *Midwest Studies in Philosophy, Volume XII: Ethical Theory: Character and Virtue* (Notre Dame, NY: Notre Dame University Press, 1988), p. 5.
[136] Aristotle, *Nicomachean Ethics*, 1140b10–1140b20.
[137] Ibid., 1144b15–1144b35.
[138] Doyle, *Empires*, ch. 6.
[139] Ibid., ch. 3. It was neither the Sicilian disaster nor the Persian support of Sparta nor the abandonment of its allies that finally brought Athens down, but its loss of political unity.

domestic and international politics alike. What my discussion adds to Doyle's empirical findings is that the political unity in question had to be of the right kind. In other words, in light of the connections between politics and the good life, unity had to be grounded in conventions that were properly used and such unity was seen to be the source of both power and excellence.

Thucydides saw the matter similarly. Political unity, when founded upon the right institutions, was a source of greatness for Athens as well as Sparta. Both were considered to have achieved political excellence in their forms of government, albeit in different ways. Hence, Pericles declares that the Athenian constitution and way of life is what makes Athens great in excellence and power.[140] 'And to show that this is no empty boasting for the present occasion, but real tangible fact,' Pericles continues, 'you have only to consider the power which our city possesses and which has been won by those very qualities which I have mentioned'.[141] Furthermore, the Athenian envoys in Sparta claim that institutions like the rule of law and the impartial administration of justice provided the grounds for moderate Athenian imperialism in accordance with the practice of excellence, at least in the initial stages of imperial expansion before the empire was transformed into a tyranny that rested solely on fear.[142] Finally, Thucydides himself highly praises the new constitution drawn up by the Five Thousand in Athens:

> Indeed, during the first period of this new regime the Athenians appear to have had a better government than ever before, at least in my time. There was a reasonable and moderate blending of the few and the many, and it was this, in the first place, that made it possible for the city to recover from the bad state into which her affairs had fallen.[143]

Here again, a good constitution was the source not only of moderate politics, but also of power, as illustrated by the victory at Cynosemma that immediately followed the establishment of the Five Thousand.

In like manner, Thucydides records how the Spartan constitution has been a source of greatness. 'For rather more than 400 years, dating from the very end of the late war,' the historian writes, 'they have had the same system of government and this has been not only a source of internal strength, but has enabled them to intervene in the affairs of other states'.[144] The external interventions Thucydides has in mind here are laudable; as discussed in the same passage, the Spartans helped 'put down tyranny in the rest of Greece' and undertook the initial leadership of the common effort to repel the Persian invasion. The Corinthian representatives in Sparta, in their desire to ignite Spartan fervour for war in light of traditional Spartan slowness, confirm this evaluation. 'Spartans, what makes you somewhat reluctant to listen to us and others, if we have ideas to put forward, is the great trust and confidence which you have in your own constitution and in your own way of life. This is a quality which certainly makes you moderate in your judgements'; the Corinthians snap.[145] King Archidamus, described by Thucydides as 'a man who had a reputation for both intelligence and moderation', further confirms the Corinthian

---

[140] Thucydides, II.36.
[141] Ibid., II.41.
[142] Ibid., I.76–I.77.
[143] Ibid., VIII.97.
[144] Ibid., I.18.
[145] Ibid., I.68.

analysis in noting how the Spartan laws, customs, and 'well-ordered life' are a source of courage, self-restraint, and wisdom, as well as power.[146] Evidently, the historian sees proper institutions as conducive to both power and excellence, in domestic as well as international affairs.

Thucydides wrote his *History* as a possession for all times. In his own words, his subject matter 'was the greatest disturbance in the history of the Hellenes, affecting also a large part of the non-Hellenic world, and indeed I might almost say, the whole of mankind'.[147] Interested in unearthing the truth about the human condition, he strove to attain the utmost accuracy in his narrative. From his knowledge of particular episodes in the war, he aspired to derive general principles that could be of use to future generations. 'My work is not a piece of writing designed to meet the taste of an immediate public,' he wrote, 'but was done to last forever'.[148] Time has proven him correct. The *History* is not only an excellent resource on ancient Greek politics, history, and culture, but also a unique source of brilliant insights on fundamental political questions that we still grapple with today. It is this eternal character of the *History* that structural Realists appeal to in rallying Thucydides for their cause. I have argued that the structural Realist appropriation, which focuses on the centrality of the struggle for power in politics, does not do justice to the complexity of Thucydides' thought since it fails to place key Thucydidean observations in the context of meaning that defined their main message. Critics of the structural Realist reading offer very good descriptions of the institutions and practices of co-operation that ordered the pursuit of power in the ancient Greek international system. While these critical accounts are extremely valuable for providing a more nuanced picture of the complex realities of ancient Greek politics, I have suggested that they do not go far enough, either. This is because most such accounts stop short of recognizing the critical links between co-operative practices and institutions and their moral foundations. These links were articulated in the effort to respond to the fundamental problem of securing political unity—a problem that dominated ancient Greek politics at the time Thucydides wrote. Re-reading the *History* in the light of these links reveals the historian's preoccupation with enunciating the political prerequisites of the good life. Deeply troubled by the ever-lurking possibility of degeneration into the equally menacing extremes of anarchy and tyranny, Thucydides set himself the task of identifying the foundations of lasting political unity, neither espousing nor rejecting any one source outright in his quest, but critically endorsing the proper use of a multiplicity of conventional possibilities. To that end, he placed his hopes in tying the pursuit of power and peace to the practice of excellence, so as to promote moderation and practical wisdom in politics, domestic and international. This, if anything, is the timeless wisdom of Thucydides.

---

[146] Ibid., I.79, I.84.
[147] Ibid., I.1.
[148] Ibid., I.22.

Before sovereignty: society and politics in *ancien régime* Europe

ANDREAS OSIANDER

In the discipline of International Relations (IR), it seems to be an uncontroversial point that the passage of European civilization from the middle ages to the early modern period was also the transition from a system with a single supreme secular regent, the emperor, to one with plural supreme regents. This is implied in the ubiquitous view that the Thirty Years' War was a struggle between the 'medieval' conception of imperial suzerainty and hegemony over christendom and the 'modern' conception of a system composed of independent 'sovereign' states, with the 1648 peace that ended the war enshrining the victory of the latter.

This interpretation of the Peace of Westphalia is far from the truth.[1] More generally, however, the entire notion of a transition from imperial preponderance (actual or, at least, claimed) to plural sovereign states recognized as such is a myth. Medieval emperors not only exercised no power over kingdoms held by others, but claimed no right to do so.[2] At no time in the middle ages did other kings defer to the emperor.[3] Certain kings at certain times acknowledged others as their liege, though this liege was not necessarily the emperor (for example, in the late thirteenth century Edward I of England obliged the Scottish king John de Balliol to recognize his suzerainty). Other rulers at times recognized the pope as their liege. The only realm that was permanently under imperial suzerainty was Bohemia, because in the eleventh century its duke received his royal title from the emperor (at first on a personal, from the late twelfth century onwards on a hereditary, basis).

The matter is beset with a great deal of conceptual and semantic confusion. What medieval people understood by concepts like empire, emperor, kingship, kingdom, king, had little to do with our modern conception of statehood. Even eighteenth-

---

[1] Andreas Osiander, *The States System of Europe 1640–1990: Peacemaking and the Conditions of International Stability* (Oxford: Clarendon Press, 1994), ch. 2; Andreas Osiander, 'Sovereignty, International Relations, and the Westphalian Myth', *International Organization*, 55 (2001), pp. 251–87.

[2] Geoffrey Barraclough, *The Mediaeval Empire: Idea and Reality* (London: Philip, 1950), esp. pp. 16–17; Marcel David, *La souveraineté et les limites juridiques du pouvoir monarchique du IXe au XVe siècle* (Paris: Dalloz, 1954), p. 22; Othmar Hageneder, 'Weltherrschaft im Mittelalter', *Mitteilungen des Instituts für Österreichische Geschichtsforschung*, 93 (1985), pp. 257–78; Robert Holtzmann, 'Der Weltherrschaftsgedanke des mittelalterlichen Kaisertums und die Souveränität der europäischen Staaten', *Historische Zeitschrift*, 159 (1939), pp. 251–64.

[3] For a case study see Dieter Berg, 'Imperium und Regna. Beiträge zur Entwicklung der deutsch-englischen Beziehungen im Rahmen der auswärtigen Politik der römischen Kaiser und deutschen Könige im 12. und 13. Jahrhundert', in Peter Moraw (ed.), *'Bündnissystem' und 'Außenpolitik' im späteren Mittelalter*. Zeitschrift für historische Forschung Beiheft, vol. 5 (Berlin: Duncker & Humblot, 1988), pp. 13–37.

century Europe was still far from the kind of international system that we take for granted. We think far too much in terms of independent territorial statehood even when talking about past ages—caught up as we are in what R.B.J. Walker calls the modern 'discourse of eternity' that represents the international system based on the sovereign territorial state as timeless in its essence.[4]

As a discipline IR continues to be puzzled by what John Ruggie has called the medieval-to-modern shift, the transition of European society from feudalism to a system of sovereign territorial states.[5] Why were the important actors in medieval Europe—all manner of feudal dignitaries ranging from minor local lords to powerful kings; bishops and abbots; the pope and the emperor; towns acting on their own or confederated into leagues; monastic or chivalrous orders—at once so heterogeneous and, seemingly, so utterly different from the important actors of the modern period, which at least since 1648 are supposed to have, uniformly, been sovereign states?

Almost all discussions of medieval politics that are offered in IR are in a positivistic mode that looks at 'objective' developments quite independent of the minds of the actors themselves. Some stress economic factors (as does Ruggie in the article referred to, basing himself on the work of Douglass C. North and R.P. Thomas).[6] Charles Tilly explains the rise of modern states out of the medieval system as a process in which continual warmaking eliminated weaker actors while it forced stronger actors to enhance continuously their ability to extract revenue from their subjects.[7] Against Tilly, Hendrik Spruyt argues that it was not so much warmaking as a coalition of interest between the crown and the bourgeoisie that caused the weakening of intermediary feudal powerholders in some parts of western Europe. According to Spruyt, this led to the establishment of centralized territorial states as well as, indirectly, to the demise of alternative political units, specifically city states and city leagues, which found themselves unable in the long run to compete with the new centralized territorial states.[8]

It is much rarer for authors to deal with the contribution of intersubjective understandings, the medieval world view, to political structure and processes in the middle ages, or to the change they went through over time. As far as I am aware, Markus Fischer is the only one, within IR, to have engaged this issue seriously, and he has done so in order to prove that it may be safely ignored.[9] Fischer argues that politics among feudal powerholders was the same as modern international politics, if not in form then at least in essence, and that differences of normative discourse—for example, between the middle ages and the modern period—do *not* translate into

---

[4] R.B.J. Walker, 'International Relations and the Concept of the Political', in Ken Booth and Steve Smith (eds.), *International Relations Theory Today* (University Park, PA: University of Pennsylvania Press, 1995), pp. 306–27.

[5] John G. Ruggie, 'Continuity and Transformation in the World Polity', in Robert O. Keohane (ed.), *Neorealism and Its Critics* (New York: Columbia University Press, 1986), pp. 131–57, esp. pp. 141 and 149.

[6] Ibid., p. 149–50. But see his qualifications of this approach in John G. Ruggie, 'Territoriality and Beyond: Problematizing Modernity in International Relations', *International Organization*, 47 (1993), pp. 139–74, p. 156 and passim.

[7] Charles Tilly, *Coercion, Capital and European States 990–1990* (Oxford: Blackwell, 1990).

[8] Hendrik Spruyt, *The Sovereign State and Its Competitors: An Analysis of Systems Change* (Princeton, NJ: Princeton University Press, 1994).

[9] Markus Fischer, 'Feudal Europe, 800–1300. Communal Discourse and Conflictual Practices', *International Organization*, 46 (1992), pp. 427–66.

differences of behaviour. For Fischer, despite the emphasis in medieval political discourse on the unity of christendom and on the need for solidarity and peace among christians, medieval politics displays the same patterns of frequently violent self-help behaviour among autonomous powerholders that Kenneth Waltz in his *Theory of Politics* describes as the inevitable characteristic of any system in which actors cannot be effectively coerced, and protected from each other, by a common superior.[10]

But even if Waltzian thinking were applicable to medieval politics, the question would remain interesting whether, to what extent, and why medieval actors were different from post-medieval ones. In the middle ages as depicted by Fischer (and in this respect I have no quarrel with his analysis), many actors were individual lords. Yet, according to conventional wisdom, actors in post-1648 Europe were, or may legitimately be treated as, 'states', that is, bounded corporate and territorial entities.

In my view, this issue cannot be tackled without reference to intersubjective understandings and normative discourse. The remainder of this article will examine the political structure of late medieval, and to some extent early modern Europe, in the light of both material constraints and opportunities on the one hand and shared normative ideas on the other. I believe that those two aspects cannot be separated if we want to gain a real understanding of the period. I suggest that the medieval-to-modern shift was much more gradual, really much less of a 'shift', than is usually implied, to the point that it was never even completed during the *ancien régime*.

It was not before the nineteenth century that the state as we know it finally established itself. This is an abstract corporate entity considered to be invested *as such* with sovereignty in the modern sense, that is (first and foremost from the perspective of IR) legal autonomy attributed to the state as a whole.[11] Crucially, however, the modern state is considered self-sufficient not only in legal terms, but also in social terms. In fact, extraordinarily, in the view both of classic (nineteenth- and twentieth-century) international law and most twentieth-century IR theory, there is no society, that is, a pattern of mutual ties of obligation or at least expectation among individual people, beyond the boundaries of the state, but only a society, or even merely a 'system' of other like entities.

It is precisely this view that cannot be projected back much beyond the end of the *ancien régime*. Looking back at the past from the point of view of our own age we tend to be prisoners of selective perception. We tend to see much more clearly those aspects of the past with which we are familiar (indeed we often see them before, historically, they appeared) while other aspects are discounted. As a corrective, this article will adopt the reverse approach. It invites readers to look at *ancien régime* Europe, not from the perspective of the twentieth century, but from the perspective of the fourteenth. It will do so by sketching the material constraints as well as the ideology and world view underlying medieval politics, examine events connected with the restoration of the imperial dignity in 1313 (after several decades without an emperor), and look at the contemporary debate on how christendom should be organized politically. In conclusion, I offer this fourteenth-century world, and its very different conception of relations not just among rulers, but, crucially, between

[10] Kenneth N. Waltz, *Theory of International Politics* (New York: McGraw-Hill, 1979).
[11] Alan James, *Sovereign Statehood: The Basis of International Society* (London: Allen & Unwin, 1986).

rulers and society (a dimension largely overlooked in twentieth-century IR theory), as an alternative template for understanding the 'classical' European system of the seventeenth and eighteenth centuries.

Material and metaphysical aspects of medieval power: the role of kings

The world of early and high medieval Europe (to about 1200) was a world of little material power. No one had very big armies, no one had very effective weapons, no one had very much money. Power could not be projected very far: powerholders found it practically impossible to coerce anyone beyond the immediate surroundings of their current abode. The main reason was that while everybody, even peasants, used money for some purposes, the economy as well as the political system were only very partially monetarized. Much of the economic surplus produced by the peasantry (the bulk of the population) was appropriated by the nobility and clergy in the form of labour services and payments in kind. Much of the latter consisted in agricultural produce that was in good part perishable and, in any case, expensive to transport. Services could not be stored at all, and labourers could not easily be uprooted from their local communities and made to travel. In these conditions, the surplus had to be used up locally and there was little possibility of accumulating and centralizing it.

This evidently favoured local powerholders. Less evidently, but importantly, in a sense it favoured supra-local powerholders too. Since no one *expected* them to be in effective control except when they were physically present, their nominal dominions could be very large indeed. The biggest medieval realms by far (if both area and population are taken into account) were the French and, especially, the German (which for most of the middle ages comprised what is now Germany, the Netherlands, Belgium, the Czech Republic, Austria, Switzerland, northern Italy and much of western France). Such huge geographical expanses did *not* form political units because their nominal rulers could keep them together by force. They existed as political units because of a sense of belonging shared, at least, by the upper strata of society, the nobility and clergy. This notional character of political units must be emphasized. If the German kingdom was considered a politically meaningful entity even though no one could coerce people so to regard it, then there was no reason why even bigger units, such as, specifically, christendom, should not be considered equally politically meaningful.

In the western middle ages, crowned heads were important not primarily as powerholders but because of their symbolic and metaphysical role. On the one hand they were the physical representatives of an ordered cosmos, which because of the cultural legacy of late antiquity (to be discussed in the next section) meant a tidy hierarchical order encompassing the whole of christendom. On the other hand they symbolized—much more than they ruled—the communities that they headed. Medieval society was essentially self-organizing, with most of the decision-making and policing taking place at the level of small, local, relatively autarchic units. In practical terms, the larger became the notional units into which christian society was divided, and the higher the social rank of the people presiding over those units, the less was the decision-making and policing affecting ordinary people. For the vast majority of people, whatever took place in the very highest reaches of the social pyramid (where kings were situated) was likely to be purely notional as far as they were concerned. And if, at the very top, there was a distant, semi-mythical figure called the emperor, the fact that nothing this person did ever seemed to affect the life of an ordinary peasant or parish priest or knight was no reason for such people to deny that, somehow, the emperor played an important part in the christian cosmos.

However, while not exactly managerial, the role of kings was not necessarily purely symbolic either. Marcel David has sought to capture the 'practical' function of medieval crowned heads by drawing on the distinction in Roman legal parlance between *potestas*, denoting the right and ability to command and enforce, and *auctoritas*, a superordinate and, even in antiquity, rather vaguely defined right of control and supervision often essentially based on social prestige. According to David, in the middle ages *auctoritas* gave its holders the right to judge the legitimacy of lower-ranking powerholders and the legality of their actions. It was this *auctoritas*, David argues, that kings exercised over their vassals and that the emperor and the pope exercised over christendom as a whole.[12] In medieval sources it is not always clear why one of those two expressions is used rather than the other, and it has even been argued that they were used interchangeably.[13] Yet whether designated by those terms or not, it is clear that the distinction was really made. Thus Lupold of Bebenburg, in a treatise on the empire of about 1340, defines the role of the emperor *vis-à-vis* other princes along precisely those lines. For him, other kings owe their office to the emperor, even though in practice his consent is tacit.[14] The emperor does not interfere directly in the running of their kingdoms, but their subjects may appeal to him if they hold themselves to have been wronged by their rulers.[15]

While it accurately describes the role of the emperor *vis-à-vis* the other princes of the Holy Roman Empire as late as (indeed in particular) the period after 1648,[16] with regard to other kings the system described by Lupold always remained purely notional, a symbolical construction inspired by the wish to portray christendom as a single order based throughout on consistent principles. Within realms, not infrequently royal *auctoritas* remained notional too—as did that of other lieges. Markus Fischer makes much of the disintegration, from the late tenth century onwards, of the control exercised by the counts of Mâcon over lesser lords nominally subordinate to them. He adduces this as evidence for his contention that the feudal hierarchy had no practical effect on medieval politics, which according to him followed the principles of Waltzian Realism as among all those (in this case the counts' vassals) who managed to keep themselves free from effective control by some superior.[17] But it is important to realise that while effective control by lieges might

---

[12] David, *La souveraineté*, esp. pp. 17, 69–70, 82.
[13] Jürgen Miethke, 'Autorität: I. Alte Kirche und Mittelalter', in *Theologische Realenzyklopädie*, vol. 5 (Berlin/New York: de Gruyter, 1980), pp. 17–32.
[14] *hi reges possunt dici constituti, seu creati a principe* [i.e. the emperor], *propter tacitum ipsius principis consensum.* Lupold of Bebenburg, *De iuribus et translatione imperii*, ed. Jakob Wimpfeling (Strasbourg: Schürer, 1508), ch. 15 (not paginated).
[15] Ibid., chs. 15–16.
[16] On this see Osiander, 'Sovereignty', pp. 269–81.
[17] Fischer, 'Feudal Europe', esp. pp. 440–3, 446–7.

be in abeyance in a given area at a given period, the right by which this control was exercised, if and when it was exercised, could not be usurped.

Thus, in the example of the Mâconnais, while the lower-ranking powerholders might be able to ignore the counts, they could not take their place, nor, for that matter, each other's—unless enfeoffed by the king or some other feudal superior. Fischer writes that in the twelfth century there came to exist 'a fairly stable balance of power among' the major castellanies of the Mâconnais.[18] I would venture to guess that this stability was not owed to any military stand-off, but to the effect of feudal law. However much individual lords might despoil their neighbours, fiefs as such could not be conquered. They *had* to be bestowed by a feudal superior, or, alternatively, bought or inherited—both means of acquisition that, *because* of feudal law, were extremely popular among the medieval nobility, for whom marriage was a much more important and efficient means of expanding their possessions than warfare.[19]

Lords, especially minor ones, could not disregard feudal law in this respect without repudiating the entire social system on which their position rested. In that sense, while the processes of medieval politics might in given instances show some congruence with Waltzian theory, the structure within which such processes took place always remained conditioned by the intersubjective construct of the feudal hierarchy. This is even true if 'structure' is understood in the Waltzian sense of being determined by the distribution of capabilities, since the lower powerholders could not aspire to control of superordinate fiefs, at least not through military means alone—and so their resources always remained limited.

This effect of the feudal hierarchy of prescribing the units within which control could be exercised was most potent at the level of kingdoms, since crowned heads had a sacred role that set them apart from other lieges. Despite the fact that their functional role is negligible, modern European monarchies survive because they are the vehicle of much symbolic meaning important to the communities they represent, and the object of an irrational fascination, indeed reverence, within and even outside those communities. Similarly, in the tenth century, monarchies like the German and French were perpetuated through the election of new rulers after the disappearance —or, in France, the marginalization—of the respective branches of the Carolingian dynasty, not because the German and French magnates could not manage on their own, or intended to give up a significant portion of their power and autonomy to their newly chosen ruler. The Capetian dynasty in particular, in the first few generations after its accession to the French throne in 987, led a rather miserable existence in the shadow of those magnates.

Rather, the crown survived even if powerless because of the strong feeling that there could be no legitimate order without it. Conversely, kings were *potentially* more powerful than other lords because they were sacred. They alone, but not other lords, were anointed and crowned and an object of popular veneration, an invaluable asset that, other things being equal, gave them an edge even over the greatest of their vassals. While their role could not be taken over by those vassals, however powerful, kings stood a good chance of subjecting vassals to their actual control, a chance that

---

[18] Ibid., p. 441.

[19] Though quite a lot of feudal warfare had to do with contested successions. It was also customary to conclude marriage arrangements in the course of negotiations to end some armed conflict, and occasionally such conflict may actually have been started with this objective in view.

could never be taken away altogether however weak the crown might be at a given period.

Royal *auctoritas* might essentially mean two things. Kings might act as supreme military leaders. Nobody owed military service indefinitely: the usual limit was forty days or six weeks per year. Also, depending on local custom, some kings were entitled to call on all their free male subjects directly, while others could only call on their immediate vassals who then would raise *their* vassals and so on. Nevertheless, even in the latter case kings had the supreme command and, in theory, more men at their disposal than anyone else in their realm.[20] Furthermore, kings might act as supreme judges. They alone could hear cases and hand down decisions anywhere, or from anywhere, in their kingdom, eclipsing lesser lords. It was a good way for monarchs to impress their special role both on those lesser lords and on the common people, and it was correspondingly exploited.[21]

Medieval society regarded the maintenance of peace as one of the biggest challenges facing it. The nobility (but also, for example, corporate entities like towns) were free to resort to self-help to settle quarrels by force. Although this was usually governed by an elaborate code of honour (for example, you were not supposed to harm clergymen, peasants, merchants, women, mills, vineyards and so on, or fighting was limited to certain days of the week), this was not necessarily very effective and, even if it was, a less than optimal solution from the point of view of society as a whole. Since at least the twelfth century kings sought to promote the peaceful settlement of disputes through adjudication. There was slow progress in this direction, though noble feuds did not disappear before the sixteenth century.

The absence of a monopoly of legitimate violence was inevitable given the absence of a centralized system of (monetary) taxation. This key point is well made by Mark Whittow when he contrasts the evolution of the eastern portion of the Roman empire that survived into the middle ages with what happened in the west:

In some ways the differences between the Byzantine empire of the early middle ages and the other post-Roman kingdoms in the west were small. Certainly in terms of economic wealth, military power or cultural sophistication the differences were not very great; but in terms of political structure, what distinguished them was fundamental. The root of these differences lies in taxation. The late Roman empire in west and east had been based on taxation. The western kingdoms naturally tried to maintain this valuable privilege, but nowhere in the west … did the ability to impose general taxation survive the sixth century …. Power now came to rest on the possession of land.

Conversely, 'behind the walls of Constantinople there was preserved the necessary expertise to maintain a system of general taxation'. Those with political influence in

---

[20] The thirteenth-century *Sachsenspiegel* (*Mirror of the Saxons*), a codification of customary law widely used in medieval central Europe, explains that the crown could call on any of its free subjects to serve for six weeks per year, with a minimum of six weeks' notice, and that no other lords might call on the same men in the six weeks preceding or following: *Lehnrecht* ch. 4 (the work is divided into three books of *landrecht* or law of the land, and one book of *lehnrecht* or feudal law). In contemporary France, however, the crown could not call on the *arrière-ban*, i.e. the vassals of its immediate vassals, directly but depended on the often doubtful loyalty of its immediate vassals for the feudal levies. In practice, the levies were increasingly complemented by mercenaries.

[21] Hans Kurt Schulze, 'Königsherrschaft und Königsmythos', in Helmut Maurer and Hans Patze (eds.), *Festschrift für Berent Schwineköper* (Sigmaringen: Thorbecke, 1982), pp. 177–86, pp.178–82. Cf. for example, *Sachsenspiegel, Landrecht* bk. 3, ch. 60.

the eastern empire, like military commanders and holders of court offices, 'were paid salaries out of tax revenue. No amount of landowning provided a real alternative.' As a result, power in the west was largely 'privatized' and passed to the great landowners, whereas 'in the Byzantine world power remained in state hands', with the imperial court retaining relatively effective central control.[22]

The disappearance of centralized taxation is the fundamental reason for the emergence of the feudal system with its decentralization of power. Conversely, both the role of the crown and efforts to replace the existing system of self-help with something less disorderly were helped by the rapid development and economic dynamism of the towns in late medieval Europe, which brought a constantly increasing amount of money into circulation. Feudal lords sought to profit, not just through rudimentary (monetary) taxation (there was as yet no acceptance of taxation on a regular basis) but through all manner of tolls and fees, the sale of privileges, or fines imposed by them in their capacity as judges.

Growing monetarization meant that, increasingly, the economic surplus was transferred in the form of coin, which in the late middle ages was increasingly substituted for labour services and payments in kind. This initiated a slow political revolution because money could easily be transported, stored and accumulated. To appropriate their share of the economic surplus, kings or other supra-local lords no longer had to come and get it (which explains the 'travelling kingship' characteristic of medieval Germany, or the fact that the actual power of the French kings was, for a long time, largely limited to the areas around Paris and Orléans, where their estates were situated). Now lords could make the surplus come to them even from faraway places. Money was, moreover, totally fungible. It could buy power, for example in the form of mercenaries that in the late middle ages increasingly supplemented and even substituted the feudal levies.

Developments like continuous kingdom-wide taxation and standing armies are not encountered before the fifteenth century. Yet even in the fourteenth century monetarization was making kings and other great lords, or some of them at least, more powerful than they had been in the past. Even discounting taxation (which did exist in inchoate fashion), the crown and its great vassals were normally the biggest landowners, and with revenues from their holdings increasingly payable in coin their power, and their ability to project it, grew, as did their competition with each other. As a result, the feudal hierarchy was being undermined. In Marcel David's terminology, what happened was that the relative importance of *potestas* and *auctoritas* was changing in favour of the former. *Auctoritas* alone was no longer satisfactory. That, in turn, raised the question of whether christendom could still be regarded as a single social order with the emperor at the top. If kings were seeking, with some success, to assert themselves over lesser lords, the emperor either had to assert himself in similar fashion over kings, or risk being regarded as obsolete. The whole process was placing growing strain on the traditional and still deeply held self-perception of western christendom as one society and one political order. Events in the early fourteenth century, and the intellectual response to them, illustrate this well.

---

[22] Mark Whittow, *The Making of Orthodox Byzantium 600–1025* (Basingstoke, UK: Macmillan, 1996), pp. 104–6.

The late antique legacy: one society, one commonwealth, and the theological importance of the Roman empire

The evolution of medieval and early modern European civilization cannot be understood without taking account of the legacy of the ancient world, especially of late antiquity, on which it built to an enormous, all-pervading extent and which accounts for much of its cultural particularity.

The area of origin of Western civilization, the Mediterranean basin, underwent a degree of cultural unification first through Hellenization (in the wake of the conquests of Alexander III of Macedon) and then Romanization (through the incorporation of all of the Mediterranean basin into the Roman empire), which produced a remarkably homogeneous Graeco-Roman culture throughout the area. The cultural and political integration achieved under the Roman empire paved the way for the spread of christianity. In turn, christianity helped to complete the process of cultural homogenization of the Roman world. Previously, Graeco-Roman culture, while cosmopolitan, had been predominantly an elite culture. Christianity, by contrast, to a much larger extent affected the population as a whole. With christianity adopted in the fourth century as the official, and increasingly exclusive, religion of the Roman empire, the church put its huge organizational resources at the disposal of the faltering Roman state. In return it was enabled to use the state apparatus to repress all rival faiths within the empire.[23] More and more, Roman-ness and christianity were equated.

With its roots in a period when the known civilized world was congruent with the single Roman society and empire, medieval christendom continued to perceive itself very strongly as both one society and, in some sense, Roman. This unity and Roman-ness was always present and visible in the one true church. The son of a Nazareth carpenter, Jesus in all likelihood had no particular interest in the Roman empire or its Graeco-Roman elite culture. Nor did he know Latin, which was not the language of any of the christian holy writings either. The fact that, in the middle ages, the church had its headquarters at Rome and that every western christian spoke Latin (if they were educated—but if not, they were still expected as a matter of course to worship in that language) had nothing to do with any obvious claim to holiness of either the city or the language but everything with the fourth-century alliance between church and empire.

Medieval thinking was predicated on what it called *ordinatio ad unum* or *reductio ad unum*, the idea that any multiplicity or diversity could ultimately be reduced to an underlying oneness, and thus harmonized.[24] Politically, this meant that there could be only one christian commonwealth, an idea that even late medieval thinkers were extremely reluctant to give up. Importantly, this commonwealth was usually identified with the Roman empire. Thus the bishop Eusebios of Kaisareia in Palestine, a main exponent of the new pro-Roman ideology of the church, explained in 336 that the pagan world suffered from worshipping plural deities that were really demons

---

[23] Cf. Andreas Osiander, 'Religion and Politics in Western Civilisation: The Ancient World as Matrix and Mirror of the Modern', *Millennium*, 29 (2000), pp. 761–90.

[24] For a good discussion see Anton-Hermann Chroust, 'The Corporate Idea and the Body Politic in the Middle Ages', *Review of Politics*, 9 (1947), pp. 423–52.

(what he calls *polutheismos*) and a concomitant plurality of rulers (what he calls *poluarchia*, denoting both the existence of plural rulers in mankind as a whole and the existence of plural powerholders within given communities); this was a world of strife and conflict. What changed all that was the coming of Christ, which, by God's will, coincided with the unification and pacification of the world through the Roman empire and the concentration, in that empire, of all power in the hands of one person.

> ... formerly all the peoples of the earth were divided. ... Because of this, continuous battles and wars, with their attendant devastations and enslavements, gave them no respite in countryside or city ... [But] as the knowledge of One God was imparted to all men and one manner of piety, the salutary teaching of Christ, in the same way at one and the same time a single sovereign [*basileus*, literally 'king'] arose for the entire Roman Empire ... two great powers—the Roman Empire, which became a monarchy [*archê monarchos*] at that time, and the teaching of Christ— ... at once tamed and reconciled all to friendship. ... For while the power of Our Saviour destroyed the polyarchy and polytheism of the demons and heralded the one kingdom of God to Greeks and barbarians and all men to the farthest extent of the earth, the Roman Empire, now that the causes of the manifold governments had been abolished, subdued the visible governments, in order to merge the entire race into one unity and concord [*eis mian henôsin kai sumphônian*].[25]

The idea of peace was central both to the ideology of the Roman monarchy and to christian theology, as evidenced for example in a famous discussion by Aurelius Augustinus (St Augustine) in what was, in the Western middle ages, probably the most widely read and most authoritative patristic text (*On the City of God*).[26] The notion that the temporal coincidence of the coming of Christ, of the creation of the Roman monarchy and of the advent of the *pax Romana* was not fortuitous but willed by God was irresistible once church and empire had reconciled themselves to each other. It is ubiquitous in late antique christian literature, to the extent that it is even acknowledged by Augustine, who is generally less enthusiastic about the empire than other patristic authors.[27] Consequently the notion of the Roman empire having in a sense been founded by God and invested by him with a redemptive purpose for all humanity is ubiquitous in medieval writings about the empire too.

The strong christian attachment to the empire is further evident in—and, in turn, was reinforced by—the late antique christian interpretation of the prophecy of the Book of Daniel. According to this four great empires would follow each other before the world would come to its end. It was taken for granted that the Roman empire was the last and greatest of these. Moreover, a highly obscure passage of the Pauline epistles, 2 Thessalonians 2.1–8, was interpreted as meaning that the fall of the Roman empire would herald the coming of the Antichrist and thus the second coming of Christ and the Day of Judgment as described in the Book of Revelations. That notion too received the blessing of the patristic authors including Augustine, and thus became an integral part of medieval faith.[28] As long as, visibly, the world had not yet ended nor seemed to be about to, it was clear that the Roman empire must still be there as well.

---

[25] Eusebios, *Trikontaetêrikos*, 16; H.A. Drake, *In Praise of Constantine: A Historical Study and New Translation of Eusebius' Tricennial Orations* (Berkeley, CA: University of California Press, 1976), pp. 119–20.

[26] Aurelius Augustinus, *De civitate Dei*, 19.

[27] Ibid. 18.64.

[28] Ibid. 20.19.

The pope—that is, the bishop of Rome—was the spiritual head of (western) christendom, and the emperor—always called either 'Roman emperor' or 'emperor of the Romans', but not 'holy'—was its highest-ranking ruler. According to the doctrine of *translatio imperii*, the pope in 800 had deprived the rulers at Constantinople of their imperial dignity and transferred it to the Frankish king Charles and his successors.[29] Among those successors, it was the German kings who, in the tenth century, secured the imperial title, which however they could acquire only if the pope was willing to crown them. Even if the pope did not crown them, however, that did not mean that there was no empire. In a wider, spiritual sense, the empire was coextensive with christendom. In a more politically concrete, narrower sense, it consisted of the dominions of the German kings. Because they were entitled to the Roman imperial dignity, from the eleventh century onwards they preferred to be known as Roman kings or kings of the Romans.

After the death of the last Hohenstaufen emperor in 1250, and his (and his predecessors') bitter conflict with the papacy, for decades the holy see refused to crown any new emperor. This worried some people. In Germany, a canon of Osnabrück cathedral, Jordanus, produced a treatise, subsequently widely read, in which he reminded his readers of the special role given to the empire by God and warned those undermining it, including the pope, of helping to bring on the Antichrist.[30] Against this, around the same time Thomas Aquinas in his commentary on 2 Thessalonians argued that if the Antichrist had not come yet it was because really the temporal Roman empire had been subsumed into the church.[31] Indeed, the holy see had long claimed that by virtue of the so-called *Constitutum Constantini*—a document quite controversial even in the middle ages and now known to be an eighth-century fake—the emperor Constantine when moving the capital of the empire to Constantinople had formally invested the bishop of Rome with power not only over that city, but over the whole of the western empire. When, in 1299, the German king, Albert of Habsburg, sent envoys to ask the pope to crown him emperor, Boniface VIII supposedly received them wearing the crown of Constantine and a sword and telling them that not only was Albert unworthy of the imperial crown but that really he, the pope, was emperor.[32] In 1302, Boniface issued the famous papal bull *Unam sanctam* in which he proclaimed full papal supremacy

---

[29] P.A. van den Baar, *Die kirchliche Lehre der Translatio Imperii Romani bis zur Mitte des 13. Jahrhunderts* (Rome: Aedes Universitatis Gregorianae, 1956); Werner Goez, *Translatio Imperii. Ein Beitrag zur Geschichte des Geschichtsdenkens und der politischen Theorien im Mittelalter und in der frühen Neuzeit* (Tübingen: Mohr/Siebeck 1958). Both works also contain much material on the other aspects of medieval thinking on the empire touched on in this article, as does Jürgen Schatz, *Imperium, Pax et Iustitia. Das Reich—Friedensstiftung zwichen Ordo, Regnum und Staatlichkeit* (Berlin: Duncker & Humblot, 2000).

[30] Jordanus of Osnabrück, 'Tractatus super Romano imperio', in Alexander von Roes, *Schriften*, ed. Herbert Grundmann and Hermann Heimpel (Weimar: Böhlau, 1949), pp. 22–33.

[31] 'Super Ad Thessalonicos II', in Thomas Aquinas, *Opera omnia*, ed. Roberto Busa, vol. 6 (Stuttgart: Frommann/Holzboog, 1980), pp. 485–9, p. 487. It is not clear whether Thomas wrote this work himself, or whether it is based on lecture notes taken by a student, but the thinking is certainly his.

[32] *Et sedens in solio armatus et cinctus ensem, habensque in capite Constantini diadema . . . ait: . . . Ego sum Caesar: ego sum Imperator . . .* Francesco Pepino, *Chronicon* 47, in Ludovico Antonio Muratori (ed.), *Rerum Italicarum Scriptores*, vol. 9 (Milan: Typographia Societatis Palatinae in Regia Curia, 1726), ..., p.745. This early fourteenth-century account may not be entirely accurate, but does show what Boniface was thought capable of.

(*potestas*) over all secular christian rulers.[33] The background of this was a quarrel between the pope and the powerful French king, Philip IV. Philip reacted by formally charging the pope with heresy and preparing to have him tried by a church council (but Boniface, spectacularly manhandled by Italian troops accompanying the French envoy, died almost immediately after).

In 1305, a Frenchman, Bertrand de Got, became pope as Clement V, giving Philip considerable leverage over the papacy.[34] Philip also pursued a policy of drawing the lords at the western periphery of the empire into his orbit, and for this reason cultivated the count of Luxemburg, Henry. The count held his lands from the German crown but, having been educated at the French court, was a native or near-native French speaker and even a French vassal by virtue of a money-fief (that is, pension) bestowed on him by Philip. Henry was also obligated to Philip because the king had weighed on pope Clement to give the prestigious archbishopric of Trier, and thus a seat in the German electoral college, to his younger brother, Baldwin. In fact, Clement may have needed little prodding as he seems to have been well-disposed towards both Henry and Baldwin in any case. Despite the fact that Baldwin lacked the minimum age and other qualifications that canon law required of a bishop, Clement granted the necessary dispensations and personally consecrated Baldwin at Poitiers in 1308; Henry was also present.

A few weeks later, king Albert was murdered in a family feud. The French king put forward the candidacy of his brother Charles of Valois to succeed Albert on the German throne. His chances seemed good since he could expect Baldwin to exert his influence among his fellow electors; he also expressly asked the pope to endorse the Capetian candidacy. Clement, however, produced only a lukewarm and ambiguous recommendation to the electors, and Baldwin (possibly abetted by Clement) in fact rallied them behind his brother, who became king as Henry VII. Henry then sent an embassy to Clement asking to grant him the imperial coronation. The pope gave the envoys the firm written pledge that they sought and hurriedly sent them off again before Philip could intervene. The coronation was to be performed at Rome by papal legates as the pope, who disliked Italy and was unpopular there, had taken up residence at Avignon (then just across the border, formed by the Rhône river, in imperial, not French, territory).

Henry was not elected German king because he was powerful (he was not), but having gained the German crown and, with it, the automatic candidacy for the imperial crown he was put in a position to exploit his *auctoritas* to become so. Thus he was able to bestow the kingdom of Bohemia on his son when it reverted to the German crown after the death of its last native ruler. Then he set out for Italy, the northern part of which was nominally part of his dominions.

Militarily, the few thousand knights and infantry with whom he crossed the Alps were a rather negligible force.[35] Rather than *potestas* Henry relied instead on his

---

[33] Text in Carl Mirbt and Kurt Aland (eds.), *Quellen zur Geschichte des Papsttums und des römischen Katholizismus*, vol. 1, 6th edn. (Tübingen: Mohr, 1967), pp. 458–60.

[34] For the events related in this and the following paragraphs see William Bowsky, *Henry VII in Italy. The Conflict of Empire and City State* (Lincoln, NE: University of Nebraska Press, 1960); Francesco Cognasso, *Arrigo VII* (Milan, 1973); Jörg K. Hoensch, *Die Luxemburger. Eine spätmittelalterliche Dynastie gesamteuropäischer Bedeutung 1308–1437* (Stuttgart: Kohlhammer, 2000), esp. pp. 25–50.

[35] "[N]ot imposing", Bowsky, *Henry VII*, p. 55; 'minuscolo', Cognasso, *Arrigo VII*, p. 131.

auctoritas as supreme judge to present himself as *rex pacificus*, the king as peace-maker. The background to this was the recurrently endemic civil war in Italy between ghibellines and guelfs. Under the Hohenstaufen dynasty (1138–1268) these had been the pro- and anti-imperial parties respectively. But their quarrels had continued even during the decades since 1268 in which the German rulers had showed little interest in Italy, and there must have been many people wishing for an end to this unhappy situation. Strikingly, the cities of Lombardy, after more than half a century of virtual independence, opened their gates to Henry. Even guelfish Milan, the powerful Lombard capital, at last did so and allowed his coronation as king of Italy (which in fact only meant Italy north of the papal territories) in its cathedral. In the cities that submitted, Henry summoned the heads of the feuding factions to appear before him and had them exchange the kiss of peace in his presence. Power in those cities passed to imperial lieutenants (*vicarii*) who raised taxes, rewrote the cities' constitutions and supervised the restoration of confiscated property to those who had been exiled but were now recalled.

Meanwhile, without breaking openly with Henry, king Philip of France sought to prevent the imperial coronation. He did so by encouraging the king of Naples, Robert of Anjou, to oppose Henry, among other things by occupying Rome. Robert was a relative of the French king but also a vassal of the pope, from whom he held his kingdom and for whom he acted as papal agent in northern Italy, giving him much influence in the whole peninsula. Sowing dissent between Robert and Henry proved an excellent means for Philip to put pressure on Clement. Perhaps to pre-empt this very strategy, Clement sought to promote some kind of marriage alliance between the families of the two rulers even before Henry left Germany, but this came to nothing.

Robert allied himself to the majority of Tuscan cities which, led by Florence, decided not to submit to Henry and to block his passage to Rome. On the point of ordering Robert to end this occupation of Rome, Clement desisted after receiving an embassy from king Philip, which apparently alerted him to negotiations between Henry and the king of Sicily which eventually did lead to an alliance between them directed against Robert. Meanwhile, Henry stayed put in Lombardy. Several of the Lombard cities rebelled. Henry, obliged to show that this would not be tolerated, besieged, took and punished Brescia as a warning to the others, delaying his departure. Also, he was desperately short of funds, having to rely on increasingly recalcitrant creditors and the sale of offices. 'For he, our king', observed a contemporary, the Milanese notary Giovanni da Cermenate, 'truly magnanimous and richly endowed with all the virtues, was very poor indeed in terms of money and gold'.[36]

Among the more vociferous of Henry's supporters was a Florentine poet deeply unhappy about the anti-imperial stance of his home town (which he had been forced to leave). He took up Henry's cause in a number of open letters. Addressing the magnates and the people of Italy, 'the humble Italian and Florentine, Dante Alighieri' urged them to seize the chance to overcome their divisions. Using the image of the bridegroom that occurs in several places in the Bible, Dante implicitly

---

[36] *Hic etenim rex noster, vere magnanimus et omnium virtutum dives, erat pecunia et auro nimium pauper.* Giovanni da Cermenate, *Historia*, ed. Luigi Alberto Ferrai (Rome: Forzani, 1889), ch. 20, p. 44.

equates Henry with Christ. 'Rejoice now, oh miserable Italy ..., for your bridegroom, the comfort of the world and the glory of your people [*mundi solatium et gloria plebis tue*], the most gracious Henry, *divus et Augustus et Cesar*, is hastening to your wedding. Dry your tears and wipe off the traces of your grief, oh most beautiful one, for he is near who will liberate you from the prison of the godless.'[37]

In another letter the 'most heinous [*scelestissimi*] people of Florence' found themselves reminded that 'the pious providence of the everlasting king [of the heavens] ... has ordained the most holy [*sacrosanctum*] Roman empire to govern [*gubernare*] human affairs', and berated for their blindness and covetousness that led them to break 'divine and human law' and to reject 'the Roman prince, the king of the world and the servant of God [*Romanus princeps, mundi rex et Dei minister*]'.[38]

Dante also addressed the king himself. 'To the most holy, glorious and successful *triumphator* and lord, the incomparable lord Henry, by God's grace king of the Romans and ever *augustus*, his most devoted followers Dante Alighieri of Florence, unjustly exiled, and with him all those in Tuscany who wish for peace: we kiss the ground before your feet.' Dante refers to Henry as 'the successor of Caesar and Augustus', 'him whom the whole world is expecting', 'the world's only protector [*preses unice mundi*]'. He chides the king for lingering in Lombardy and urges him not to be intimidated by the resistance of the Tuscan cities. In this context, perhaps somewhat ominously, Dante compares Henry to David in his fight against Goliath. But he also goes much further when again he likens the king to the Messiah. Henry's tardiness to press on for Rome 'compels us to entertain doubt and to join in the words of the precursor [that is, John the Baptist, Matthew 11.3], 'Are you he that should come, or do we look for another?" But Dante quickly reassures Henry that

nevertheless in you we put our belief and our hope, acknowledging you as a servant of God, a son of the church and a promoter of Roman glory [*Romane glorie promotorem*]. For I myself ... saw you to be most kind, and heard you to be most gracious, as befits the majesty of an emperor, when my hands touched your feet and my lips rendered their due. Then my spirit rejoiced in you [a line from the *Magnificat*, Luke 1.46ff.: 'My soul does magnify the lord, and my spirit has rejoiced in God my saviour'], and I silently said to myself: Behold the lamb of God, behold him who takes away the sins of the world [this is John the Baptist acknowledging Jesus as the Messiah, according to John 1.29].[39]

Eventually, Henry embarked his troops at Genoa and shipped them to Pisa so as not to have to cross territory controlled by Florence and its allies, which he placed under the ban of the empire. Having reached Rome, he was treated to an enthusiastic welcome by the inhabitants, but despite much fighting was unable to occupy the Vatican defended by a Neapolitan and Tuscan garrison. St Peter's thus being inaccessible, it was decided to hold the coronation in the Lateran basilica instead. The papal legates at first refused, but, finding themselves threatened by the pro-imperial Roman populace, at last performed the ceremony subject to the pope's later approval.

On 29 June 1312, Henry issued notes in which he informed the other kings of christendom (and numerous lesser dignitaries) of his coronation, on that day, as

---

[37] Letters 5.2; Dante Alighieri, *Opere*, 2nd edn. (Florence: Società Dantesca Italiana, 1960), p.389.
[38] Letters 6.1–2; ibid. 391–2.
[39] ... *velut decet imperatoriam maiestatem benignissimum vidi et clementissimum te audivi, cum pedes tuos manus mee tractarunt et labia mea debitum persolverunt. Tunc exultavit in te spiritus meus, cum tacitus dixi mecum: "Ecce Agnus Dei, ecce qui tollit peccata mundi"*. Letters 7; ibid. pp. 394–7.

Roman emperor, the first such coronation since 1220 and thus a major restoration. His chancery took care, in a lengthy preamble, to reaffirm the universally acknowledged ideological foundation on which the imperial office rested. God had willed, readers were reminded, 'that, just as all the ranks [*ordines*] of the heavenly hosts fight under him, the sole God, so also all mankind, separated into kingdoms and provinces, should be placed under a single monarchical ruler [*universi homines ... uno principi monarche subessent*] ...' The order of the universe would be the more perfect

the more, originating from one God as its creator, it is governed under one ruler and receives for itself increasing peace and unity and returns to one God and lord [*quo ab uno Deo suo factore progrediens sub uno principe moderata et in se pacis ac unitatis augmenta susciperet et in unum Deum et dominum ... rediret*] ... And whereas in previous ages this kind of princely rule [*huiusmodi principatus*] was located in various nations [*in diversis fuerit nationibus*] ..., yet at last, as the fullness of time [a common metaphor for the birth of Christ, taken from Galatians 4.4] was approaching, when that same God our lord ... desired to become human, ... the aforementioned dominion [*imperium*] providently passed to the Romans through the working of God's grace ...[40]

This did not mean that Henry was hoping to undo the separation of mankind into provinces and kingdoms—an implausible proposition given his lack of military resources, and, as we will see in the next section, at odds with contemporary political thinking. Rather, the version of the document addressed to kings expressed its expectation that its royal recipients would be the more pleased with it as the imperial dignity and the royal were 'very similar to each other through a kind of neighbourhood in glory' (*quadam glorie vicinitate consimiles*) and should be at one with each other in love and charity (*amoris participio et caritatis unione conformes*).[41]

In his reply, king Edward II of England did his best to create just that impression.

To his most cherished friend, the most excellent prince and lord, Henry, by God's grace emperor of the Romans [etc.], Edward, by God's grace [etc.] ... hail ... The son of God, who without doubt is king of kings and lord of those in power [*dominus dominantium*], having entrusted the empire to the governorship [*regimini*] of a man who is farsighted and experienced, it may be hoped that both spiritual and worldly affairs will prosper the more happily everywhere on earth [*ubique terrarum*]. Having received, with joyful hand [*leta manu*] [the letter which you have] sent us concerning your having been elected Roman emperor by the princes of Germany, ... [and] the ceremony of your consecration and coronation ..., we have heard and diligently listened to its words, greatly rejoicing in its contents ... We put our hope, then, in the lord Jesus Christ, that by your powerful efforts [*per vestre strenuitatis potenciam*] and your prudent and farsighted activities [*circumspectionis industriam providam*] the entire catholic people [*universa gens catholica*, that is, christendom] may be granted wholesome increase in the Lord [*salubria in Domino suscipiet incrementa*], to the confusion, in particular, and perpetual abasement of the enemies of Christ's cross and the exaltation of our christian faith.[42]

It is true that it took the English court the better part of a year to dispatch this reply. Among the reasons for this may have been a desire to wait first for the reaction of other players more intimately involved. The most important among these were

---

[40] *Monumenta Germaniae Historica* (MGH), series *Constitutiones Imperatorum et Regum* vol. 4.2, ed. Jakob Schwalm (Hanover: Hahn, 1909–11), no. 801, p. 802.
[41] Ibid. p. 804.
[42] Ibid. no. 812, p. 814.

Philip of France and the pope. The French king in fact answered very quickly, acknowledging Henry's new title.[43] In his reply, he paraphrases Henry's circular in rather pointed fashion by claiming that according to it all men were to be under the emperor's 'temporal power' (*temporalis potentia*); Philip also explicitly calls this *subiectio*. He observes that this language (*loquendi modus*) of the circular had caused 'not a little surprise' (*admiratio non modica*) among those in his realm who had received it. We must remember that ten years earlier, when Boniface VIII spoke of subjecting him to his *potestas*, Philip not only rejected that claim but, spectacularly, sought to have the pope deposed.

This time, rather than challenge this strong formulation of imperial overlordship Philip actually accepted it, for the rest of christendom, by insisting merely that it could not apply to the French kingdom, which the emperor in his circular ought to have exempted (*excipere debuisset*). In an allusion to the doctrine that the emperor as protector of the church wielded the secular sword on its behalf, Philip argues that the christian religion had always been so secure in France that that realm had received from Christ himself the 'unique privilege' (*singularis prerogativa*) of exemption from imperial suzerainty: 'For it is widely and generally acknowledged by all and everywhere that from the time of Christ onwards the kingdom of the Franks [French] has only had its own king, under Jesus Christ as king of kings and lord of lords…, knowing or having no other temporal superior, no matter which emperor was reigning'. In support of this extraordinary claim the French document refers to unnamed ancient historical writings (*veterum historiarum veridica narratio*). Addressing his reply, Philip named himself first and the emperor in second position (*Philippus Dei gratia Francie rex illustri principi Henrico eadem gratia Romanorum imperatori … salutem*), unlike Edward, who properly named the emperor first (*Excellentissimo principi domino Henrico Dei gratia etc. … Edwardus eadem gratia etc. … salutem*).

In light of the fact that he had been snubbed by Henry's election as German king in the first place, and tried to prevent his becoming emperor, Philip's quick acceptance of Henry's imperial title may appear surprising. But, as mentioned, Philip consistently avoided any open break with Henry. As long as possible the presence in Rome of Neapolitan troops under the brother of the king of Naples was explained by the intention of that brother to represent the Neapolitan king at the coronation. And when that pretext was exposed, rather than contest the legitimacy of the coronation on the technicality of its having taken place in the Lateran (for which there was a precedent) Philip clearly thought it better to concede his defeat. For the alternative would have been open insubordination to the emperor's sacred *auctoritas*, which would have alienated many in christendom without offering any compensating political advantage.

At the same time, it was a shrewd move to pretend to understand Henry as claiming the effective *subiectio* of christendom to him. In fact this expression does not occur in the circular. *Subesse*, literally 'to be under', is the strongest term it uses, and while it is clearly meant to denote a hierarchy within christendom this was almost certainly meant to be simply symbolic. Nor, unlike the bull *Unam sanctam*, does the circular claim *potestas* or *potentia* for the emperor. Its phraseology is distinctly more moderate, indeed rather hazy, and its chief motive seems to be a

[43] Ibid. no. 811, p. 813–14.

desire to justify Henry's new title in terms of the venerable and powerful notion of *ordinatio ad unum*. However, the restoration of the imperial dignity after such a long time was an event whose consequences could not yet be gauged. After all, rulers were becoming more powerful than ever, as Philip was well placed to know. With few troops and almost no money, but making skilful, charismatic use of his legitimacy as *Romanus princeps*, Henry had already come a long way from his comparatively humble origins. He was only in his late thirties, and there was no telling what he would yet prove capable of. It was advisable, then, to guard against the possibility, however remote, that one day he or his successors *would* claim suzerainty over neighbouring realms. On the other hand, one of those successors might yet be a Capetian, in which case it would actually be useful to have stated the role of the emperor in strong terms.

Meanwhile, in Italy, the new emperor still had Florence and Naples to deal with. Unable to take Florence, Henry lifted the siege and decided to direct his efforts against Robert. If he could be eliminated, the rebellious cities of northern Italy would be deprived of their most important ally. And his position was not secure. For the sake of convenience he has so far been referred to here as 'king of Naples'. But he really styled himself 'king of Sicily', and the kingdom of Sicily theoretically comprised both southern Italy (Naples) and Sicily proper. In fact, it was divided between Robert and another claimant, Ferdinand of Aragon, who held the island of Sicily as well as parts of Calabria on the mainland but likewise claimed the whole kingdom. Moreover, many south Italian nobles apparently did not like and did not much obey Robert, and the majority of the population seems to have been pro-imperial.

On the other hand, Robert had formidable supporters—his relative the French king, and the pope, whose vassal Robert was. The clash, fomented by Philip, between Robert and Henry put Clement in an extremely uncomfortable position. Abandoning his vassal and protégé to Henry would have meant not only a loss of face but an open challenge to Clement's compatriot and powerful neighbour, king Philip. In response to Henry's circular, the pope sent a gruff acknowledgement. Mostly it dwells, in rather sharp tone, on the relationship between Henry and Robert and the need for Henry to patch it up, urging the emperor to pursue the marriage project cherished by Clement.[44] But Henry ignored this.

On arriving in Italy he had surrounded himself with lawyers, among them the famous Cino da Pistoia, with the obvious intention of making the most of the strong position that Roman law accorded to the emperor to compensate for his lack of material resources. All formal legal training in this period was based on the *Corpus Iuris* of the emperor Justinian, the massive sixth-century compilation of Roman law. Few medieval lawyers would have dared to question that the strong position of the emperor as reflected in this compilation was still the one that any current successor of Justinian could claim by right. If the *Corpus Iuris* was not quite the Bible, in medieval eyes it did not come far behind.[45] A formula had already been coined, by Italian jurists in the late thirteenth century, according to which not only the emperor but any king (though, significantly, not other lords) was entitled to the prerogatives that the

---

[44] Ibid. no. 810.
[45] On the reverence in which the *Corpus* was held see, for example, Hans Hattenhauer, *Europäische Rechtsgeschichte* (Heidelberg: C.F. Müller Juristischer Verlag, 1983), p. 255; Peter G. Stein, *Römisches Recht und Europa. Die Geschichte einer Rechtskultur* (Frankfurt/Main: Fischer, 1996), p. 82.

Corpus attributed to the emperor: on this view, a king was emperor in his own realm (*rex imperator in regno suo*). But this was still quite a novel notion.[46]

Now that he had formally been crowned emperor Henry was even better placed to harness Roman law to his purposes. He summoned Robert of Anjou to appear before him and, when he failed to obey, sentenced him to death for *crimen laesae maiestatis*, in other words, failing to heed the emperor's authority.[47] This was very much a Roman law thing to do, not a feudal law thing. His right to judge Robert was somewhat problematic. Henry was not Robert's liege—the pope was. But Henry proclaimed that there could be no order in the world if the Roman empire was in upheaval (*Romanum imperium, in cuius tranquillitate totius orbis regularitas requiescit*) and that both divine and human law required every individual to submit to the Roman emperor (*nedum humana, verum etiam divina precepta, quibus iubetur quod omnis anima Romano principi sit subiecta*).[48]

This sounds ambitious but, again, should probably not be interpreted as indicating any desire to subject all christendom to the effective rule of the emperor. It was more *ad hoc* than that: Henry urgently needed legal grounds for taking action against Robert to oppose to the predictable papal veto. Henry could not quarrel with the pope's suzerainty over southern Italy (at least not without losing any lingering hope of papal support). So basing his jurisdiction on Roman law was the only solution, and an ideologically potent one to boot because of the near-metaphysical authority of the *Corpus Iuris*.

On learning of Robert's condemnation, the pope reacted in the manner that Henry must have feared he would. Clement announced that he would excommunicate anyone who took up arms against Robert. Henry concluded an alliance with Ferdinand of Sicily, sent an embassy to the pope to try to conciliate him and, without waiting for the reply, set out with his army from Pisa. But he was already a sick man and succumbed to his malaria shortly afterwards, after an imperial reign of just over a year.

Philip of France tried to get his son, the future Philip V, elected German king but failed again. Clement V produced a papal bull (*Pastoralis cura*) containing an array of reasons (not very consistent with one another) why the sentence against Robert was invalid in the first place and why, even if it was not, the pope was competent to quash it.[49] The Florentine poet, in the work for which he is chiefly famous, awarded a place in Paradise to the soul of 'the august Henry, who [came] to raise up Italy when she [was] not yet ready',[50] and, while he was at it, inveighed some more against his fellow Florentines. Decades later, they, in fact, paid Henry's grandson and successor, the emperor Charles IV, the substantial sum of 100,000 florins to have their condemnation by Henry repealed.[51]

---

[46] On this formula see Francesco Calasso, *I glossatori e la teoria della sovranità. Studio di diritto comune pubblico*, 3rd. edn. (Milan: Giuffrè, 1957).

[47] MGH *Constitutiones* 4.2. no. 946.

[48] Ibid. no. 929, p. 965.

[49] Ibid. no. 1166.

[50] *l'alto Arrigo, che a drizzar l'Italia verrà in prima ch'ella sia disposta*. Dante Alighieri, *Divina commedia, Paradiso*, 30.137–8.

[51] In 1355. Bowsky, *Henry VII*, p. 183 explains the payment in this fashion. According to Hoensch, *Die Luxemburger*, p. 141 the sum represented tax arrears. In any case, the money was apparently also paid to keep Charles, who was on his way to Rome for his imperial coronation, from visiting Florence. Like his grandfather, he caused great popular excitement in Italy and repeatedly found himself the object of appeals from the local opposition in the cities where he did appear, enabling or even forcing him to intervene in their politics.

The intellectual response: *Respublica christiana* and the problem of peace

It is worth emphasizing that the theological role attributed to the Roman empire did not presuppose the exercise of actual power by the Roman emperor or king over the whole of christendom. In fact, it was fashionable to point out that the medieval empire (in the narrower, political sense) was a mere shadow of what it had been in antiquity. Thus in the 1140s, Otto of Freising, a relative of the emperor Frederick I, could write that 'as a result of so many vicissitudes, especially in our own day, the monarchy of the Romans has been transformed from the most eminent almost to the most insignificant'.[52] Robert of Anjou, in a document composed shortly after Henry's death to urge the pope not to crown any more emperors in the future, also emphasized this: 'Where is the matchless and outstanding monarchy of the Romans, reduced now from controlling almost the entire world to a very small number of lands subject to it?'[53] Around the same time, the abbot of Admont in Styria, Engelbert, in his treatise *On the Origin and End of the Roman Empire*, states that for many people the empire had 'already lost so much of its rights and strength [*in tantum iam ... in suis iuribus et viribus defecisse*] that it would likely soon fail entirely and cease to exist'.[54] Although, for Engelbert, the 'end' of the empire mentioned in the title of his treatise was still self-evidently a future occurrence which would trigger the apocalypse, he explained the empire's weakness as a result of the fact that it was so old, having lasted longer already than any of its three predecessors. At one point mention is made of one 'Henry, seventh of that name, who in our time has taken the helm of the empire as the ninety-seventh emperor since Augustus himself'.[55] In this perspective, the end of the world could not be that far off.

Engelbert's defence of the empire is on a par (at least) with the more famous *Monarchia* of Dante Alighieri. Both were written under the impact of the restoration of the imperial dignity by Henry. Engelbert and Dante employ many of the same arguments despite the fact that almost certainly they knew nothing of each other, showing that those arguments represent a widely shared discourse. Needless to say, both authors develop the theology of the empire already briefly outlined in this article. But both also redefine it in line with the neo-Aristotelian thinking fashionable at the time.

In accordance with all the political thinkers of the period Engelbert and Dante understand christendom as a single commonwealth (*respublica*) organised as a hierarchy of communities (*communitates*). This latter notion had developed quickly as a result of the rapid and enthusiastic appropriation, in the second half of the

---

[52] *regnum Romanorum ... ex tot alternationibus, maxime diebus nostris, ex nobilissimo factum est pene novissimum*; Otto von Freising, *Chronik*, ed. Adolf Schmidt (Darmstadt: Wissenschaftliche Buchgesellschaft, 1990), Otto's preface, p. 12.

[53] *ubi Romanorum singularis et precipua monarchia, que fere de tocius mundi dominio ad brevissimum terrarum subiectarum sibi numerum est reducta?* MGH, *Constitutiones*, 4.2 no. 1253, p. 1372.

[54] Engelbert of Admont, *De ortu et fine Romani imperii*, ed. Gaspar Bruschius (Basel: Oporinus, 1553), preface, p. 16–17. The re-edition of the Latin text by Wilhelm Baum (ed.), *Engelbert von Admont. Vom Ursprung und Ende des Reiches und andere Schriften* (Graz: Leykam, 1998), contains quite a few obvious errors and, while more accessible, is thus inferior to the 1553 *editio princeps*; nor is the parallel German translation particularly good. I have not seen the new English translation in Cary J. Nedermann and Thomas M. Izbicki (eds.), *Three Treatises on Empire* (Bristol: Thoemmes Press, 2000).

[55] Ibid. ch. 16, p. 86.

thirteenth century, of Aristotle's *Politics* after it became available in Latin. There, medieval thinkers discovered the analysis of society as consisting of three tiers: households (*oikoi, domus*), village communities (*kômai, vici*), and cities (*poleis, civitates*). Adapting this approach to their own time, medieval thinkers followed Thomas Aquinas and his influential pupil Giles of Rome (Aegidius Romanus) in positing a fourth level, the *regnum* or kingdom.[56] When Thomas and Giles wrote, there was no emperor, and Thomas, as we have seen, solved the puzzle of the missing Antichrist by arguing that for eschatological purposes the Roman empire was sufficiently represented by the universal Roman church. But once Henry of Luxemburg had renewed the imperial dignity Engelbert and Dante promptly posited a further, supreme *communitas*, encompassing the *regna* and coextensive with mankind.

Each *communitas* was seen as self-organizing to the extent that it was autarchic, and subject to intervention from the next higher level only to the extent that it was not. At the same time, however, supervision was always necessary because the interest of the smaller group, that is, of a group at a lower level, must give way to that of the larger group. For example, a single household had no right to disturb the peace of the village, and to that extent could legitimately be coerced by the village.

Engelbert unusually divides mankind into six *communitates*—household, village, city, *gens, regnum, imperium*, with the addition of *gens* unique to him (as far as I am aware). He defines the *gens* as sharing a common language, a common homeland, and common customs and laws (*communitas unius linguae et patriae, et morum ac legum*).[57] In situating it below the level of the *regnum* Engelbert reflects the fact that a large kingdom like the German or French one comprised a multitude of regional legal systems (and *communitas linguae* presumably refers to regional dialects as much as to separate languages in the strict sense). Kings had to respect those local laws—even Louis XIV in the seventeenth century was unable to impose a unified legal code on his subjects.[58] To my knowledge, the (sparse) literature on Engelbert has not elucidated the reason why he introduces the *gens* into the hierarchy of *communitates*—indeed, it hardly even comments on the fact. But it is central to his whole theory.

Engelbert evidently drew on his knowledge of the Justinianic *Corpus Iuris*. It contains a beginner's textbook of jurisprudence, the *Institutiones*, which states at the very outset that

All peoples [*populi*] that are governed by laws and customs use in part their own law and in part the law of all mankind [*omnium hominum ius*]. For what each people lays down for itself as its law is peculiar to the citizenship as such [*ipsius proprium civitatis*] and is called civil law [*ius civile*]. But what natural reason lays down among all men [*quod naturalis ratio inter omnes homines constituit*] is observed equally by all peoples and is called the law of nations [*ius gentium*].[59]

---

[56] Thomas introduced this notion in a short, unfinished work variously known as *De regimine principum* or *De regno* (*Opera* vol. 3, pp. 595–601). Giles developed it in his own *De regimine principum* (On the government of princes), which, written about 1280 and dedicated to the future Philip IV of France, became one of the most widely read books of the late middle ages. See Aegidius Romanus, *De regimine principum*, ed. Hieronymus Samaritanus (Rome: Zannettus, 1607; facsimile reprint: Aalen, Scientia Verlag, 1967), esp. ch. 3.1.5.

[57] Engelbert, *De ortu* ch. 12, p. 59.

[58] Pierre Goubert, *Louis XIV et vingt millions de Français* (Paris: Hachette-Pluriel, 1993), p. 128.

[59] *Institutiones* 1.2.1.

This distinction between the law of the individual *populi* and the law of all mankind was clearly the starting point for Engelbert's reflection. He could not use *populus* as a name for an intermediary *communitas* because in his day the term was too strongly associated with christendom as a whole, *populus christianus* being a standing expression. Therefore he preferred the alternative *gens* which was less commonly associated with christendom (although this usage occurs too, as in Edward II's reply to Henry: *universa gens catholica*). In the middle ages (and long afterwards) legal systems often were not kingdom-wide so the *gens* had to be fitted in between *civitas* (used here with the meaning 'city' as in the Latin translation of the *Politics*) and the *regnum* or kingdom.[60] To the extent that the *gentes* needed supervision it was provided by kings, that is, on the next higher level. But that left, precisely, the *populus christianus*, if not mankind, as a whole, and *its* law, the *ius naturale*. Like others, Engelbert uses this expression as a synonym for *ius gentium*, which, as stated in the quoted passage from the *Institutiones*, was the law dictated by natural reason.

Kings could not be entrusted with its defence because each of them was only in charge of a fragment of christendom. Someone had to be in charge of all christendom, if not humanity, and the law that all of it (or all *gentes*) shared. For Engelbert, the *regna* certainly had their legitimacy, but taken individually none of them was indispensable. The empire had a higher legitimacy because its existence alone was dictated by nature. Just as the good, or interest (*bonum*) of the household was subordinated to (*ordinatur ad*) that of the village, the good of the village to that of the city and so on, 'so too the several kingdoms of the world, and their good, are subordinated to the one natural kingdom and empire'.[61]

Engelbert sums up the core of his theory thus:

> … just as the law … is distinguished into natural law, which is the common law of all *gentes* [*ius commune omnium gentium*], and positive law [*ius positivum*], which varies in accordance with the diversity of the *gentes*, … so too the individual *gentes* have individual kings, who govern [*gubernare*] each of them in accordance with the laws peculiar to them [*secundum suas leges proprias*]… But at the same time, it is not only possible, but necessary and useful that all kingdoms obey [*obedire*] the Roman empire in accordance with natural law, common to all *gentes* and kingdoms, or according to that part of Roman law that can justly and usefully be applied to all *gentes* and kingdoms, to ensure the peace and quiet [*pacem et quietem*] which all *gentes* and kingdoms are bound to observe both among themselves and with respect to outsiders, as in the christian kingdoms, and, at a minimum, to ensure that the christian kingdoms are not invaded, or disturbed, by those outsiders, as in the kingdoms of the infidels and pagans, which, in this respect, are bound to defer to the Roman empire [*Romano imperio subesse tenentur*]. For it is not just the law of christians, but also the law of *gentes* [*ius gentium*], and of all human beings in their capacity as such [*ius omnium hominum in quantum homines*], to grant each that which is his and preserve it for him, and not to harm another unjustly [*suum unicuique tribuere et servare, et alterum iniuste non laedere*: Engelbert is quoting from *Institutiones* 1.1.10]. By law [*de iure*] even infidels and pagans can and must be forced by the empire to observe this in their dealings with christian kingdoms.[62]

---

[60] Evidently, this means that 'nations', the usual rendering of *gentes* in the expression *ius gentium*, is not an apt translation here so I leave the term untranslated from now on.

[61] *sic etiam multa regna mundi, et bonum ipsorum, ordinantur ad unum naturale regnum et imperium.* Engelbert, *De ortu*, ch. 15, p. 77.

[62] Ibid. ch. 18, p. 106–7.

In Engelbert's view, even though it need not be the same for all, let alone total, *some* kind of subordination to the empire was required to preserve the unity of christendom:

It is better, and more just ... for all kingdoms and all kings to defer [*subesse*] to, and obey, the one empire and the one christian emperor, to the extent that by law, or by reasonable and longstanding custom each single kingdom is bound to do so, than for each individual kingdom or king to stand alone, without any subjection [*subiectio*] or obedience to the empire, like many heads on the one body of the christian commonwealth [*christiana respublica*], which is one, the commonwealth of the one christian people [*populus christianus*], and as such has only one head for all [*unum caput omnium*], unless someone wants to turn that commonwealth and the one christian people into a many-headed monster [*multorum capitum monstrum*].[63]

Dante in his *Monarchia* employs the same comparison, indicating that it must have been common: 'Oh human race, how many storms ..., how many shipwrecks do you have to suffer while, turned into a many-headed beast [*bellua multorum capitum*], you strive in opposite directions!'[64] He looks back nostalgically to the days of the *divus Augustus* and his *monarchia perfecta*. At that time 'the human race was happy in the tranquillity of universal peace, as all historians, the great poets, and also he who wrote of the meekness of Christ deigned to testify; indeed Paul described that most happy state as the fullness of time'.[65] However, the empire advocated by Dante is very much medieval and bears no resemblance to the one ruled by Augustus.

The *Monarchia* stipulates five *communitates*: household, village, city, kingdom and *humanum genus*, the human race. Since the interest of the larger group takes priority over that of a smaller one, the highest good is that of mankind as a whole. But for mankind to attain perfection, it has to be able to live in peace. Like Engelbert (and also Thomas Aquinas and Giles of Rome), Dante argues that unity and peace are better served by monarchical than by collective rule. So, like the other *communitates*, mankind too should be under one ruler, the emperor (Dante does not distinguish between christendom and the rest of mankind, perhaps because he conceives of the empire as limited entirely to temporal matters). Again like Engelbert Dante sees the emperor not as someone who actively intervenes in the life of the lower *communitates*, but only as a guarantor of peace.

To say that the human race can be ruled [*regi*] by a single supreme prince does not mean that the smallest decisions of each municipality [*minima iudicia uniuscuiusque municipii*] can come directly from this single person. ... For nations [*nationes*], kingdoms and cities have peculiarities of their own, which it is necessary to regulate [*oportet regulari*] by different laws .... Rather, the statement means that the human race should be ruled by him with respect to those things that it shares in common, that concern everybody [*secundum sua comunia, que omnibus competent*], and that it should be governed in accordance with a common rule so as to maintain peace [*ut ...comuni regula gubernetur ad pacem*]. It is this rule or law that the individual princes [*particulares principes*] ought to receive from him.[66]

Engelbert did not believe that the empire would ever be as strong again as it once was. As the preface to his treatise makes clear, he aimed it at those who thought that

---

[63] Ibid. ch. 18, p. 98–9.
[64] Dante Alighieri, *Monarchia* 1.16.4. Quotations from this work appear in my own translation.
[65] Ibid. 1.16.1–2.
[66] Ibid. 1.14.4–7.

the empire was a lost cause, unnecessary, indeed illegitimate while suggesting that such people were numerous. Dante may have hoped that the restoration of the imperial dignity by Henry heralded a new beginning for the empire. But almost certainly he wrote his *Monarchia* when Henry was already dead, so his mood cannot have been exactly triumphant either. Widely debated, the notion of universal empire was also struggling. Importantly, however, even those inclined to reject it were not prepared to abandon the notion of a single christian commonwealth along with it. Among them was the French lawyer, Pierre Dubois.

In his treatise *De recuperatione Terre Sancte* (On the recovery of the Holy Land), written between 1305 and 1307, Dubois dismisses universal empire as unsuitable for the present age:

I doubt if there is a man of sound mind who thinks that at this late stage of time there can be a single temporal monarch for the whole world, who would rule all things and whom all would obey as their superior. If there were a tendency in this direction there would be wars, rebellions, and dissensions without end. There would be no one who could quell these disturbances because of the multitude of people and the distant areas involved, local differences, and the natural inclination of men toward strife.[67]

Dubois briefly discusses the contemporary *imperium Romanum*, held by the *reges Alemannie*, the kings of Germany. He treats it as no different from any other christian realm; indeed the possibility that it might be special is not even raised.[68] But then (as he asks in a different context),

what of those cities and the many princes who recognize no superior authority on earth [*superiores in terris non recognoscentes*] possessing the power to judge them [*qui justiciam faciant de ipsis*] in accordance with local laws and customs? When these cities and princes engage in controversies, before whom shall they institute proceedings and conduct litigation?[69]

The fundamental problem, for Dubois as for Engelbert and Dante, is the unity of christendom and the maintenance of peace within and among its constituent parts. To solve it, Dubois separates the concept of the single christian commonwealth from the concept of universal empire, reproposing the former without reference to the latter. It is necessary, he announces at the outset, 'to establish peace among all Christians—at least those obedient to the Roman Church—on such a firm basis that they will form a single commonwealth so strongly united that it cannot be divided'.[70]

Una respublica: this is the essence of Dubois' programme. Mantra-like, though with constant semantic variation, the idea of christendom forming a single common-wealth occurs again and again in his text.[71] In his view, even the christian cities and

---

[67] Pierre Dubois, *The Recovery of the Holy Land*, trans. Walther I. Brandt (New York: Columbia University Press, 1956), ch. 63, p. 121–2. Brandt oddly renders Dubois's *in hoc fine seculorum* by 'in this day and age'; I have substituted 'at this late stage of time'. For the original text see the editions by Ch.-V. Langlois (Paris: Picard, 1891) and Angelo Diotti (Florence: Olschki, 1972).

[68] Ibid. ch. 13.

[69] Ibid. ch. 12, p. 78–9.

[70] *Idcirco inter catholicos omnes, saltem ecclesie romane obedientes, pacem firmari taliter expedit quod una sit respublica, sic fortiter unita quod non dividatur*. Ibid. ch. 2, p. 71. Brandt translates 'that they will form in effect a single commonwealth'. I have deleted 'in effect' as having no basis in the original.

[71] For example, *respublica christicolarum ecclesie romane obedientium* (ch. 3), *respublica catholicorum* (ch. 27), *respublica totius sancte religionis christicolarum* (ch. 46), *omnium credentium una respublica* (ch. 64).

princes that do not recognize a suzerain nevertheless have a duty not to attack each other, for nothing is worse than war among christians.[72] Dubois advocates a general council of all christendom, at which *principes et prelati* shall sign an undertaking, binding themselves and their successors, to renounce violence in their mutual dealings. If those princes and prelates do recognize a temporal suzerain, they shall pledge themselves to have any quarrel adjudicated by that suzerain—a suggestion indicating how little this could be taken for granted. If they recognize no temporal suzerain, then they shall pledge themselves to have any quarrel adjudicated by an arbitral court set up *ad hoc*, whose decision can be appealed to the pope.[73]

The participants in the council are to accept this system in sworn pledges to be deposed at, and published by, the holy see. But what if somebody ignores this undertaking? Then, Dubois explains, they shall be proclaimed outlaws by the pope, creating an obligation for everybody else to do what is in their power to resist them. It should be noted that, without discussion, Dubois envisages participation in his council by autonomous and non-autonomous actors alike. Similarly, no difference is to be made between autonomous and non-autonomous actors when it comes to punishing those breaking the peace. In a hypothetical example, Dubois lets the duke of Burgundy make war on his overlord, the king of France: following an appropriate declaration by the pope, all christian rulers, autonomous or not, would then have an obligation to assist the king in putting down this rebellion.[74]

In his discussion of the *imperium Romanum* in *De recuperatione* Dubois laments that the elective nature of the imperial crown invites internal strife each time the throne falls vacant, and recommends that the crown be made hereditary. This, he asserts, will greatly help 'the welfare and prosperity of the commonwealth, the kingdom, and empire of such noble peoples'.[75] The expression 'commonwealth', *respublica*, could be taken to refer to the empire but Dubois means christendom, as is made clear by the context and also by a very similar passage in a slightly later work: in his *Pro facto Terre Sancte* of 1308, Dubois likewise excoriates those who rebel against the elected German/Roman monarch, 'doing the greatest harm to the Roman church, the empire, the Holy Land and the entire commonwealth of the worshippers of Christ.'[76]

Yet another work of Dubois, known variously as *Summaria brevis* or *De abreviacione* and written in 1300, offers advice to Philip IV on how to put down rebellions against the crown. Here Dubois complains that 'the vice of disrespect for the welfare and interest of the commonwealth has hitherto become more ingrained in the kingdom of France than in other parts of the world.'[77] Since he never uses the

---

[72] *Guerre catholicorum inter se sunt pessime*, ch. 2.

[73] I follow here the interpretation of Merriam Sherwood, "Pierre Dubois and the Arbitration of International Disputes", in John H. Mundy/Richard W. Emery/Benjamin N. Nelson (eds.), *Essays in Medieval Life and Thought. Presented in Honor of Austin Patterson Evans* (New York: Bilbo and Tannen, 1965), pp. 138–49.

[74] Ch. 5.

[75] *salus et exaltatio reipublice, regni et imperii tam nobilium populorum*. Brandt translates 'of that noble people', but the original uses the plural. Dubois, *Recovery*, ch. 13, p. 80.

[76] *in gravissimum preiudicium ecclesie Romane, imperii, terre sancte tociusque reipublice christicolarum*. Quoted in Hellmut Kämpf, *Pierre Dubois und die geistigen Grundlagen des französischen Nationalbewußtseins um 1300* (Leipzig/Berlin: Teubner, 1935), p. 50.

[77] *Vicium autem contemptus salutis et utilitatis reipublice plus in regno Francie quam in aliis mundi partibus hactenus inolevit*. Quoted ibid., p. 72.

expression *respublica* other than to denote christendom, this again shows that for him strife in any individual kingdom is bad for christendom as a whole. Conversely, pacifying even a mere individual kingdom like France is good for christendom, prompting Dubois to devise, in *De recuperatione*, a system under which it would be the duty of all christian rulers to defend each other against challenges to their authority—with no distinction being made between 'internal' and 'external' challenges. It is precisely this distinction which, evidently, did not even occur to Dubois in this context.

Conclusion

Two main arguments have been developed and analysed in this article. First, concerning the role of the empire, it should be clear by now that it was not primarily power-political. As with any other christian crown, it owed its status largely to metaphysical considerations, based in this instance on theology and the christian interpretation of history, rather than to its power. Other medieval kings generally granted to the emperor (when there was one) a kind of primacy of honour, but this was a courtesy that reflected, essentially, widely shared assumptions concerning the *theological* role of the empire. This must not be confused with any acknowledgment of suzerainty.

Henry VII's Italian expedition is a fine example of royal *auctoritas*—mirrored in Dante's reverent formulations—being operationalized to achieve political ends even in the absence of adequate material resources and coercive power. Yet despite its partial successes and the fact that it clearly caused anxious moments even to some powerful actors, it also shows the inherent fragility of this kind of strategy. Had the German crown been able, at this juncture in the evolution of the medieval world, to enhance its *potestas* in a way comparable to what was happening for example in France, then it is conceivable that it might have created a real political hegemony over christendom. But this was always unlikely. Princely power might be growing and increasingly supra-local. Yet its ability to exercise effective control over large territories should not be overrated, nor the staying power of lower-ranking actors and their means to resist centralization neglected. Medieval kings had enough on their hands trying to assert themselves *within* their realms and were in no position to try to dominate christendom as a whole.

Even when the Habsburg dynasty briefly managed, in the reign of the emperor Charles V in the sixteenth century, nominally to unite much of Europe under one ruler through a policy of dynastic marriages, it proved quite incapable of creating an effective central government for the territories subject to it. Indeed, it did not try, and likewise never even attempted to get other European kings to accept its suzerainty. Fourteenth-century defenders of the empire like Engelbert and Dante illustrate the fact that the medieval ideology of empire was backward-looking and nostalgic rather than expansionist and aggressive, and that it never called in question the existence and legitimacy of plural christian kingdoms.[78]

---

[78] Markus Fischer writes repeatedly that feudal discourse denied the legitimacy of individual kingdoms or other autonomous units within christendom ('Feudal Europe', pp. 436, 461). This is quite untrue.

Second, and conversely, the reaction of rulers like Edward II of England and Philip IV of France to the restoration of the imperial dignity by Henry VII shows that even if they were not prepared to take orders from the emperor (as Philip emphasizes) they nevertheless readily shared in a political discourse that emphasized their common christianity, and their obligation to the christian cause, above all else. Edward expresses the standard view of the period that the success of individual rulers is good for christendom as a whole. So, very emphatically, do the writings of Pierre Dubois. Dubois shows that in this period there was no perceived incompatibility between a strong desire to enhance the power of individual monarchs (enabling them to pacify their dominions) and an equally strong commitment to the christian commonwealth.

The important lesson to be derived from this is that, in the middle ages and the early modern period, the sense of belonging to a single christian society was not predicated on effective government of that society by a single person. Consequently, it was not undermined either by the predictable failure of the medieval (and post-medieval) emperors to gain, indeed even to try to gain, power over rulers outside the Holy Roman Empire in the same way that many of those rulers strengthened their power over their vassals.

Contrary to what Thomas Hobbes was to posit in the seventeenth century, society in the *ancien régime* was not seen as presupposing subjection to a 'sovereign'. Desirous to justify royal absolutism, Hobbes was to claim, in rather extremist fashion, that without subjection to a power capable of coercing them individuals would inevitably remain in the pre-social state of nature, and thus war, and that their existence would therefore be 'solitary, poor, nasty, brutish, and short'.[79] His novel concept of both government *and society* being based on a *pactum subiectionis*, by which individuals wishing to enjoy the benefits of social life had to agree to surrender their freedom to the sovereign, was at the origin of the modern conception of the state. The modern state is not just seen as exercising effective government over those within its jurisdiction, but as creating society among them. As, for Hobbes, society presupposes subjection to the sovereign, the commonwealth thus formed cannot have social ties beyond its borders. His general approach of regarding the state and society as twin phenomena and coterminous slowly gained ground in the eighteenth century and culminated in the late nineteenth-century nation state with its *sacro egoismo*.

By contrast, in the *ancien régime* rulers, even if called sovereign, were not seen as creating society. Society existed independently of rulers. It existed even if they were ineffective, or worse; indeed medieval people must often have felt that society survived not because of its lords but despite them. Because society existed independently of the power of rulers, it did not end at the borders of their dominions either. It was limited not by the boundaries of anybody's power but defined by a common culture and belief system.

Conversely, even the most powerful individuals within this society remained precisely that: individuals. Sovereignty even as redefined by Jean Bodin was vested in rulers, not in corporate entities. As individuals, those rulers remained members of a society that went beyond the borders of their jurisdiction, and they remained, were considered, and perceived themselves to be, obligated to that wider society even

---

[79] Thomas Hobbes, *Leviathan*, ch. 13.

though their primary responsibility might be to their subjects. To take just one example, the peace treaty between 'Britain' and 'France' of 1713 was actually concluded, as the text makes clear, between two individuals, king Louis of France and queen Anne of Britain; there is no suggestion of corporate entities as parties to the agreement. In the preamble of the British copy, which is in Latin, the two contractants are described as 'equally mindful of the interest of their subjects and concerned for the perpetual … tranquillity of the whole christian world [*totius christiani orbis tranquillitati prospicientes*]'. The French copy (in French) even reverses the order: '*remplis du désir de procurer … une tranquillité perpétuelle à la chrétienté, et portés par la considération de l'intérêt de leurs sujets.*'[80]

It is this which is at the heart of the 'international society' phenomenon dear to the English School in IR. Both Martin Wight and Hedley Bull have described this international society as essentially a society of 'states'.[81] But it was no such thing. In the *ancien régime*, which even in the eighteenth century remained in many ways visibly rooted in the medieval world, this larger society was not a society among 'states'. In a nutshell, the crucial difference is this: we see society as existing within states. By contrast, the *ancien régime* saw rulers as existing within society.

[80] Quoted in Osiander, *States System*, p. 112.
[81] Martin Wight, *Power Politics* (2nd edn.), ed. Hedley Bull and Carsten Holbraad (Harmondsworth, UK: Penguin, 1986), ch. 10; Hedley Bull, *The Anarchical Society: A Study of Order in World Politics* (Basingstoke, UK: Macmillan, 1977), p. 13 and passim.

The eighteenth century international system: parity or primacy?

JAMES R. SOFKA[1]

'No man profits but by the loss of others'
—Montaigne, *Essays*, I: 21

The conceptual foundations of the eighteenth century international system, long neglected in narrative diplomatic histories, are enjoying increased attention with the recent contributions of Jeremy Black, Paul Schroeder, and Michael Doyle. Nevertheless, in political science literature the period is routinely treated as an interesting— yet quickly dispatched—'prequel' to the post-1815 order which matured in the Bismarckian alignments of the late nineteenth century. Indeed, as a field of study the period has been all but ignored in the discipline of international relations.[2]

For this reason, interpretive characterizations of the period between the War of The Spanish Succession and the advent of Napoleon have not changed significantly from 1907, when Arthur Hassall concisely titled his study of *ancien régime* diplomacy *The Balance of Power*. In the intervening years Ludwig Dehio, Inis Claude, and Edward Gulick echoed the same theme: the eighteenth century system revolved, as a Copernican model, around the idea of a 'balance of power' in which no state could escape its gravity. Indeed, Paul Schroeder invokes the late eighteenth century period as an archetypical balance system directed by clearly articulated 'rules' in order to establish the pivot point for his declared conceptual 'transformation' in international relations after 1815. The interpretation Hassall provided almost a century ago was reaffirmed by Michael Doyle as late as 1997 when he proclaimed that eighteenth century Europe 'constituted as perfect a laboratory of classical balance of power politics as history is likely to afford'.[3]

For over ninety years, therefore, the assumption that the eighteenth century system was evocative of and dictated by balance of power theory has been a

[1] The author wishes to thank the Center for Governmental Studies at the University of Virginia as well as the Thomas Jefferson Memorial Foundation for their support of this research as well as the important comments and suggestions of Michael Cox, Stanley J. Michalak, and Katherine M. Martini.

[2] See, for example, Michael Doyle, *Ways of War and Peace* (New York, 1997), ch. 5; Paul Schroeder, *The Transformation of European Politics, 1763–1848* (Oxford, 1994), ch. 1; Jeremy Black, *The Rise of the European Powers 1679–1793* (London, 1990) and *British Foreign Policy in An Age of Revolutions, 1783–1793* (Cambridge, 1994), esp. ch. 11; T.C.W. Blanning, *The Origins of the French Revolutionary Wars* (London, 1986).

[3] Doyle, p. 175. M.S. Anderson offered a similar hypothesis in 1993, noting that 'the eighteenth century ... saw the balance of power more generally accepted as a guide to the conduct of states than ever before or since'. In an important qualification, however, he continues that 'Yet it was also an age

reflexive impulse in international relations literature. Indeed, the establishment of this 'truth' has served a critical intellectual purpose: *ancien régime* diplomacy is frequently invoked as a contrast and 'baseline' for surveys of later state ambitions. The 'hegemonic' campaigns of Napoleon are routinely delineated from the 'moderation' of the eighteenth century, and the French Revolution has—until recently—been invoked as a fundamental turning point in the development of the international system from an era of classical/limited war to a period of revolutionary/total war. The events of 1789–1793, therefore, are interpreted as the genesis of a 'new' or 'transformed' international system, much in the same manner as 1648 or 1945.[4] Given that the prevailing assumptions as to its workings have seldom been questioned, the eighteenth century system has served as a useful and necessary theoretical foundation against which to analyse the actions and motives of later generations of statesmen.

Yet as the superstructure of international relations theory has matured upon this axiom, and as an ever-increasing weight of 'balance' literature and historical parallels is added to it, the soundness of this foundation must be surveyed. As Black and Blanning have proved with reference to the continuity of political alignments after the French Revolution, careful scrutiny of the period reveals structural weaknesses in the traditional interpretation.[5] Constructed upon a shaky footing, balance of power interpretations of the eighteenth century have become elasticized to the point of vagueness and have been seriously corroded by recent research. Indeed, a general review of the period indicates a more disturbing pattern: instances where balance theory applies in the eighteenth century are more exceptions than norm.

Rather than attempt to rebuild a structure whose underpinnings are less than secure, it seems safer to construct a new architecture upon a different premise. An examination of the broad patterns of Great Power politics after Utrecht reveals that the major states operated according to hegemonic, rather than balance of power, objectives. While an unsteady balance of power may have been the unintended effect of eighteenth century international relations, balance of power calculations and motivations were seldom the cause of political action. The thesis of this study is that the ambition for primacy, rather than the attainment and maintenance of parity with rival states, governed the diplomatic calculations of the major powers throughout the century. There was, in fact, greater continuity between the *ancien régime* and

---

during which the whole idea was subjected to often very hostile criticism'. *The Rise of Modern Diplomacy, 1450–1919* (London, 1993), p. 176. See also his earlier and extremely perceptive 'Eighteenth Century Theories of the Balance of Power' in R.M. Hatton and M.S. Anderson (eds.), *Studies in Diplomatic History* (London, 1970). For an interesting brief counterpoint, see Black, 'The Theory of the Balance of Power in the First Half of the Eighteenth Century: A Note on Sources', *Review of International Studies*, 9 (1983), pp. 55–61. On the persistence of the balance of power interpretation in general, see Schroeder, *Transformation of European Politics*, pp. 5–11; Arthur Hassall, *The Balance of Power 1715–1789* (London, 1907); John Wolf, *The Emergence of the Great Powers, 1685–1715* (New York, 1951), ch. 3; Ludwig Dehio, *The Precarious Balance* (New York, 1962), chs. 2 and 3; Inis L. Claude, Jr., *Power and International Relations* (New York, 1962); Edward Gulick, *Europe's Classical Balance of Power* (New York, 1955).

[4] In the political science literature this pattern of creating a post-1789 'Revolutionary' or 'Napoleonic' system distinct from the preceding period began with the pioneering and influential—but not extensively researched—work of Hans J. Morgenthau, who interpreted the French Revolution as a paradigmatic shift in international relations. See *Politics Among Nations*, 3rd. edn. (New York, 1961), ch. 14.

[5] Black, *British Foreign Policy*, ch. 11; Blanning, *Origins of the French Revolutionary Wars*, conclusion.

Revolutionary order than has been assumed. The failure of various states to secure hegemony does not negate hegemonic impulses: Napoleon merely succeeded in his ambitions where his precursors did not.

The shortcomings of balance theory: the myth of a '*status quo*' in the eighteenth century

It is beyond the scope of this study to offer a thorough examination of balance of power literature, which has been ably provided elsewhere.[6] While the balance is a relatively straightforward concept in theory, its protean nature makes it difficult to isolate in practice.[7] Central to balance theory is the idea of multiple state actors possessing roughly equivalent capabilities and operating in an anarchic international system. Balance theory posits that wars are likely to be limited due to the security dilemma: a state's ambitions must be measured against the costs of pursuing them.[8] According to balance theorists, peace results because states will be deterred from hegemonic and system-disruptive campaigns by mutually reinforcing external and internal restraints. Externally, the pressure imposed by rival powers limits competition to modest goals. Internally, statesmen will ideally conform to a 'cult of restraint' and seek only 'moderate' aims in the framing of policy, thus making the system self-regulating. Ambition, in the Madisonian formulation, will be made to counteract ambition and a parity of assets will tend to yield stability, if not general peace.

To be sure, eighteenth century authors spoke glowingly about a 'balance' of power and the concept was celebrated in both philosophical and press literature.[9] Enlightenment texts routinely analogized politics to astronomy, geometry, chemistry, physics, magnetism, gravity, and other neatly compartmentalized scientific phenomena.[10] This Newtonian political logic, with its emphasis on countervailing forces of producing an 'equilibrium,' was unquestioned by 1750. Indeed, Frank Manuel noted that the 'whole vocabulary of international politics was an adaptation from the materialist philosophy and scientific language of the age'. Anderson bitingly commented—with some justice—that the 'balance' literature was so extensive and consuming in the eighteenth century that the idea was often invoked simply 'to inhibit thought'.[11]

---

[6] Most notably by Doyle, ch. 5; Gulick, *Europe's Classical Balance of Power*; Dehio, *The Precarious Balance*; Claude, *Power and International Relations*; Kenneth N. Waltz, *Theory of International Politics* (New York, 1979), ch. 6; Hedley Bull, *The Anarchical Society: A Study of Order in World Politics* (New York, 1977), ch. 5; Arnold Wolfers, 'The Balance of Power in Theory and Practice', in *Discord and Collaboration*, (Baltimore, MD, 1962). An entire issue of *The Review of International Studies* (vol. 15) was devoted to the theory and practice of the balance of power in 1989 and should be consulted.

[7] Inis Claude noted that 'the trouble with the balance of power is not that it has no meaning, but that it has too many meanings'. *Power and International Relations*, p. 13.

[8] See Doyle, ch. 3; Glenn Snyder, *Alliance Politics* (Ithaca, NY, 1997), pp. 192–9.

[9] Black has commented on this extensively: see 'The Theory of the Balance of Power'; and *British Foreign Policy in the Age of Walpole* (Edinburgh, 1985), ch. 8; *Rise of the European Powers*, pp. 157–62.

[10] See Anderson, *Rise of Modern Diplomacy*, pp. 166–70 and 'Eighteenth Century Theories of the Balance of Power'.

[11] Frank Manuel, *The Age of Reason* (Ithaca, NY, 1951), p. 114; Anderson, 'Eighteenth Century Theories', p. 185.

Certainly eighteenth century monarchs and diplomats echoed the same formulas used in descriptions of the natural world in their political writings. References to 'the balance of Europe', 'equilibrium,' and 'the natural repose of the continent' are strewn throughout the papers of Fleury, Kaunitz, Vergennes, Frederick II, and Panin, to name but a few. Virtually every important treaty signed after 1713 offered obliging references to the balance of power as a 'natural' or desired state of the international system.[12] Given this glut of writings, it is not surprising that many have assumed that balance theory carried prescriptive weight. By linking contemporary references with the absence of conspicuous hegemonic wars, many scholars have concluded that the 'balance of power' was both cause and effect in eighteenth century international relations. The relative 'moderation' of international politics, the argument goes, was created by general acceptance of the ideology of 'equilibrium'. As Enlightenment authors would put it, Nature, in both its scientific and political dimensions, imposed constraints and limits on behaviour: a state would no more rationally seek hegemony than an individual could defy the law of gravity. Through deductive logic, statesmen could use the balance model to arrive at a 'natural' policy for their state to pursue.[13]

An essential ingredient in both the theory and practice of the balance of power is the concept of the *status quo*, against which states are frequently classified as conservative system-maintainers (the norm of balance theory) or revisionists (the departure from balance theory).[14] As Waltz notes, all states will tend to support the system and its 'rules' and will rationally seek security through competitive, rather than absolute, means.[15] States that do seek to radically—and, under the theory, irrationally—alter the existing system will be deterred by countervailing powers, all of which, despite heterogeneous interests, will reject subjugation to one dominant power.

Applied to the eighteenth century this *status quo*, or commonly accepted frame of reference as to the architecture of the international system, is generally assumed to be the 1713 Treaty that ended the Wars of the Spanish Succession. Utrecht is routinely invoked as the 'breaking point' with the seventeenth century, much as nineteenth century international politics is said to begin in 1815. This *status quo*, it is assumed, lasted for fifty years, was revised after the Seven Years' War, and endured until 1792. Hence balance logic would indicate that the eighteenth century can be separated into three systems: 1713–1756; 1763–1792, and 1792–1815. Balance theorists

---

[12] See Franz A.J. Szabo, 'Prince Kaunitz and the Balance of Power', *International History Review*, 1 (1979), pp. 399–408. Frederick II's 'Political Testament' (1768) is littered with balance of power language.

[13] Indeed Black notes that 'the idea of policies "natural" to each particular state was very common in the period. Each state was believed to possess only one policy, and any alteration from it was a distortion, a perversion of sound policy wrought by corruption or incompetence, the product of misguided monarchs and evil ministers ... such a mechanistic interpretation was in accord with and essential to the concept of the balance of power. A few brave spirits dismissed the balance of power as a childish and erroneous concept, but most saw it as essential to any correct operation of the international system'. Jeremy Black, *The Collapse of the Anglo-French Alliance, 1727–1731* (New York, 1987), p. 87.

[14] Gulick, pp. 37–42 develops the status quo aspect of balance theory with particular reference to the late eighteenth century. See also Wolfers, 'The Pole of Power and the Pole of Indifference', in *Discord and Collaboration*, op. cit. on this point.

[15] See Waltz, *Theory of International Politics*, pp. 117–21; Schroeder, *Transformation of European Politics*, pp. 5–11; Doyle, pp. 161–74.

routinely invoke the Aix-la-Chapelle treaty of 1748, which ended the War of the Austrian Succession on roughly *status quo ante bellum* terms, as evidence of the balance in action, as well as the Treaty of Teschen of 1779, which resolved the Bavarian succession crisis on essentially conservative principles.

This idea of an agreed-upon *status quo* is essential if the balance of power is to be followed as a model, or set of 'rules': without it a balance system cannot endure. If all powers are revisionist, and few accept the *status quo* as legitimate, a major war is all but assured unless a new formula can be improvised. This was the case, for example, in the Locarno Pact of 1925, which refined the Western European security provisions of the Versailles Treaty. Without an accepted or recognizable *status quo* the balance of power as a temporary condition may exist by 'fortuitous' means, yet the notion of the balance as guide to state behaviour and policy calculations is virtually meaningless, and the causal linkage of balance thinking to state behaviour is greatly diminished.[16]

In my view, two essential attributes of balance of power theory were absent throughout much of the eighteenth century, and this void seriously weakens mono-causal explanations of state behaviour in balance terms. First, as the following analysis will make clear, the idea of a viable and commonly accepted *status quo* was decisively rejected by all of the major powers throughout the century. All powers were, at some time after 1713, revisionist: Britain in America, India, and the Carribean after 1739; France in America and Central Europe in the 1750s and again under Choiseul after 1770; Austria against France in 1725 and in Germany after 1748; Frederick II with Silesia in 1740 and again in Bavaria in 1778; and Catherine II consistently in Poland and in the Balkans after 1768. In these instances states rejected balance logic with its emphasis on limited objectives and instead attempted to achieve hegemonic ambitions.

Second, the self-regulating aspect of balance theory—that is, the internally and inherently understood constraints on state behaviour in relation to diplomatic ends—was lacking throughout the century. Balance logic teaches that statesmen will limit their appetites to avoid disrupting the system; hence wars will be fought for clearly limited ambitions.[17] In simple terms, powers recognize ambiguous yet commonly understood parameters in the international system over which they dare not tread for fear of provoking war. Thus, in the ideal, the balance of power sustains and enforces itself.

Again, the empirical evidence refutes this logic. Throughout the eighteenth century monarchs and statesmen displayed ingenious and ruthless attempts to dismember, depopulate, demilitarize, and destroy rivals without regard to fidelity to a doctrinal set of rules. Often this was attempted through manipulation of a dynastic crisis, as with Austria in 1740, Poland in 1733 and 1763, Sweden in 1773 and Bavaria in 1778, to name but the most conspicuous examples. Partition schemes were legion and the ambition of the complete destruction of an opponent—usually thought to begin with Napoleon—was painfully evidenced throughout the century, though such attempts usually failed in practice. France supported uprisings in Scotland against Britain in 1715 and 1745; Russia and Prussia, beginning in the late seventeenth century, contemplated dividing Poland and Sweden several times;

---

[16] See Robert Gilpin, *War and Change in World Politics* (Cambridge, 1981), ch. 1, esp. pp. 12–15.
[17] Bull, *Anarchical Society*, ch. 5.

Britain sought to annihilate France's position in North America and the Carribean after 1754; Kaunitz sought the destruction of Prussia, and not just the return of Silesia, in 1756; Catherine contemplated the evisceration of the Ottoman Empire, Poland, and for a brief period Sweden; Austria was a favourite target of Bourbon partition schemes throughout the century; Austria and Spain contemplated annexing parts of France in 1725. This is, of course, but a cursory list. Indeed, eighteenth century diplomats are better characterized as frustrated Napoleons rather than parity-seeking power 'balancers'.[18]

What prevented the attainment of these grandiose revisionist impulses was not the teachings of balance doctrine, but rather the limited resources available to most eighteenth century governments.[19] Only Britain was able to raise the resources necessary to achieve its objectives under Newcastle and Pitt during the Seven Years' War, but at prohibitive cost. Enormous debts and the tremendous expenditures of raising mercenary armies and expensive navies made sovereigns and ministers reluctant to risk these assets in extended campaigns, while the administrative and logistical support necessary to maintain prolonged combat was only slowly developed after the 1760s. France's debt after the Seven Years' War, compounded by Choiseul's frantic naval construction, highlighted the obstacles faced by *ancien régime* governments in pursuing their ambitions of primacy. With tax structures that protected the clergy and nobility and armies that fought solely for pay, governments could finance hegemonic wars only rarely, if at all. This pursuit of formidable objectives with exceedingly slim budgets yielded incessant, yet inconclusive and relatively brief, wars after 1713.[20]

To credit balance of power theory with producing this 'moderate' international system is misleading. The gulf between hegemonic objectives and military and financial means was unbridgeable throughout most of the century. Even in debt-ridden France, Turgot's cold-blooded appraisal of the dire straits of the Treasury did not deter Louis XVI and Vergennes from entering the American War in 1778.[21] Rather than view the political equation through the traditional allegory of chess, a

---

[18] Dennis Showalter sums it up admirably: 'In diplomatic contexts the eighteenth century's principled commitment to balance of power politics must not be exaggerated. Major and middle-sized powers regularly contemplated and frequently attempted significant aggrandizement ... [Yet] pragmatically, even the best of the *ancien régime's* armed forces could not hope to dominate its adversaries enough to implement the diplomat's grand designs'. *The Wars of Frederick the Great* (London, 1996), p. 3.

[19] On this point see Eric Robson, 'The Armed Forces and the Art of War', in J.O. Lindsay (ed.), *The New Cambridge Modern History*, vol. 7: *The Old Regime, 1713–1763* (Cambridge, 1957); M.S. Anderson, *Europe in the Eighteenth Century, 1713–1783*, 3rd. edn. (London, 1987), ch. 7; Showalter, ch. 1; Black, *European Warfare, 1660–1815* (New Haven, CT, 1994).

[20] On the British debt issue and its relation to international politics, see John Brewer, *The Sinews of Power: War, Money, and the English State, 1688–1783* (New York, 1989); Nancy Koehn, *The Power of Commerce: Economy and Governance in the First British Empire* (Ithaca, NY, 1994), ch. 1; Lawrence H. Gipson, *The British Empire Before the American Revolution*, vol. 9 (New York, 1965). On France, J.C. Riley's *The Seven Years' War and the Old Regime in France: The Economic and Financial Toll* (Princeton, NJ, 1986) is definitive. See also H.M. Scott, 'The Importance of Bourbon Naval Reconstruction to the Strategy of Choiseul After the Seven Years War', *International History Review* 1 (1979), pp. 17–35. On the ends/means relationship of war to political objectives, see Blanning, *Origins of the French Revolutionary Wars*, ch. 1, Black, *European Warfare*, ch. 3; Michael Howard, *War in European History* (Oxford, 1976), ch. 3.

[21] See Orville Murphy, *Charles Gravier, Comte de Vergennes: French Diplomacy in the Age of Revolution, 1719–1787* (Albany, 1982), ch. 20, and Jonathan Dull, 'France and the American Revolution Seen as Tragedy', in Ronald Hoffman and Peter Albert (eds.), *Diplomacy and Revolution: The Franco-American Alliance of 1778* (Charlottesville, VA, 1981) for a development of this argument.

more accurate metaphor would be poker: eighteenth century governments played ambitious moves without sufficient resources to cover their bets. This led to the conspicuous faith in a 'grand strategy' which could potentially stack the deck in one's favour and which were offered, in Kaunitz's phrase, as 'geometric proofs'.[22]

Contrary to the predictions of balance theory, the eighteenth century system remained a zero-sum game in which gains for one state invariably came at the significant expense of another. The 'Ricardo principle' of balance theory expressed in the law of comparative advantage—under which states would seek modest gains in a competitive system similar to that of firms in a market economy—simply did not obtain.[23] The international system was not sufficiently organized or ordered to allow for this rational actor behaviour. As one British offical noted in 1773, 'there is no real system anywhere, no grand bond of union and therefore not knowing who and who is together, every court stands upon his own bottom, and lives from hand to mouth without any great principle of policy'.[24] Rather, a drive for monopoly, with its emphasis on primacy rather than mutual vulnerability through competition, remained the dominant leitmotif. If a 'balance' did exist, as in North America from 1748–54, Germany after 1740, or Poland from 1773–95, it was usually to everyone's dissatisfaction rather than delight and occurred in spite, rather than because, of calculated policy. Throughout the century, each state desired more than the prevailing system provided.[25]

This thesis can be sustained through an overview of two mutually reinforcing axes of the eighteenth century system: the maritime struggle between France and Britain, particularly in North America, and the tripolar central European axis between Russia, Austria, and Prussia in Germany and Poland. In both spheres, the restraining influences of balance theory were overtaken by a ruthlessly predatory hegemonic policy. In most cases the means of diplomacy and warfare could not match these ends; yet, the limited gains that resulted did not radically transform intended objectives, which continued to view primacy as the Polar Star in the charting of foreign policy.

The colonial axis: the Anglo-French contest for commercial hegemony

As David Horn notes, the struggle for mastery between Britain and France was the 'single dominant idea running right through the century' after 1713. Indeed, with the exception of the 'astonishing' *entente* between the two powers from 1716–31, Britain and France were either in a state of 'cold' or real war after 1735.[26] This chronic hostility can largely be attributed to the mercantilist ideology underscoring their

---

[22] Szabo, 'Kaunitz and the Balance of Power', Anderson, *Rise of Modern Diplomacy*, p. 167. In doing so *ancien régime* governments inadvertently proved Morton Kaplan's legendary maxim that states will fight rather than forego potential gain. *System and Process in International Politics* (New York, 1962), p. 23.

[23] For a development of the market analogy to balance theory, see Gilpin, *War and Change*, ch. 3.

[24] Cited in Black, *Rise of the European Powers*, p. 207.

[25] A development which affirms Claude's perceptive conclusion that 'the balance of power works best when it is little needed'. 'The Balance of Power Revisited', *Review of International Studies,* 15 (1989), pp. 77–85, at p. 80.

[26] David B. Horn, *Great Britain and Europe in the Eighteenth Century* (Oxford, 1967), pp. 382; 44–5.

respective trade policies. This economic theory, which equated wealth with power and posited the supply of economic resources as fixed, led British and French ministers to conceive of the chief areas of colonial rivalry—North America, the Carribean islands, and India—in zero-sum terms. One British merchant expressed this logic with unusual astringency by noting that 'our trade will only improve by the total extinction of theirs'.[27]

Governed by this relentless and predatory economic orthodoxy, both British and French ministries practised overt hegemonic policies in relation to the colonial axis of the international system. The 'Balance of Trade', as Hume noted, was the 'balance of power' and under this mercantilist ethos a mere parity of resources was an insufficient guarantor of security.[28] On the continent, Britain viewed France in negative terms; that is, it sought to prevent France from allying with a third power and distracting London from its lucrative overseas trade.[29] After Walpole's ministry, successive British governments frequently expected other European states to be as Francophobic as the Board of Trade and tended to interpret European politics through the prism of respective support or opposition to France.[30] France, for its part, began seeking hegemony in Europe under Fleury and favoured alliances— particularly the Prussian entente in the 1740s—only if its partners 'were prepared to accept an international system presided over by France and in which French interests were given free rein'.[31]

The curious Anglo-French entente of 1716–31, which may be termed a 'diplomatic revolution', was the only aberration in this century of apocalyptic rhetoric and incessant hostilities between the two powers.[32] In the 1720s both London and Paris recognized the domestic political imperative of maintaining European peace, given the fragility of the Hanoverian succession in Britain after 1714, the equally uncertain succession question in Regency France, as well as mutual concerns about the direction of Spanish policy. Although Black argues that the entente could have formed a primitive collective security system for Europe, much in the fashion of the

---

[27] Cited in Walter Dorn, *Competition for Empire, 1740–1763* (New York, 1940), p. 9. On mercantilism and its relationship to international politics in this period, Eli Heckscher's *Mercantilism*, 2 vols. (London, 1935) remains standard. See also Richard Pares, *War and Trade in the West Indies, 1739–1763* (Oxford, 1936); E. Lipson, *The Economic History of England*, vol. 3: *The Age of Mercantilism* (London, 1943); Klaus Knorr, *British Colonial Theories, 1570–1850* (Toronto, 1944), chs. 3–4; Charles Andrews, *The Colonial Period of American History*, vol. 4 (New Haven, CT, 1964); Jacob Viner, 'Power Versus Plenty as Objectives of Foreign Policy in the Seventeenth and Eighteenth Century', *World Politics,* 1 (1948), pp. 1–30; Charles Cole, *Colbert and a Century of French Mercantilism* (New York, 1939), Jeremy Black, *Natural and Necessary Enemies: Anglo-French Relations in the Eighteenth Century* (London, 1986), ch. 5.

[28] David Hume, 'Of the Balance of Trade' (1752) Eugene Miller (ed.), *Essays Moral, Political, and Literary* (Indianapolis, 1987). As Dorn succinctly noted, 'power politics and economic policy became interchangeable terms'. Dorn, *Competition for Empire*, p. 9.

[29] A strategy brilliantly dissected by Pares in 'American versus Continental Warfare, 1739–1763', *English Historical Review*, 51 (1936), pp. 429–65.

[30] Pares, 'American versus Continental Warfare', p. 433.

[31] Black, *Natural and Necessary Enemies*, p. 33. See also the excellent study by Arthur Wilson, *French Foreign Policy During the Administration of Cardinal Fleury, 1726–1743* (Cambridge, MA, 1936), esp. ch. 11. He observes that, by 1740, 'So completely had Fleury isolated the British that it actually became discreet for him to challenge them in their own element. It was a policy coolly considered, and by no means foolhardy.' P. 324.

[32] Richard Lodge notes that the pact 'is quite as deserving to be called a diplomatic revolution as the Austro-French alliance of 1756, to which the term is usually applied'. 'The Anglo-French Alliance, 1716–1731', in A. Coville and H.V.W. Temperley (eds.), *Studies in Anglo-French History* (Cambridge, 1935), p. 3.

Conference System of the 1820s, the alliance never enjoyed enough support in either capital to become an institutionalized feature of the international system. Rather, the pact was a contingency of international relations rather than a norm: As Horn notes, the most amazing feature of the entente is that it lasted as long as it did.[33]

Indeed, the 1716–31 agreement proved incapable of transforming the fundamental assumptions governing both powers' approach to the international system; rather, it merely suppressed their hostile effects until the domestic political structures of both states became more secure after 1725. The axiom that trade was the lifeblood of the state, institutionalized by Colbert and Law in France and the Board of Trade in Britain, led to an increasingly acrimonious relationship between the two powers and a corresponding inability to compromise. Any gain for one side was an automatic loss for the other and security could only be obtained through the destruction of the other side's resources and assets. This tendency was particularly pronounced in North America: William Shirley, the Governor of Massachusetts, put it best in 1749 when he noted that 'I can't but look upon the point now coming on in Dispute, as what must finally determine the Mastery of this Continent between His Majesty and the French King'.[34]

French officials perceived the stakes to be equally high. Governor Vaudreuil of New France reported in 1716 that 'should a new war break out with the English ... it cannot be, for an instant, doubted but the English ... would employ all their efforts to seize the whole of Canada, and consequently the entirety of North America, whence might follow the loss of Mexico, from which they would expel the Spaniards in a few years without any resistance. ... It is impossible to express how much the power of England would increase should she seize the remainder of North America, and how formidable that power would be in Europe'.[35] This eighteenth century variant on the 'domino theory' led to entrenchment on the part of both powers: in a zero-sum system to compromise was to lose, and 'balance' was at best a temporizing measure. For this reason both Britain and France aggressively sought to prevent neutral states such as Sweden, the United Provinces, or Russia from encroaching on their established trade networks.[36]

Given the prevailing view of the international system on the part of both London and Paris it is not surprising that wars between them were so common or their objectives so vast. A 'balance', if one could even be said statistically to exist in the century, was certainly a less desirable outcome than undisputed domination of lucrative trade routes, and the latter remained the *ultima ratio* of foreign policy throughout successive ministries in both states from the 1740s to the 1780s.

---

[33] The best study of the issue is Black's *The Collapse of the Anglo-French Alliance, 1727–1731* (New York, 1987). He notes that 'the efforts in the late 1710s and early 1720s to preserve the Utrecht settlement and to prevent any major change in international relations can be seen as an important attempt to use a system of collective security to maintain peace and a given international order'. *Rise of the European Powers*, p. 163. Horn, *Great Britain and Europe*, p. 45.

[34] Shirley to the Duke of Bedford, May 10, 1749; cited in Max Savelle, *The Origins of American Diplomacy: The International History of Angloamerica, 1492–1763* (New York, 1967), p. 550. This important work should be consulted in relation to developing the thesis of 'inevitability' of conflict in Anglo-French relations after 1748. See esp. ch. 18.

[35] Vaudreuil to the Duc de Orléans, February 1716. cited in Savelle, *Origins of American Diplomacy*, p. 233.

[36] See Pares, *Colonial Blockade and Neutral Rights, 1739–1763*, (Oxford, 1938), and Isabel de Madariaga, *Britain, Russia, and the Armed Neutrality of 1780* (New Haven, CT, 1962), chs. 1–3.

Indeed, the only Anglo-French pact concluded on even remotely 'balance of power' terms—the Aix-la-Chapelle pact of 1748—proved unworkable and undesirable from the moment it was signed.[37] Reaction to the Treaty, which generally restored territories seized during the War of the Austrian Succession, was scathing in both London and Paris. The lack of consensus on a *status quo*, which the Treaty ostensibly preserved, led both French and British statesmen to castigate the agreement as worthless, and skirmishes in the Ohio Valley and Carribean began almost as soon as the ink was dry. The agreement was little more than a 'breathing space' in a period of general war, similar to the Amiens pact of 1801 during the Napoleonic Wars. Indeed, Parisian wits coined a new expression at the Treaty's expense: 'bête comme la Paix'.[38]

This drive for hegemony became most pronounced during the Seven Years' War, which began in 1754 over a dispute as to the Anglo-French border in the Ohio Valley. Pitt's energetic conduct of the war after three years of defeat, along with the ministry's willingness to greatly augment the national debt, contributed to the unprecedented magnitude of the British victory in 1763.[39] France, whose allies Austria and Russia could not win the decisive victory over Prussia that Kaunitz predicted, received little tangible support in its American campaign and large segments of its army were required to remain in Europe.[40]

Ironically Britain's gains in 1763 did not fundamentally transform the primacy-seeking security concerns synonymous with the mercantilist ideology. Its enormous debt and growing problems in the American colonies left its gains open for potential French reprisals, which were realized with the resumption of war with the Bourbons after 1778. Britain's fixation with consolidating the victory in the colonies left it exposed in Europe, with no allies and little or no influence over political dynamics in the East, especially Poland and the Balkans.[41] France, while effectively marginalized in North America, continued an aggressive policy in the Carribean during the 1778–83 war and again after 1793.[42] Given the parameters imposed by mercantilist

---

[37] In an interesting epitaph Lodge termed it 'perhaps the nearest approach in history to that "peace without victory" that President Wilson at one moment seemed to regard as the ideal ending of a war. It cannot be said that this particular peace gives much support to the President's view. The war in its erratic course had raised a number of problems, but the treaty settled none of them'. Richard Lodge, *Studies in Eighteenth Century Diplomacy, 1740–1748* (London, 1930).

[38] Basil Williams, *The Whig Supremacy, 1714–1760* (Oxford, 1939), p. 251.

[39] See Richard Middleton, *The Bells of Victory: The Pitt-Newcastle Ministry and the Conduct of the Seven Years' War, 1757–1762* (Cambridge, 1985), chs. 2–3. Much of this expense went to Berlin in the form of subsidies, thus adding some weight to Pitt's famous assertion that 'America was conquered in Germany'. See Lodge, *Great Britain and Prussia in the Eighteenth Century* (Oxford, 1923) and the important study by Carl Eldon, *England's Subsidy Policy Towards the Continent During the Seven Years' War* (Philadelphia, 1938).

[40] The cost of this struggle for primacy was enormous. Koehn notes that 'between 1689 and 1793, England fought five major wars with France. The two powers spent 36 of these 94 years in expensive combat. During the war years, the British government devoted an average of 67 per cent of its total expenditures to military purposes. If we include debt service charges, the proportion of total public outlay committed to war costs rises to between 75 and 85 per cent in each of the 36 years'. *Power of Commerce*, p. 4. On French policy in general, see Frank Brecher, *Losing a Continent: France's North American Policy, 1753–1763* (Westport, CT, 1998).

[41] For a gifted analysis of England's approach to the international system after 1763, see Scott, *British Foreign Policy in the Age of the American Revolution* (Oxford, 1990), ch. 3.

[42] See Blanning, *Origins of the French Revolutionary Wars*, ch.1; Scott, 'Bourbon Naval Reconstruction', R.E. Abarca, 'Classical Diplomacy and Bourbon *Revanche* Strategy, 1763–1770', *Review of Politics*, 32 (1970), pp. 313–37, and John F. Ramsey, *Anglo-French Relations 1763–1770: A Study of Choiseul's Foreign Policy* (Berkeley, 1939).

logic, conflict was interpreted as a routine form of statecraft and both British and French ministers throughout the century sought hegemony rather than parity, an objective that endured as long as the fundamental assumptions motivating behaviour on both sides went unchallenged.[43]

In short, balance of power theory cannot be invoked as a causal explanation of British and French colonial policy in the eighteenth century, as the zero-sum nature of the mercantilist system was in direct opposition to balance ideology. When 'balances' were contrived, such as in 1748 and again in 1783, they never endured because both powers desired to transcend a *status quo* and seek security at the expense of the other.[44] Only in the Seven Years' War was the objective of primacy briefly attained by London; however, this victory was unusual, given the dynamics of the European war which forced France to conserve resources on the continent along with atypical British willingness to float massive amounts of debt. Nevertheless, the hegemonic objectives of statecraft on the part of both governments was remarkably consistent—the 'expedient' peace of 1716–31 notwithstanding—from 1713 to 1815. Neither power viewed security as a divisible concept, and both pursued strategies aimed at the total capitulation of its rival. There was, in brief, little daylight between the fundamental strategic intentions of Pitt in America from 1757–60 and those of Napoleon in Europe from 1805–1807.

The continental axis: the contest for mastery in central and eastern Europe

On the continent similar hegemonic ambitions prevailed, and evidence of satiated powers is exceedingly sparse. Power dynamics rotated around two mutually reinforcing poles: the growth of 'dualism' in Germany between Austria and Prussia and the meteoric rise of Russia after 1763.[45] With Spain's role on the continent rapidly declining, Britain all but impotent in Central Europe after the loss of the Prussian alliance in 1762, and France vainly struggling to reassert its traditional role in Poland and the Ottoman Empire, these three powers largely determined the course of politics in Central and Eastern Europe.[46]

In Germany the seemingly impulsive Prussian invasion of Silesia in December 1740 further weakened the already fragile Holy Roman Empire and cost Maria Teresa one of the wealthiest provinces of the Habsburg Monarchy. Vienna's inability

---

[43] One British author noted in 1723 that 'France and Great Britain are as natural enemies, as old Rome and Carthage were, and the power of the former can never be increased with safety to the latter'. Cited in Black, *Natural and Necessary Enemies*, p. 99. This logic animates popular characterizations of the eighteenth century as a period of a second Hundred Years' War between the two powers.

[44] One British author noted in 1744 that 'the pretence [for war with France] is the Balance of Power. What this Balance of Power is no Parliament ever yet has explained nor one member ever yet once mentioned it in the House of Commons though it has cost the nation above 300 millions'. Cited in Black, *Rise of the European Powers*, p. 161.

[45] Anderson notes that 'the growth of Austro-Prussian antagonism, of "dualism" in Germany, was the most important development in the politics of eighteenth century Europe apart from the emergence of Russia'. *Eighteenth Century Europe*, p. 306.

[46] For a general overview of this dynamic, see Schroeder, *Transformation of European Politics*, pp. 12–52; Madariaga, *Russia in the Age of Catherine the Great*, chs. 12–15; McKay and Scott, ch. 8; Scott, *British Foreign Policy in the Age of the American Revolution*, ch. 7; Black, *Rise of the European Powers*, ch. 3; Blanning, *French Revolutionary Wars,* ch. 2.

to wrest control of Silesia by force during the ensuing War of the Austrian Succession led Austrian policy to shift towards a more anti-Prussian, rather than anti-French, direction. Kaunitz's legendary 'diplomatic revolution', by which Austria allied itself with France and later with Russia against Prussia, was designed as a means of crushing the 'upstart' Prussian state, regaining Silesia, and partititioning the Brandenburg kingdom. Austria's aims in the Seven Years' War were no less than the dismemberment of Prussia, rather than the maintenance of a 'balance' in Central Europe similar to the model of the German Confederation after 1815.[47]

Prussia's victory in the Seven Years' War, partially obtained by lucrative British subsidies and poor co-ordination by the three allies, confirmed its Great Power status but did not recreate the *status quo* of 1740. Both Austria and Prussia were drained militarily and financially by the war, yet they continued to manouevre for primacy in central Europe. In 1778 the death of the Elector of Bavaria touched off renewed war. Yet mutual reluctance to sacrifice large armies so soon after the destructive conflict of 1756–63 led to a relatively bloodless 'campaign' which ended with the Russian-mediated settlement at Teschen in 1779.[48]

While both Austria and Prussia ultimately accepted the 1779 Treaty, at least until the Napoleonic period, neither was wholly content with the arrangement. Certainly the idea of power balancing satisfied none of the chief actors involved and it clearly did not carry prescriptive weight in the charting of foreign policy, Frederick's protestations to the contrary in his Political Testament notwithstanding. Maria Teresa, Kaunitz, and Joseph II fumed over the loss of Silesia and the rapid ascendancy of Prussian power, while Frederick sought to consolidate his gains and expand upon them. Central Europe remained, therefore, in a state of cold war between Vienna and Berlin, and no constructive settlement of the German question was offered until Metternich's proposals in 1815. Any rapprochement between these powers throughout the latter half of the century was, in Frederick's own words, 'as inconceivable as an alliance between fire and water'.[49]

The German powers' struggle for primacy was compounded and augmented by the ascension of Russia after 1762 under Catherine II. With the relative weakening of Berlin and Vienna through the Seven Years' War, Russia emerged as the decisive actor on the continent in the 1760s and 1770s. Indeed, one British official noted that 'the Russians may now be considered as the arbiters of Germany, since it is evident that their conjunction with either [Austria or Prussia] must overwhelm the other'.[50]

---

[47] On Kaunitz's 'reversal of alliances' and its motives, see the brilliant analysis by Horn, 'The Diplomatic Revolution', in J.O. Lindsay (ed.), *The New Cambridge Modern History*, vol. 7: *The Old Regime, 1713–1763* (Cambridge, 1957). See also Doyle, ch. 5 and the older—yet still perceptive—study of the alliance by Richard Waddington, *Louis XV et le renversement des alliances, 1756* (Paris, 1896).

[48] A development which, as Schroeder correctly notes, 'had nothing to do with the moderate aims of the belligerents'. *Transformation of European Politics,* p. 29. On Teschen, see Madariaga, *Russia in the Age of Catherine the Great*, pp. 380–92; Scott, *British Foreign Policy*, pp. 300–4.

[49] Cited in Wolfgang Michael, 'Great Britain under William Pitt the Elder', in A.W. Ward, et al. (eds.), *The Cambridge Modern History*, vol. 6: *The Eighteenth Century* (Cambridge, 1934), p. 398.

[50] Cited in Black, *Rise of the European Powers*, p. 130. In a masterful summary Otto Hötzsch argued that Catherine's diplomacy was based on 'the consistent assertion of the strength of Russia in the interests of Russia; nor was it devoid of a Machiavellian note. Catherine never allowed her country to be taken in tow by another Power. To her, alliances and understandings were, simply and solely, means for increasing the strength of Russia with a view to securing for it the status of a really European power. And herein she was so successful, that, apart from the acquisition of territory,

With the central axis of Europe dominated by the bipolar division of Germany, Catherine embarked on a two-pronged expansionist policy in the 1760s. The 'Greek Project' aimed at securing the Crimean Peninsula and other adjacent Black Sea territory from the Ottomans and projecting Russian power to the south, and the 'Northern System' sought to neutralize Swedish or Prussian opposition to Russian trade and naval power in the Baltic. In both the Balkan and Baltic spheres, therefore, Catherinian Russia followed a careful yet deliberate policy of annexationism.[51]

Frederick's realization of Russian hegemonic ambitions in Central and Northern Europe—expressed in his famous aphorism that he feared nothing so much as Russia—led him to seek an alliance with Catherine in 1764.[52] Eager to gain Russian support for his inconclusive struggle with Austria, Frederick cultivated Catherine, even though many Russian diplomats viewed Prussia as obstructing Russian designs on Poland.[53] Frederick supported Catherine's candidate for the Polish throne in 1763–64, much to the distress of France, which had gone to war in 1733 over the succession in Warsaw.[54]

The Ottoman declaration of war against Russia in 1768 formally opened the 'Eastern Question', as it would come to be known in the next century. Catherine's victories against Turkey in 1769–70 alarmed both Austria and Prussia, both of which recognized Russian dominion of the Black Sea and Balkan regions as hostile to their interests. Frederick's 1771 proposal for the partition of Polish territory between Russia and Prussia was intended to distract Catherine from her expansionist policy in the Balkans by compensating Russia in an area susceptible to Prussian monitoring and influence.[55]

The First Partition, though rationalized in terms of classical balance of power logic, was in fact a fallback position for Catherine.[56] Unwilling to risk war in Central

---

which in itself furthered her aims, she almost attained to the position of arbitress in the affairs of central Europe. She was able to avail herself of the strong antagonism between Prussia and Austria, siding now with one and now with the other, and thus dependent on neither. In … 1778, both Powers sought her help at the same time; so that she could announce her intention to stand surely for the Consititution of Germany, thus assuming a role hitherto played by France…an indication of the change in the European status of Russia, even as compared with that reached under Peter. It was at Teschen that Catherine laid the foundation of the political influence exercised by Russia in Germany, and more importantly in Prussia, which lasted far into the nineteenth century'. 'Catherine II', in Ward (ed.), op. cit., p. 676–7. On Catherine's general policy after 1763, see Madariaga, *Russia in the Age of Catherine*, ch. 12.

[51] Madariaga, *Russia in the Age of Catherine*, chs 12–15; Schroeder, *Transformation*, pp. 20–3; Both projects appealed to different constituencies in St. Petersburg, and Catherine sought to placate both camps. See D.M. Griffiths, 'The Rise and Fall of the Northern System: Court Politics and Foreign Policy in the First Half of Catherine II's Reign', *Canadian American Slavic Studies*, 4 (1970), pp. 547–69.

[52] He wrote to his brother Prince Henry in 1769 that 'Russia is a terrible Power which in half a century will make all of Europe tremble'. Cited in Albert Sorel, *The Eastern Question in the Eighteenth Century* (New York, 1969), p. 40.

[53] Indeed Elizabeth I's Foreign Minister, Count Bestuzhev, anticipated as early as 1755 that Prussia was an obstruction in Russia's designs for Eastern Europe, similar to Sweden in the 1710s. McKay and Scott, pp. 185–6.

[54] Scott, 'Frederick II, the Ottoman Empire, and the Origins of the Russian-Prussian Alliance of April 1764', *European Studies Review*, 7 (1977), pp. 153–75; Sorel, chs. 1–2; Schroeder, *Transformation*, pp. 11–18; Herbert Kaplan, *The First Partition of Poland* (New York, 1962), pp. 20–2.

[55] Schroeder, *Transformation*, pp. 12–12. As he notes, 'partition … came about mainly as a by-product of events, a means to other ends'.

[56] Madariaga, pp. 221–5; Schroeder, *Transformation*, p. 12: 'Catherine and her advisers would have preferred to maintain Poland outwardly intact under Russian domination'.

Europe and the Balkans simultaneously, and persuaded that maintaining the Prussian alliance temporarily served Russian interests, Catherine agreed to divide a third of Polish territory with Prussia and Austria in 1772 to prevent a rupture with these powers while she continued the war against the Ottomans. Kaunitz, 'uneasingly tagging along' in the partition in order to prevent the outbreak of war, remained sceptical of Russian motives and manoeuvred to replace Prussia as Russia's German ally, a move which was consummated in the Austrian-Russian entente of 1787.[57]

The First Partition was hardly a decisive Russian triumph; indeed, Kaplan convincingly argues that Catherine ideally desired both the entirety of the Polish state in addition to considerable gains in the Balkans.[58] Again, the fundamental contradiction in ends and means became strikingly apparent in the East: Russian eagerness for primacy was checked by a reluctance to fight an Ottoman and possible German war simultaneously and by Catherine's desire to maintain Prussian co-operation until the Balkan war was concluded. The anti-Russian coup in Sweden in 1772–73 further reinforced the need for a Baltic ally.[59] The precise disposition of Polish territory, despite considerable Prussian concerns regarding Danzig, was effect rather than cause of the Partition. Frederick desired Catherine's support for a future decisive contest with Austria; Catherine, for her part, masterfully manipulated German tensions yet sought to minimize conflict in Central Europe while her armies fought for gains from the Porte.

Both French and British officials clearly perceived the hegemonic objectives of Russian policy. In 1773 French Foreign Minister D'Aiguillon proposed an Anglo-French entente reminiscent of the 1716–31 pact to restrict further Russian penetration of eastern Europe and the Balkans, a proposal at first welcomed by George III but later rejected by the ministry. Commenting on this development, a British official noted after the tripartite partition of Poland that 'one could say that these three powers are the sovereign masters of the Continent and could partition it as they wish, and I am very afraid that they already have plans to achieve this'.[60]

Russian gains in the 1780s and 1790s were considerable. Catherine's triumphant role as mediator in Germany secured a Russian claim to influence in Central Europe by 1780; the Treaty of Kutchuk-Kainairdji of 1774 had given Russia unprecedented gains in the Balkans; the Crimea was annexed in 1783; a new war with the Turks brought additional gains from 1787–91; Poland was partitioned again in a manner favourable to Russia in 1793 and 1795. By the time of her death in 1796 Catherine had secured a decisive role for St. Petersburg in Europe and achieved her objective of Russian primacy in Poland and the Black Sea. 'Who gains nothing, loses', she noted in a revealing aphorism in 1794.[61]

---

[57] Scott, *British Foreign Policy*, p. 192. On the 1787 Austro-Russian agreement, see Madariaga, *Russia in the Age of Catherine*, chs. 24–25.

[58] In a controversial conclusion, Kaplan argues that the partition was in some respects a 'failure' for Catherine given the strong Austro-Prussian pressure applied against her in Central Europe. *First Partition of Poland*, p. 189.

[59] Indeed, Anderson suggests that the Swedish coup was the only serious defeat Catherine suffered in international politics throughout her 34 year reign, a verdict that is difficult to challenge. *Eighteenth Century Europe*, p. 268.

[60] Cited in Black, *Rise of the European Powers*, p. 125. On French and British reaction to the First Partition, and to eastern developments generally, see Blanning, French Revolutionary Wars, ch. 2; Scott, *British Foreign Policy*, chs. 7–8; Black, *British Foreign Policy in an Age of Revolutions, 1783–1793* (Cambridge, 1994), chs. 2 and 4; Murphy, *Vergennes*, chs. 10–11.

[61] Cited in McKay and Scott, p. 211.

As in the colonies, the continental dimension of the eighteenth century international system was dominated by hegemonic ambitions. Balance of power logic, with its emphasis on parity and satiation, was useful only as a temporary respite at times when powers were engrossed in multiple conquests, as in the case of Russia from 1768–74. The desire to avoid conflict soon after the costly Seven Years' War led to a 'balanced' solution to Poland in 1772, yet the arrangement satisfied none of the partitioning powers and was revised twenty years later. Russia scored commanding gains through the 1774 and 1783 settlements with the Porte and its annexationist objectives were conspicuous, much to the dismay of Vergennes and Pitt by the 1780s.

In Germany, both Austria and Prussia were dissatisfied with the 1763 settlement and desired revision. Frederick sought Russian support in 1764 and Austria followed in 1787; yet, Catherine prudently saw no reason to sanction a major central European War, and preferred to focus Russian attention to the south. The rejection of bipolarity, and the mantra of one power emerging triumphant in the dualist contest for Germany, was a constant refrain in official circles in both Vienna and Berlin. Mutual suspicion about Russian motives in the Balkans and the course of French politics after 1791 provided the only point of common interest between the capitals.[62]

In brief, the eastern dynamic between 1740–1791 represented a two-tiered contest for primacy: between Austria and Prussia for Germany and Russia against the Ottomans and, at times, the German powers for mastery in the Baltic, Poland, and Balkans. The only restraint on state ambitions was the issue of cost: neither Austria nor Prussia desired a repetition of the Seven Years' War, especially with France weakened; hence, the Bavarian War was relatively brief.[63] Catherine approached foreign policy objectives sequentially and was wary of overextension: the First Partition provided less than she initially desired, but came without the cost of a two-front war. To argue, as Schroeder does, that the Central and Eastern European dynamic of the international system 'conformed to all the eighteenth century balance of power assumptions—indeed, to realist assumptions in any age' is misleading.[64] Each power was continuously seeking more than the *status quo* provided and the 'balance' in Poland in 1772 or Teschen in 1779 was more effect than cause. These arrangements were ephemeral and did not deter ministries from their ultimate objective: dominance in Central and Southeastern Europe.

Conclusions: the prescription of primacy: hegemonic impulses reviewed

Our investigation of the continental and colonial axes of the eighteenth century state system has revealed a conspicuous absence of balance of power theory in practice. Each of the five major powers pursued hegemonic policies aimed at attaining primacy at the cost of the territorial amputation, economic ruination, or in

---

[62] A development which culminated in the Pillnitz Declaration of 1791. Blanning notes, however, that 'the Austro-Prussian *rapprochement* was not an instinctive reaction to the collapse of the old regime in France', pp. 80–9.
[63] Showalter, *Wars of Frederick the Great*, pp. 341–52.
[64] Schroeder, *Transformation*, p. 19.

some cases physical eradication of rival states. That these sweeping aims were not realized in practice owed more to the constricted budgets of *ancien régime* ministries and their reliance on expensive mercenary armies. Ambition, in brief, outran power. Eighteenth century international relations represents a curious and striking imbalance of ends and means: declared objectives could not be met with existing capabilities, yet limited resources only grudgingly—and rarely—translated into reduced appetites. Hence systemic conflict was common throughout the post-1713 period and peace settlements were inherently temporary as they failed to address the underlying causes of state action: the tendency to seek predominance rather than maintain an equilibrium.

The modern attraction of balance theory as an explanatory device is certainly understandable given the 'moderate' *effects* of eighteenth century politics as well as the copious references to this 'scientific' model in Enlightenment texts. Certainly a rough balance of measurable forces existed at specific periods in the century, most notably in the mid-1730s, early 1750s, and mid-1780s, yet interpreting the international system as regulated by balance doctrine is to mistake effect for cause. International politics operated in an exceedingly competitive and unstable universe, which was frought with contingencies: any disruption, such as the death of a sovereign or minor territorial gain, could trigger a general war. If a contemporaneous philosophical or literary allegory to the state system must be offered, it would be the predatory and conquest-oriented salons of Laclos rather than the ordered and harmonious political laboratory of Holbach.

The implications of these hegemonic impulses are considerable both for interpretations of the period as well as broader themes in international relations. Conceiving of the systemic dynamics in this manner enables us to see beyond the traditional—yet artificial—division of *ancien régime* and Revolutionary foreign policy: through this lens 1789, 1792, and 1799 appear as less dramatic points of departure than frequently assumed. As Black notes in a specific reference to France, yet one capable of generalization, 'though revolutionary emotion altered much of the tone of French policy it had much less effect on its substance and thus the situation after 1792–3 was one of the pursuit by greatly expanded means of aims which were not in themselves essentially new'. The restructuring of the taxation system in France and the *levée en masse* provided Napoleon with resources that Louis XV or Vergennes could not have imagined, even though diplomatic aims remained constant. Looked at solely in terms of objectives, the shift from an '*ancien régime*' to a 'Napoleonic' international system is almost imperceptible.[65]

Therefore, the Revolution did not 'transform' the international system from a balance of power to a hegemonic model. Rather, it made the the achievement of primacy now appear possible, especially for politically, socially, economically, and militarily restructured France. Reading back into the eighteenth century antecedents of the conservative maintenance structures of the Bismarck period ignores the

---

[65] Black, *British Foreign Policy in an Age of Revolutions*, p. 542. He further argues that 'However radical the speeches made by revolutionary orators, many of the presuppositions underlying government policy were usually to a large extent traditional'. Blanning concurs with this judgment, noting that after 1792 'the old European alignments reasserted themselves in a manner that would not have seemed strange to Europe before 1756: France allied to Spain versus Great Britain and Austria plus, occasionally, Russia. The old firms were back in business again'. Blanning, *French Revolutionary Wars*, p. 207.

fundamental reality of *ancien régime* politics: a predatory struggle for dominance rather than a system composed and preserved by more or less satiated powers. As Charles Andrews put it in a succint epitaph, 'In international relations states were construed as in a condition of perpetual conflict with each other, each endeavouring to gain all it could at the expense of the rest. Whether the contest was for territory, or for markets, trade routes, staple products, negroes, gold, silver or other metals, or for such commercial advantages as would enrich one state at the expense of the others, the situation was the same—what one state gained another state lost'.[66]

This is a far cry from Bismarck's dictum that parity and alliances would yield stability or Metternich's insistence that a general war was injurious to the interests of all powers. Peace was not interpreted by responsible ministers as the natural or even desired state of international relations—as Clausewitz later noted, the best intentions of Enlightenment philosophers could not make two and two equal five in politics. The idea of a satisfied major power did not exist in the eighteenth century system and with this assumption went the rejection of conservative balance of power policies aimed at preserving or only marginally revising a *status quo*. The rapid deterioration of pledged agreements whenever deemed advantageous to a state—such as in the cases of the Austrian Pragmatic Sanction in 1740 or the Aix-la-Chapelle agreement of 1748—is evidence of the ephemerality of eighteenth century attempts at stability. Kant was more correct than he may have imagined when he remarked in 1792 that to achieve 'a permanent universal peace by means of a so-called European balance of power is a pure illusion'.[67] The desire for primacy, which seemingly offered greater security than the comparative advantage model of the balance of power, remained the motivating force of international relations on the part of all major powers throughout the eighteenth century.

---

[66] Andrews, *Colonial Period of American History*, vol. 4, p. 8.
[67] 'Theory and Practice', in Hans Reiss (ed.), *Kant's Political Writings*, 2nd. edn. (Cambridge, 1991), p. 92.

The long nineteenth century in Europe

HUDSON MEADWELL

Histories of European international politics are punctuated by turning points. Typically, these watersheds have been connected to major wars. What do such histories have to tell us about nineteenth century Europe? What, if anything, is left out in the telling? My purposes in posing these questions are, first, to suggest that these histories focus too narrowly on war and, second, to propose an alternative perspective on modern European politics.

This perspective does not dispute the importance of war in European history. Rather, it frames the phenomenon of war in a particular way. Thus, I discuss what I term 'the long nineteenth century'—a phase of European history that is initiated with the French Revolution and that ends with the military defeat of fascism. Such a perspective offers an alternative to other accounts of European history. First of all, it picks out different dates, 1789 and 1945. The analysis does not begin in 1800, a chronologically convenient turning point, or in 1815. And this phase of European history does not end in 1914, or in 1918. So war counts in this story but not in the typical way, since I treat the long nineteenth century as a protracted phase of democratization in Europe.

There are four parts to this essay. In the next section, I consider two important arguments about war and change in European society that pick out the Congress of Vienna and the Concert system as a decisive watershed in European and international politics. In the second section, I emphasize the revolutionary background to the Congress and Concert. This discussion includes an analysis of the strategic structure of revolution when democratic republicanism is introduced into a social system composed of dynastic states. In the third section, I continue the discussion of democratic republicanism and its impact in France and Europe. In the final section, I consider a different republican experiment, conducted under different conditions, and its consequences for democratic development in Europe at the end of the long nineteenth century.

War and change in European politics

A frequently invoked turning point in the nineteenth century is the Congress of Vienna. This is often also considered a watershed in a longer sequence of development that begins in 1648 with the Treaty of Westphalia. European international politics, according to the authoritative work of Paul Schroeder, was transformed in the years 1813–1815. 'A fundamental change occurred in the governing rules, norms and practices of international politics'. The rules, norms and practices of the balance of power gave way to those of 'political equilibrium'.[1] Ikenberry, as well, associates the Vienna settlement with an emergent historical pattern. 'Beginning with the 1815 settlement and increasingly after 1919 and 1945, the leading state [after major war] has resorted to institutional strategies as mechanisms to establish restraints on indiscriminate and arbitrary state power and 'lock-in' a favourable and durable post-war order'.[2] Moreover, these three moments are linked parts of a larger dynamic in both accounts; they are not independent events. To study the meaning of 1815, 1914 and 1945 is not to study a random sample of events; there is serial correlation among these dates.

Ikenberry's work in fact provides support for an assumption made by Schroeder. '[T]he history of international politics is not one of an essentially unchanging, cyclical struggle for power or of the shifting play of the balance of power, but a history of systemic institutional change—change essentially linear, moving overall in the direction of greater complexity, subtlety, and capacity for order and problem-solving'.[3] This is precisely the story told by Ikenberry about 1815, 1919, and 1945. 'Over time, post-war settlements have moved in the direction of an institutionalized order'.[4] The settlement established in 1945 was superior to the settlement of 1919, and the latter was superior to the settlement of 1815. And this assessment is consistent with the criteria proposed by Schroeder: one international system is superior to another when it more satisfactorily meets the demand for order, legitimacy and welfare.[5]

Their two stories converge. There has been progress in history; moreover the 'history of systemic institutional change' as recounted by Ikenberry is 'essentially linear'. In each iteration, beginning in 1815, there is more constitutional order than in the previous settlement. There are three ways to account for this pattern. One way is through learning. This would be consistent with the arguments of Schroeder who proposed that what happened in 1815 '... was a general recognition by the states of Europe that they could not pursue the old politics any longer and had to try something new and different. ... European statesmen, taught slowly and painfully by repeated defeats and disaster, finally and suddenly succeeded in learning how to conduct international politics differently and better'.[6]

Ikenberry, however, does not rest his work about the rebuilding of order after war on learning processes. Rather he has two other arguments. A second way to account for this pattern would be to emphasize how the composition of the states involved changed over time. Ikenberry indicates that the twentieth century settlements were truly global.[7] The 1815 settlement was more strictly a European affair. But in 1919,

---

[1] Paul Schroeder, *The Transformation of European Politics, 1763–1848* (Oxford: Clarendon Press, 1984), p. viii.

[2] G. John Ikenberry, *After Victory: Institutions, Strategic Restraint and the Rebuilding of Order After Major Wars* (Princeton, NJ: Princeton University Press, 2001), p. 4.

[3] Schroeder, *The Transformation of European Politics*, p.xiii.

[4] Ikenberry, *After Victory*, p. 19.

[5] Schroeder, *The Transformation of European Politics* , p. 803. Schroeder draws on the work of Edward Kolodziej here. See his 'The Cold War as Co-operation', in R. Kanet and E.W. Kolodziej (eds.), *The Cold War as Co-operation* (Baltimore, MD: Johns Hopkins University Press, 1991).

[6] Schroeder, *The Transformation of European Politics*, p.viii-ix. See also Jack S. Levy, 'The Theoretical Foundations of Paul W. Schroeder's International System', *International Historical Review,* 16 (1994), pp. 715–44.

[7] Ikenberry, *After Victory*. p. 8.

and even more powerfully in 1945, the European post-war settlement was influenced by the United States. The third and final way to account for this historical pattern, initiated in 1815, is a centrepiece of Ikenberry's argument. He argues that '[d]emocracies are better able to create binding institutions and establish credible restraints and commitments than non-democracies'. 'The great divide' he argues, 'was really the twentieth-century settlements—in which the major parties to the post-war settlements were democratic—and the earlier settlements, which were basically between non-democracies'.[8] So this process of linear change and progress, which begins in 1815, depended on the diffusion of democratic institutions in domestic politics. 'The rise of democratic states and new institutional strategies allowed states capacities to develop new responses to the old and recurring problem of order'.[9]

This is where Ikenberry and Schroeder part theoretical company. There are two important and related differences. First, Ikenberry takes more seriously the distribution of types of regime. In 1815, for example, although Britain was 'an emerging constitutional democracy', the other major European states were 'mostly monarchical and autocratic'.[10] This matters for the degree of constitutionalism present in the post-war order. Schroeder, on the other hand, downplays the importance of 'monarchic solidarity' in the Congress and Concert system.[11] The political equilibrium that emerged in 1815 had little to do with the domestic regimes characteristic of participants at the Congress of Vienna. Second, Schroeder is at pains 'to go beyond unit-level analysis to systemic analysis'. '[I]nternational politics does belong in history on its own terms, as an equal and autonomous element …'.[12] However, domestic democratic political cultures and institutions are unit-level properties. Thus Ikenberry's analysis is far more rooted in the unit-level.

This is also the point where problems arise for each of these arguments. The problems are curiously symmetrical. After identifying them, I will propose a solution. And I will use this solution to recast some of the central features of the long nineteenth century in Europe.

The problem for Schroeder is that the mechanism by which this transformation in international politics is accomplished in 1815 remains rather mysterious, even after we try to set our understanding of it within some theory of political learning. The problem for Ikenberry is that he does specify a mechanism, in some theoretical detail, but it still remains a mysterious historical process. A great deal in his argument about international order depends on the rise of democratic states, but he says nothing about the process of democratization in any case, or anything about the diffusion and extension of democracy. There are two stories in Ikenberry's work, one told, the other untold. The story he tells is one of order-making after war in international politics since 1815. The story he does not tell is the story of democratic development, which remains untold despite its importance to his arguments. Ikenberry's argument requires that there be democratic states after war because only these types of regimes have the qualities that conduce to constitutional international

---

[8] Ibid., pp. 75, 78.
[9] Ibid., p. 18.
[10] Ibid., p. 78.
[11] Schroeder, *The Transformation of International Politics*, pp. 801–2.
[12] Ibid., p. ix.

orders. Yet his argument also requires that democratic qualities be only weakly present in the *status quo ante* before war. Otherwise there would be no war to puzzle over, since by hypothesis democracies do not fight each other.[13] There has to be at least one non-democracy in an international subsystem for war to occur.

Moreover, neither argument can be used to correct the problems of the other. Schroeder cannot fill in the gaps left in Ikenberry's analysis because Schroeder's work is too committed to a systemic level of analysis. And Ikenberry cannot fill in the gaps in Schroeder's analysis for exactly the same reason—the two arguments are working at different levels of analysis and the two levels are watertight compartments. Schroeder is more self-conscious about this feature of his work, but much of what Ikenberry says about *international* order reduces to the patterns and consequences of domestic variables.

I believe that some of these difficulties may be resolved by considering what is distinctive about 1815, when this date is considered along with other dates that are usually considered turning points in European and international political history: 1648, 1713, 1763, 1815, 1919, 1945. All of these dates mark the end of wars, but only 1815 marks the end of a war which was closely associated with revolution. Neither Schroeder nor Ikenberry note this feature. Rather, they argue that the Congress and Concert system was distinctive because it marked a new way of doing international politics.

Much of the debate about the Congress of Vienna and the Concert system in international relations theory has focused on this question: Was it a balance of power?[14] To argue that it was is to suggest, as Gulick did in his now-dated but influential study,[15] that there was more continuity than rupture in interstate relations after the Napoleonic Wars. To argue otherwise is to see in the Congress and the Concert system new mechanisms of adjustment among states and to emphasize changes in interstate practices. Both Schroeder and Ikenberry take this point of view. But in taking this position, they have settled on an answer to a narrowly-framed question. Another question to ask is this: What was the relationship of the Congress and Concert to the French Revolution? This is a different question with correspondingly different implications for how we think about nineteenth and twentieth century European politics.

Schroeder has no choice—theoretical consistency compels him to deny that there was any causal relationship between the French Revolution and interstate war. However, theoretical consistency also has implications for the arguments of Ikenberry. As I suggested above, much of his analysis turns on a phenomenon—

---

[13] There is a massive literature on the democratic peace. See for example, Michael Doyle, 'Kant, Liberal Legacies and Foreign Affairs', *Philosophy and Public Affairs*, 12 (1983), pp. 205–35, 323–53; Bruce Russett, *Grasping the Democratic Peace: Principles for a Post-Cold War World* (Princeton, NJ: Princeton University Press, 1993); Spencer R. Weart, *Never at War: Why Democracies Will Not Fight Each Other* (New Haven, CT: Yale University Press, 1998).

[14] See for example, AHR Special Forum, 'Did the Vienna Settlement Rest on a Balance of Power?' *American Historical Review*, 92 (1992), pp. 683–735; Ian Clark, *The Hierarchy of States: Reform and Resistance in the International Order* (Cambridge and New York: Cambridge University Press, 1989), pp. 91–130; Robert Jervis, 'From Balance to Concert: A Study of International Security Cooperation', *World Politics* 38 (1985), pp. 58–79; Charles A. Kupchan and Clifford A. Kupchan, 'Concerts, Collective Security, and the Future of Europe', *International Security*, 16 (1991), pp. 114–161; Richard Elrod, 'The Concert of Europe: A Fresh Look at An International System', *World Politics*, 28 (1976), pp. 159–74.

[15] Edward Gulick, *Europe's Classic Balance of Power* (Ithaca, NY; Cornell University Press, 1955).

democratic change—that remains exogenous to his model of order-building. If one were to write the political history of democratic change in the modern world, the French Revolution would occupy a central place. If Ikenberry had in fact made explicit the story that remains untold in his work, it is not 1815 that might have loomed large, but 1789. But this could introduce into the narrative of progress something about democratic change that does not neatly fit his argument. The process of democratization and the rise of democratic states may contribute to war rather than, or as well as, contribute to constitutional order-building in international politics in the aftermath of war.[16]

In one account of order, primarily of order in a European setting, no mention is made of the French Revolution despite the attention in this account to unit-level variables and types of domestic political regimes; in another account, the causal relevance of the French Revolution is explicitly denied, primarily because of the systemic theoretical orientation of the author. In the remainder of this article, I attempt to remedy this state of affairs by arguing for the importance of the French Revolution to the nineteenth century political order in Europe.

The long nineteenth century in Europe has a coherence—a dynamic—that stems from the diffusion of political innovations associated with the French Revolution. More specifically, the pattern of war and revolution that characterizes this phase of European political history from 1789 to 1945 is associated with how these innovations were simultaneously taken up and resisted in Europe after the Revolution. Domestic revolution initiates the 'long nineteenth century'. Interstate war, and more specifically the defeat of fascism, concludes it.

Fascism substituted conquest for trade and equilibrium for growth. 'At the best this equilibrium would be achieved by an increasingly nationalistic and autarchic economy withdrawing by stages from the international economy. At its worst, as in the case of Germany, it implied the extension by conquest of that autarchy to large areas of Europe'. As Milward has argued, '[t]he economic developments in Germany after the National Socialist revolution were meaningless in the long run if confined to one country …' Fascism had to have at its heart the integration of domestic and foreign policy. 'The expression of this integral nature was the New Order, involving nothing less than a total economic and political reconstruction of Europe'.[17] The long nineteenth century thus ended as it began—with revolution and war.

This history is explicitly about the process of European-wide democratization. In general, it is a history of halting, limited, unstable and unconsolidated democratic development. The primary obstacles to democracy were endogenous to European civilization. It was not simply levels of economic development, or class structure in a narrow economic sense that was a barrier to democratic change in the long nineteenth century. Rather it was the dynastic quality of European states and the corresponding importance of aristocratic political cultures within them that made democratic innovations difficult to instantiate and reproduce over time. These qualities particularly came into play because democratic reform was closely associated with republicanism, especially after the French Revolution.

---

[16] See Edward D. Mansfield and Jack Snyder, 'Democratization and the Danger of War', *International Security*, 20 (1995), pp. 5–38.

[17] Alan S. Milward, *The New Order and the French Economy* (Oxford: Clarendon Press, 1970), quotations at pp. 21, 2, 295.

This phase of political history that begins in 1789 and ends in 1945 suggests further that democracy was not self-sustaining in Europe. The consolidation of democracy in Europe, beginning in 1945, depended on outside leadership provided by a stable, consolidated republic which had been able to develop in a geopolitical context relatively unfettered by dynastic and aristocratic resistance and by interstate rivalry.[18]

In the next section, I discuss the strategic structure of the French Revolution. This section provides an argument about the relationship between revolution and war and, more specifically, about the relationship of the Revolution and 1815, a crucial turning point for both Schroeder and Ikenberry. Furthermore, it also specifies some of the obstacles to the extension of democratic republicanism in Europe. The commitments of democratic republicans were radical and they pro-voked substantial counter-mobilization within and outside France.

Republics in modern Europe were rare and unstable forms of government until 1945. Before 1914, there were only three, Switzerland, France and Portugal.[19] By the end of 1918, there were ten new republics created by the collapse of autocratic empires. All of these republics, except Switzerland, Finland and France, failed in the inter-war period.[20] It took the military defeat of fascism to clear the way for republican consolidation. By the 1980s, of the seventeen democracies of Western Europe, only eight were monarchies (excluding mini-states such as Liechtenstein).[21]

The strategic structure of revolution

This discussion is abstract and simplified; it is a way of describing the dynamics that I consider essential to the interaction of dynastic states in an interdependent social system when confronted with a republican challenge. I assume (1) a social system composed of several territorially organized political communities, (2) each of these territorial communities is a dynastic state and (3) revolution occurs in one of these communities.[22] Revolution has these minimal features: it is a local option designed to transform a local situation of monarchical rule *via* a process of regime change and institutional redesign. The process of transition transforms subjects of a monarch into the citizens of a democratic republic.

---

[18] There is a counterfactual implied here: leaving aside the American contribution to the conduct of the war and its military outcome, would the same patterns of European political and economic reconstruction after the war have been sustained, absent American participation? On counterfactual reasoning in social science and history, see Philip E. Tetlock and Aaron Belkin (eds.), *Counterfactual Thought Experiments in World Politics* (Princeton, NJ: Princeton University Press, 1996); Niall Ferguson (ed.), *Virtual History: Alternatives and Counterfactuals* (London: Picador, 1997); Jon Elster, *Logic and Society: Contradictions and Possible Worlds* (New York: John Wiley, 1978).

[19] Vernon Bogdanor, 'European Constitutional Monarchs', in David Butler and D.L. Low (eds.), *Sovereigns and Surrogates: Constitutional Heads of State in the Commonwealth* (New York: St. Martin's Press, 1991), p. 274.

[20] Mark Mazower, *Dark Continent: Europe's Twentieth Century* (New York: Alfred K. Knopf, 1998), p. 3.

[21] Bogdanor, 'European Constitutional Monarchs', p. 21.

[22] This discussion draws on an argument presented in Hudson Meadwell, 'Lords, States and Peasant Revolts', *Social Science Information*, 29 (1994), pp. 775–9.

The revolution is local, but it has universal implications. These monarchical regimes are similar. They are all associated with dynastic states, and are organized around the courts and household economies of the ruling family. The principles used locally to challenge the political *status quo* have a wider extension. They can be used to challenge similar patterns of authority in all of the units of the subsystem.

Is the independent construction of a complete local republican society possible in such a society? Is 'republicanism in one country' feasible? In considering these questions, consider also these features of republican political culture in France and in Europe. There was nothing intrinsically 'French' about the democratic republican moment of the Revolution. Indeed, political actors in the Revolutionary conjuncture who invoked republicanism were seeking legitimating principles that stood outside French history. Moreover, the republican understanding of patriotism implied that a patriot was committed to the cause of free association, wherever it was limited by despotism. Free association would be stable only when despotism was eliminated not only locally but also universally. The stability of local republicanism in the long run depended on system-wide change.

The *status quo ante* before revolution, in other words, combines two elements. There are multiple sovereigns and they are all monarchs. Both elements are inconsistent with democratic republicanism. By separating these two dimensions, we can say that democratic republicans rejected both universal monarchy and multiple sovereignty.

Republican ideology was sensitive to the problems of local revolution. The strategic structure of this situation was systemic. The interdependent choices that were generated within it spanned all of the social system and they were not identified simply with the territorial boundaries of particular communities.

Suppose now that all of the princes in this system have devised a self-enforcing convention, such that a local revolution is explicitly recognized to be a revolution against the principle of kingship, wherever that principle is instantiated in the social system. The convention produces co-ordinated resistance among princes to the revolution. Revolution then must be more than local to be successful. It might be co-ordinated across the system—simultaneously local and universal. Or, revolution might be sequential. That is, the revolution could be secured locally and then exported or imitated. Such a sequence, however, depends on initial local success, and this is likely to be difficult given the assumption of a self-enforcing convention to respond to republican revolution wherever it occurs. Such a convention makes local republican revolution more difficult to achieve and encourages the formation of more modest goals associated with reform rather than revolution, whether this change is tactical or more or less permanent.

Suppose that this co-ordination among princes is imperfect. It does not include all of the princes, for example, or even if the alliance is universal, it is not perfectly co-ordinated. A local transition to republicanism might then be more likely to succeed because resistance to it is more likely to be purely local or only incompletely co-ordinated amongst princes.

And it does not follow that republican consolidation is assured, if a transition does occur. The new republic is still surrounded by hostile princes. They have the opportunity to co-ordinate once again, either to attempt to remove the new republic or, failing that, to resist the extension of republican principles to other parts of the social system. They can also pursue similar goals by acting unilaterally.

Princes are motivated to co-ordinate because they are vulnerable in similar ways. Their vulnerability does not arise because their rule is territorial, but because the revolutionary challenge threatens to do away with princes wherever they are located. If co-ordination is successful (and its success might be assessed by the number and importance of the princes inside the arrangements and the extent of their individual commitment), an encompassing coalition emerges. At the limit, this coalition approaches a universal alliance, constructed to defend a widespread principle and political practice   kingship and dynastic rule—against another potentially universal principle and practice—democratic republicanism.

These principles represented two different versions of cosmopolitanism. Metternich, for example, could feel at home anywhere in Europe—which he considered his fatherland[23]—only if an aristocratic way of life could be preserved across it. A democratic republican could feel at home anywhere in Europe only if Europe was democratic and republican. The important cleavages in this social system were not defined simply by territory—that is, by conflict among states—but by the differences between princes and republicans.

Clearly it is still important that this social system was stratified by territorially-ordered political communities. It is this feature that makes co-ordination among princes difficult to achieve if it is deemed socially necessary, whatever the shared interest that princes might have in resisting democratic republican transitions. And yet it is also this feature that makes co-ordinated system-wide revolution difficult.

The primary intention of the alliance introduced in the above discussion is not to eliminate or regulate war among princes but to eliminate revolution. It is not the conventions of the alliance *per se* that lower the incidence of wars among princes, but rather the fear of revolution. Peace is not incidental, but it is a by-product of the desire to avoid revolution. In this model of revolution and reaction, this desire is the primary source of those conventions that regulate relations among members.

Princes, or their delegates, constructed the European Concert. This feature was an important source of similarity among the contracting parties. The parties were not simply '... historic states that had been major actors in European diplomatic relations since at least the middle of the seventeenth century ... [and that] all had undergone a common set of historical experiences and the socializing effects of diplomacy, war and peacemaking'.[24] A principle of monarchical solidarity was put down on paper, once the occupation of France was ended, and Louis XVIII had been returned to the throne. The protocol was signed at Aix-la-Chapelle on November 15, 1818 by the Foreign Ministers of Prussia, France, Austria, Russia and Britain. 'The intimate union established among the Monarchs associated with this

---

[23] Alan Sked, ' The Metternich System, 1815–1848', in Alan Sked (ed.), *Europe's Balance of Power, 1815–1848* (New York: Barnes and Noble, 1976), p. 99; R.J.W. Evans, 'Liberalism, Nationalism and the Coming of the Revolution', in R.J.W. Evans and Hartmut Pogge von Strandmann (eds.), *The Revolutions in Europe, 1848–1849: From Reform to Reaction* (Oxford: Oxford University Press, 2000), p. 12; Axel Körner, 'Ideas and Memories of 1848 in France: Nationalism, République Universelle, and Internationalism in the Goguette between 1848 and 1890', in Axel Körner (ed.) *1848: A European Revolution?* (London: Macmillan Press, 2000), pp. 92–8.

[24] K. J. Holsti, 'Governance without Government: Polyarchy in Nineteenth-Century European International Politics', in James N. Rosenau and Otto Cziempl (eds.), *Governance Without Government: Order and Change in World Politics* (Cambridge and New York: Cambridge University Press, 1992), p. 52.

system by their principles, no less than by the interest of their Peoples, offers to Europe the most sacred token of its future tranquility'.[25]

Monarchical solidarity, which extended a weak version of the principle of dynastic legitimacy, was a 'consensus principle' at Vienna and the corresponding convention was 'if kingship was in danger anywhere, all rulers had a duty to intervene to uphold it'.[26] The prominence of this convention contributed to the 'non-reestablishment of earlier non-dynastic actors (Genoa, Venice, Poland) … it helped to prevent the destruction of another (Saxony).[27] As Osiander indicates, this was the first attempt to establish a criterion of membership in the states system of Europe.

What I have done to this point in this section is to ask the question: What social interdependencies were implied in European society by the convention of monarchical solidarity? I have been led as a consequence to consider cleavages in European society that were not territorial. The Congress and Concert system were part of a larger pattern of interaction between princes and democratic republicans in European society, a pattern that was crystallized, if not initiated, by the French Revolution. This discussion accords well with some features of Ikenberry's work. He is sensitive to the implications of regime type in general, and within the Concert system. On the other hand, it is more difficult to reconcile this discussion with the arguments of Schroeder.

His examination of the European Concert after 1815 drew six central conclusions. First, the Vienna settlement did not rest on a balance of power but rather on 'political equilibrium'. 'The international system [constituted after 1815] required and rested on political equilibrium … mutual consensus on norms and rules, respect for law and an overall balance among the various actors in terms of rights, security, status, claims, duties, and satisfactions rather than power … a balanced political order'.[28] Second, and closely related, the Vienna settlement was not a revival of the competitive eighteenth-century balance of power. 'A move away from the eighteenth-century balance of power politics to a different kind of politics was an essential element in the revolutionary transformation of European politics in 1813–1815'.[29] Third, the Concert initiated a golden age of interstate peace, markedly different than the eighteenth-century history of interstate warfare. Fourth, the break in European society came in the early 1800s. Fifth (actually an assumption that is regarded by Schroeder as confirmed by the detailed historical research), the explanation for the revolutionary break can be located at the systemic level. Schroeder argues that '… it is vital to show how systemic rules and structural limits influenced and shaped these outcomes [of international politics]'.[30] By 'system', Schroeder means 'essentially what I understand Michael Oakeshott to mean by the constituent rules of a practice or a civic association: the understandings, assumptions, learned skills, and responses,

[25] Annexe C, Déclaration des 5 cours sur les Arrangements conclus à Aix-la-Chapelle' *British and Foreign State Papers 1818–1819* (London : Ridgway, 1835), vol. 6, p. 18.
[26] Andreas Osiander, *The States System of Europe, 1640–1990* (Oxford and New York: Oxford University Press, 1994), p. 221.
[27] Ibid., p. 223.
[28] Paul W. Schroeder, 'Did the Vienna Settlement Rest on a Balance of Power?' *American Historical Review*, 57 (1992), pp. 694, 695.
[29] Ibid.
[30] Schroeder, *The Transformation of European Politics*, p. xi.

rules, norms, procedures and so on, which agents acquire and use in pursuing their individual divergent aims within the framework of a shared practice ... the practice of international politics'.[31]

Although Schroeder does not deny that the late eighteenth-century revolutions had 'profound structural effects on Europe and the world',[32] he argues, sixth, that the French Revolution had little to do with the outbreak of war that provided the final catalyst for the transformation of the international politics of Europe. 'Europe in the 1780s was not heading inexorably toward revolution, but toward war, whether or not there was revolution. Revolution was contingent, war systemic and structural'.[33] 'The French Revolution, considered as an event which occurred in 1789, was not inevitable ... [yet] during the same period, no state seriously threatened by war avoided it in the long run. The explanation is structural, not contingent'.[34]

Revolution could have been avoided, even if it was not, and for this reason, the Revolution apparently has an inferior causal status. The wars that broke apart the old world would have occurred, even if the revolution had not happened.

According to Schroeder, it was the Polish, rather than the French, Revolution that was integrally linked to international politics.[35] The Polish Revolution was more important precisely because it was not an independent event. The explanation for the Polish Revolution is structural and systemic, and thus the French Revolution is different. It was a contingent bundle of events and, as should now be clear, associated with unit-level properties and processes. Schroeder identifies contingency with unit-level properties, such that system-level constitutive rules map neatly on to non-contingent causes. In the end, however, the argument about the French Revolution appears to be that the Revolution had causes independent of the constitutive rules of the game in the international system. The Polish Revolution did not, which in turn implies that it had no independent ontological status, other than as an instantiation of the dynamics of the systemic level.

These conclusions summarize a powerful explanation of large-scale political change in Europe. This explanation is located at the systemic level of analysis. It individuates the European interstate system into two different types: the balance of power system and the Concert system of political equilibrium. Each is a 'shared practice' and, by extension, a 'civil association', but they are not constituted by the same rules of practice. And the transition from one set of shared practices to another is explained endogenously.

This implies that the causes of breakdown (and transition) were internal to the balance of power system. This implication further suggests that the balance of

---

[31] Ibid. p.xii. His arguments here might resonate with recent work on constructivism in international relations theory. On the latter see, for example, the discussions in Alexander Wendt, *Social Theory of International Politics* (New York: Cambridge University Press, 1998); Steve Smith, Ken Booth and Michael Zaleski (eds.), *International Theory: Positivism and Beyond* (Cambridge: Cambridge University Press, 1996). But the interest in Oakeshott also suggests an affinity with the 'English School' of international relations theory. See Robert Jackson, *The Global Covenant: Human Conduct in a World of States* (Oxford: Oxford University Press, 2001), pp. 37, 61, passim.

[32] *The Transformation of European Politics*, p. 51.

[33] Ibid., p. 52.

[34] Ibid., p. 51. See also H. M. Scott, 'Paul W. Schroeder's International System: The View from Vienna', *International Historical Review*, 16 (1994), pp. 661–80, and Stephen Walt, *Revolution and War* (Ithaca, NY: Cornell University Press, 1996), p. 118.

[35] *The Transformation of European Politics*, p. 74.

power system was incoherent at some level. That is, its constitutive rules were contradictory, or the balance of power system, as a system, was dynamically unstable or inefficient. Its breakdown was inevitable, or at least a major war was inevitable, and this seems to be an indicator of thoroughgoing breakdown according to Schroeder.

These ways of explaining endogenous change may collapse one into the other, as variations on a single theme. I leave that issue aside, in order to point to a problem with this kind of explanation. To invoke contradiction, instability or inefficiency is to introduce a criterion external to these practices themselves, which is used, for example, to assess inefficiency. Hence a claim of this sort—that transition from one type of system to another occurs endogenously—is potentially inconsistent, or is incompletely specified.

While Schroeder emphasizes that the Revolution and international politics were 'only tenuously linked by contingent events and developments', he does concede that there was another way in which they were 'organically connected'. The Revolution changed the nature and rules of the international game.[36] Having made this concession, however, he quickly abandoned its implications and went on to argue that the Revolution did not immediately pit France against the great monarchies of Europe. What he appeared to mean at this point was that the French Revolution did not necessarily have to pit France against these powers. That it did at a later stage in the Revolutionary process was, once again, merely a contingent outcome of a contingent event.

His overarching argument about late eighteenth and early nineteenth century Europe is largely dependent on endogenous change at the systemic level, whatever the attention to unit-level detail in the actual historical narrative. Schroeder is singleminded. He wants to relegate everything that is not systemic to an inferior explanatory role. He is intent on arguing that the balance of power system itself, and it alone, was responsible for the military contests of late eighteenth and early nineteenth century Europe. Anything that appears to have an existence independent of the balance of power system is rendered contingent and thus less important. Schroeder firmly believes that a balance of power system is bound to result in major war. Major war can be extinguished by entrenching a superior set of constitutive practices at the systemic level. He is led to argue that anything that is not thoroughly structured by these constitutive practices, whether in a balance of power system or a system of political equilibrium, can in effect be shunted off to one side in explanation.

In the end, therefore, I want to separate two parts of Schroeder's argument about the French Revolution. I agree that it was contingent in the following specific sense: 'The French Revolution … was not inevitable; it came about because reform programs designed to avoid it happened to fail'.[37] The Revolution was a classic example of a political transition that could not be controlled by those actors who initiated demands for reform. I believe I can take this argument on board without accepting the larger claims that Schroeder wants to make about the Revolution and its importance.

[36] Ibid. pp. 70–72.
[37] *The Transformation of European Politics*, p. 52.

It is ironic that the French Revolution, considered a contingent event by Schroeder, has been treated in comparative politics as a determined outcome in a larger process of structural change. Moreover, this literature brings the international system into the explanation of the Revolution, usually through the effects of war and interstate military competition on the fiscal sociology of the state. Theda Skocpol has developed these arguments the most forcefully and the most successfully.[38] Her 'nonvoluntarist structuralist perspective'[39] on the causes and processes of social revolutions, including the French Revolution, takes as a problem to be solved the gap between intentions and outcomes in the revolutionary process. The intentions of the actors were not revolutionary, but the outcome of the process of change set in motion in 1789 was a social revolution. This gap was reason for Schroeder to propose that the revolution was contingent; yet it is for Skocpol reason to argue that the French Revolution, like other great historical revolutions, was determined by structures. To explain revolution, Skocpol argued, one must focus '... simultaneously upon the institutionally determined situations and relations of groups within society and upon the interrelations of societies within world-historically developing international structures'.[40] Such an explanation is 'impersonal and nonsubjective' and superior to any 'voluntarist' account of revolution because the latter is, by implication, personal and subjective.

Her argument was both structuralist and historicist. Given the path of French history, the Revolution was inevitable. But what was inevitable: the initiation of a process of reform, or the outcomes that emerged from a complex phase of political competition? If it was the former, Skocpol cannot specify the political processes that shaped the transition. Her theory is structuralist, yet the French Revolution is an example of a political transition that could not be controlled by those actors who sought reform, and structural theories have limitations in the analysis of political transitions. To admit a gap between reformist intentions and actual outcomes, and to leave this gap unexplained, is actually to acknowledge the weakness of a structuralist theory of revolution. It is to admit that a structuralist theory can say little or nothing about the process by which a revolution unfolds. But this does not entail that a systematic account of this process cannot be developed. It simply means that such an account is not structuralist. Further, if it was the actual outcome that was determined by the path of French history, rather than the initial demand for reform, Skocpol would be hard put to explain the quite specific political behaviours, patterns and institutions that constituted the 'outcome'. A structuralist explanation of the French Revolution that sees the latter as a determined outcome thus is unlikely to be a convincing alternative to Schroeder's emphasis on the contingency of the Revolution.

Skocpol modified the earlier work of Barrington Moore by adding arguments from the work of Max Weber and Otto Hintze to Marx in constructing a theory of revolution. At about the same time as Skocpol was working, some historians of France were modifying their approaches, also by revising their dependence on Marx.

---

[38] See Theda Skocpol, *States and Social Revolution* (Cambridge and New York: Cambridge University Press, 1979); Jack Goldstone, *Revolution and Rebellion in the Early Modern World* (Berkeley and Los Angeles, CA: University of California Press, 1991); Walt, *Revolution and War*.
[39] Skocpol, *States and Social Revolution*, p. 14.
[40] Ibid., p. 18.

Furet, in particular, but also Baker, Hunt and Sewell argued that the events of the Revolution had an autonomous dynamic that could not be read off from the structural context (especially economic structures) of old regime France.[41] But they took this to be a weakness of structural theory, rather than a reason to stop where a structuralist explanation left off. The influences were diverse: de Tocqueville for Furet, cultural anthropology (and some literary theory) for Sewell, Baker and Hunt. They agreed that the Revolution was fundamentally a political and cultural process, although some drew much more on the 'new cultural history' than others. The autonomy of politics and culture during the revolutionary conjuncture—this was their way of breaking with the Marxist emphasis on the 'bourgeois revolution' in France. Skocpol modified Marx by introducing another set of structures associated with states. These historians broke with Marx by emphasizing the autonomy of elements of the 'superstructure' during periods of political reform, although their work had varying emphases. More recent investigations have continued in this vein, but without the strong commitment to culturally-informed theory. The work of Tackett, Woloch and Walt, for example, looks in detail at the politics of revolution in France.[42]

A revolutionary republican political culture did emerge in France in the 1790s. We can agree with Schroeder that this development was not an inevitable result of the attempts at reform. But should we be surprised that a republican option emerged? A central claim in the politics of republicanism was constitutional: a republican regime was superior to a monarchical regime, even a constitutionally limited monarch. In a period of challenge to a monarch, then, republican ideology might understandably become a focal point for challengers.

The republican moment of the Revolution combined a non-monarchical political principle and a legitimating ideology organized around the importance of republican virtue.[43] Its specific weight and centre of gravity was neither liberal nor nationalist. A liberal nationalist outcome of the reform process would probably have produced a constitutionally limited monarchy. The politics of republican virtue sought more—to break free of the conventions of the old regime. Republicans harked back to earlier republics in the classical world, in a sense attempting to abandon the French past in the search for a new beginning.

Republicanism implied commitments that distinguished it from liberalism. Republicans sought to define an alternative route out of old regimes that did not culminate in liberal markets and states. Liberals found it easier to accomodate themselves to constitutional monarchs and representative government, to market

---

[41] See François Furet, *Intrepreting the French Revolution*, trans. Elborg Foster (Chicago, IL: University of Chicago Press, 1981[1978]); Keith Baker, 'On the Problem of the Ideological Origins of the French Revolution', in Dominick LaCapra and Steven A. Kaplan (eds.), *European Intellectual History: Reappraisals and New Perspectives* (Ithaca, NY: Cornell University Press, 1982); Lynn Hunt, *Politics, Culture and Class in the French Revolution* (Berkeley and Los Angeles, CA: University of California Press, 1984); William H. Sewell, 'Ideologies and Social Revolutions: Reflections on the French Case', *Journal of Modern History*, 57 (1985), pp. 57–85. For Skocpol's response to Sewell, see Theda Skocpol, 'Cultural Idioms and Political Ideologies: A Rejoinder to Sewell', *Journal of Modern History*, 57 (1985), pp. 86–96.

[42] See Timothy Tackett, *Becoming a Revolutionary: The Deputies of the French National Assembly and the Emergence of a Revolutionary Culture (1789–1790)* (Princeton, NJ: Princeton University Press, 1996); Walt, *Revolution and War;* Isser Woloch, *The New Regime: Transformations of the French Civic Order, 1789–1820s* (New York: W.W. Norton, 1994).

[43] The next four paragraphs draw on Hudson Meadwell, 'Republics, Nations and Transitions to Modernity', *Nations and Nationalism* 5 (1999), pp. 19–51.

economies, and to modern states in an anarchical international society, and thus to specialized professional armies. Republicans opposed absolutist monarchy and, often, constitutional monarchs. In juxtaposing virtue and commerce, they opposed or were ambivalent about market relations, commercial society and capitalism. Republicans also harboured reservations about the institutions of representative government. They opposed standing armies and favoured citizen-militias.

Holsti remarks that Jacobinism is merely a pejorative label used by conservatives to describe liberals.[44] Democratic republicans, however, rejected the political commitment that was characteristic of European liberals: constitutional monarchy. Liberals also tended to favour limited political participation, much more so than the extensions to the suffrage supported by democratic republicans. Liberals, moreover, were less concerned with replacing organized religion with a civil religion. Republicanism, especially in Catholic societies that escaped the liberalizing effects of the Reformation, provided a way to challenge the Catholic Church and republicans in these societies often wanted to implement a civil religion. Liberals, as well, could consistently be nationalist. The political concept of the 'nation' was compatible with a restored relationship between a constitutionally-limited monarch and the body politic. Republicanism, however, was more radical than this liberal nationalist position, which used the notion of the nation to legitimate liberal limitations on monarchs. Republicans rejected foreign rule and valued self-government. Yet republican patriots denied that they were nationalists and associated nationalism with the politics of dynastic states.

Finally, republicanism also enlarged the range of options that nineteenth century radical democrats and socialists could draw upon. Their ambivalence toward representative institutions, their hostility toward market society, their attitudes toward militarism and standing armies, drew on republican ideology. The basic Marxist distinction between exchange and use value, which was central in much of radical political economy, drew on republican political economy. Not all of these republican influences were filtered through the French Revolution. However, French democratic republicanism, one of the first manifestations of a truly active communist party according to Marx, packaged together seminal ideas and organizational models. The Decembrists, for example, introduced the political principles of republicanism and a Jacobin model of organization to the intelligentsia of the Russian empire. This emergent dissident stream was joined to Marxism later in the century.

The domestication of republicanism in France

The French revolution left an enduring legacy in French politics: political competition around the principles of the republic. This competition influenced French politics in important ways from the onset of the counter-revolution up to the formation of the Fifth Republic. This competition helps to account for the combination of regime instability and territorial consolidation that was characteristic of political modernization in France. War continued to shape the relationship of nation

---

[44] Holsti, 'Governance Without Government', p. 38.

and republic. Military defeat in 1870 weakened the Right and opened the door to republican political consolidation to an important degree and this consolidation, following on the Commune, separated republicanism from revolution. Yet it still nurtured, in reaction, an integral nationalism that drove a wedge between the republic and the nation.[45]

Eugen Weber has provided an influential description of the process of political modernization in France, aptly captured in the phrase 'peasants into Frenchmen'. Military defeat in 1870, he argued, produced a 'new nationalism'[46] and its domestic success, he argued, could be measured by the mobilization in 1914. His arguments have a specific time frame bounded by military conflict in 1870 and 1914. Weber appears to document another instance of how nationalism trumped all other forms of solidarity in the outbreak of the War. Weber also appears to confirm the central importance of war in shaping domestic politics. This new nationalism was caused by military defeat and contributed to domestic solidarity. Thus Weber appears to fit nicely within the conventional explanation of the centrality of interstate war in European political development.

However, the late nineteen-thirties and the early forties provide evidence that the 'new nationalism' was not a complete success. Extending the time line forward from 1914 leads to the divisions over the armistice with Germany, to Vichy, and the 'fraticide' of the resistance.[47] This new nationalism had not fully settled the issue of republicanism. It was not caused simply by military defeat. It was a response as well to the most important challenge to dynastic principles within France. The domestic enemy of the new nationalists was republicanism, which had sapped France of its military spirit. The new nationalism was related to the enduring importance of the republican question and the regime transition to non-revolutionary, parliamentary republicanism in the Third Republic.

Weber analysed rural modernization as a process structured politically around the nation, as his notable phrase suggested. Yet it is a striking feature of Weber's argument that the last phase of rural modernization coincided with the beginnings

[45] Zeev Sternhell in fact argues that the origins of fascist ideology are French. See, for example, his book *La droite révolutionnaire. Les origins francaises du fascisme, 1885–1914* (Paris: Éditions du Seuil, 1978), and the discussion in Michel Winock, *Nationalism, Anti-Semitism and Fascism in France*, trans. Jane Marie Todd (Stanford, CA: Stanford University Press, 1998), pp. 195–205. Paxton extends the arguments of Sternhell by proposing that 'fascisms take their first steps in reaction to claimed failings of democracy'; thus, 'it is not surprising that they should appear first in the most precocious democracies, the United States and France'. According to Paxton, the functional equivalent of fascism in America was the emergence of the Klu Klux Klan in the South after the Civil War. But he also argues that it is not necessarily the first fascisms that take political root and become 'parties capable of acting decisively on the political stage'. In his comparative analysis of fascism in Europe, Linz notes the much stronger commitment to royalism in French proto-fascism, while 'other fascist movements were in principle republican, even when they, like Mussolini, ended in accepting the monarchy'. See Robert O. Paxton, 'The Five Stages of Fascism', *Journal of Modern History*, 70 (1998), pp. 12–13, and Juan J. Linz, 'Some Notes Toward a Comparative Study of Fascism in Sociological Historical Perspective', in Walter Laqueur (ed.), *Fascism: A Reader's Guide* (Berkeley and Los Angeles, CA: University of California Press, 1978), p. 106.

[46] Eugen Weber, 'The Nationalist Revival before 1914' [1958] in Eugen Weber, *My France: Politics, Culture, Myth* (Cambridge, MA: Harvard University Press. 1991); idem, *Peasants into Frenchmen* (Stanford, CA: Stanford University Press, 1976).

[47] Douglas Johnson, 'The making of the French nation', in Mikuláš Teich and Roy Porter (eds.), *The National Question in Europe in Historical Context* (Cambridge and London: Cambridge University Press, 1993), pp. 53–6. See also Marc Bloch, 'Pourquoi je suis républicain' [1943], in Marc Bloch, *La étrange défaite* (Paris : Armand Colin, 1957).

of republican government in the late 1870s. When peasants became Frenchmen, the mould was republican as well as national.[48] In regions where monarchists and intransigent Catholics could resist republican penetration, it was unlikely that socialists could do better than republicans. There were few conversions from monarchism to socialism. Socialists had to pass through republicanism first. For the same reason, where republicanism had not penetrated, efforts of the left would be directed at consolidating the Republic, rather than at undermining it through political attack. Although the political expression of class was shaped by republicanism, it does not follow that republican political cleavages were a result of political manipulation by economic classes. This would reduce the constitutional question to the class question.

Republicanism no longer carried the threat of civil war or revolution, but parliamentary republicans in the Third Republic built their networks in the provinces through excluding those who were considered their opponents.[49] This practice continued to politicize the issue of political regime. Republicans used regime resources and manipulated state institutions in order to maximize republican support and minimize counter-mobilization by anti-republicans. The consolidation of republicanism during the Third Republic depended on the politics of patronage, in contrast to the ascetic ideals of the republican moment of the revolution. This change illustrates both the routinization of republican charisma, and the domestic divisions that it continued to produce.

This process of moderation had occurred progressively over the course of the nineteenth century. In terms of diplomatic practice in the 1790s, '[e]ven as they struggled against it, the revolutionaries found themselves enmeshed in the old system… the new diplomacy increasingly resembled the old as the revolutionaries found themselves making compromises with the demands and practices of the old diplomacy'.[50] In 1848, Lamartine reassured Europe that the proclamation of the Second Republic did not mean war. 'Reassure yourselves if in error you take the Republic of 1848 for the Republic of 1792! We are not a revolutionary anachronism, we are not going against the stream of civilization'.[51] By 1871, no such reassurance

---

[48] 'Relatively secure in their urban political base in the early 1870s, the republicans knew that their ultimate victory depended critically on the extension of their support in the countryside'. Sudir Hazareesingh, 'The *Société d'Instruction républicaine* and the propagation of civic republicanism in provincial and rural France', *Journal of Modern History*, 71 (1999), pp. 271–307. See also Hudson Meadwell, 'The Politics of Language: Republican Values and Breton Identity', *Archives européennes de sociologie*, 31 (1990), pp. 263–85; idem, 'The Catholic Church and the Breton language in the Third Republic', *French History*, 5 (Fall, 1991), pp. 325–44, idem, 'A Rational Choice Approach to Political Regionalism', *Comparative Politics*, 23 (1991), pp. 401–23.

[49] On republican political culture and institutions, see Claude Nicolet, *La république en France* (Paris : Gallimard, 1992); François Furet and Mona Ozouf (eds.), *Le siècle de l'avènement républicain* (Paris : Gallimard, 1993); Serge Berstein and Odile Rudile (eds.), *Le modèle républicaine* (Paris: Presses Universitaires de France, 1992); Odile Rudelle, *La république absolue : Aux origines de l'instabilité constitutionelle de la France républicaine* (Paris : Publications de la Sorbonne, 1986).

[50] Linda Frey and Marsha Frey, '"The reign of the charlatans is over": The French Revolutionary Attack on Diplomatic Practice', *Journal of Modern History*, 65 (1993), pp. 740, 741. See also T.C.W. Blanning, *The Origins of the French Revolutionary Wars* (London: Longman, 1983) and Walt, *Revolution and War*.

[51] Quoted in Lawrence Jennings, *France and Europe in 1848: A Study of French Foreign Affairs in Time of Crisis* (Oxford: Oxford University Press, 1973), pp. 10–11. Breuilly notes that this reassurance implied uncertainty within Europe about French intentions. See John Breuilly, '1848: Connected or Comparable Revolutions', in Axel Körner (ed.), *1848–A European Revolution?* , p. 33. On the effects of uncertainty about intentions on the likelihood of war after revolution, see Walt, *Revolution and War*.

was necessary, whatever the domestic rhetoric about *revanche*.[52]

In terms of domestic political competition, republicans gradually gave up the instrument of violent revolution. Revolution had led in the 1790s to foreign invasion. Revolution in 1848 yielded a coup in 1851. After the Bonapartist coup in particular, republicans began to abandon the dream of a radically new beginning.[53] The final acknowledgement of the reality of republicanism in one country evidently went hand in hand with a new political strategy in domestic partisan politics.

Still, the routinization of republican charisma is not the same as its complete effacement. Cleavages around the republican question distinguished France from the quintessential liberal case—Britain. Changes that could be linked to liberal innovation in France—the expansion of democracy, the separation of church and state, the reform of the military[54]—were closely associated with republicanism. Liberals had far greater reservations about democratic expansion in the nineteenth century, particularly universal (male) suffrage, than did republicans.[55] The separation of church and state was also republican; it was explicitly linked by Emile Combes, in the government of republican defence, to the substitution of a republican civil religion for Catholicism. Republicans, finally, opposed standing armies, militarism and too powerful military elites[56] although their reforms to the military were not very deep.

Republicanism in France was domesticated over the course of the nineteenth century, but it was still exceptional within Europe. '[D]emocratic movements', Nord has argued, 'had a hard time of it in mid-nineteenth century Europe. There was one exception to this rule, and it was France which became the first of the great powers to adopt a democratic constitution'. 'Gambetta and Ferry ... rubbed shoulders with the like of Garibaldi and Virchow', yet outside of France, he argues, 'the democratizing thrusts were blunted or absorbed'.[57]

In effect, the French case suggests that there was another way to escape fascism, other than liberal democracy.[58] To speculate to some degree by considering the implications of this statement, fascism on the European continent might be accounted for, not by the absence of liberal democratic political institutions or culture, but by the failure of republican consolidation. Where republicanism failed to be consolidated, there was political contestation around the republican question and it contributed to fascist revolution; where republicanism was consolidated, there

---

[52] Bertrand Joly, 'La France et la revanche (1871–1914)', *Revue d'histoire moderne et contemporaine*, 46 (1999), pp. 325–47.

[53] Francois Furet, *La gauche et la révolution au milieu du XIX siècle : Edgar Quinet et la question du Jacobinisme, 1865–1870* (Paris, 1986).

[54] See Ronald Rogowski, *Commerce and Coalitions. How Trade Affects Domestic Political Alignments* (Princeton, NJ: Princeton University Press, 1989), pp. 34–8.

[55] Raymond Huard, *Le suffrage universel en France, 1848–1946* (Paris: Flammarion, 1990); Pierre Rosanvallon, 'La république du suffrage universel', in François Furet and Mona Ozouf (eds.), *Le siècle de l'avènement républicain*.

[56] Pierre Birnbaum (ed.), *La France de l'affaire Dreyfus* (Paris : Gallimard, 1994).

[57] Philip Nord, *The Republican Moment : Struggles for Democracy in Nineteenth-century France* (Princeton, NJ: Princeton University Press, 1995), p. 250.

[58] On social democracy and consociational democracy as other alternatives in inter-war Europe, see Gregory Luebbert, *Liberalism, Fascism or Social Democracy: Social Classes and the Political Origins of Regimes* (New York: Cambridge University Press, 1991) and Arend Lijphart, *The Politics of Accommodation: Pluralism and Democracy in the Netherlands* (Berkeley and Los Angeles, CA: University of California Press, 1968).

may have been contestation and conflict, but not enough to contribute to fascist revolution. The republican route to modernity was a dangerous political route because if republicanism failed, the door was open for a different form of popular political integration—that is, fascism.

The problem of popular integration within republican institutions took on particular importance within Catholic societies, or societies with substantial Catholic populations. For in these circumstances, the issue was how to integrate Catholics. These were societies that had escaped the Reformation or had rolled back Protestant advances during the Counter-Reformation. In Catholic societies, republicanism became a way of attacking the social and political position of the Catholic Church. It was a substitute for Protestant and liberal challenges to Catholicism. Where the latter challenges were successful, the resulting political regime tended to be monarchical, although with constitutional limitations on the monarch. In Catholic societies, the politics of republicanism was not only anti-monarchical, but also drew on a tradition of hostility to the Church. This made the popular integration of Catholics within republican institutions and culture difficult. Even in France, where republicanism was more consolidated, there were limits to the integration of Catholics. 'Most Catholics welcomed the end of the Third Republic and the sweeping away of a political class for whom anticlericalism had been an article of faith, and identified with the declared intention of the regime to organize a 'National Revolution' which would be based largely on a return to Christian moral values'.[59]

Varieties of fascism not only crowded out republicanism on the continent, but also the most important political vehicle for the popular integration of Catholics— Christian democracy. However, when republics were constituted in Italy and renewed in France and Germany after the military defeat of fascism, it was with the support of modernizing political coalitions that gave a central place to Christian democrats.[60] The importance of Christian democratic parties in post-war settlements,[61] an importance encouraged by the occupying powers especially the Americans, helped to reassure Catholics about their prospects under republican constitutions. This contributed to republican consolidation in all of these cases, but this consolidation was possible only after fascism was no longer a viable option in European politics.

One other transition to a republican constitution in this same time period in Europe can be remarked upon. In 1948, a coalition government led by Fine Gael implemented a republican constitution, gave up Ireland's Dominion status within the imperial constitution, and led Ireland out of the British Commonwealth. This completed a lengthy political transition that, in an earlier phase, had culminated in the formation of the Irish Free State in 1922. Catholic Ireland had never been fully politically integrated into the liberal and Protestant framework of imperial Britain.

---

[59] James F. Macmillan, 'France', in Tom Buchanan and Martin Conway (eds.), *Political Catholicism in Europe, 1918–1965* (Oxford: Clarendon Press, 1996), p. 55.

[60] Noel D. Cary, *The Path to Christian Democracy: German Catholics and the Party System from Windthorst to Adenauer* (Cambridge, MA: Harvard University Press, 1996); Jean-Claude Debreil, *Centrisme et Démocratie-chrétienne en France. Le Parti Démocrate populaire des origines au MRP* (Paris : Publications de la Sorbonne, 1990); John Pollard, 'Italy', in Buchanan and Conway (eds.), *Political Catholicism in Europe*; Robert Leonardi and Douglas A. Wertman, *Italian Christian Democracy: The Politics of Dominance* (New York: St. Martin's Press, 1989), pp. 47–60.

[61] Charles Maier, 'The two postwar eras and conditions for stability in twentieth century western Europe', *American Historical Review* 86 (1981), p. 332.

This was a Catholic population that could not find a political home within a constitutional monarchy. The Anglo-Irish Agreement of 1921 demonstrated the hostility of the British imperial government to republicanism, as well as to full-scale Irish independence. A republican constitution was out of the question if Ireland was to remain within the Commonwealth. Republicanism was strictly incompatible with empire. The reaction of the new political elite in the South of Ireland to the terms of the 1921 agreement also demonstrated the symbolic importance of the republic within Ireland. It was the issue of imperial association and the oath of allegiance to the monarch, more than the issue of Irish unity, which provoked the factional infighting that resulted in a brief period of civil war. Britain maintained its imperial identity by denying that a republic could be a part of the empire in 1921; Ireland confirmed its distinctiveness in 1948 by becoming an independent republic. Catholics chose a republic.

Philip Nord notes the exceptionalism of the Third Republic in Europe. Indeed, in his emphasis on French exceptionalism in Europe, Nord provides support for my earlier argument that democratic change in Europe in the long nineteenth century was limited, and unstable. Yet in acknowledging the weaknesses of the French Third Republic, he also notes the existence of another unnamed republic. 'Sister republics exist that have their own paranoid style, their own marginalized populations, their own elites none too respectful of democratic procedure. And if such republics have survived the hard blows of twentieth century history, it may be—happily for them—that their democratic mettle has not been put to the ultimate test, the heavy bludgeoning of total defeat in war'.[62] When recognizing the imperfections of republican France, he notes also that '… it is easy to think of at least one democratic culture, riven with globalist, moralizing, and racist impulses, that has survived and even prospered'.[63]

He is referring, of course, to the United States and, in a backhanded way, to the contributions that the United States made to European political and economic reconstruction. This discussion of the long nineteenth century in Europe is not complete without attention to this 'sister republic'.[64] I turn therefore to my earlier argument that democracy was not self-sustaining in Europe and to the argument that consolidation depended on outside leadership provided by a stable, consolidated republic which had been able to develop in a geopolitical context relatively un-fettered by dynastic and aristocratic resistance and by interstate rivalry.

I do not examine the American role in Europe in 1945;[65] rather, I look at some features of the republican regime that evolved in America, without which it would be difficult to imagine why and how the United States was in a position to support democratic change in Europe in 1945.[66]

They key moment in the evolving relationship between Europe and America was the emergence of Wilsonian internationalism. When the Americans entered World War I, Wilson sought to construct a foreign policy that would not be based on the

---

[62] Nord, *The Republican Moment*, p. 249.

[63] Ibid., p. 246.

[64] Nord's reference is to Patrice Higonnet, *Sister Republics: The Origins of French and American Republicanism* (Cambridge, MA: Harvard University Press, 1988).

[65] There is an excellent analysis in Ikenberry, *After Victory*, pp. 163–214.

[66] The next three paragraphs draw on Hudson Meadwell, 'States, Secession and International Society', *Review of International Studies*, 25 (1999), pp. 375–6.

tradition of *realpolitik*, and that would express the exceptionalism of America. 'The history of the United States', he wrote, 'is modern history in broad and open analysis, stripped of a thousand elements which, upon the European stage, confuse the eye and lead the judgement astray'.[67] If in 1897, Wilson had commented that the nation was 'unfinished, unharmonized, waiting still to have its parts adjusted',[68] he wrote four years later that '[a] nation hitherto wholly devoted to domestic develop-ment now finds its first task roughly finished and turns about to look curiously into the tasks of the great world at large, seeking its special part and place of power'.[69]

In questioning the balance of power, and its presupposition of interstate anarchy and self-help, Wilson used the principle of self-determination to support the position that interstate war was associated with the distribution of types of domestic political regimes. His liberalism was closely tied to the belief that American power had a special character. As carried forward by Wilson, the principle of national self-determination had its origins in American political culture—through a reworking of the tradition of states-rights, a tradition that had some roots in Wilson's Virginia background. Wilson had conceded that the commonwealths of 1774 were states, and states they remained after they entered the union of 1789.[70] He further allowed that '... the right of secession may have existed (theoretically) at the first' [that is, 'the first years of the century']. But, he further argued, the right of secession 'did not exist at the time the South sought to exercise it'. This right had 'ceased to exist by reason of the growth of national sentiment'.[71] The principle for which the South fought was retrograde, and 'protected a belated order of society'. The victory of the North freed the American nation from internal contradictions,[72] and preserved the territorial integrity of the American Union. The secession of the South could not, in this view, be justified by a principle of national self-determination. The refusal of the national government to accept the withdrawal of the South, and the decision to protect the integrity of the Union, were quite consistent with a principle of national self-determination. Self-determination established internal sovereignty. National self-determination in America thus was associated with the extension and consolidation of liberal republicanism. There was no contradiction in nineteenth century America between national self-determination and territorial integrity. Territorial integrity and self-determination were separated, and potentially in conflict, outside America—particularly in the old world because of the continuing importance of imperial and monarchical rule within it.

Wilson may have failed at Versailles but he stands behind Roosevelt's Four Freedoms speech of 1941 and the Atlantic Charter of the same year. And behind Wilson stands one hundred-odd years of republican hegemony. America was unusual because its ideology of nationhood was republican. The same could not be said for the states of Europe where anti-republicans could always invoke a national past against republicans. It was not true of Spanish America, where republicanism

---

[67] Woodrow Wilson, 'The Significance of American History' [1901], *Papers of Woodrow Wilson* (Princeton, NJ: Princeton University Press, 1966), vol. 12, p. 180.
[68] Wilson, 'The Making of the Nation', *Atlantic Monthly*, LXXX (1897), p. 10.
[69] Wilson, 'The Significance of American History', p. 184.
[70] Wilson, 'A Review of *A System of Political Science and Constitutional Law*', *Atlantic Monthly*, LXVII (1891), p. 698.
[71] Letter to William Henry Bartlett [draft], 3 May, 1893. *Papers*, vol. 8, p. 206.
[72] Woodrow Wilson, 'State Rights', *Cambridge Modern History* (London, Macmillan, 1903), p. 442.

was quickly and thoroughly challenged. Even as America made the transition from a federal union to a federal state, liberal republicanism continued to inform America's sense of its distinctiveness and its place in the world. Some legacies die hard, even in a world of sovereign states.

Republicanism in America

This discussion of republicanism in America provides some support for my earlier claims about the strategic structure of republicanism in a monarchical world. There has been republican continuity in America since the Founding and the geopolitical context in America was dramatically different to that in Europe. The differences shaped the strategic structure of republicanism and contributed to its hegemony in America.

No movement challenged the emerging American regime by drawing on a monarchist alternative, unlike post-Revolutionary Europe, where divisions between republicans and monarchists very much influenced political competition. The most aristocratic faction in American politics—the planter elite of South Carolina—in fact attempted to hoist fellow Americans by their republican commitments.[73]

In this light, the assertion that republicanism was the ideology of American nationhood[74] does not seem remarkable. And it would further suggest that the polemical charges of monarchy and aristocracy deployed in political debate in the Founding period carried primarily symbolic weight.[75] Jefferson's quarrel with Hamilton was not an opposition between republican virtue and monarchical ambition but, rather, a debate between different virtues[76] inflected against a background of shared political convictions. 'Instead of repression and revenge, ideological passions in the US found an outlet in polemics and party organization'.[77] This remark points to a useful contrast between Europe and America in the wake of revolution, which might help to place in sharper relief the unusual situation of republicanism in America.

In America, the protracted European war slowly transformed elite attitudes about the source of foreign threats. In the early years of his administration, Jefferson had treated England as the 'contemporary culprit and historic enemy'.[78] He attributed the lingering crisis in Anglo-American affairs to the unfinished business of the

---

[73] See Mark D. Kaplanoff, 'Charles Pinckney and the American Republican Tradition', in Michael O'Brien and David Moltke-Hansen (eds.), *Intellectual Life in Ante-Bellum Charleston* (Knoxville, TN: University of Tennessee Press, 1986); Lacy K. Ford, *Origins of Southern Radicalism: The South Carolina Upcountry, 1800–1860* (New York: Oxford University Press, 1988).On the relationship between political radicalism in the *ante-bellum* South and republican political thought, see also Eric H. Walther, *The Fire-Eaters* (Baton Rouge, LA and London: Louisiana State University Press, 1992), particularly the Conclusion.

[74] Burton Spivak, *Jefferson's English Crisis: Commerce, Embargo and the Republican Revolution* (Charlottesville, VA: University Press of Virginia, 1979), p. ix.

[75] Joyce Appleby, *Capitalism and A New Social Order: The Republican Vision of The 1790s* (New York: New York University Press, 1984), p. 75.

[76] Kurt Walling, *Republican Empire: Alexander Hamilton On War and Free Government* (Lawrence, KS: University Press of Kansas, 2000), p. 10ff.

[77] Appelby, *Capitalism and A New Social Order*, p. 6.

[78] Spivak, *Jefferson's English Crisis*, p. 103.

American Revolution.[79] But by late 1807, Jefferson increasingly feared all of Europe. And as the European war ended, American policymakers continued to believe 'that Europe's absolutist regimes viewed the United States as a standing challenge to legitimate rule and monarchical government'.[80] 'The Royalists everywhere detest and despise us as republicans' wrote John Adams in 1816. 'Our government', Monroe wrote in 1815, 'makes all the govts. of Europe our enemies'.[81]

These were real fears, but at the same time, since the 1780s policymakers had recognized that the two 'neighborhoods'—Europe and America—were very different. Republican America simply was not in the same strategic situation as republican France. These differences, which tended to be elided in these American reactions after the Congress of Vienna, were the very reasons for optimism in America about the future of republicanism.

From the American point of view, there were no sovereign competitors in America to the project of republicanism. This was a condition, moreover, which had to be maintained in order to ensure the success of the republican experiment. Multiple sovereignty implied competition among technologically comparable societies; this in turn implied standing armies and national debts to support soldiers in the field, and such a society of states implied balance of power politics and a situation of permanent insecurity. The goals of the American Revolution, it was feared, would be difficult to preserve under such conditions. It was essential then, as Lewis argues, to pursue federal union. 'Unless a single union included all of the states, separate sovereignties would interact in some form of a balance of power system'.[82] This union was imagined by some, particularly Jefferson, as a 'republican empire, an empire without a powerful metropolis or an aristocratic ruling class'.[83]

The American union was something more than an anarchy, and it was more centralized than the European Concert. A concert offers no permanent solution to the security dilemmas associated with interstate anarchy, and the European Concert was not a stepping-off point for political union. The Concert decayed with time and its decay reinforced the interstate system of European society.[84] Since the American union was already more than a concert, however, its transition path was more likely to be toward deeper political integration. The federal union internalized political conflict, unlike the European Concert. While interstate conflict and war threatened the European concert, it was the possibility of secession that threatened the American union.

The hegemonic power of republicanism was actually confirmed in the Civil War. The South Carolina elite argued that their institutions and practices represented a truer form of republicanism than the institutions and practices of the North. Slavery was essential in a true republic, they argued, thus confirming the power of republicanism as a legitimating ideology in America. They sought to exploit the

---

[79] Ibid., p. 94.
[80] James E. Lewis Jr., *The American Union and the Problem of Neighborhood: The United States and the Collapse of the Spanish Empire, 1783–1829* (Chapel Hill, NC and London: University of North Carolina Press, 1998), p. 75.
[81] Ibid., p. 75.
[82] Ibid., p. 6.
[83] Peter S. Onuf, *Jefferson's Empire: The Language of American Nationhood* (Charlottesville, VA and London: University Press of Virginia, 2000), p. 45.
[84] Jervis, 'From Balance to Concert'.

Federalist synthesis of states' rights and national government by denying another central claim that had been central to the early debate—namely that an extended republic feasibly protected liberty. The planter elite in South Carolina was drawn instead to earlier justifications for the small republic—that the extended republic could not resolve the problem of faction. The run-up to the Civil War thus continued some of the debate of the Founding period.

Relations among the states in the American union in its early years were more peaceful than relations among the newly independent states of Latin America. This held for all types of war, from systemic to civil to small wars.[85] 'With large armies on hand, the new states readily sought military solutions to internal and external disputes. War broke out first between Buenos Aires and Brazil and later between Colombia and Peru'. And in the same year, 1825, military leaders took power in a number of Spanish American states,[86] marking the beginning of the militarization of public life in Spanish America.[87] Internal divisions plagued the new nations, including factional disputes and unresolved constitutional issues.[88] All of the revolutions had been incomplete, and had left in their wake characteristic conflicts among post-independence conservatives, moderates who were liberal, constitutional monarchists and radical republicans.[89] These conflicts were not so different from the divisions between monarchists and republicans that were crystallized in continental Europe after the French Revolution.[90] In Spanish America, however, public life was far more militarized. In the language of one observer, the *caudillo*-ridden Latin American republics looked like militarized *haciendas*.[91] Hence conservatives were not always monarchists. They could co-ordinate around a military dictatorship even if the constitution was formally republican. Such an option was not beyond the pale for European conservatives but it was much less likely to be invoked in the first instance. Monarchies in Europe still had considerable support and staying power after the French Revolution. The 'legitimist' peace settlement of Vienna[92] demonstrated the continuing presence and importance of monarchical regimes in Europe.

American policymakers, particularly Adams, Clay and Monroe, had hoped to encourage general adherence among the new states of Spanish America to a 'North

---

[85] Melvin Small and J. David Singer, *Resort to Arms: International and Civil Wars, 1816–1980* (Beverley Hills, CA: Sage Publications, 1982); Erik Goldstein, *Wars and Peace Treaties, 1816–1991* (London: Routledge, 1992).

[86] Lewis, *The American Union*, p. 204.

[87] Tulio Halperin-Donghi, *The Aftermath of Revolution in Latin America* (New York: Harper and Row, 1973), p. 1–43.

[88] Harold Eugene Davis, 'Relations during the Times of Troubles, 1825–1860', in Harold Eugene Davis, John F. Finan and F. Taylor Peck (eds.), *Latin American Diplomatic History* (Baton Rouge, LA and London: Louisiana State University Press, 1977), p. 67.

[89] For a particularly clear description of these divisions in Mexico, see Donald Fithian Stevens, *Origins of Instability in Early Republican Mexico* (Durham and London: Duke University Press, 1991), pp. 110–11. Compare his discussion of the conflicts in Mexico with the analysis of political conflict in the European revolutions of 1848, in Jonathan Sperber, *The European Revolutions, 1848–1851* (Cambridge and New York: Cambridge University Press, 1994), pp. 64–86.

[90] Hudson Meadwell, 'Republics, Nations and Transitions to Modernity'.

[91] Mark Thurner, *From Two Republics to One Divided: Contradictions of Post-Colonial Nationalism in Andean Peru* (Durham and London: Duke University Press, 1997), p. 4.

[92] Samuel Flag Bemis, *The Latin American Policy of the United States* (New York: W.W. Norton, 1976 [1943]), p. 34.

American model of diplomacy, politics and economics'[93]—that is, adherence to neutral rights, republican government and liberal principles on trade. But by the nature of events in Spanish America, they also had to confront precisely what the federal union had been designed to eliminate—multiple sovereignty in the Americas. Republicans had always feared that multiple sovereignty would lead to balance of power politics, which was considered inimical to republican politics. The federal union was the political bedrock on which to build a republican America because it solved the problem of multiple sovereignty. Yet there was now more than one sovereign power in the Americas. And American policymakers could do little about it. Could they have refused to recognize republican governments in Spanish America as the Spanish American Empire disintegrated? Once they had recognized these new entities as legitimate international actors, the neighbourhood had changed.

As the neighbourhood changed, so did the internal structure of the United States. There were ambiguities in the Federalist synthesis of state rights and national government that could be exploited in ways that would force a domestic reworking of the internal logic of the federal union. A right to secede could be justifiably invoked in the South, supporters of secession argued, because the United States was a compact of states. If a right to secede existed and the act of seceding occurred, it was precisely because the United States was not a state. The units to which the right to secede was attached were semi-sovereign. They were states in a union. This political use of the concept of secession was designed to establish that the United States was not a state but a compact of states.

The political debate in *ante-bellum* America was about how secession was to be conventionally understood. More particularly it was about how to describe the United States in constitutional terms and how any description could be made compelling. In describing secession as a process of withdrawal of a state from a compact, the political elite in the South forced the North to deny this description of the United States and to substitute a rival description.

The position of the South could be challenged in several ways. One way would have been to concede the description used in the South, namely that the United States was a compact of states, but then deny that such an arrangement created a right to secede. Another challenge would have been to concede this description and to concede that it entailed a right to secede, but to deny that this right extended automatically to the Southern states. A third way to challenge the constitutional language of the South was to argue that a right to secede that was grounded in a compact theory could not be invoked because the United States was not a compact. The North made real this latter claim that the United States was a state and not merely a compact through the use of force, 'resolving once and for all where sovereignty lay'. In so acting it took on board the most important trappings of a territorial state. 'A state proves itself as a sovereign state by demonstrating that it has an overwhelming monopoly on the legitimate use of physical force'.[94] The Civil War not only consolidated republicanism; it also consolidated the territorial foundations

---

[93] Lewis, *The American Union*, p. 203.
[94] John Patrick Diggins, *Max Weber: Politics and the Spirit of Tragedy* (New York: Basic Books, 1996), p. xv. Diggins here echoes earlier arguments of Wilson. 'The Reconstruction of the United States', *Atlantic Monthly*, LXXXVII (1901), pp. 11–12.

of the American federal state and eliminated any future threat of secession as America continued to expand.

The dreams of a federal union and a republican empire were dead by the middle part of the nineteenth century. Both of these models of political arrangements were particularly sensitive to patterns of authority within and across political boundaries. As authority began to be dispersed amongst multiple sovereign actors in the Americas, political authority within the United States became increasingly concentrated. But the political culture of republicanism did not disappear with these changes. Rather, republicans in America were forced to consider how liberal republicanism could continue to make a distinctive contribution to public life, both within and across political boundaries. Liberal republicanism continued to motivate policymakers when they defined American identity and its role in the world.

Conclusion

The long nineteenth century stretched from 1789 to 1945. It began in revolution and ended in war. This period is treated here as a protracted European-wide democratic transition. My analysis thus treats differently the turning points typically emphasized in international histories of European politics in the nineteenth and twentieth centuries. So, for example, 1815 is relevant for my arguments, not because the Congress of Vienna begins a transformation in international politics, but because it is a post-war settlement resulting from the consequences of social and political revolution. And for my purposes, 1945 is relevant because it marks the military defeat of the National Socialist revolution in Germany and the consolidation across much of Europe of a long process of democratic change.

My arguments are explicitly rooted in the unit level. However, I also take into account social interdependencies in European society associated with the distribution of types of political regime and with territorial stratification—that is states. I have emphasized in particular the consequences of democratic republicanism within a social system composed of dynastic states.

These arguments about European society show how difficult it is to sustain an exclusively systemic perspective on war and change in European society. They show why it is important to take seriously the preferences of revolutionary actors, and the structures within which they act. And they illustrate, as well, some of the consequences of broaching in argument the theoretical importance of domestic regimes.

Furthermore, if this period is of one piece as I have proposed, then we should be able to rethink, or frame in some new ways, other events such as the revolutions of 1848 or the Great War. We might also be able to rethink the cleavage structures of European politics in more systematic ways for a number of cases by taking into account the political conflicts associated with republicanism. In any event, these are ways in which the arguments of this article might be taken forward.

American power and the empire
of capitalist democracy

G. JOHN IKENBERRY*

The United States is today a global superpower without historical precedent. It stands at the centre of an expanding democratic-capitalist world order that is itself, fifty years after its creation, the dominant reality in world politics. Despite expectations that American hegemony would disappear and trigger the emergence of a new and unstable multipolar post-Cold War order, the opposite has in fact happened. American power has grown even greater in the decade since the collapse of the Soviet Union. Although American power is not uniformly welcome around the world, serious ideological challengers or geopolitical balancers are not to be found. Scholars who a decade ago were debating the prospect of co-operation and conflict in a post-hegemonic world are now debating the character and future of world politics within an American unipolar order.

The rise of American unipolarity is surprising. Many observers expected the end of the Cold War to usher in a new era of multipolarity. Some anticipated a return to the balance of power politics of the late nineteenth century. Others saw signs of regional blocs that would return the world to the instabilities of the 1930s. But the distribution of power took a dramatic turn in America's favour. The sudden collapse of the Soviet Union, the decline in ideological rivalry, lagging economic fortunes in Japan and continental Europe, growing disparities in military and technological expenditure, and America's booming economy all intensified power disparities in the 1990s.

The United States began the 1990s as the world's only superpower and it had a better decade that any of the other great powers. Between 1990 and 1998, the American economy grew 26 per cent, while Europe grew 17 per cent and Japan 7 per cent. The United States has reduced its military spending at a slower rate than other countries. It has also been steadily distancing itself from other states in the range and sophistication of its military power.[1] The global reach and multifaceted character of American power separates the American unipolar moment from earlier eras of hegemonic dominance. 'The United States of America today predominates on the economic level, the monetary level, on the technological level, and in the cultural area in the broadest sense of the word', observed French Foreign Minister Hubert Vedrine in a speech in Paris in early 1999. 'It is not comparable, in terms of power and influence, to anything known in modern history'.[2]

* The author would like to thank Christopher Jones, Jonathan Kirshner, and participants at a Cornell University Government Department seminar for helpful comments on an earlier draft of this essay.

[1] Calculated from OECD statistics (July 1999 web edition). GDP measures are calculated at 1990 prices and exchange rates. Reflecting the sharp disparities in military power—and its likely continuation well into the future—80 per cent of world defence research and development takes place in the United States. For this and other empirical indicators of American unipolar power, see William Wohlforth, 'The Stability of a Unipolar World', *International Security* (Summer 1999).

[2] Quoted in Craig R. Whitney, 'NATO at 50: With Nations at Odds, Is It a Misalliance?' *New York Times*, 15 February 1999, p. A7.

But disparities in material capabilities do not capture the full character of American unipolarity. The United States is a different type of hegemonic power. It is not just a powerful state that can throw its weight around—although it is that as well. The United States also dominates world politics by providing the language, ideas, and institutional frameworks around which much of the world turns. The extended institutional connections that link the United States to the other regions of the world provide a sort of primitive governance system. The United States is a central hub through which the world's important military, political, economic, scientific, and cultural connections pass. No other great power—France, Germany, the United Kingdom, Japan, or China—has a global political or security presence. The European Union has a population and economic weight equal to the United States but it does not have a global geopolitical or strategic reach. It cannot project military power or pursue a unified foreign policy toward, for example, China. Japan, who many thought a decade ago might emerge as the next great world power, is struggling under the weight of political gridlock and economic malaise. America's far flung network of political partnerships and security commitments—together with the array of global and regional institutions—provide what passes for global governance.

To look at the current world order with realist eyes—focusing on anarchy and great power politics—misses the deeper structures of hierarchy and democratic community that prevail today. It is remarkable that fifty years after their defeat in World War II, Japan and Germany—now the second and third largest economies in the world—are still dependent on the American security commitment and station American military forces on their soil. If empires are coercive systems of domination, the American-centred world order is not an empire. If empires are inclusive systems of order organized around a dominant state—and its laws, economy, military, and political institutions—than the United States has indeed constructed a world democratic-capitalist empire.

The United States is not just a unipolar power. It is also the dominant state within a unipolar world order. This world order—perhaps best called the American system—is organized around American-led regional security alliances in Europe and Asia, open and multilateral economic relations, several layers of regional and global multilateral institutions, and shared commitments to democracy and open capitalist economies. It is an order built around American power and a convergence of interests between the United States and other advanced industrial democratic states. Shared values and interests help give shape to the American system, but it is also an engineered political order that is built around a series of political bargains between the United States and its European and Asian partners after World War II and renewed and expanded over the decades.

But how stable is this order? The answer depends on what the precise character of this order actually is. Some argue that behind the fascade of democracy and institutional co-operation lies a predatory and imperial American state. Chalmers Johnson argues that the American 'empire' is as coercive and exploitative as the Soviet empire and anticipates a backlash in which America's resentful junior partners will wreak their revenge and bring the entire imperial edifice down.[3] This is an echo of a revisionist tradition that sees American global dominance driven by expansionary and exploitative capitalists or a crusading national security state.

[3] Chalmers Johnson, *Blowback: The Costs and Consequences of American Empire* (New York: Metropolitan Books, 2000).

American Cold War-era interventionism in Latin America and elsewhere around the world provides ample material to make this claim.[4] Some intellectuals in the West even suggest that an arrogant and overbearing America brought the terrorism of 11 September, 2001, on itself.[5] Taking the opposite view, John Gaddis argues that the American empire is fundamentally different to the old Soviet empire. The habit of democracy and reciprocity has given American relations with Europe and Asia a more benign and legitimate cast.[6] Realists, such as Kenneth Waltz, argue that the American unipolar order is inherently unstable not because of any special malign American characteristics but because of the inherent insecurity that unequal power confers on weaker states. In anarchic orders, weaker states are threatened by extreme concentrations of power and will seek protection in counter-hegemonic groupings. The balance of power will reassert itself.[7] But the debate about whether there is a coming backlash begs the question: what is the character of American unipolar order as a political formation?

I argue that American unipolarity is an expansive and highly durable political order. It is not a transitional phase in international relations but is a political formation with its own character and logic. Nor is it a political formation that falls easily into a particular historical category—empire, superpower, hegemonic order. The American order is built on power—at least at its core. The extended system of American-led security protection in Europe, the Middle East, and Asia is an essential element of this order and it can only be sustained by dominant military capabilities, which in turn depends on continuing American economic and technological strength. But the American order is sustained by more than power and therefore its political dynamics—and historical trajectory—are not intelligible from a narrow realist perspective.

The American unipolar order has deep foundations. It is unlikely that any other state or alternative political order will soon arise to replace it. Nor is the world likely to return to a more traditional multipolar world of great power politics. The reason is that the sources of American dominance—and the stability of the American-centred liberal capitalist world order—are remarkably multidimensional and mutually reinforcing. Critical features of the order make American power less threatening and therefore reduce the incentives that other states have to distance themselves from or balance against the United States.

There are four major facets of the American order that make it robust and durable. One dimension is identified by realist theorists of hegemony, such as Robert Gilpin, who focus on power as the essential glue—power manifest in American security protection, market dominance, and the international role of the dollar. A second dimension is found in the special circumstances of American geography and historical staging. American power is offshore—geographically isolated from the other major powers—making that power less threatening and more useful in stabilizing regional relations. The United States also rose to power as an anti-

---

[4] See, for example, Noam Chomsky, *Turning the Tide: US Intervention in Latin America and the Struggle for Peace* (Boston, MA: South End Books, 1986).

[5] See, for example, Steven Erlanger, 'In Europe, Some Say the Attacks Stemmed from American Failings', *The New York Times*, 22 September 2001; and Elaine Sciolino, 'Who Hates the US? Who Loves It? *The New York Times*, 23 September 2001.

[6] John Lewis Gaddis, *We Now Know: Rethinking Cold War History* (New York: Oxford University Press, 1997), ch. 2.

[7] Kenneth Waltz, 'Structural Realism after the Cold War', *International Security* (Summer 2000).

colonial and post-imperial state with strategic interests that could be pursued by articulating universal principles of state relations. A third dimension of American unipolarity is the distinctive way in which democracy and international institutions have provided the United States with mechanisms to make itself less threatening to the rest of the world. The liberal character of American hegemony allows the United States unusual capacities to make commitments and restrain power. Finally, the deep forces of modernization and the distinctive principles of the American polity—civic nationalism and multi-cultural identity—also give the United States unusual influence and political congruence with world political development. The durability of the American order is not simply sustained by the exertion of American power—activity shaping and managing the world. Rather it is the country's deep alignment with global developmental processes—and the 'project of modernity'— that gives the American system its durability and global reach.

This article will examine these facets of the American order. It will conclude by looking at the underlying political bargain that the United States has made with the rest of the world and discuss whether that bargain is coming unstuck or not. The American system has a long future if its leaders understand its logic and rules.

Balance of power, hegemony, and the American system

In explaining the character and future of American unipolarity, structural realism provides the most elegant and time-honoured theory. International order is the result of balancing by states under conditions of anarchy to counter opposing power concentrations or threats. In this view, the rise of the American order was itself a creature of the Cold War and bipolar balancing. The Soviet threat provided the essential stimulant for American-led post-war order building in the non-communist world. But with the end of the bipolar threat, American preponderance is unsustainable: now it poses a danger to other states and balancing reactions are inevitable. Kenneth Waltz provides the logic of this realist expectation. The underlying condition of anarchy leads weaker states to resist and balance against the predominant state. Security—indeed survival—is the fundamental goal of states, and because states cannot ultimately rely on the commitments or guarantees of other states to insure their security, states will be very sensitive to their relative power position. When powerful states emerge, secondary states will seek protection in countervailing coalitions of weaker states. The alternatives risk domination. As Waltz argues: 'Secondary states, if they are free to choose, flock to the weaker side; for it is the stronger side that threatens them. On the weaker side they are both more appreciated and safer, provided, of course, that the coalition they join achieves enough defensive or deterrent strength to dissuade adversaries from attacking'.[8] Alliances emerge as temporary coalitions of states formed to counter the concentration of power. As the distribution of power shifts, coalitions will also shift. American unipolar power is manifestly unstable.

---

[8] Waltz, *Theory of International Politics*, p. x. See also Waltz, 'The Emerging Structure of International Politics', *International Security*, 18:2 (1993); and Waltz, 'Structural Realism after the Cold War', *International Security* (Summer 2000).

Yet it is remarkable that despite the sharp shifts in the distribution of power, the other great powers have not yet responded in a way anticipated by balance of power theory. Despite the disappearance of the Soviet threat, it is difficult to discern a significant decline in alliance solidarity between the United States and its European and Asian partners. 'Rather than edging away from the United States, much less balancing against it, Germany and Japan have been determined to maintain the pattern of engagement that characterized the Cold War', argues Michael Mastanduno. 'Neither China nor Russia, despite having some differences with the United States, has sought to organize a balancing coalition against it. Indeed, the main security concern for many countries in Europe and Asia is not how to distance from an all-too-powerful United States, but how to prevent the United States from drifting away'.[9] Both NATO and the US-Japan alliance have recently reaffirmed and deepened their ties. Nor have wider realms of political and economic co-operation or accompanying multilateral relations declined in serious ways. Trade and investment has expanded across the Atlantic and Pacific and an increasingly dense web of intergovernmental and transnational relations connect these countries. Despite the most radical shifts in international power in half a century, the relations among the major states have remained remarkably stable and continuous.

For Waltz, the expectation of a return to a global balance of power requires patience. Realist theory clearly expects that 'balances disturbed will one day be restored', but it cannot predict when national governments will respond to these structural pressures. In Waltz's structural realist view, unipolarity is the least durable of international configurations that inevitably will provoke actions and responses by the dominant and weaker states that will ultimately return the system to a more traditional balance of power order. A unipolar state is fundamentally unrestrained —and this makes its foreign policy less disciplined and more dangerous to other states. Resistance and counter-balancing will follow. Indeed, Waltz claims that one can observe 'balancing tendencies already taking place'.[10]

Aside from balance of power theory, a second realist theory holds that order is created and maintained by a hegemonic state which uses power capabilities to organize relations among states.[11] The preponderance of power by a state allows it to offer incentives—both positive and negative—to the other states to agree to ongoing participation within the hegemonic order. According to Gilpin, an international order is, at any particular moment in history, the reflection of the underlying distribution of power of states within the system. Over time, this distribution of power shifts, leading to conflicts and ruptures in the system, hegemonic war, and the eventual reorganization of order so as to reflect the new distribution of power capabilities. It is the rising hegemonic state or group of states, whose power position has been ratified by war, which defines the terms of the post-war settlement —and the character of the new order.

In the strong version, hegemonic order is built around direct and coercive domination of weaker and secondary states by the hegemon. The dominant state manipulates the world to its purposes. But actual hegemonic orders have tended to

---

[9] Michael Mastanduno, 'Preserving the Unipolar Moment: Realist Theories and US Grand Strategy after the Cold War', *International Security*, 21:4 (1997), p. 58.

[10] Waltz, 'Structural Realism after the Cold War', *International Security* (Summer 2000).

[11] See Robert Gilpin, *War and Change in World Politics*.

be more complex and less coercive. Gilpin depicts the British and American hegemonic orders as ones built around dominant military and economic capabilities but bolstered as well by mutually beneficial trade relations and shared liberal ideology. Indeed, he argues that hegemony without a commitment to liberalism is likely to lead to imperial systems, regional blocs, and the imposition of severe restrictions on lesser states.[12] Hegemonic orders can be relatively benevolent and non-coercive—organized around reciprocal, consensual, and institutionalized relations. The order is still organized around asymmetrical power relations but the most overtly coercive character of domination is muted. In a highly imperial hegemonic order, weaker and secondary states are simply unable to counter-balance. Domination itself prevents the escape to a balance of power system. In more benign and consensual hegemonic orders, where restraints on hegemonic power are sufficiently developed, it is the expected value of balancing that declines. Balancing is an option for weaker and secondary states, but the benign character and institutional limits on hegemonic power reduce the incentives to do so.

Following this observation, it is possible to identify three variants of hegemonic order. The first is based on coercive domination. Weaker and secondary states are not happy about their subordinate position and would actively seek to overturn the order if they were capable of doing so. But the prevailing power distribution provides insufficient capabilities for these states to challenge the dominant state. This is in effect an informal imperial order.[13] Power—and in the final instance coercive domination—keeps the order together.[14]

A second type of hegemonic order is held together by some minimal convergence of interests. The dominant state might provide 'services' to subordinate states that these states find useful—and sufficiently useful to prevent them from actively seeking to overturn the order. In this order, the dominant state's security or economic assets can be used or employed in one way or other by weaker partner states—the leading state provides security protection or access to its market—and these opportunities for gain outweigh the dangers of domination or abandonment. America's extended security role in Western Europe, East Asia, and the Middle East, for example, is welcomed by states in these regions because it allows them to stabilize local rivalries. Finally, in a

---

[12] See Gilpin, 'Economic Interdependence and National Security in Historical Perspective', in Klaus Knorr and Frank Trager (eds.), *Economic Issues and National Security* (Lawrence, KS: Regents Press of Kansas, 1977), pp. 19–66.

[13] For discussion of empires—their sources of order and variation—see Michael Doyle, *Empires* (Ithaca, NY: Cornell University Press, 1986); Alexander Motyl, *Revolutions, Nations, Empires: Conceptual Limits and Theoretical Possibilities* (New York: Columbia University Press, 1999); S.N. Eisenstadt, *The Political Systems of Empires: The Rise and Fall of the Historical Bureaucratic Societies* (New York: Free Press, 1969); and Karen Dawisha and Bruce Parrott, *The Disintegration and Reconstruction of Empires* (Armonk: M. E. Sharpe, 1966). For a discussion of European empire and reactions to it, see Philip D. Curtin, *The World and the West: The European Challenge and the Overseas Response in the Age of Empire* (New York: Cambridge University Press, 2000). For a broad historical survey of types of international orders in historical and comparative perspective, see Barry Buzan and Richard Little, *International Systems in World History: Remaking the Study of International Relations* (New York: Oxford University Press, 2000).

[14] In a variation of this view, William Wohlforth argues that it is the sheer preponderance of American power that prevents a return to traditional patterns of balance. The power disparity is such that a countervailing coalition is not possible. 'No other major power is in a position to follow any policy that depends for its success on prevailing against the United States in a war or an extended rivalry', Wohlforth argues. 'None is likely to take any step that might invite the focused enmity of the United States'. Wohlforth, 'The Stability of a Unipolar World', *International Security*, p. x.

third variant, hegemonic order might even be more thoroughly institutionalized and infused with reciprocal processes of political interaction so that the hierarchy of the order is all but obscured. This is quasi-rule-based and open hegemony. In such a benevolent hegemonic formation, where there are real institutional restraints on the exercise of power, the resulting order begins to reflect less faithfully the underlying distribution of power. This is reflected in the American hegemonic order, where the web of institutional relations—security, political, and economic—that the United States spun after World War II and in later decades has transformed the sharp power disparities into a more principled and mutually acceptable order.

Security alliances, markets, and the dollar

American power—military, political, economic—is the not-so-hidden hand that built and sustains the American system. The realist narrative is straightforward. The United States emerged from World War II as the leading global power and it proceeded to organize the post-war system in a way that accorded with its interests. In 1947, the British scholar Harold Laski wrote: 'America bestrides the world like a colossus; neither Rome at the height of its powers nor Great Britain in the period of its economic supremacy enjoyed an influence so direct, so profound, so pervasive ...'[15] America's allies and the defeated axis states were battered and diminished by the war, whereas the United States grew more powerful through mobilization for war. The American government was more centralized and capable, and the economy and military were unprecedented in their power and still on an upward swing. America's position was also enhanced because the war had ratified the destruction of the old order of the 1930s, eliminated the alternative regional hegemonic ambitions of Germany and Japan, and diminished the viability of the British imperial order. The stage was set for the United States to shape the post-war order.

The extraordinary power disparities of the moment were not lost on American officials. George Kennan pointed to this reality in 1948: 'We have about 50 per cent of the world's wealth but only 6.3 per cent of its population. ... Our real task in the coming period is to devise a pattern of relationships which will permit us to maintain this position of disparity without positive detriment to our national security'.[16] Kennan is expressing a quintessentially realist sentiment that the United States needed to construct a post-war order that would allow it to retain its power and advantages but do so in a clever enough way so as not to provoke resistance.

Two sorts of strategic objectives became attached to the exercise of American power in the 1940s. One dealt with the geoeconomic organization of the post-war order: the United States sought to build an order that would avoid the return to the antagonist regional blocs of the 1930s. The United States wanted to situate itself in an open order that would allow multilateral trade and resource access with the other regions of the world. America's other great ambition emerged later—countering Soviet communism by creating a worldwide system of alliance partnerships and pursuing containment.

---

[15] Harold J. Laski, 'America–1947', *Nation*, 165 (13 December, 1947), p. 641.
[16] 'Memorandum by the Director of the Policy Planning Staff [Kennan] to the Secretary of State and Under Secretary of State [Lovett]', 24 February 1948, *Foreign Relations of the United States*, 1948, vol. 1, p. 524.

During the 1930s, the United States saw its geopolitical operating space shrink as the other great powers begin to construct closed and competing regional blocs. Germany pursued a series of bilateral trade agreements with Eastern European countries in order to consolidate an economic and political sphere of influence in the region. Japan pursued an even more overt campaign to create a Greater East Asian Co-Prosperity Sphere. In a less obvious or aggressive way, Britain also was pursuing a strategy of discriminatory economic co-operation with its Commonwealth partners - a non-territorial economic bloc built around the imperial preferential system. By the end of the 1930s, the world was effectively carved up into relatively insular economic blocs—antagonistic groupings that American officials understood to be at least partly responsible for the onset of war.[17]

This is where American strategic thinkers began their debates in the 1930s. The question these thinkers pondered was whether the United States could remain as a great industrial power within the confines of the Western Hemisphere. What were the minimum geographical requirements for the country's economic and military viability? For all practical purposes this question was answered by the time the United States entered the war. An American hemispheric bloc would not be sufficient; the United States must have security of markets and raw materials in Asia and Europe.[18] If the rimlands of Europe and Asia became dominated by one or several hostile imperial powers, the security implications for the United States would be catastrophic. To remain a great power, the United States must seek openness, access, and balance in Europe and Asia.

This view that America must have access to Asian and European markets and resources—and must therefore not let a potential adversary control the Eurasian landmass—was also embraced by post-war defence planners. As the war was coming to an end, defence officials began to see that America's security interests required the building of an elaborate system of forward bases in Asia and Europe. Hemispheric defence would be inadequate.[19] Defence officials also saw access to Asian and European raw materials—and the prevention of their control by a prospective enemy—as an American security interest. Melvin Leffler notes that 'Stimson, Patterson, McCloy, and Assistant Secretary Howard C. Peterson agreed with Forrestal that long-term American prosperity required open markets, unhindered access to raw materials, and the rehabilitation of much—if not all—of Eurasia along liberal capitalist lines'.[20] Indeed, the base systems were partly justified in terms of their impact on access to raw materials and the denial for such resources to an adversary. Some defence studies went further, and argued that post-war threats to Eurasian access and openness were more social and economic than military. It was

---

[17] For arguments that the great mid-century struggle was between a open capitalist order and various regional, autarkic challengers, see Bruce Cumings, 'The Seventy Years' Crisis and the Logic of Trilateralism in the New World Order', *World Policy Journal* (Spring 1991); and Charles Maier, 'The Two Postwar Eras and the Conditions for Stability in Twentieth-Century Western Europe', in Maier, *In Search of Stability: Explorations in Historical Political Economy* (New York: Cambridge University Press, 1987).

[18] The culmination of this debate and the most forceful statement of the new consensus was presented in Nicholas John Spykman's *America's Strategy in the World: The United States and the Balance of Power* (New York: HarcourtBrace, 1942).

[19] See Melvyn P. Leffler, 'The American Conception of National Security and the Beginning of the Cold War, 1945–48', *American Historical Review*, 48 (1984), pp. 349–56.

[20] Leffler, 'The American Conception of National Security', p. 358.

economic turmoil and political upheaval that were the real threats to American security, as they invited the subversion of liberal democratic societies and Western-oriented governments. A CIA study concluded in mid-1947: 'The greatest danger to the security of the United States is the possibility of economic collapse in Western Europe and the consequent accession to power of Communist elements'.[21] Access to resources and markets, socioeconomic stability, political pluralism, and American security interests were all tied together.

By the late 1940s, the twin objectives of openness and containment came together. The building of security partnerships and open economic relations with Western Europe and East Asia were essential to fighting the Cold War, while the imperatives of the Cold War reinforced co-operation with America's partners and created domestic support for American leadership. Robert Gilpin argues that the Soviet threat was critical in fostering cohesion among the capitalist democracies and providing the political glue that held the world economy together. Over time, in his view, an elaborate American-led political order emerged that was built on two pillars: the US dollar and the American security umbrella. The American military guarantee to Europe and Asia provided a national-security rationale for Japan and the Western democracies to open their markets. Free trade helped cement the alliance, and in turn the alliance helped settle economic disputes. In Asia, the export-oriented development strategies of Japan and the smaller Asian tigers depended on America's willingness to accept their imports and live with huge trade deficits; alliances with Japan, South Korea, and other Southeast Asian countries made this politically tolerable.[22]

The importance of American power in post-war order building was most evident in the occupation and security binding of Germany and Japan. American troops began as occupiers of the two defeated axis states and never left. They eventually became protectors but also a palpable symbol of America's superordinate position. Host agreements were negotiated that created a legal basis for the American military presence—effectively circumscribing Japanese and West German sovereignty. West German rearmament and restoration of its political sovereignty—made necessary in the early 1950s by a growing Cold War—could only be achieved by binding Germany to Europe, which in turn required a binding American security commitment to Europe. Complex and protracted negotiations ultimately created an integrated European military force within NATO and legal agreements over the character and limits of West German sovereignty and military power.[23] A reciprocal process of security binding lay at the heart of the emerging American system. John

---

[21] CIA, 'Review of the World Situation as It Relates to the Security of the United States', 26 September, 1947. Quoted in Leffler, 'The American Conception of National Security', p. 364.

[22] Robert Gilpin, *The Challenge of Global Capitalism: The World Economy in the 21st Century* (Princeton, NJ: Princeton University Press, 2000), ch. 2.

[23] A treaty governing the relationship between the new German state and Britain, France, and the United States was signed in 1952, and specified ongoing 'rights and responsibilities' of the three powers. 'Convention on Relations between the Three Powers and the Federal Republic of Germany, 26 May, 1952, as modified by the Paris Accords of October 1954', reprinted in Department of State, *Documents on Germany, 1944–1985* (Washington, DC: Department of State, 1986), pp. 425–30. See also Paul B. Stares, *Allied Rights and Legal Restraints on German Military Power* (Washington, DC: Brookings Institution, 1990). Later, when speculation arose in the 1950s that a German Social Democratic leader might be elected and request the Americans to leave, an Eisenhower official quipped that if this were to happen the United States would respond by doubling the size of its forces in Germany. See Mark Trachtenberg, *A Constructed Peace: The Making of the European Settlement, 1945–1963* (Princeton, NJ: Princeton University Press, 2000).

McCloy identified the 'fundamental principle' of American policy in the early 1950s: that 'whatever German contribution to defence is made may only take the form of a force which is an integral part of a larger international organization. ... There is no real solution of the German problem inside Germany alone. There is a solution inside the European-Atlantic-World Community'.[24]

Japan was also brought into the American security and economic orbit during the 1950s. The United States took the lead in helping Japan find new commercial relations and raw material sources in Southeast Asia to substitute for the loss of Chinese and Korean markets.[25] Japan and Germany were now twin junior partners of the United States—stripped of their military capacities and reorganized as engines of world economic growth. Containment in Asia would be based on the growth and integration of Japan in the wider non-communist Asian regional economy—what Secretary of State Dean Acheson called the 'great crescent' in referring to the countries arrayed from Japan through Southeast Asia to India. Bruce Cumings captures the logic: 'In East Asia, American planners envisioned a regional economy driven by revived Japanese industry, with assured continental access to markets and raw materials for its exports'.[26] This strategy would link together threatened non-communist states along the crescent, create strong economic links between the United States and Japan, and lessen the importance of European colonial holdings in the area. The United States would actively aid Japan in re-establishing a regional economic sphere in Asia, allowing it to prosper and play a regional leadership role within the larger American post-war order. Japanese economic growth, the expansion of regional and world markets, and the fighting of the Cold War went together.

Behind the scene, America's hegemonic position was also backed by the reserve and transaction-currency role of the dollar. The dollar's special status gave the United States the rights of 'seigniorage': it could print extra money to fight foreign wars, increase domestic spending, and go deeply into debt without fearing the pain that other states would experience. Other countries would have to adjust their currencies, which were linked to the dollar, when Washington pursued an inflationary course to meet its foreign and domestic policy agendas. Because of its dominance, the United States did not have to raise interest rates to defend its currency, taking pressure off its chronic trade imbalances. In the 1960s, French President Charles de Gaulle understood this hidden source of American hegemony all too well and complained bitterly. But most of America's Cold War allies were willing to hold dollars for fear that a currency collapse might lead the United States to withdraw its forces overseas and retreat into isolationism.

In this post-war bargain, American security protection, its domestic market, and the dollar bound the allies together and created the institutional supports of the stable political order and open world economy. Because the US economy dwarfed other industrial countries, it did not need to worry about controlling the distribution of gains from trade between itself and its allies. The United States provided its

---

[24] Quoted in Thomas Schwartz, *America's Germany: John J. McCloy and the Federal Republic of Germany* (Cambridge, MA: Harvard University Press, 1991), p. 228.

[25] Michael Schaller, 'Securing the Great Crescent: Occupied Japan and the Origins of Containment in Southeast Asia', *Journal of American History*, 69 (September 1982), pp. 392–414.

[26] Bruce Cumings, 'Japan's Position in the World System', in Andrew Gordon (ed.), *Postwar Japan as History* (Berkeley, CA: University of California Press), p. 38.

partners with security guarantees and access to American markets, technology, and supplies within an open world economy. In return, East Asian and European allies would become stable partners who would provide diplomatic, economic, and logistical support for the United States as it led the wider American-centred, non-communist post-war order.

Geography and historical staging

The geographic setting and historical timing of America's rise in power have also shaped the way American primacy has been manifest. The United States is the only great power that is not neighboured by other great powers. This geographical remoteness made the power ascent of the United States less threatening to the rest of the world and it reinforced the disinclination of American leaders to directly dominate or manage great power relations. In the twentieth century, the United States became the world's pre-eminent power but the location and historical entry point of that power helped shaped how this arrival was greeted.

In the 1870s, the United States surpassed Britain as the largest and most advanced economy but because of its geographical remoteness this development— and its continued growth—did not destabilize great power relations. America's era of territorial expansion took place without directly threatening other major states. The European powers had stakes in the New World but not fundamental interests or even—at least by the mid-nineteenth century—a direct presence. The United States purchased territory from France rather than acquiring it by conquest. Indigenous peoples were the main losers in the American pursuit of manifest destiny. Later in the nineteenth century, the United States became the leading industrial power without triggering new interstate rivalries. Germany, of course, was not as geographically lucky and the expansion and unification of Germany unleashed nationalist rivalries, territorial ambitions, arms races, and ultimately world war.[27] More generally, power transitions—with rising powers overtaking *status quo* powers—are dangerous and conflict-prone moments in world history.[28] As European great powers grew in strength, they tended to trigger security dilemma-driven conflict and balancing reactions in their regional neighborhood. But America's remoteness lessened the destabilizing impact of its transition to global pre-eminence.

The open spaces of the new world also meant that American political and economic advancement could take place—at least until 1914—without the development of a war-making strong state.[29] The United States became a world power through the gradual expansion of its industry and economy rather than by the

[27] A.J.P. Taylor, *The Course of German History* (London: Hamish Hamilton, 1945).
[28] On power transitions and hegemonic wars, see Robert Gilpin, *War and Change in World Politics*.
[29] On divergent European and American state building experiences, see Samuel Huntington, *Political Order in Changing Societies* (New Haven, CT: Yale University Press, 1968); Charles Tilly, 'Reflections on the History of European State-Making', in Tilly (ed.), *The Formation of National States in Western Europe* (Princeton, NJ: Princeton University Press, 1975), pp. 3–83; Charles Tilly, *Coercion, Capital, and European States, AD 990–1990* (Oxford: Blackwell, 1990); and Michael Mann, *The Sources of Social Power*, vol. 2: *The Rise of Classes and Nation-States, 1760–1914* (Cambridge: Cambridge University Press, 1993).

orchestration or command of the central government. American power was latent—rooted in an expanding civil society, productive economy, and stable constitutional democracy. Even on the eve of the European war in 1914, the United States had a tiny standing army and little capacity to mobilize or project military force. This made the United States less able to directly manoeuvre among or deter the other great powers but it also made the United States less threatening. American power was submerged within its society and removed from the territorial battlegrounds of the other great powers, thereby allowing it to grow unimpeded and unchecked.

When the United States was drawn into European power struggles, it did so primarily as a offshore balancer.[30] This was an echo of Britain's continental strategy which for several centuries was based on aloofness from European power struggles, intervening at critical moments to tip and restore the balance among the other states.[31] This offshore balancing role was played out by the United States in the two world wars. America entered each war relatively late and tipped the balance in favour of the allies. After World War II, the United States emerged as an equally important presence in Europe, Asia, and the Middle East as an offshore military force that each region found useful in solving its local security dilemmas. In Europe, the reintegration of West Germany into the West was only possible with the American security commitment. The Franco-German settlement was explicitly and necessarily embedded in an American-guaranteed Atlantic settlement. In Joseph Joffe's apt phrase, the United States became 'Europe's pacifier'.[32] In East Asia, the American security pact with Japan also solved regional security dilemmas by creating restraints on the resurgence of Japanese military power. In the Middle East a similar dynamic drew the United States into an active role in mediating between Israel and the Arab states. In each region, American power is seen less as a source of domination and more as a useful tool.

Because the United States is geographically remote, abandonment rather than domination has been seen as the greater risk by many states. As a result, the United States has found itself constantly courted by governments in Europe, Asia and elsewhere. When Winston Churchill advanced ideas about post-war order he was concerned above all in finding a way to tie the United States to Europe.[33] British Foreign Minister Ernest Bevin had similar thoughts when he heard Secretary of State George Marshall's celebrated speech in June 1947 announcing aid for Europe. 'The first thought that came into his mind was not that this gave a prospect of American economic help for Europe. He saw that, and grasped the chance with both hands; but first came the realization that his chief fear had been banished for good. The Americans were not going to do as they had done after the first World War and retreat into their hemisphere. ... The keystone of Bevin's foreign policy had swung into place'.[34] As Geir Lundestad has observed, the expanding American political

---

[30] On the notion of offshore balancing, see Christopher Layne, 'From Preponderance to Offshore Balancing', *International Security*, 22:1 (1997).

[31] See Paul Kennedy, *The Rise and Fall of the Great Powers: Economic Change and Military Conflict from 1500 to 2000* (New York: Vintage Books, 1989).

[32] Joseph Joffe, 'America: Europe's Pacifier', *The National Interest*. See also Robert Art, 'Why Western Europe Needs the United States and NATO', *Political Science Quarterly*, 111 (1996), pp. 1–39.

[33] See Ikenberry, *After Victory*, ch. 6.

[34] Sir Oliver Franks, in *Listener*, 14 June 1956. Quoted in John W. Wheeler-Bennett and Anthony Nicholls, *The Semblance of Peace: The Political Settlement after the Second World War* (London: Macmillan, 1972), p. 573.

order in the half century after World War II has been in important respects an 'empire by invitation'.[35] The remarkable global reach of American post-war hegemony has been at least in part driven by the efforts of European and Asian governments to harness American power, render that power more predictable, and use it to overcome their own regional insecurities. The result has been a durable system of America-centred economic and security partnerships.

Finally, the historical timing of America's rise in power also left a mark. The United States came relatively late to the great power arena, after the colonial and imperial eras had run their course. This meant that the pursuit of America's strategic interests was not primarily based on territorial control but on championing more principled ways of organizing great power relations. The world had already been carved up by Japan and the European states. As a late-developing great power the United States needed openness and access to the regions of the world rather than recognition of its territorial claims. The American issuance of its Open Door policy toward China reflected this orientation. Woodrow Wilson's championing at Versailles of democracy and self-determination and FDR's support of decolonialization several decades later were also statements of American strategic interests issued as principled appeals.[36] American officials were never fully consistent in wielding such principled claims about order and they were often a source of conflict with the other major states. But the overall effect of this alignment of American geostrategic interests with enlightened normative principles of order reinforced the image of the United States as a relatively non-coercive and non-imperial hegemonic power.

Institutions, democracy, and strategic restraint

The American unipolar order is also organized around democratic polities and a complex web of intergovernmental institutions—and these features of the American system alter and mute the way in which hegemonic power is manifest. One version of this argument is the democratic peace thesis: open democratic polities are less able or willing to use power in an arbitrary and indiscriminate manner against other democracies.[37] The calculations of smaller and weaker states as they confront a democratic hegemon are altered. Fundamentally, power asymmetries are less threatening or destabilizing when they exist between democracies. This might be so for several reasons. Open polities make the exercise of power more visible and easy to anticipate. Accountable governments make the exercise of power more predictable and institutionalized. Democracies are more accessible from the outside than non-

---

[35] Geir Lundestad, 'Empire by Invitation? The United States and Western Europe, 1945–1952', *The Journal of Peace Research*, 23 (September 1986), pp. 263–77. See also Charles Maier, 'Alliance and Autonomy: European Identity and US Foreign Policy Objectives in the Truman Years', in Michael J. Lacey (ed.), *The Truman Presidency* (New York: Cambridge University Press, 1989), pp. 273–98; and David Reynolds, 'America's Europe, Europe's America: Image, Influence, and Interaction, 1933–1958', *Diplomatic History*, 20 (Fall 1996).

[36] See Tony Smith, *America's Mission: The United States and the Worldwide Struggle for Democracy in the Twentieth Century* (Princeton, NJ: Princeton University Press, 1994).

[37] See Bruce Russett and John Oneal, *Triangulating Peace: Democracy, Interdependence, and International Organizations* (New York: Norton, 2001).

democracies. Leaders who rise through the ranks within democratic countries are more inclined to participate in the 'give and take' with other democratic leaders than those who rise up in autocratic and authoritarian states.

In these various ways, European and Asian countries are more willing to co-operate with America because hegemonic power is wielded by a democracy. Processes of interaction between democracies make crude and manipulative exercise of power less likely or consequential. Institutions and norms of consultation and reciprocal influence are manifest in relations across the democratic world. As a result, asymmetries of power do not generate the sort of strategic insecurities and security dilemmas that would otherwise pervade such sharp disparities of power. These facets of democracy are stressed by John Gaddis: 'Negotiation, compromise, and consensus-building came naturally to statesmen steeped in the uses of such practices at home: in this sense, the American political tradition served the country better than its realist critics—Kennan among them—believed it did'.[38]

It is possible to identify several features of American-style hegemony that distinguish it from past hegemonic or imperial powers. Rooted in democratic culture and institutions, American hegemonic is unusually reluctant, open, and highly institutionalized. The reluctant character of American hegemony is seen in the absence of a strong imperial impulse to directly dominate or manage weaker or secondary states within the order. One aspect of this reluctant hegemony has been manifest—ironically—in the very ambitiousness of America's order-building proposals in the twentieth century. The United States has frequently sought to reshape the world precisely so that it would not need to manage it. Woodrow Wilson championed a democratic revolution in Europe because a rising tide of democracy would ensure the working of the League of Nations and a peaceful functioning post-war order. When Wilson presented his Fourteen Points in January 1918, it looked as if the tide of European politics was moving in the liberal and social democratic direction. The revolution in Russia seemed to confirm the democratic revolution that was sweeping the major industrial societies. The United States would lead the world to democracy but it would not rule the world or provide traditional security commitments to Western Europe. An expanding community of democracies would govern itself.[39] To British and French leaders, Wilson seemed to be the very embodiment of the arrogant and pushy American leader—preaching to Europe to reform its politics but stopping short of making real and practical commitments to the security of the continent. But Wilson wanted to transform the world precisely so the United States would not need to rule it.

The same logic informed America's plans for the post-1945 world economy. It is revealing that the initial and most forcefully presented American view of post-war order was the State Department's proposal for a post-war system of free trade. This proposal did not only reflect an American conviction about the virtues of open markets, but it also was a vision of order that would require very little direct American involvement or management.[40] The system would largely be self-regulating, leaving the United States to operate within it, but without the burdens of direct

---

[38] Gaddis, *We Now Know: Rethinking Cold War History*, p. 50.
[39] This argument is made in Ikenberry, *After Victory*, ch. 5.
[40] Ikenberry, 'Rethinking the Origins of American Hegemony', *Political Science Quarterly*, 104 (1989), pp. 375–400.

and ongoing supervision. This general characteristic was not lost on the Europeans, and it mattered as America's potential partners contemplated whether and how to co-operate with the United States. It meant that the Europeans would need to actively seek to court American involvement in Europe rather than resist it, and it provided some reassurance that the United States would operate within limits and not use its overwhelming power position simply to dominate.

Another aspect of this imperial reluctance is the American eagerness to construct a legitimate international order—that is, an order that is recognized as acceptable and desirable by the countries operating within it. This desire for legitimate order has led the United States to make extensive compromises in its foreign policy goals so as to achieve a mutually agreeable settlement. This orientation was reflected during World War II in the compromises that the United States made in accommodating European views about the post-war world economy. The British and the continental Europeans, worried about post-war depression and the protection of their fragile economies, were not eager to embrace America's stark proposals for an open world trading system, favouring a more regulated and compensatory system.[41] The United States did attempt to use its material resources to pressure and induce Britain and the other European countries to abandon bilateral and regional preferential agreements and accept the principles of a post-war economic system organized around a nondiscriminatory system of trade and payments.[42] The United States knew it held a commanding position and sought to use its power to give the post-war order a distinctive shape. But it also prized agreement over deadlock, and it ultimately moved a great distance away from its original proposals in setting up the various post-war institutions.[43]

Another aspect of the non-imperial American hegemonic orientation is manifest in the lack of a singular grand strategic vision to inform the construction of the American-led post-war order. There is an old quip that Great Britain acquired its Indian empire 'in a fit of absence of mind'. In important respects this is also true of America as it acquired a global order. There was as much inadvertence and unintended consequence as grand design. As the realist narrative presented earlier suggests, important aspects of the American order were engineered—particularly the security alliances—as part of post-war political bargains with Western Europe and Asia. As the same time, however, it is difficult to discern a singular vision or grand strategy in this order. Even after World War II, when the foundations of the American order were put in place, there were many different ideas and projects. Different bureaucracies and political groups, each with its own agenda, went about building a slice of the post-war order. There were the United Nations activists, the free trade groups, and the geopolitical strategists. The post-1945 order was cobbled

[41] The strongest claims about American and European differences over post-war political economy are made by Fred Block, *The Origins of International Economic Disorder* (Berkeley, CA: University of California Press, 1977).

[42] The 1946 British Loan deal was perhaps the most overt effort by the Truman administration to tie American post-war aid to specific policy concessions by allied governments. This was the failed Anglo-American Financial Agreement, which obliged the British to make sterling convertible in exchange for American assistance. See Richard Gardner, *Sterling-Dollar Diplomacy* (New York: McGraw Hill, 1969); and Alfred E. Eckes, Jr., *A Search for Solvency: Bretton Woods and the International Monetary System, 1944–1971* (Austin, TX: University of Texas Press, 1971).

[43] Ikenberry, 'A World Economy Restored: Expert Consensus and the Anglo-American Postwar Settlement', *International Organization*, 46 (1991/92), pp. 289–321.

together. The United States did strike a bargain with the rest of the world but it was largely implicit and manifest in a rolling process of piecemeal institutional agreements and security relationships.

A second major way in which the power asymmetries were made more acceptable to other countries was the liberal democratic structure of the American polity. The open and decentralized character of the American political system provided opportunities for other states to exercise their voice in the operation of hegemonic order, thereby reassuring these states that their interests could be actively advanced and processes of conflict resolution would exist. In this sense, the American postwar order was a 'penetrated hegemony', an extended system that blurred domestic and international politics as it created an elaborate transnational and transgovernmental political system with the United States at the centre.[44]

There are several ways in which the penetrated hegemonic order provided ways for the United States to restrain and commit its power. To begin with, America's mature political institutions organized around the rule of law have made it a relatively predictable and co-operative hegemon. The pluralistic and regularized way in which American foreign and security policy is made reduces surprises and allows other states to build long-term, mutually beneficial relations. The governmental separation of powers creates a shared decision-making system that opens up the process and reduces the ability of any one leader to make abrupt or aggressive moves toward other states. An active press and competitive party system also provide a service to outside states by generating information about United States policy and determining its seriousness of purpose. The messiness of democracy can frustrate American diplomats and confuse foreign observers. But over the long term, democratic institutions produce more consistent and credible policies than autocratic or authoritarian states.

The institutional opportunities for foreign officials to actively work within the American system—exercising voice opportunities—also reduces worries about American power.[45] The fragmented and penetrated American system allows and invites the proliferation of a vast network of transnational and transgovernmental relations with Europe, Japan, and other parts of the world. Diffuse and dense networks of governmental, corporate, and private associations tie the system together. The United States is the primary site for the pulling and hauling of trans-Atlantic and trans-Pacific politics. European and Asian governments do not have elected officials in Washington but they do have representatives.[46] Although this access to the American political process is not fully reciprocated abroad, the openness and extensive decentralization of the American liberal system assures other states that they have routine access to the decision-making processes of the United States.

---

[44] See Daniel Deudney and Ikenberry, 'The Sources and Character of Liberal International Order', *Review of International Studies*, 25:2 (1999), pp. 179–96.

[45] The notion of 'voice opportunities', drawn for Albert Hirschman's distinction between exit and voice, is discussed in Joseph Grieco, 'The Maastricht Treaty, Economic and Monetary Union and the Neo-Realist Research Programme', *Review of International Studies*, 21, pp. 21–40.

[46] Thomas Risse finds a similar pattern in his study of American-European relations within NATO. See Risse-Kappen, *Cooperation among Democracies* (Princeton, NJ: Princeton University Press, 1994). For patterns in US–Japanese relations, see Peter J. Katzenstein and Yutaka Tsujinaka, '"Bullying", "Buying", and "Binding": US–Japanese Transnational Relations and Domestic Structures', in Thomas Risse-Kappen (ed.), *Bringing Transnational Relations Back In* (Cambridge: Cambridge University Press, 1995).

A final way in which the United States overcame fears of domination was through binding itself institutionally to other states. Security binding means establishing formal institutional links between countries that are potential adversaries, thereby reducing the incentives for each state to balance against the other.[47] Rather than responding to a potential strategic rival by organizing a counter-balancing alliance against it, the threatening state is invited to participate within a joint security association or alliance. By binding to each other, surprises are reduced and expectations of stable future relations dampen the security dilemmas that trigger worst-case preparations, arms races, and dangerous strategic rivalry. Also, by creating institutional connections between potential rivals, channels of communication are established which provide opportunities to actively influence the other's evolving security policy. When states employ institutional binding as a strategy, they are essentially agreeing to mutually constrain themselves. In effect, institutions specify what it is that states are expected to do and they make it difficult and costly for states to do otherwise. In binding itself to its weaker partners, the leading state is giving up some policy autonomy and discretion but gains the non-coerced co-operation of the other states by making itself less threatening.

The United States and its allies built the post-war order around binding institutions. They built long-term political and security commitments—the alliance system itself most importantly—that were difficult to retract. NATO and the US–Japan security treaties were the most important binding institutions in the American system. The old saying that NATO was created to 'keep the Russians out, the Germans down, and the Americans in' is a statement about the importance of the alliance structures for locking in long-term commitments and expectations. The American-Japanese security pact has had a similar 'dual containment' character. These institutions have not only served as alliances in the ordinary sense as organized efforts to balance against external threats, they also provided mechanisms and venues to build political relations, conduct business, and regulate conflict.[48] The binding logic of NATO allowed France and the other Western partners to acquiesce in Germany's military rearmament during the Cold War. Even today, the United States and its European and Japanese partners ward off rivalry and balancing among themselves by maintaining their security alliances. It is the binding logic—more so than the response to external threats—that makes these institutions attractive today.

American-led economic and security institutions provide Germany and Japan with a political bulwark of stability that far transcends their more immediate and practical purposes. Germany has had more opportunities to bind itself to Western Europe and the Atlantic order than Japan has had opportunities in East Asia. The European Community—and later European Union—and the NATO alliance have

[47] See Paul Schroeder, 'Alliances, 1815–1945: Weapons to Power and Tools of Management', in Klaus Knorr (ed.), *Historical Dimensions of National Security Problems* (Lawrence, KS: University of Kansas Press, 1976), pp. 227–62.

[48] On security binding, see Schroeder, 'Alliances, 1815–1945: Weapons to Power and Tools of Management', in Klaus Knorr (ed.), *Historical Dimensions of National Security Problems*. On more recent formulations, see Joseph M. Grieco, 'State Interests and Institutional Rule Trajectories: A Neorealist Interpretation of the Maastricht Treaty and European Economic and Monetary Union', *Security Studies*, 5:3 (1996); and Daniel Deudney, 'The Philadelphian System: Sovereignty, Arms Control, and Balance of Power in the American States-Union', *International Organization*, 49 (Spring 1995), pp. 191–228.

given Germany a layer of institutions with which to bind itself to neighbours and thereby reduce security dilemma instabilities. Indeed, the Christian Democrat Walther Leisler Kiep argued in 1972 that 'the German-American alliance ... is not merely one aspect of modern German history, but a decisive element as a result of its pre-eminent place in our politics. In effect, it provides a second constitution for our country'.[49] Japan—because of geography, history, and politics—does not have as many regional institutional options. The US–Japan alliance is currently the only serious institution with which Japan can signal restraint and commitment. As a result, the bilateral alliance has become even more indispensable to Japan and the region.[50]

Modernization and civic nationalism

American power has been rendered more acceptable to the rest of the world because the United States 'project' is congruent with the deeper forces of modernization. The point here is not that the United States has pushed other states to embrace its goals and purposes but that all states are operating within a transforming global system—driven by modernization, industrialization, and social mobilization. The synchronicity between the rise of the United States as a liberal global power and the system-wide imperatives of modernization create a sort of functional 'fit' between the United States and the wider world order. If the United States were attempting to project state socialist economic ideas or autocratic political values, its fit with the deep forces of modernization would be poor. Its purposes would be resisted around the world and trigger resistance to American power. But the deep congruence between the American model and the functional demands of modernization both boost the power of the United States and make its relationship with the rest of the world more harmonious.

Modernization is a slippery notion that is difficult to specify but generally refers to the processes whereby historically evolved institutions are adapted to the changing demands and opportunities created by ongoing scientific, technological, and industrial revolutions.[51] These processes had their origins in the societies of Western Europe but in the last two centuries have extended to societies in other regions and have resulted in a worldwide transformation in human relations. Some accounts have been concerned primarily with political modernization while others have focused on societal changes that accompany industrialization.[52] Theorists of industrial modern-

---

[49] Quoted in Thomas Schwartz, 'The United States and Germany after 1945: Alliances, Transnational Relations, and the Legacy of the Cold War', *Diplomatic History*, 19:4 (1995), p. 555.

[50] For a discussion on this basic difference between Japan and Germany, see Erica Gould and Stephen D. Krasner, 'Germany and Japan: Binding *versus* Autonomy', in Wolfgang Streeck and Kozo Yamamura (eds.), *Germany and Japan: The Future of Nationally Embedded Capitalism in a Global Economy* (forthcoming).

[51] See C. E. Black, *The Dynamics of Modernization: A Study in Comparative History* (New York: Harper and Row, 1966; and Edward L. Morse, *Modernization and the Transformation of International Relations* (New York: Free Press, 1976). For a survey of modernization ideas, see Krishan Kumar, *Prophecy and Progress: The Sociology of Industrial and Post-Industrial Society*, (New York: Penguin Books, 1978).

[52] Huntington, *Political Order in Changing Societies*; and Ralf Dahrendorf, *Class and Class Conflict in Industrial Society* (Stanford, CA: Stanford University Press, 1959).

ism have focused specifically on industrial society and emphasized variations and contingencies in the ability of societies to adapt and take advantage of unfolding advances in science, technology, and industrialism.[53]

Industrialization is a constantly evolving process and the social and political characteristics within countries that it encourages and rewards—and that promote or impede industrial advancement—change over time and as countries move through developmental stages. In this sense, the fit between a polity and moderniz-ation is never absolute or permanent, as the changing virtues and liabilities of the Japanese developmental state makes clear.[54] Industrialism in advanced societies tends to feature highly educated workforces, rapid flows of information, and pro-gressively more specialized and complex systems of social and industrial organiz-ation. These features of industrial society—sometimes called late-industrialism—tend to foster a citizenry that is heterogenous, well educated, and difficult to coerce.[55] From this perspective it is possible to see why various state socialist and auth-oritarian countries—including the Soviet Union—ran into trouble as the twentieth century proceeded. The old command order impeded industrial modernization while, at the same time, industrial modernization undercut the old command order.[56] In contrast, the American polity has tended to have a relatively good fit with the demands and opportunities of industrial modernization. European and Asian forms of capitalist democracy have also exhibited features that seem in various ways to be quite congruent with the leading edge of advanced industrial development.[57] The success of the American model is partly due to the fact that it used its post-war power to build an international order that worked to the benefit of the American style of industrial capitalism. But the success of the American model—and the enhanced global influence and appeal that the United States has experienced in recent decades—is also due to the deep congruence between the logic of moderniz-ation and the American system.

The functionality between the United States polity and wider evolutionary developments in the international system can also be traced to the American political identity—which is rooted in civic nationalism and multi-culturalism. The basic distinction between civil and ethnic nationalism is useful in locating this feature. Civic nationalism is group identity that is composed of commitments to the nation's political creed. Race, religion, gender, language, or ethnicity are not relevant in defining a citizen's rights and inclusion within the polity. Shared belief in the country's principles and values embedded in the rule of law is the organizing basis for political order, and citizens are understood to be equal and rights bearing

---

[53] See Raymond Aron, *The Industrial Society: Three Essays on Ideology and Development* (New York: Clarion Books, 1966); Leon Lindberg (ed.), *Politics and the Future of Industrial Society* (New York: David McKay, 1976); and Clark Kerr, *The Future of Industrial Societies: Covergence or Continuing Diversity?* (Cambridge, MA: Harvard University Press, 1983).

[54] See Meredith Woo-Cumings (ed.), *The Developmental State* (Ithaca, NY: Cornell University Press, 1999).

[55] See Daniel Dell, *The Coming of Post-Industrial Society* (New York: Basic Books, 1973).

[56] See Daniel Deudney and G. John Ikenberry, 'Soviet Reform and the End of the Cold War: Explaining Large-Scale Historical Change', *Review of International Studies*, 17 (1991), pp. 225–250.

[57] For a discussion of the variety of advanced industrial democratic forms, see Herbert Kitschelt, Peter Lange, Gary Marks, and John D. Stephens, 'Convergence and Divergence in Advanced Capitalist Democracies', in Kitschelt, Lange, Marks, and Stephens (eds.), *Continuity and Change in Contemporary Capitalism* (Cambridge: Cambridge University Press, 1999).

individuals. Ethnic nationalism, in contrast, maintains that individuals' rights and participation within the polity are inherited—based on ethnic or racial ties.[58]

Civic national identity has four sorts of implications for the orientation—and acceptability—of American hegemonic order. First, civic identity has tended to encourage the American projection outward of domestic principles of inclusive and rule-based international political organization. The American national identity is not based on ethnic or religious particularism but on a more general set of agreed-upon and normatively appealing principles. Ethnic and religious identities and disputes are pushed downward into civil society and removed from the political arena. When the United States gets involved in political conflicts around the world it tends to look for the establishment of agreed-upon political principles and rules to guide the rebuilding of order. Likewise, when the United States promotes rule-based solutions to problems it is strengthening the normative and principled basis for the exercise of its own power—and thereby making disparities in power more acceptable.

Second, because civic nationalism is shared with other Western states it tends to be a source of cohesion and co-operation. Throughout the industrial democratic world, the dominant form of political identity is based on a set of abstract and juridical rights and responsibilities which coexist with private ethnic and religious associations. Just as warring states and nationalism tend to reinforce each other, so too do Western civic identity and co-operative political relations reinforce each other. Political order—domestic and international—is strengthened when there exists a substantial sense of community and shared identity. It matters that the leaders of today's advanced industrial states are not seeking to legitimate their power by making racial or imperialist appeals. Civic nationalism, rooted in shared commitment to democracy and the rule of law—provides a widely-embraced identity across most of the American hegemonic order. At the same time, potentially divisive identity conflicts—rooted in antagonistic ethnic or religious or class divisions—are dampened by relegating them to secondary status within civil society.[59]

Third, the multicultural character of the American political identity also reinforces internationalist—and ultimately multilateral—foreign policy. John Ruggie notes that culture wars continue in the United States between a pluralistic and multicultural identity and nativist and parochial alternatives, but that the core identity is still 'cosmopolitan liberal'—an identity that tends to support instrumental multilateralism. '[T]he evocative significance of multilateral world order principles— a bias against exclusive bilateralist alliances, the rejection of discriminatory economic blocs, and facilitating means to bridge gaps of ethos, race, and religion—should resonate still for the American public, insofar as they continue to reflect its own sense of national identity'.[60] The American society is increasingly heterogenous in race, ethnicity, and religion. This tends to reinforce an activist and inclusive foreign

---

[58] This distinction is made by Anthony D. Smith, *The Ethnic Origins of Nations* (Oxford: Blackwell, 1986). For an important reconceptualization of nationalism—emphasizing the strategic use of national identity by elites—see Michael Hechter, *Containing Nationalism* (Oxford: Oxford University Press, 2000).

[59] See Daniel Deudney and G. John Ikenberry, 'The Nature and Sources of Liberal International Order', *Review of International Studies*, 25:2 (1999).

[60] John Gerard Ruggie, *Winning the Peace: America and World Order in the New Era* (New York: Columbia University Press, 1996), p. 170.

policy orientation and a bias in favour of rule-based and multilateral approaches to the organization of hegemonic power.[61]

Finally, the American civic identity has tended to give the United States an unusual ability to absorb and integrate immigrants within a stable yet diverse political system. This integrative capacity will grow in importance. The mature industrial democracies are all experiencing a decline in their birth rates and a gradual population ageing. In the decades ahead, many of these countries—most notably Japan and Italy—will see their populations actually shrink with a smaller workforce unable to support an ageing demographic bubble. Immigration is increasingly a necessary aspect of economic growth. If Japan and other industrial societies are to maintain their population size and social security provisions they will need to open the door wide to immigration—but these imperatives are fiercely resisted.[62] The American willingness and ability to accept immigrants—putting it on the receiving end of the brain drain—already gives it an edge in knowledge and service industries. These advantages will only grow in the future and keep the United States at the dynamic centre of the world economy. Multinational and multi-ethnic empires of the nineteenth century ultimately failed and were broken apart in the twentieth century. Built on a civic national base, the United States has pioneered a new form of multicultural and multi-ethnic political order that appears to be stable and increasingly functional with the demands of global modernization.

Conclusion

The world has seen many great powers rise up to dominate the international system. Charles V, Louis XIV, Napoleon I, Wilhelmine and Nazi Germany—each became a hegemonic threat to Europe and triggered a backlash that rearranged the geopolitical landscape. Today it is the United States that looms about all other states and the question that many observers pose is: will the United States suffer a similar fate? 'There is one ideology left standing, liberal democratic capitalism, and one institution with universal reach, the United States', observes Fareed Zakaria. 'If the past is any guide, America's primacy will provoke growing resistance'.[63] Resistance has in fact appeared and may be growing. But it is remarkable that despite the sharp shifts in the distribution of power, the other great powers have not yet responded in a way anticipated by balance of power theory.

This article argues that American power—and the American unipolar order—is different and less threatening to other states than that which is envisaged in theoretical and historical claims about the balance of power. A variety of features associated with American hegemony—rooted in geography, history, ideology,

---

[61] On the ways in which American ethnic groups encourage foreign policy activism, see Tony Smith, *Foreign Attachments: The Power of Ethnic Groups in the Making of American Foreign Policy* (Cambridge, MA: Harvard University Press, 2000).

[62] See Christian Joppke, *Immigration and the Nation-State* (New York: Oxford University Press, 1999).

[63] Fareed Zakaria, 'The Empire Strikes Out', *New York Times Magazine*, 18 April 1999, p. 99. For views along these lines, see Peter W. Rodman, 'The World's Resentment: Anti-Americanism as a Global Phenomenon', *The National Interest*, no. 60 (Summer 2000), pp. 33–41; and Samuel Huntington, 'The Lonely Superpower', *Foreign Affairs*, 78:2 (March/April 1999), pp. 35–49.

democracy, institutional structures, and modernization itself—make it different from past great powers. These characteristics of American power mute and restrain that power and alter the risk calculations of weaker and secondary states. It also matters that these restraining characteristics are deeply rooted in the American polity. American power is reluctant, open, and highly institutionalized. It is also situated offshore from the other great powers which spares it from regional antagonisms and rivalries. American power is also able to deploy its power to solve problems for other states —particularly regional security dilemmas—and this weakens the incentives other states might have to engage in counter-balancing.

The United States used its power in the 1940s and afterwards to build a world order. An entire system of alliances, multilateral institutions, and entangling relations have emerged, such that it is possible to talk about American unipolarity as a distinctive political formation. *Pax Americana* is not just a powerful country throwing its weight around. It is a political formation with its own logic and laws of motion. It is an order that was created and sustained by American power but it is also not simply a reflection of that power. Indeed, it is the ability of this order to mute the impact of power symmetries that give it its durability. The deep congruence between the internal American political system—and its civic and multicultural identity—and the long-term project of modernity also gives the unipolar order robustness. The United States remains at the core of this order but it is an order that now has a life of its own.

The Russian-Soviet empire:
a test of neorealism

WILLIAM C. WOHLFORTH*

Russia is by some measures the most successful imperial enterprise in history. Surpassed in size only by the British and Mongol empires, Russia and its Soviet successor proved far more durable than either one. It retained its peak territorial extent longer than any other empire, and for most of the last 400 years it has been the largest polity on earth.[1] Moreover, both St. Petersburg and Moscow were hugely successful as great powers, playing major roles in European and world politics for the three centuries after 1700. And their influence as great powers peaked in the nineteenth and twentieth centuries—an era in which states based on nations appeared to have the competitive edge over old-fashioned polyglot empires.

Russia's brilliant career at the centre of the world political stage, however, came at a high price. Frequent and costly wars reinforced the empire's inefficient institutions, ultimately locking in Russia's backward position *vis-à-vis* its western rivals. The sprawling empire in both Tsarist and Soviet forms subsumed and truncated the Russians' own sense of national identity, and required St. Petersburg and Moscow to rule over scores of peoples—some with more developed national identities than the Russians themselves—sparking endless and draining expenditures of blood and treasure. Expansion eventually engendered opposition from other, wealthier great powers, producing costly arms races and rivalries that Russia could not win over the long run. And notwithstanding all the sacrifices, the state and empire collapsed twice in the twentieth century. The tawdry spectacle of early twenty-first century Russia—an oversized 'Upper Volta with missiles', as one popular article put it— drives home this message of ultimate failure.[2]

At the root of Russia's grandeur and tragedy is a bias toward expansion. That is, both Imperial Russia and the Soviet Union were biased toward the acquisition and retention of territory, for which they were willing to pay high costs. Territory acquired was rarely given up without a fight. The underlying preference for holding territory fed a willingness govern it by strong central control whenever challenged internally, which further raised the costs of empire. There is thus no disagreement on

* I am grateful to Mathew Rendall for commenting on an earlier draft of this essay.

[1] Rein Taagepera, 'Expansion and Contraction Patterns of Large Polities: Context for Russia', *International Studies Quarterly*, 41:3 (1997), pp. 475–504.

[2] Jeffrey Tayler, 'Russia is Finished,' *The Atlantic Monthly* (May 2001), pp. 35–52. A more graphic example of popular turn-of-the century views of Russia is the following from John Robson, Deputy Editorial Page Editor of *The Ottawa Citizen*, 'Normal for Russia is filthy, corrupt, menacing and hollow. Nothing good has ever happened there, nor will it. Russia is a lump of dung wrapped in a cabbage leaf hidden in an outhouse.' Cited in Dmitry Mikheyev 'Russia: Myths and Reality', Johnson's Russia List, no. 5292 (10 June 2001).

the key 'dependent variable' for IR theory. Russia appears to have suffered from an expansionistic bias that saddled it with too many territories and enemies and too few resources to deal with either.

How to explain this ultimately self-defeating propensity to expand? On this question turn a great many debates about both general IR theory and the explanation of particular cases. The standard approach in the field today is to assess a state's behaviour in a limited set of cases against a theoretically informed baseline account of the international system's imperatives. Scholars generally select cases that span a few years or at most a few decades. Within this restricted temporal domain, they normally find that the international system's incentives as described by Kenneth Waltz's neorealist theory cannot account for the given state's behaviour.[3] That is, the standard neorealist explanatory model—the imperative of survival in anarchy given the distribution of power—is either indeterminate or predicts a defensive non-expansionary stance on the part of the state. The conclusion follows that costly expansionism can only be explained by reference to domestic politics, ideas, or some combination thereof.[4]

These studies have contributed a great deal to our knowledge of international relations. Indeed, the basic approach taken in this literature is close to being the conventional wisdom in the field today. But the conventional approach presents an ambiguity. Neorealist theory concerns long-term structural pressures, not the explanation of specific events or even a limited series of events.[5] The theory is bound to be indeterminate concerning specific cases over short periods. Any finding concerning a temporally limited case, or even the cumulation of many such findings, cannot alter the theory's status. Intentionally or not, most of the case study literature is applying rather than truly testing the theory, a practice that has the effect of reinforcing its influence. The result is a growing body of empirical literature that appears to undermine neorealist theory, yet the theory continues to be used as a baseline for analysing state behaviour. There are few if any attempts to test it on its own terms: as an explanation of subtle structural influence over long stretches of time. In the absence of such tests, what grounds do scholars have for using neorealism as a baseline?

This Special Issue of the *Review* is thus fortuitous. It provides an opportunity to examine the neorealist explanation in exactly the domain to which it purports to

---

[3] Kenneth N. Waltz, *Theory of International Politics* (Reading, MA: Addison-Wesley, 1979). It is important to stress that here I evaluate not the whole family of neorealist theories, but the central aspects of the theory set forth in Waltz's text that bear on the explanation of expansionism.

[4] For reviews of this literature, see Richard Rosecrance and Arthur A. Stein (eds.), *The Domestic Bases of Grand Strategy* (Ithaca, NY: Cornell University Press, 1993); Richard Rosecrance, 'Overextension, Vulnerability, and Conflict: The "Goldilocks Problem" in International Strategy', *International Security*, 19:4 (1995), pp. 145–63. Premier examples include: Jack Snyder, *The Ideology of the Offensive* (Ithaca, NY: Cornell University Press, 1984); Snyder, *Myths of Empire; Domestic Politics and International Ambition* (Ithaca, NY: Cornell University Press, 1991); and Charles A. Kupchan, *The Vulnerability of Empire* (Ithaca, NY: Cornell University Press, 1994). On Russia, see Snyder, *The Ideology of the Offensive,* chs. 6–7. On the Soviet Union, see Matthew Evangelista, 'Internal and External Constraints on Grand Strategy: The Soviet Case', in Rosecrance and Stein (eds.), *Domestic Bases of Grand Strategy;* Snyder, *Myths of Empire,* ch. 6. Ted Hopf, *Peripheral Visions: Deterrence Theory and American Foreign Policy in the Third World, 1965–1990* (Ann Arbor, MI: University of Michigan Press, 1994); and Richard D. Anderson, Jr, *Public Politics in an Authoritarian State: Making Foreign Policy During the Brezhnev Years* (Ithaca, NY: Cornell University Press, 1993).

[5] Waltz, *Theory of International Politics;* and Waltz, 'International Politics is Not Foreign Policy', *Security Studies,* 6:1 (Autumn 1996), esp. pp. 54–57. Cf. Colin Elman, 'Horses for Courses: Why *Not* Neorealist Theories of Foreign Policy?', *Security Studies* 6:1 (Autumn 1996), pp. 7–53.

apply. For Russia's career as empire and great power is precisely coterminous with the seventeenth–twentieth century 'Westphalian' system. If neorealism is to be considered a useful theory of long-term structural causation, then it should be able to generate a broadly accurate explanatory account of major patterns of inter-national behaviour over the entire three-century career of a great power within this system. If major schools of historical scholarship on the Russian and Soviet imperial past persistently question the existence and causal importance of the mechanisms that neorealist theory predict ought to have been in play, then we may fairly con-clude that it has suffered a blow on its home turf and that its status as a 'baseline' theory has been impugned.[6]

My purpose in this article is to conduct such an evaluation, subject to the obvious space constraints. Given the frequency with which Waltz's project has been declared to be a 'degenerating' research programme or a fatally 'ahistorical' approach (as well as my own prior expectation based on my previous work), the result is surprising: neorealist theory turns out to have powerful explanatory leverage over the larger pattern of Russian and Soviet strategic choices.[7] From the standpoint of the historio-graphy of Russian and Soviet imperialism, the problem with neorealism is not that it is wrong but that it is obviously true. The contention that international anarchy generates pervasive security problems that powerfully constrain states and influence their identities and domestic political arrangements is a truism for students of Russian and Soviet history. Moreover, Waltz's structural approach to theory, which highlights socialization and selection rather than strict rational choice as the key causal mechanisms, resonates strongly with the empirical literature on Russia. Neorealist theory clearly fails to tell experts much about the Russian and Soviet past that they did not already know, but it does provide a deductively based explanation for perennial forces that they regard as central to Russian and Soviet history.

Applying one of the most abstract IR theories ever written to a specific case does require one additional, though widely accepted assumption. For neorealist theory to explain important patterns of Russian-Soviet behaviour, one must accept that strategic choices are path-dependent. If an actor adapts successfully to environ-mental pressures, the probability of continuing down that adaptive path increases because the relative costs of switching back to some previously possible adaptive path increase.[8] States' adaptation to systemic pressures is therefore 'sticky' in that the costs imposed by initially successful but eventually suboptimal adaptations fre-quently must rise dramatically to prompt a change of course. States may therefore follow apparently inefficient strategic paths for long periods. When states do reverse course, the resulting changes may be sudden and dramatic—defying prediction and

---

[6] In other words, this is what Stephen Van Evera calls a 'hoop test', because neorealist theory is very likely to fit the Russian-Soviet case of expansion. 'To remain viable, the theory must jump through the hoop this test presents, but passage of the test still leaves the theory in limbo'. See Van Evera, *Guide to Methods for Students of Political Science* (Ithaca, NY: Cornell University Press, 1997), p. 31. It is a less rigorous version of Harry Eckstein's 'most likely' test. See Eckstein, 'Case Study and Theory in Political Science,' in Fred I. Greenstein and Nelson Polsby (eds), *Handbook of Political Science*, vol. 7: *Strategies of Inquiry* (Reading, MA: Addison-Wesley, 1975): pp. 79–137.

[7] Paul W. Schroeder, 'Historical Reality versus Neorealist Theory', *International Security*, 19: 1 (Summer 1994), pp. 108–48; John A. Vasquez, 'The Realist Paradigm and Degenerative versus Progressive Research Programs', *American Political Science Review*, 91:4 (1997), pp. 899–912.

[8] Paul Pierson, 'Increasing Returns, Path Dependence, and the Study of Politics', *American Political Science Review*, 94: 2 (2000), pp. 251–68.

appearing to defy explanation based on the immediate initial conditions. Timing and sequencing matter: actors' initial advantages in a formative period have important consequences for their behaviour in subsequent periods.[9] All of these themes—timing, sequencing, inefficiency, sudden and dramatic reversals—are central in Russian history. That is why the *longue durée* perspective favoured in this Special Issue is so important for assessing arguments about the veracity of neorealist theory. The periods of Russian and Soviet history that appear in hindsight to present the greatest challenges to neorealist theory are in part explained by path dependency.

Three pervasive themes in the empirical literature on Russian and Soviet imperial history reflect the explanatory purchase of neorealism: the primacy of the security problem; the influence of geopolitics on identity and domestic institutions; and the causal salience of socialization and adaptation to external pressures. I consider these themes in the sections that follow. I then reconsider briefly a period of expansionist behaviour most analysts regard as particularly anomalous: Soviet policy from Brezhnev to Gorbachev. I conclude with a discussion of implications for theory and explanation.

The primacy of the security problem

Neorealist theory posits that the interaction of several states in anarchy renders their security problematic and encourages them to compete. Does the system induce an expansionistic bias on the part of states? Realists themselves frequently disagree on this question, with 'offensive realists' arguing that anarchy encourages such a bias while 'defensive realists' hold that such a bias is inexplicable without reference to the internal properties of states.[10] Conceptual differences do divide these theoretical strains, particularly over how to model human decision-making.[11] But often their differences turn on disagreements over the existence and causal effects of 'structural modifiers' (such as geography and military technology) that might reduce the benefits of conquest and decrease systemic incentives for security competition. So both may be more or less true in different degrees for different international systems in different periods, and the question of which applies in a given instance—and therefore whether an observed bias toward expansion is optimal—is often an empirical one.[12] While different strains of realist theory may generate different predictions concerning the optimality of expansion in general, they may converge on particular cases. There are three reasons, each one a major theme in the historical literature, that for most of its history Russia faced particularly severe security problems and therefore that the origins of its expansionistic bias lay in international rather than domestic politics.

[9] Robert Jervis, *System Effects: Complexity in Political and Social Life* (Princeton, NJ: Princeton University Press, 1997), ch. 4.

[10] For a review of this debate, see Jeffrey W. Taliaferro, 'Security Seeking under Anarchy: Defensive Realism Revisited', *International Security*, 25:3 (Winter 2000/01), pp. 128–161.

[11] Stephen G. Brooks, 'Dueling Realisms', *International Organization*, 51:3 (1997), pp. 445–77.

[12] Stephen M. Walt, 'The Enduring Relevance of the Realist Research Tradition', in Ira Katznelson and Helen Milner (eds.), *Political Science: The State of the Discipline* (Washington, DC: The American Political Science Association, forthcoming 2002).

Geography

First, the flat geography of the Eurasian plain bred a genuinely Hobbesian inter-national system in which a bias toward expansion was the only means of survival. Muscovy developed its statehood as the great nomadic Mongol empire that had sprung from the endless steppes to the south and east had begun to break down. There were no natural borders. The vast territory from the Carpathians and the Caucasus mountains north to the Baltic and east to the Pacific lies no more than 100 metres above sea level (excepting the Ural mountains that rise no more than 600 metres). There was no defence against offensively powerful rivals except for the resources and strategic depth provided by territory. A comparatively small and sedentary agricultural principality, Muscovy lay wide open to the offensively potent successor steppe khanates to the south and east, and the rapidly expanding Polish and Lithuanian kingdoms to the west. The units in this system were offensively powerful but defensively weak owing both to geography and to the susceptibility of domestic factions to manipulation by outside powers. It was characterized by expansive, unpopulated or sparsely populated tracts of land that were easy to conquer and potentially valuable strategically. National sentiments were weak and presented comparatively few barriers to conquest. Sovereignty was tenuous. International rela-tions were carried out in the temporal shadow of an Empire that had stretched from the Himalayas and the Pacific to the Danube. The possibility that a rival might reunite seemingly independent units, and quickly obtain the capabilities necessary to eliminate the sovereignty of all members of the system, remained in peoples' consciousness.

Anyone familiar with this system would find the notion that a state could overcome the security dilemma by 'signalling benign intentions', or 'creating non-offensive defence' derisory. The system obviously did not determine which state would survive. Systemic pressures clearly do not explain why of all the Russian principalities it was Muscovy that succeeded. One must clearly look inside the units to explain why it was Russia and not Lithuania, Poland, or a Mongol successor state that prevailed. Much of the historical literature is rightly concerned with explanation at this level. But implicit in these studies is the finding that the unit that survived in this system would be big. Everything we know about the international politics of Eurasia in the fourteenth–sixteenth centuries suggests that there was no equilibrium in which a small eastern Slav state could have survived.

It was a game of conquer or be conquered. But successful conquest offered no lasting security, only the chance to play another round as it brought contact with a new neighbour and a new potential enemy. Those new challenges kept the pressure on for further expansion, whenever and wherever feasible. Russia solved the threat from the steppes by expanding until it became a great Eurasian empire, but in so doing it placed itself in the path of other more powerful and often far more efficient states. Thus, the Tatar khanates and Poland-Lithuania were eventually replaced by Sweden and Turkey, which were followed in time by even more formidable powers to the west. And the regional system where this contact took place—where western Eurasia, Asia Minor and Eastern Europe met—was as a rule more dangerous and sanguinary than the western European system with which many IR scholars are most familiar. Wars were continuous in both systems, but were bloodier in the east. Borders were unstable in both, but more so in the east. States were eliminated from the map in both, but more frequently in the east. Geography in this system was only marginally more suited to the defence than that further East in Eurasia. If the European states system ever approximated the hellishly competitive world described by offensive realist theory, then it was in the seventeenth–eighteenth centuries. Russia lived in that system's most dangerous neighbourhood. And it stayed dangerous until the twentieth century, as a comparison of the casualty statistics from the eastern and western fronts of World War II shows.

Relative backwardness

The transition from the steppe system to the more developed and thus more lethal eastern reach of the European states system brings up the second reason Russia's security problem was so severe: relative backwardness. In competitive systems, states can either emulate the practices of successful rivals or maximize their own comparative advantages. The choice is contingent on timing and sequencing. It depends on past choices; and on whatever a state's initial advantage seems to be at the moment when the security problem happens to become especially acute. In the steppe system, Russia chose to emulate some of the successful practices of its local competition, particularly regarding autocracy (the Mongol khans were absolute autocrats), expansionism and diplomatic strategy. But since it was already a sedentary realm based on peasant agriculture, the costs of trying to become nomadic were fearsome, so it perforce exploited whatever advantages its existing practices conveyed. What turned out to be key was a mode of expansion that generated more capabilities than similar expansion by steppe rivals. Moscow would slowly penetrate the territory, co-opt some of the local aristocracy, dispossess some of their land, distribute some of the spoils to nobles who served the tsar, and seize some for the crown. The whole process was marked patience and persistence, with generations sometimes passing before local independence was totally eliminated.

By the time Russia had seriously to contend with more advanced rivals to the west, it was already a vast multinational empire. Peter the Great's response to this new challenge was once again to emulate the new rivals' more successful practices where possible, but much more fundamentally to exploit the initial comparative advantages of his empire's very backwardness: the sheer size of its territory and population mobilized by an especially ruthless autocratic regime. As William Fuller has shown, this spectacularly expensive effort to exploit Russia's initial advantage turned out to be brilliantly successful in competing with more advanced rivals for more than a century after the Russians' victory over the Swedes at Poltava in 1709.[13] During the latter nineteenth century, Fuller and many other scholars argue, the advantages of backwardness declined *vis-à-vis* western rivals. When the Bolsheviks seized power in 1917, Russia's old problem of backwardness was more sharply posed than it had been since the eighteenth century.[14] This set the context for Stalin's horrendously costly industrialization drive. Though many contemporaries saw it as modernization, in hindsight most scholars see it as reinforcing the old Russian

---

[13] William C. Fuller, Jr., *Strategy and Power in Russia: 1600–1914* (New York: The Free Press, 1992).
[14] Stephen M. Walt, *Revolution and War* (Ithaca, NY: Cornell University Press, 1996).

pattern of adaptation by exploiting the advantages of size, resources, and centralized state power.[15] Once again, this costly effort seemed, initially at least, to be successful for the purposes of international security competition.

Success, however, had its price. As Jack Snyder has argued, the Russian-Soviet adaptation to competitive coexistence with more advanced great powers intensified the security dilemma in a number of ways.[16] Russia's adaptive response generated military-industrial rather than commercial power, which exacerbated the security dilemma—especially with commercial-naval rivals such as Britain and the United States. The mix of resources available to a state critically affects the costs and benefits of various strategies. Commercial capabilities convey reward power; military capabilities favour coercive power.[17] In general, this incommensurability between the kinds of capabilities available to Russia and its rivals complicated their relations.[18] When signalling intent, commercial and naval capabilities offer more flexible options than military capabilities. Russia's only option in signalling intent was often the mobilization and movement of ground forces or the seizure of bits of territory. This reduced bargaining manoeuvre and heightened the security dilemma with differently endowed rivals.

In a more general vein, Snyder notes:

Backward Russia constituted a vulnerable yet provocative target for its European competitors. Huge and lumbering, Russia always seemed an immense threat, but one that could be neutralised by a bold stroke aimed at one of its innumerable weak points. The size of Russia's army fuelled worst case analysis about its aggressive capabilities and intentions, while the relative immobility of its forces convinced opponents that aggressive containment would fend off the threat. … At the same time, the sharp fluctuations in Russian power, linked to the stop-and-go nature of its efforts to catch up to the West, created strong incentives for preventive war initiated by Russia's foes.[19]

Snyder's phrase 'vulnerable but provocative' captures the essence of the way its adaptive response tended to exacerbate the security dilemma. Examples of these dynamics are legion. In the lead up to the Crimean War, Russia's only method of signalling its intentions was to occupy two principalities of the Ottoman Empire, a move with the unfortunate side effect of looking like preparation for attack.[20] As the crisis spiralled into war, Britain invaded Russia to defend itself in Europe and India against the Tsarist Empire's might, yet at the same time contemplated pushing Russia back to its seventeenth century borders in order to eliminate the threat for good.[21] Germany went to war in 1914 ostensibly out of fear of rising Russian power,

---

[15] Jack Snyder, 'Russian Backwardness and the Future of Europe', *Daedalus*, 123:2 (1994), pp. 179–87; Alexander Gershenkron, *Economic Backwardness in Historical Perspective* (Cambridge, MA: Belknap Press, 1962).

[16] Snyder, ibid., and *Myths of Empire*.

[17] Military capabilities do offer some ability to offer rewards to elicit desired behaviour, just as commercial capabilities can be used to coerce. However, military capabilities yield relatively more coercive power than commercial capabilities. The interaction between these different kinds of power is a central tenet of social exchange theory. See David A. Baldwin, *Paradoxes of Power* (New York: Basil Blackwell, 1989).

[18] This is a theme in William Curti Wohlforth, *The Elusive Balance: Power and Perceptions During the Cold War* (Ithaca, NY: Cornell University Press, 1993).

[19] Snyder, 'Russian Backwardness'.

[20] See John Shelton Curtiss, *Russia's Crimean War* (Durham, NC: Duke University Press, 1979, pp. 148–150.

[21] Hermann Wentler, *Zerstörung der Großmacht Rußland? Die britischen Kriegsziele im Krimkrieg* (Göttigen and Zürich: Vandenhoek and Rupprecht, 1993).

but with a war plan that assumed Russia could be eliminated quickly. The Soviet General Staff assumed it could not win a war against the full economic might of the United States, so it devised a war plan for denying US access to Eurasia. Unfortunately, 'denying US access to Eurasia' was indistinguishable in practice from 'invading and occupying western Europe', which helped unite the West against Moscow. American war planners saw their Russian counterparts' strategy as a reflection of aggressive intent, and contemplated preventive nuclear war before another upward spurt of Russian power made it invulnerable. And so on.

Security dilemmas of empire

The key to Russia's adaptive response to a threatening environment was size, which brings up the third reason Russia faced particularly acute security challenges. Russia became a great Eurasian empire in order to survive in an unforgiving international environment. Had it not become a multinational empire, Russia would likely have ended up as provinces of Poland, Sweden and Turkey. But an empire is an international system waiting to emerge, so the imperial centre must pursue a bi-level deterrence strategy, one directed outward toward other states and another directed inward toward internal groups that might choose to become states. Applied to empires, standard deterrence theory predicts that the imperial centre will want to have a reputation for resolve. The theory's assumption of interdependence—that resolve demonstrated in T1 will carry over to T2 and that resolve demonstrated on issue *X* will carry over to issue *Y*—is most applicable to centre-periphery relationships in empire. The relationship is continuous, carried out within a well-defined framework, and concerns a single set of recurring issues.

Thus, the imperial centre will place extraordinary emphasis on its reputation for resolve that will, in turn, feed a bias against relinquishing territory. These 'domestic' reputational concerns constitute a powerful constraint on imperial foreign policy. In Russia's case, the Polish problem is an example. For almost two centuries, Russian fear of a Polish uprising was a constant constraint on St. Petersburg. In 1812, Napoleon bragged that his Grand Duchy of Warsaw was a pistol aimed at Russia's heart, and Alexander agreed, concluding that he had to break out of Tilsit at nearly any cost. Thereafter, Russians ruled out many territorial concessions that they may have thought optimal for external purposes for fear of their consequences for the touchy Polish question.[22] Needless to say, precisely these concerns re-emerged in East Central Europe after the Second World War. Fear that external concessions on the German Question or other issues in European security could destabilize the Warsaw Pact was a staple of Cold War Soviet policy, as were the high costs Moscow had to pay internationally for its internal reputation for resolve.

Securing an empire in a world of empires is one thing; doing so in a world of states is quite another. Russia's initial move toward empire took place in a world without modern nationalism. Immense security benefits accrued. With time, however, the challenge of being a multinational empire intensified as the European system of states based on nations strengthened. Many theories of empire predict a

---

[22] William C. Fuller, Jr., provides a brilliant analysis of this constraint in *Strategy and Power In Russia*.

tendency toward decay and decline even without international competition.[23] The implication is that old-fashioned polyglot empires faced particularly intense security challenges in a system based on states that exploited national sentiment to solve collective action dilemmas and generate power. The toughness of any system can be measured by the survival rate of its members. The systems of the Eurasian steppe and early modern Europe were fairly demanding, judging by the relative frequency with which states 'fell by the wayside'. In the nineteenth and twentieth centuries the European system matured and survival rates for great powers increased. But this was not the case for empires. The Ottoman and Austro-Hungarian empires were in terminal decline throughout the nineteenth century. All three polyglot empires collapsed in World War I. The nation-state based overseas empires were on the retreat after 1918, and clearly on the way out after 1945. Russia and the Soviet Union faced a true dilemma. Their empires were their main source of both security and insecurity. International pressures severely limited the degree to which they could be flexible in governing their empires. Internal pressures severely limited the degree to which they could be flexible in managing relations with other great powers.

Insecurity and empire

In sum, Russia had to become a great multinational empire to survive on the Eurasian plain. But once it came into direct contact with the powerful European states system lying to its west, it had to become a great power in that international society in order to remain a multinational empire. Unless Russia was a member of that society, it would end up its victim. To be secure, it was necessary to play—and influence—the European balance of power game. Otherwise, it could fall prey to an aggressive alliance of these powerful states, all on the prowl for land and resources to use in their mutual rivalries. And the main resource it had to achieve that status was its vast empire. Maintaining and periodically extending this empire were thus necessary in order to attain and retain great-power status, which was necessary to defend the empire. The Bolsheviks came to power contemptuous of the European international system and its rules. Once they realized that their revolution would not soon spread, however, they came to appreciate the security imperative of active participation in that system, and that one of their main assets in the balance of power game was the sheer size and resources of the territory they controlled. This mutually reinforcing relationship between great power status, security and empire goes a long way toward explaining the larger pattern of Russian-Soviet expansionism.

Realists may argue over the degree to which anarchy generates a universal bias toward expansion. Concerning the Russian case, however, the theory is unambiguous. Even if we take the lead from defensive realist theory and consider the 'fine-grained structure of power', we find in Eurasia and Eastern Europe Hobbesian systems. For most of their history Muscovy, Russia and the Soviet Union existed in

---

[23] See David A. Lake, 'The Rise, Fall and Future of the Russian Empire', in Karen Dawisha and Bruce Parrott (eds.), *The End of Empire? The Transformation of the USSR in Comparative Perspective*, (Armonk, NY: M.E. Sharpe, 1997); Carlo M. Cipolla (ed.), *The Economic Decline of Empires* (London: Methuen, 1970); Robert Gilpin, *War and Change in World Politics* (Cambridge: Cambridge University Press, 1981); and Alexander Motyl, 'From Imperial Decay to Imperial Collapse: The Fall of the Soviet Empire in Comparative Perspective', in Richard L. Rudolph and David F. Good (eds.), *Nationalism and Empire: The Hapsburg Empire and the Soviet Union* (New York, 1992).

dangerous international systems that fostered expansion as a solution to the security problem. It is true that both Russia's and the Soviet Union's solution to the security challenge began to obsolesce late in the history of both empires. Whether these periods present important anomalies for a neorealist explanation requires a far more nuanced specification of the dependent variable than one usually encounters.

Domestic institutions and ideas are endogenous to systemic constraints

In many explanatory accounts of the Russian-Soviet bias toward expansion, domestic institutions and identity take on autonomous causal powers. The upshot of the foregoing discussion, however, is that the Russian Empire was in important ways a product of systemic pressures. It follows that the institutions necessary to govern it and the ideas needed to make sense of it were also endogenous to the international system. To be sure, the further into the specifics we go, the weaker the systemic influences may appear. Neorealist theory does not predict the precise nature of institutions and ideas; it merely predicts the rough manner in which states will be shaped by the international system. This predicted endogeneity is strongly present in the Russian and Soviet cases.

Insecurity, autocracy, and Russia's 'imperial identity'

The importance of systemic pressures in explaining the European state-building process is a well-established finding in social science.[24] Given the especially competitive nature of the Eurasian and Eastern European systems, it is not surprising to find that this theme is even stronger in the literature on the origins of the Russian autocracy. As might be expected, specialists debate the causal weight that ought to be attributed to external pressures. When one compares the literature on Russian state building with that concerning other countries, however, the greater salience of external factors in the Russian case is striking. 'The fundamental fact was the primacy of external concerns', writes Robert C. Tucker.[25] Dominic Lieven summarizes his conclusion as follows: 'The demands of international power politics and of membership of the European and then global system of great powers were of overwhelming importance in Russian history. More probably than any other single factor they determined the history of modern Russia'.[26] So many and so tight are the links between insecurity, expansion, and the emergence of the institutions of autocracy—the power of the Tsar over the aristocracy, serfdom, the creation of the service nobility, and the subordination of the Church—that it is not possible to construct a narrative of the origins of Russian state structure without according major importance to them.

---

[24] See S. E. Finer, *The History of Government from the Earliest Times*, 2 vols. (Oxford: Oxford University Press, 1997); and Charles Tilly (ed.), *The Formation of National States in Western Europe* (Princeton, NJ: Princeton University Press, 1975).

[25] Robert C. Tucker, *Stalin in Power: The Revolution from Above* (New York: Norton, 1990), p. 15.

[26] Dominic Lieven, *Empire: The Russian Empire and its Rivals* (London: John Murray, 2000), p. ix.

The same goes for the origins of Russia's imperial identity. Given what we know about the Eurasian international system in the fourteenth–fifteenth centuries, Moscow's seemingly fateful choice of identity as the 'gatherer of the Russian lands' functioned also as a grand strategy for survival as an independent polity. There was a catch, however. Ivan III's expansion to the north and east gave Moscow the resources without which it could not have deflected the last major effort by the lower Volga khanates to subordinate it in 1480. Moreover, this expansion yielded the means eventually to halt and reverse the rapid westward advance of Poland-Lithuania, a rival claimant to the identity of 'gatherer of Russian lands'. But in expanding to the east Ivan was already 'gathering up' non-Russian land and people (Tatars and Finno-Ugric tribes). When Ivan IV absorbed the khanates of Kazan' and Astrakhan, he gathered up large, coherent, territorially defined non-Russian and non-Orthodox polities. It was this expansion to the east that gave Russia the resources it needed to survive the Time of Troubles, during which it came perilously close to being partitioned among Poland, Sweden and the Ottoman Empire. However, this resource base came at the cost of Russia's original identity as the gatherer together of the Russian people *and* its nascent identity as successor to Byzantium and leader of the Orthodox faith. Neither of those identities would do for a state whose geopolitical position required the acquisition of territories inhabited by Moslem Tatars.

This captures one of the most important themes of Russian history: in the end, the empire defined the identity, rather than *vice versa*.[27] The fateful distinction between *rossiskiy* (having to do with the Russian imperial state) versus *russkiy* (having to do with the Russian nation) and the perennial ambiguity between identifying with Europe or Asia—both of which dog contemporary Russia—have their origins in the imperative to build and maintain an empire in response to systemic pressures. The Russians became just one of many peoples—indeed, worse off than many—within an empire run by a multinational elite. Ukranians, Poles, Tatars and eventually other non-Russians were welcomed into the imperial aristocracy. Baltic German aristocrats staffed the foreign ministry and army. A German Princess became Empress. Territories inhabited by nations with more developed national identities, such as the Poles and the Finns, were acquired and granted special freedoms. For over a century, this imperial identity served its purpose brilliantly, creating another instance of the path-dependency problem. In the nineteenth century, however, Russian rulers began to sense the competitive advantages their rivals obtained by exploiting national sentiment. They could either mimic their rivals or fall back on further entrenching the imperial identity. The costs and benefits of these alternatives were powerfully constrained by past choices. The Russians were numerous, and might form a national core, especially if Ukranians and Byelorussians could be induced to become Russian. But the power of Russian national feeling could only be tapped at the risk of alienating numerous non-Russian imperial subjects in the ruling class as well as the intelligentsia and peasantry, thus exacerbating the internal security problem and escalating the governance costs of empire.

---

[27] This is a central theme in Geoffrey Hosking, *Russia: People and Empire, 1552–1917* (Cambridge, MA: Harvard University Press, 1997). He carries it to the Soviet period in Hosking, *Russia and the Russians: A History* (Cambridge, MA: Belknap Press, 2001). For a brilliant analysis of the Europe-Asia identity tension, see Marc Bassin, 'Russia Between Europe and Asia: The Ideological Construction of Geography', *Slavic Review* 50: 1 (1991), pp. 1–17.

Socializing the Bolsheviks

The Russian Revolution provides a wonderful test for social science theory, though a tragic and costly one for the Russians and other subjects of the empire. A new Bolshevik elite came to power, imbued with radical new ideas and the motive to create new institutions. Yet it confronted the same security pressures as its Tsarist predecessors, and still had to contend with the effect of past Russian solutions to those pressures; that is, backwardness and empire. To be sure, the revolution itself exacerbated the security dilemma, and revolutionary ideology impeded co-operation with the west.[28] But systemic pressures in the dangerous multipolarity of the inter-war years powerfully influenced Soviet choices throughout the fateful years of the revolution. The result was a series of compromises between the revolutionary identity and the twin problems of security and the imperial legacy in which the latter continually and steadily gained at the expense of the former.

The story of the uneven but inexorable 'socialization' of Bolshevik ideas and institutions to international system pressures is well documented. The main intellectual rationales were survival and competitiveness. The Bolsheviks had to adjust ideas and institutions to permit or explain actions deemed necessary to continue in power. In international politics as described in neorealist theory, survival over the long run requires competitiveness. Given the failure of the revolution to spread as expected, the revolutionaries' hopes perforce resided in their state, and the security of that state became paramount. If in the long run the state could not compete materially with rivals, the original revolutionary purpose would be lost. The logic of competition implied the standard mix of emulation of and asymmetrical response to rivals, however in this instance it was supplemented by the Bolsheviks' ideological commitment to modernism. The Tsarist autocracy was chained to its traditions. The Bolshevik dictatorship was ideologically committed to modernism. Because the Soviet Union's main international rivals were modern states, the commitment to modernism facilitated emulation. But because the Soviets inherited the same territory and mix of resources as their Tsarist predecessors, they found themselves opting for some of the same strategies to exploit the comparative advantages of backwardness.

Several studies have traced the precise intellectual process by which experience in international politics shoved and shaped Soviet ideas.[29] Intellectual socialization began almost immediately upon the Bolsheviks' seizure of power with tactical concepts, but over time it proceeded to encompass causal beliefs, worldviews, and the political elite's conception of its collective identity. The essential change was the steadily increased salience of the state. Tactically, Bolsheviks moved from orchestrating revolutionary movements to overthrow governments, to using them to influence governments, and finally to subordinating them entirely to balance-of-power considerations. The institutional career of the Comintern reflects this progression. At the level of causal beliefs, Marxism portrays the state as a reflection of deeper causes. It is an easy step intellectually to begin to focus on state behaviour as an indicator of these causes until the state becomes, *de facto,* an autonomous actor in operational thinking if not official doctrine. This process can be seen in Stalin's and Molotov's application of Lenin's theory of imperialism to the day-to-day analysis of

---

[28] Walt, *Revolution and War.*
[29] I trace this process in *Elusive Balance.*

Soviet foreign policy. For many members of the official class whose public lives were defined by manning a massive state apparatus, the worldview shifted from revolution to state building. To be 'revolutionary' was to make the Soviet Union modern and powerful. Eventually, the elite began to identify itself more with the state and its achievements—its vast territory, military victories, and status in international society—than the radical ideals on which it was ostensibly founded. Hence the original revolutionary identity became in time a 'revolutionary imperial', and for many simply an updated state-imperial identity.[30]

The mixture of system pressure, path dependence on earlier Tsarist adaptations, and the Bolsheviks' impulse to modernism is evident in the reacquisition and reorganization of the empire. In order to win the Civil War, the Bolsheviks concluded that they needed to reconquer the empire to deny bridgeheads to rivals (White forces and/or the 'imperialist' powers). They thus appealed to national self-determination where and when it would undermine adversaries, and reverted to the orthodox Marxist insistence on the priority of workers' class interest (represented, of course, by the Bolsheviks or their dependable allies) where 'bourgeois' nationalist leaders of former imperial territories seemed likely to opt for independence.[31] The logic was simple and very often identical to the thinking that had led to the Tsars' conquest of the same territories in the first place: imperial provinces lost to the Bolsheviks would end up dependent on hostile foreign powers. The result was that the new revolutionary state ended up territorially identical to the former empire minus Finland, Russian Poland, and the three Baltic states.

But the Bolsheviks had no interest in recreating an old-fashioned Eurasian empire. Empires of that type were obvious losers. Moscow was now competing with modern nation-state based empires like Britain and France. The Soviets wanted to retain the strategically valuable territory of the Russian empire yet use whatever advantages they had to undermine their rivals' analogous assets. The solution was 'non-imperialist colonialism', which stressed economic and cultural development in order to distinguish the USSR from both its Tsarist predecessors and its contemporary British and French rivals.[32] They built a state that radically concentrated political and economic power in Moscow; yet it was formally organized as a federation based on the national principle and it granted non-Russian nationalities far more cultural rights than they had ever had under the old regime. In hindsight, the fatal contradictions in this policy seem obvious. The USSR is now seen as the great incubator and constructor of Eurasian national identities.[33] But for many decades it appeared to be a brilliant competitive adaptation. It was highly effective for Soviet anti-colonial propaganda. It increased the appeal of Soviet Union Republics to co-nationals living immediately across the border. And it facilitated Soviet 'non-imperialist' expansion by incorporating new territory into existing Union Republics rather than 'Russia' or

---

[30] Vladislav Zubok and Constantine Pleshakov, *Inside the Kremlin's Cold War* (Cambridge, MA: Harvard University Press, 1996).

[31] Richard Pipes, *The Formation of the Soviet Union: Communism and Nationalism, 1917–1923* (Cambridge, MA: Harvard University Press, 1954); Edward Hallet Carr, *A History of Soviet Russia*, vol. 3 (London: Macmillan, 1950).

[32] Francine Hirsch, 'Empire of Nations: Colonial Technologies and the Making of the Soviet Union, 1917–1939', Ph.D. thesis, Princeton University, 1998.

[33] Ronald Grigor Suny, *The Revenge of the Past: Nationalism, Revolution, and the Collapse of the Soviet Union* (Stanford, CA: Stanford University Press, 1993).

even adding new Union Republics, as in the case of Moldova and the Baltic states. As late as the 1960s, 'soviet colonialism' was seen as a far more effective form of imperialism than its Western counterpart.[34]

The most fateful and controversial question is the relationship between international systemic pressures and the Soviet political economy of autarkic forced-draught industrialization funded by a new enserfment of the peasantry on collective farms. As E. H. Carr discovered, any effort to defend this regime as somehow necessary given international pressures invites accusations of justifying a morally revolting system.[35] But as Stephen Kotkin has observed, the opening of archives has prompted a renewed emphasis on the political and international-political context of Soviet history, as opposed to the Cold War preoccupation with the 'totalitarian model'.[36] And this has brought back some of the themes if not the tone of Carr's work. Carr defended Stalin's violent 'revolution from above' because it appeared to be the only way to meet two critical criteria: (1) that the Soviet Union build 'socialism'—some system that was not capitalism and so did not rely on markets and private property; and (2) that it be capable of meeting the security challenge. Morally odious though they were, Stalin's policies can only be understood in light of the fact that they achieved these two objectives, which was no easy feat.

Ideology thus accounted in part for the high costs of Stalinism by foreclosing a capitalist road such as the Chinese took in the 1980s. But it is important to remember that without geopolitical pressure, the ideas would not have generated Stalinism. Moreover, in selecting a non-capitalist adaptive path, the Soviets were not consciously sacrificing international competitiveness. On the contrary, in the 1920s and 1930s, state planning and heavy industry were synonymous with both modernity and competitiveness. Given capitalism's performance in the 1930s, it was hard to see that system as optimal for the generation of power in international politics. Thus it was not the Soviets but the capitalists who were thought to be sacrificing state effectiveness to ideology or greedy domestic interests. And like so many Russian adaptations in the past, Stalin's was effective in meeting the security challenge in the medium term. Unlike many, it seemed to observers inside and outside the USSR to be progressive and modern. The fact that the kind of 'planning' envisioned in the Soviet official image was impossible in the slide-rule era was known only to those very close to the system. The fact that the giant 'Fordist' industrial enterprises built at such sacrifice would one day hinder rather than abet international competition would be known only to future generations.

Neorealist theory, ideas and institutions over the long term

In summary, neorealist theory cannot fully explain domestic institutions and ideas. But the Russian-Soviet case shows that the evolution of institutions and ideas

---

[34] See, for example, Michael Rywkin, *Russia in Central Asia: How Soviet Colonial Policy Operates and What it Portends* (New York: Collier, 1963). 'Confronted with the Soviet design for a world state', another scholar wondered in 1960, 'can the non-Soviet world confine itself to a precarious patchwork of expedients or must it not … hammer out some common plan for its own survival, which might ultimately foster the genuine integration of all nations?' Elliot R. Goodman, *The Soviet Design for a World State* (New York: Columbia University Press, 1960), p. xviii.

[35] Carr, *History of Soviet Russia*.

[36] Stephen Kotkin, '1991 and the Russian Revolution: Sources, Conceptual Categories, Analytical Frameworks', *The Journal of Modern History*, 70:2 (1998), pp. 384–425.

cannot be explained without reference to the causal forces neorealism identifies. The salience of these causes depends critically on timing and case selection. If one focuses on periods of major adaptive effort, the 'second image reversed' argument is very strong. In the Russian-Soviet case, momentous adaptive efforts were frequently executed by strong leaders—Ivan IV, Peter I, Stalin—against the inclinations of the existing domestic interests and ideas. If one focuses on cases that occur in periods in which the last adaptive effort has begun to obsolesce, then the institutions and ideas shaped by that last great effort appear to hinder rational responses to system incentives. In the Russian-Soviet case, weaker leaders like Nicholas II or Brezhnev held the helm of state during such periods. The apparent deficiencies of these leaders and the regimes they headed are partly the results of their unavoidable dependence on past adaptations to security pressures.

Structural effects: socialization and adaptation

Surprisingly, given neorealism's poor reputation among those historians who have acquainted themselves with it, the modes of Russian behaviour featured in many historical accounts correspond closely to the theory's predictions. It is important to stress that neorealism is not a strict rational-choice theory in two senses. [37] First, Waltz places 'the notion of "selection" in a position of central importance' in his theory. [38] This does not mean that states are utterly insensitive to relative costs and benefits over the long run. It simply means that the mechanism through which system pressures 'shape and shove' states in particular ways is not rational optimization of each decision problem but rather socialization, adaptation, and selection—subtler processes that operate over a much longer-term period. Second, as Stephen Brooks has argued, 'neorealism does not have expected utility foundations'.[39] Instead, it assumes that rather than calculating the precise *probability* of various outcomes, decision-makers are generally driven by the mere *possibility* of worst case disasters.[40] The theory thus predicts that states will follow decision rules that are biased by systemic pessimism in ways that violate the assumptions necessary to make expected utility models work.

---

[37] Waltz states unequivocally that his 'theory requires no assumptions of rationality', *Theory of International Politics,* p. 131. My claim here is simply that the theory is not one of strict rational choice in the two senses discussed in the text below. There is considerable debate on this issue, much of which revolves around how narrowly to construe the concept of rationality. Cf. Robert O. Keohane, 'Theory of World Politics: Structural Realism and Beyond', in Keohane (ed.), *Neorealism and its Critics* (New York: Columbia University Press, 1986), and Jeffrey W. Legro and Andrew Moravscik, 'Is Anybody Still a Realist?', *International Security*, 21: 2 (Fall 1999), pp. 5–55; with Miles Kahler, 'Inventing International Relations: International Relations Theory After 1945', in Michael W. Doyle and G. John Ikenberry (eds.), *New Thinking in International Relations Theory* (Boulder, CO: Westview Press, 1997) and Randall Schweller and William Wohlforth, 'Power Test: Updating Realism in Response to the End of the Cold War', *Security Studies*, 9:2 (2000), pp. 60–107.

[38] Kenneth N. Waltz, 'Reflections on *Theory of International Politics:* A Response to My Critics', in Keohane (ed.), *Neorealism and its Critics*, p. 118.

[39] Stephen G. Brooks, 'Dueling Realisms', p. 454. Other scholars contend that the 'possibilistic' assumption Brooks identifies as intrinsic to Waltz's neorealist theory actually only assumes this role in 'offensive' neorealist theory.

[40] Ibid., pp. 447–50.

The Russian models of adaptation and expansion

When considered over the long term, Russian and Soviet behaviour falls into repetitive patterns that strike analysts as distinct and identifiable models. These models frame a great many secondary accounts. The best known of these is the 'adaptive model,' featuring a strong leader and a brutal state-led adaptation to external pressures. Less well known but equally important is the 'expansion model' into which many historians fit the extraordinary growth of the Russian empire.

The adaptive model is already implicit in the foregoing discussion.[41] It encompasses three stages. First, an innovative leader perceives or precipitates some new or impending challenge and forces the state through a wrenching adaptation to meet it. The adaptation tends to be crisis-driven and *ad hoc*; a series of hasty innovations in response to impending disasters followed by further frenzied responses to the unforeseen problems created by these innovations. This costly adaptation does not emanate from within, but is imposed by a leader preoccupied by external concerns. Ivan IV, Peter I and Stalin are the classic examples. But Ivan III's innovations necessitated by his 'gathering up' of Novgorod also fit on a smaller scale, as do Catherine II's revamping of Peter's earlier adaptation, and Alexander II's post-Crimean revitalization programme.

In the second stage, the adaptation turns out to be successful in international competition for a generation or more. Thus, the initial adaptation to the pressures of the steppe system produced the central features of a tsarist state that turned out to be 'one of the most effective mechanisms for territorial expansion ever known', as Dominic Lieven put it.[42] This initial comparative advantage in territorial expansion naturally affected the relative costs and benefits of subsequent adaptations to external challenges. As William Fuller has shown, Peter's asymmetrical response exploited the tsarist state's initial advantages and proved brilliantly successful for over a century after 1709.[43] By contrast, Stalin's reorganization of the empire and industrialization drive remained competitive for only about 40 years. In the third stage, the adaptation loses its competitive edge, and pressure builds for a new adaptation, though path dependency creates lags between the general recognition of a problem and a major effort to address it. Thus, defeat in Crimea exposed the new competitive weakness of Peter's adaptation, setting the stage for the reforms of Alexander II.

The Russian model of expansion is similar, except that it generally falls into four stages.[44] First, prodded by leaders, the state adopts a basic expansionistic bias. Again, the bias does not emerge from within the polity; it is imposed by the monarch. The reasons for doing so are many, but among them is always the expected long-term security dividend that will accrue from expansion. The bias generates a simple rule: expand where feasible until you come to a natural geographical frontier or the border of a strong state with which you can establish predictable relations.

---

[41] A concise description is Snyder, 'Russian Backwardness'. See also Fuller, *Strategy and Power.*

[42] Lieven, *Empire*, p. 262.

[43] Fuller, *Strategy and Power.*

[44] See, for general discussions, Marc Raeff, 'In the Imperial Manner', in Raeff (ed.), *Catherine the Great: A Profile* (New York: Hill and Wang, 1972); Raeff, 'Patterns of Russian Imperial Policy Toward the Nationalities', in Edward Allworth (ed), *Soviet Nationality Problems* (New York: Columbia University Press, 1971); and S. Frederick Starr, 'Tsarist Government: The Imperial Dimension', in Jeremy R. Azrael (ed.), *Soviet Nationality Policies and Practices* (New York: Praeger, 1978).

Take the territory now; we'll figure out what to do with it later. Implicit in the rule is the assumption that the costs and benefits of expansion are impossible to discern precisely in each instance, but over the long run expansion will probably pay. The bias derives from an underlying pessimism about security: threats will emerge, no matter what we do; territory will prove valuable in impending struggles, even if such struggles are not immediately in the offing. Generally, the technique of expansion is an adaptation of whatever worked last time to the new circumstances. Thus Ivan IV tried out on the khanates of Kazan' and Astrakhan the basic expansion model Ivan III had developed in gathering up Novgorod and other Russian principalities. The techniques that worked on steppe Tatars were tried out on Crimean Tatars, and then on Caucasian peoples to the south, and so on.

Second, the new territory often turns out to be quite costly to conquer and/or difficult to incorporate in the near-term. At times, overly ambitious rulers like Ivan IV and Peter I try to expand too far and suffer costly defeats. Often, the original rationales for acquiring the territory are quickly proved false by experience. And, the model of imperialism updated from the last expansionist enterprise frequently fails in the new circumstances, producing unexpected costs. Caucasian mountain peoples responded very differently than steppe Tatars to Russian tactics, fighting a bloody war against Russia for over half a century. The Poles proved impervious to Russian imperial strategies that had worked elsewhere for centuries. But reputational concerns prevent relinquishing such territory unless forced to do so.

Third, however, in the long term—sometimes a generation or two after conquest—the territory frequently proves immensely valuable for security and/or wealth, providing fresh evidence in favour of the original bias toward expansion and justifying the immense initial costs. Peter's costly acquisition of the Baltic provinces yielded only tiny amounts of land, but proved critical in the dramatic expansion of the empire's trade in the eighteenth century, and also provided the services of the extraordinarily talented Baltic German aristocracy and bourgeoisie. Catherine's expansion to the Black Sea eventually made Ukraine secure so it could prosper and become Europe's breadbasket and a major exchange earner for Russia. The process of taking Crimea ruined its economy, but the peninsula eventually proved valuable strategically. The partitions of Poland brought Catherine over seven million new subjects whose comparative wealth filled her treasury's coffers. The revenues and strategic depth provided by her westward expansion later proved critical in fending off Napoleon's Grand Army in 1812. The Transcaucasus expansion eventually put the Baku oilfields in Russian hands. In some cases, however, the expansion model extends to a fourth stage: in the very long term changing conditions that could not have been foreseen once again make the territory problematic, but the same concerns for internal and external reputation impede efforts to shed it. The rise of nationalism in the nineteenth century slowly changed the cost-benefit calculus for many lands that had formerly been successfully incorporated into the empire.

The Russian behavioural models and neorealist theory

These Russian models of adaptation to systemic pressure and territorial expansion raise two important issues. First, they exactly fit neorealist theory as described by

Waltz and Brooks. They were 'selected' by system pressures, and reflect biased decision rules that violate the basic precepts of expected utility models in the direction of neorealist worst-case pessimism. They discount the utility of rigorous cost-benefit calculations of any given decision to expand or adapt. They are thus consistent with a systematic inattention to finely grained expected utility calculations and the absence of institutions able to conduct them. They reflect the assumption that the uncertainty inherent in any given decision to expand or adapt is intractable; no *ex ante* measurement of costs and benefits is possible. Expansion is less a choice than an environmentally conditioned disposition reflecting an underlying pessimism. As Geoffrey Hoskings put it, 'like a cumbersome and nervous amoeba, [Muscovy] expanded to fill the space it was able to dominate, and was impelled into a perpetual dynamic of conquest'.[45] Similarly, Russian-Soviet adaptations are not usefully understood as calculating strategic plans with coherent sets of corresponding institutions but rather as frantic bursts of activity that haphazardly make the best of the mix of resources Russia happens to have at that moment.

It follows, secondly, that both neorealist theory and the Russian-Soviet patterns of adaptation are consistent with institutional arrangements and decision-making styles that appear suboptimal from the standpoint of a strictly rational 'logic of consequences'. As Waltz stresses, 'one cannot expect of political leaders the nicely calculated decisions that the word "rationality" suggests'.[46] This is important because neither Russian nor Soviet institutions and leaders were such as to inspire confidence in their capacity for optimally rational decision-making. Perhaps for this reason, evidence on decision-making is often thought to offer strongest support for explanations rooted in domestic institutions and identity. Behind nearly every decision that produced seemingly suboptimal results, one can uncover a decision-making process that looks deeply flawed. This connection between deficient institutions and flawed individual decision-making styles, on the one hand, and blundering, bellicose statecraft that produced seemingly avoidable costs, on the other hand, is at the centre of the mainstream literature that treats the behaviour as incompatible with system pressures.

For anyone familiar with late imperial or Soviet history, it is difficult to deny the appeal of this argument. Both regimes in their last years seem to epitomize incompetence.[47] But a longer-term perspective does undermine the significance of this connection between poor governance and poor foreign policy outcomes by revealing selection bias. If one looks at behaviour that seems in hindsight to have led to failure, one finds institutional and individual departures from the strict rationalist ideal of decision-making. But if one looks at apparent successes, one frequently finds the same thing. Territorial expansion that ultimately added immeasurably to the wealth and security of the empire, such as the expansion to control the course of the Volga River, or later to Siberia and Ukraine, or the acquisition of access to the Caspian, Black and Baltic Seas, occurred under rulers and regimes following decision rules just as biased as those who undertook seemingly unnecessary and ultimately costly expansion. Strategic adaptations that turned out to work spectacu-

[45] Hoskings, *Russia,* p. 4.
[46] Waltz, 'Reflections on *Theory of International Politics*', p. 118.
[47] On late imperial Russia, see especially David Schimmelpenninck van der Oye, *Toward the Rising Sun: Russian Ideologies of Empire and the Path to War with Japan* (DeKalb, IL: Northern Illinois University Press: 2001). Compare, however, Dominic Lieven, *Nicholas II: Emperor of all the Russias* (London: John Murray, 1993), which stresses the path dependency problem highlighted here. On Brezhnev's Soviet Union, see Anderson, *Public Policy in an Authoritarian State*; and Hopf, *Peripheral Visions*.

larly were undertaken under leaders and institutions who were just as far from rationalistic optimality as those which stubbornly refused or bungled reforms.

Peter the Great is a case in point. His reputation among historians, as compared, say, to that of Nicholas II, is clearly not merely a product of hindsight. He was an unusually competent leader. He beat Sweden, secured access to the Baltic and won 'great power' status for his empire. But his chaotic strategic *modus operandi* bears scant resemblance to the rationalist ideal. True, he was adept at technical and tactical matters, and could cobble together institutions to manage them. When it came to designing a ship or directing a military campaign, few leaders were his equal. But he simply did not devote his formidable energy to the task of clearly articulating the strategic logic behind his relentless and astonishingly costly imperialism. If his expansionism was the result of expected utility calculations, he left no record of them. One historian stresses Peter's 'reluctance—inability even—to produce clear-cut policy statements'.[48] He frequently overreached his empire's capabilities, as in the campaigns to the Caspian and Central Asia. His real competence lay in putting the larger Russian patterns of adaptation and expansion into effect. Biographers portray him as in many ways the personification of these patterns. Expansion was less a strategic choice than a basic disposition.[49]

In sum, historians' analyses of the patterns of Russian expansion and adaptation strongly correspond to expectations of neorealist theory. Decision-making styles and institutional arrangements that seem maladaptive in certain periods are consistent with these larger patterns. Whether such patterns and decision rules were suboptimal given the state interest in security cannot be answered by examining only cases of apparent failure.

Reconsidering anomalies: the Soviet empire from Brezhnev to Gorbachev

If the foregoing discussion suggests that neorealist theory provides a valid explanation for the general Russian-Soviet propensity toward costly expansion, what about the specific periods that the standard literature views as anomalous? To be sure, as a theory of long-term structural causation, neorealism is always a limited tool in explaining specific cases. But the theory's ability to account for the longer-term pattern of behaviour may alter the way we interpret the cases that are generally seen as challenging to the theory.

The period that has attracted the greatest attention from IR scholars is the Soviet Union's continued expansionist bias in the years after its acquisition of a secure second-strike nuclear capability. Many analysts assume that the essential scope (though not the particular form) of Stalin's wartime expansion in the Baltics and Central Europe, as well as the creation of an informal empire in Central Europe in 1945–48, was strongly influenced by security concerns. Recent archival research buttresses this general interpretation.[50] But once the USSR obtained a secure

---

[48] Lindsey Hughes, *Russia in the Age of Peter the Great* (New Haven, CT: Yale University Press, 1998), p. 61.

[49] Ibid., M. S. Anderson, *Peter the Great* (London: Thames and Hudson, 1978).

[50] See Mark Kramer, 'The Soviet Union and Eastern Europe: Spheres of Influence', in Ngaire Woods (ed.), *Explaining International Relations Since 1945* (Oxford: Oxford University Press, 1996); Mark Kramer, 'Ideology and the Cold War', *Review of International Studies*, 25:4 (1999), pp. 539–76; and Vojtech Mastny, *The Cold War and Soviet Insecurity: The Stalin Years* (New York: Oxford University Press, 1996).

second-strike capability by the mid-1960s, subsequent willingness to pay high costs for an informal empire in Central Europe appears puzzling. Three answers emerge from the analysis here.

First, the security benefits of the informal empire transcended the region's role as a defensive *glacis* against NATO and a forward base for the Red Army's offensive war plan. Lacking the great commercial power of its US rival, the Soviet Union retained influence over European security policy, and indeed significant leverage over Washington, partly by courtesy of its informal empire in Central Europe. That is, the Soviet Union was still using its comparative advantage in territorial control to obtain a greater voice on European security matters than its economy and techno-logical level would warrant. And unlike their predecessors in Moscow's Kremlin, Leonid Brezhnev and his foreign policy team had managed to extract undeniable security benefits from their forward positions in Europe that continued to matter even in an era of nuclear deterrence.

The much-maligned Brezhnev took power in 1964, when the Western economies were in the midst of the greatest boom in capitalism's history, and the United States was engaged in a furious military build-up. In a scant seven years, he and Foreign Minister Gromyko had attained favourable *modus vivendi* with West Germany, secured international recognition of the German Democratic Republic and most of their wartime conquests, and were engaged in a *détente* with the world's pre-eminent power, the United States, on formal terms of parity. A major source of Moscow's influence on these questions was its position in Central Europe. The costs and benefits of the informal empire were thus harder to calculate than scholars often assume. To be sure, Moscow's forward position was one factor helping to unite NATO. On the other hand, it gave Moscow the wherewithal to elicit deference from powerful NATO countries on crucial security questions. Whether it was better to have more influence over a relatively coherent NATO (and NATO perennially seemed on the verge of a major crisis in these years), or less influence over a less united NATO was a tough call for Moscow.

Second was the old imperial problem. In retirement at his dacha in the mid 1970s, Molotov entertained a Georgian fighter pilot—a hero of the Great Fatherland War—who emphatically reaffirmed his willingness to die for the 'motherland'. 'You mean Georgia?' Molotov asked. 'No! Our Soviet Motherland'! his guest insisted.[51] The Old Bolshevik was under no illusions about the imperial nature of the Soviet federal 'state'. And he and his contemporaries knew well that the geopolitical expansion that had brought Russia the Baltic States, Moldova, and a major swath of new territory for Ukraine were linked historically with the creation of the informal empire after the war. Hence, retrenchment from the outer empire would be very hard to separate from the inner empire. The pact Molotov had negotiated with Ribbentrop in 1939 brought Russia back into Poland and the Baltics. If Poland were set free, pressure would rise in the Baltics, and thence, perhaps, to the Georgian motherland of his war hero guest. The old imperial problem reasserted itself. The flexibility that might be optimal for external purposes contradicted the internal requisites of empire.

Third, given the remaining security benefits and the imperial problem, any decision to retrench from the outer empire looked very costly indeed. Hence, it

---

[51] Feliks Chuev, *Sto sorok besed s Molotvym: Iz dnevnika F Chueva* (Moscow: Terra, 1991), p. 54.

would take prolonged and salient evidence of rising relative costs to prompt a policy departure. As it turned out, the costs of empire increased steadily, but at about the same time oil prices boosted Moscow's ability to absorb them. Thus, the crunch truly intensified in the 1980s, as imperial costs soared and oil revenues plummeted. The result was building pressure throughout the decade to put the relationship on a new footing.

The decline and fall of the Soviet Union serves as an illustration of many of the arguments made herein. The perception of Moscow's willingness to enforce its dominion in Central Europe militarily appears to have been a necessary condition of its external empire. In 1953, 1956 and 1968, Soviet rulers decided to pay the international costs of repressing perceived or anticipated defection. But during the 1970s and 1980s, Moscow also responded to the classic problems of the decay of its imperial rule by devolving considerable authority to local agents in Central Europe and in the Union Republics of the USSR. By the time Gorbachev took the helm, the policy of dealing with principal-agent problems by increased decentralization was already well entrenched. Gorbachev's response combined continued devolution in Central Europe with intermittent efforts at re-centralization in the inner empire. Externally, he began to implement a policy of careful appeasement that required dispelling external perceptions of the Soviet threat. This proved to be a volatile mix of policies: dispelling the Soviet threat abroad did deliver *détente*, but it also dispelled Moscow's reputation for resolve in the outer empire, which rapidly became unglued. The collapse of the outer empire then fed into the centre-periphery struggle in the Soviet Union itself, as Moscow's centralizing effort to control local agents clashed against its declining reputation for coercive sanction.

Gorbachev tried the policies of retrenchment and reform that are the obvious alternatives to the expansionist bias favoured by his predecessors. On balance, those policies should be applauded for minimizing the bloodshed that accompanied the end of the Cold War and the collapse of the Soviet Union. But, it does need to be pointed out that those policies failed miserably in achieving Gorbachev's goals. It is simply much more difficult than often realized to make the case that Russia was too concerned with territory and status and too reluctant to consider retrenchment and reform as solutions to imperial decline. When Nicholas II decided in 1914 to fight for status, his empire collapsed. When Gorbachev declined to fight for status and banked instead on retrenchment and reform, his empire collapsed. The two decisions and their consequences speak volumes about the intrinsic difficulty of the task both men faced. The argument that Russia was too concerned with territory and status suggests that alternative policies were available that could have maintained the empire longer, or as long at smaller cost. The analysis here suggests otherwise.

Conclusion

Neorealism occupies a paradoxical position in contemporary IR. It is the theory that is most frequently proclaimed dead; and it is the theory that is most frequently proclaimed dominant. The reason is that the theory's main role is as a foil for scholarly research. It serves as the ubiquitous baseline argument against which any case study's findings, no matter how limited, may seem to loom large. But neorealism's actual claim to be a theory of very long-term structural causation that accounts for persistent patterns of state behaviour is never subjected to focused empirical evaluation. The origins of this lacuna may lie in American IR's bias against historical research. But whatever the cause, the absence of such studies makes it difficult to justify the theory's continued influence as a baseline account. In this article, I conducted such a review in the broad-brush manner dictated by space constraints. I found that Russia and the Soviet Union are good cases for neorealism. The theory provides an explanation for pronounced patterns of Russian-Soviet behaviour that finds very strong validation in the historical literature. Given the prior expectation that would follow from recent discussions of neorealism as a 'degenerating research programme,' the finding is strikingly favourable to the theory. However, the evaluation conduced here was perforce a cursory one, and the Russian-Soviet case may well be an especially good one for the theory. If this finding tends to be replicated in other cases, then neorealism's baseline role may rest on firmer foundations.

This is not to conclude that the Russian-Soviet historical experience contains no lessons for neorealist theory. Even when applied over long spans of time, the theory's reliance on the elusive concept of 'power' is a central weakness. The experience of the Russian-Soviet empire shows that the imperative of survival under anarchy fosters power maximization. The system socialized Russian and Soviet leaders to maximize power, but they remained uncertain about how to measure it. In practice, how do we know when we are more 'powerful' and thus more secure? Russian and Soviet leaders responded by exploiting their comparative advantage in territorial expansion and monitoring the results over the very long term. Overall, this bias toward expansion worked in securing an inherently insecure state over centuries.

However, the evidence shows that Russian and Soviet leaders did have a more fine-grained approach to measuring 'power' and thus monitoring the effectiveness of their power-maximizing strategy. They appear frequently to have used status as an index of power. The Russian and Soviet affection for status in international society is a ubiquitous theme in the historical and diplomatic literatures. The quest for status is a standard explanation for late imperial Russian expansion, as well as Khrushchev's and Brezhnev's competitive behaviour in the Third World. Russian and Soviet statesmen frequently appear to have selected strategies with an eye toward eliciting formal indicators of deference on the part of other states. Using status as a metric for power is especially compelling for backward states playing catch-up ball with the system's leaders, as both Russia and the Soviet Union had to do. Measuring status demands a keen sensitivity to the symbols, signals, and discourse that indicate degrees of deference. It involves monitoring the relationship between recent policy choices and status—a task subject to error, to be sure, but one that may yield information extremely valuable to decision-makers.

If the quest for status becomes an end in itself, divorced from power politics and security, it may fit far more comfortably into a British School or constructivst theoretical framework than neorealism. The Russian experience would then be seen as a story of socialization to a particular and contingent sort of status society that happened to take shape in western Europe around the time Russia became a major power. On the other hand, Russia's strong preference for high standing in the interstate hierarchy may be consistent with neorealist theory. The theory would portray status-seeking as endogenous to insecurity. The more insecure a social system is, the more any member's fate is contingent upon its rank in the social hierarchy. The more insecure a member of a system is, the more it will seek reassurance of its relative rank. States exist in a primitive society, and thus care about their standing in that society not just for the intrinsic gratification it brings but also because of the security it conveys. Russia faced particularly acute security challenges, and thus placed greater emphasis on its status than relatively more secure powers.

The relationship between status seeking, power maximization and security has yet to be worked out in realist theory or IR more generally. Russia's historical experience may provide useful material for advancing our understanding of these relationships. And such understanding has more than theoretical implications. For Russia's sense of insecurity, its problems of backwardness and its sensitivity to its status in international society did not disappear with the Soviet empire. All of these themes frame the discourse in Moscow, as well as Beijing, Delhi and other capitals. Historical research on long-term patterns has much to add to an explanation of their interconnections.

Another 'double movement': the great transformation after the Cold War?

IAN CLARK

This collection of essays grapples, historically, with the complex issues involved in understanding system transformation. Often these transformations have taken the form of a shift along the spectrum of independence-centralization, and it is within the framework of such declining or emerging imperial systems that the degree of change has tended to be measured. The task of this contribution is to locate the specific case of the end of the Cold War within the broader reflections on these themes. It will respond to this challenge by applying a different litmus test for change from that already found in the existing literature about the significance of the end of the Cold War. Instead, it will broach the topic by an examination of prevailing concepts of legitimacy within international society.[1] In short, it argues that a study of the role of legitimacy might be a useful way of documenting and measuring the kinds of changes taking place within an international system. Moreover, while the end of the Cold War might be thought to have nothing to say about the issue of empire as such (beyond recording the expiry of the Soviet version), it will additionally be suggested that the resultant extension of shared concepts of international legitimacy can be understood as a defining attribute of the contemporary imperial project.

This argument is itself couched within a broader claim. As a counterpart to Polanyi's[2] analysis of the 'double movement' created by the exposure to the market, and the reactive quest for forms of social and political protection, there is another Great Transformation that needs to be documented by the historians of international relations. For Polanyi, the great formative force during the nineteenth century was the vulnerability of society, under industrial capitalism, to the full effects of the unregulated market. As a reaction to this, forms of state welfarism and interventionism were developed by the middle twentieth century to cushion its effects. The 'double movement' thus consisted in the fact that 'markets spread all over the face of the globe', but then, in response, 'a network of measures and policies was integrated into powerful institutions designed to check the action of the market'.[3]

A parallel development took place in international relations, and the logics of both should be understood as connected, not coincidental. In international relations,

---

[1] This article forms part of a larger study that will be published as *Legitimacy in International Society* by Oxford University Press.
[2] K. Polanyi, *The Great Transformation: The Political and Economic Origins of Our Time* (New York: Farrar and Rinehart, 1944).
[3] Polanyi, *Great Transformation*, p. 76.

the first movement took the form of the creation during the late nineteenth and first two-thirds of the twentieth centuries of an international society that had finally become fully global in scope. However, as a 'double movement' associated with this expanding formalistic society, there also emerged, from within, a thicker version, committed to a set of particular economic and political values. An alternative vision has, at least since 1919 but more vigorously since 1945, sought to fashion a more intense style of international society. This was developed as a form of social and economic 'protection' for the bloc of Western states that found itself exposed to the vagaries and inconveniences of the increasingly open political 'market' of the global state system, as it developed in the twentieth century. The logics of both sets of movements were thus being driven by a single process. While society had to be protected from the unregulated global market, in the interests of restoring domestic and international political stability, so the core states of the international system sought to guard their existing privileges in the unregulated global state system by deploying the institutions of the embedded liberal solution at the international level also. It is important to understand, however, that this was not simply the working out of any natural liberal progressivism, but was intended also to shape a new international society best suited to preserving the advantages already enjoyed by the Western states.

The end of the Cold War needs to be understood in this context, not as the inculcation of any new set of principles, but rather as an important stage in the advancement of this 'double movement' towards a more overtly normative style of international society, as defined by the core states within it. This has been wrought by the direct application of a revised standard of civilization, as the appropriate test for membership. In short, the 'expansion' of international society that accompanied the zenith and subsequent decline of the imperial age has evoked a second and counter tendency in the shape of an 'intensification' of international society emanating from its imperial core. This 'double movement' is now far advanced and has become coextensive with significant sections of the global state system. In that sense, international society is undergoing a process of 'reinvention',[4] and the end of the Cold War marks a critical phase in that development.

The key argument set out here is that, as part of this process, the principles of international legitimacy should be considered not to have changed with the end of the Cold War. In fact, they were to be substantially reaffirmed. These legitimizing principles revolved around three central and interconnected ideas: principles of multilateralism and a commitment to a global economy; a collectivization of security; and adherence to a set of liberal rights values.[5] These principles had pervaded the post-1945 international order but, in the context of the Cold War, had operated as a principle of 'exclusion', rather than of inclusion.[6] With the end of the Cold War, these self-same principles became agents of admission to the inner international society, justifying the changes that had been made *via* the post-Cold War settlement, but also legitimizing the induced changes in the economic and political structures of

---

[4] T. Dunne, *Inventing International Society: A History of the English School* (Houndmills, UK: Macmillan, 1998).

[5] I. Clark, *The Post-Cold War Order: The Spoils of Peace* (Oxford: Oxford University Press, 2001).

[6] P. W. Schroeder, 'A New World Order: A Historical Perspective', in B. Roberts (ed.), *Order and Disorder after the Cold War: A Washington Quarterly Reader* (Cambridge, MA: MIT Press, 1995).

the former East. In that respect, they served a similar function to earlier applications of the standard of civilization. The role of that principle has been depicted in the following terms:

> By the turn of the century, the standard had emerged sufficiently to define the legal requirements necessary for a non-European country like China to gain full and 'civilized' status in 'civilized' international society. Included in these requirements were the ability of the country to guarantee the life, liberty, and property of foreign nationals; to demonstrate a suitable governmental organization; to adhere to the accepted diplomatic practices; and to abide by the principles of international law.[7]

Thus construed, the principles of legitimacy have operated as a second standard of civilization, and as part of the 'double movement' accelerated by the end of the Cold War. They permit 'full membership' within all aspects of international society to those members of the former communist bloc that had hitherto been semi-detached from important aspects of it, particularly in the economic sphere, but also with regard to adherence to liberal democratic norms. These principles did not change as a result of the end of the Cold War. The key question is whether or not they have been used to legitimate new practices, such as in Wheeler's suggestion that there is now greater acceptance of an entitlement to, not to mention a duty of, humanitarian intervention.[8] The principles might also be thought to have legitimized a practice of encouragement of democratization, as an acceptable dimension of international intercourse.[9]

But are any such changes to be understood as the natural development of solidarist norms within international society, or simply as structural principles inculcated for the advantage of particular interests? What this raises is the key, and problematic, relationship between legitimacy and power. Entailed by this is the basic issue of whether or not legitimacy is a separate way of understanding international society and its workings, or merely an expression of power and interests. At the very least, some claim, 'power and legitimacy … are not conflicting concepts but rather are complementary ones'.[10] We need to do more to understand, internationally, 'the role of power … in making an institution legitimate'.[11] As is often noted, actors can comply for three basic reasons: coercion, self-interest, or because 'they think the norms are legitimate and therefore *want* to follow them'.[12] Posed in these terms, what is the contemporary status of principles of international legitimacy? Are they symptomatic of a gradual universalism that is tightening the normative bonds of international society, and is it for this reason that the end of the Cold War symbolizes the transformations currently underway? Or, more cynically, are these

---

[7] Gerrit W. Gong, 'China's Entry into International Society', in H. Bull and A. Watson (eds.), *The Expansion of International Society* (Oxford: Oxford University Press, 1984), p. 179.

[8] N. J. Wheeler, *Saving Strangers: Humanitarian Intervention in International Society* (Oxford: Oxford University Press, 2000).

[9] M. Cox, G. John Ikenberry, and T. Inoguchi (eds.), *American Democracy Promotion: Impulses, Strategies, and Impacts* (New York: Oxford University Press, 2000).

[10] M. N. Barnett, 'Bringing in the New World Order: Liberalism, Legitimacy, and the United Nations', *World Politics*, 49:4 (1997), p. 544.

[11] I. Hurd, 'Legitimacy and Authority in International Politics', *International Organization*, 53:2 (Spring 1999), p. 402.

[12] A. Wendt, *Social Theory of International Politics* (Cambridge: Cambridge University Press, 1999), pp. 268–73; Hurd, 'Legitimacy and Authority'.

principles simply a reflection of current power plays, and an instrument for encouraging the compliance of other states with the West's own preferred rules of the game?

Assessing the end of the Cold War

How then might an examination of principles of international legitimacy assist in the task of mapping the degree of change resulting from the end of the Cold War? Before this train of thought can be pursued, we need to reflect upon the existing debates about how fundamental have been the post-Cold War transitions, and how such assessments have been reached. This will set the scene for the specific framework within which the remainder of this argument is set.

The confidence with which the end of the Cold War was initially greeted as marking a fundamental watershed in world affairs was soon matched only by a profound uncertainty as to what it was, after all, that had changed as a result. As such, that transition offered a good test case for exploring wider theoretical issues about systems and systemic change.[13] The case was particularly apposite as an illustration of the problems in distinguishing between fundamental systemic change, on the one hand, and varying degrees of lower level change, on the other. In summary, part of the fascination with the end of the Cold War resided in its intimation that we might possibly 'be on the brink of another transformation of the international system'.[14] And yet, by many other theoretical measures, the end of the Cold War seemed to betoken much more modest forms of change than this implied. According to these, its implications were confined to uncertain adjustments to the system's polarity and stability. Occupying the middle ground between these two verdicts, there was a position that, although falling some way short of the apocalyptic, the end of the Cold War remained nonetheless *symptomatic* of other, much wider, processes of transformation that were already underway. If not itself the cause of these changes, it could nevertheless be understood as symbolic of their potency in general. The end of the Cold War thus represented these changes, even if not itself the precipitant of them.

The pervasive assessment at the time was that the end of the Cold War should be counted as one of history's great 'punctuation points',[15] and that it marked a 'clear and pronounced break'.[16] It was understandable that this should have been the reaction when viewed from close up to the tumbling walls. However, once we had gained some distance from, and perspective upon, these events, commentators became less persuaded that the world had, indeed, been turned upside down. Since a number of important features had palpably *not* changed, we were reminded that the

---

[13] R. Gilpin, *War and Change in World Politics* (Cambridge: Cambridge University Press, 1981), pp. 39–49; G. John Ikenberry and M. W. Doyle, 'Conclusion' in Doyle and Ikenberry (eds.), *New Thinking in International Relations Theory* (Boulder, CO: Westview Press, 1997), p. 274.

[14] B. Buzan and R. Little, *International Systems in World History: Remaking the Study of International Relations* (Oxford: Oxford University Press, 2000), p. 349.

[15] J. L. Gaddis, 'The Cold War, the Long Peace, and the Future', in M. J. Hogan (ed.), *The End of the Cold War: Its Meaning and Implications* (Cambridge: Cambridge University Press, 1992), p. 22.

[16] B. Hansen and B. Heurlin, 'Introduction', in Hansen and Heurlin (eds.), *The New World Order: Contesting Theories* (Houndmills, UK: Macmillan, 2000), p. vii.

'landscape in 1999 may look very different to 1989, but there are still some very familiar landmarks'.[17] The issue of whether to be more impressed by what had changed, or by what remained constant, revealed itself, on closer scrutiny, as an instance of the generic problem of theory-dependence. 'The changes which occurred during "the end of the Cold War"', Patomaki observed early in the development of this debate, '... can be analysed only within a theoretical framework. ... Hence, every theory of international relations defines what the world is, what it is like, and what its *possible* transformations are'.[18] The end of the Cold War, for that reason, became inextricably caught up in the theoretical webs spun around it.

So what was to be the relevant theory for this particular purpose? The desultory debate about the character of the post-Cold War order soon clarified the full nature of the problem as one of seeming 'incommensurability'.[19] It largely took place within the territory marked out by Buzan and Little as referring to two of the three types of systems change, namely 'process' and 'structure',[20] and was in large measure about the relationship between them. The border between these two spheres was sometimes respected and treated as inviolate (as in the debate about power, balancing, polarity and unipolarity); it was regarded by others as being still important, but increasingly permeable (as in debates about collective security, concerts, humanitarian intervention, and the constructivist challenge in general); or it was elsewhere widely dismissed as largely irrelevant (as in many of the presentations on globalization). There could be no agreement on how significant was the end of the Cold War without reaching a prior agreement on the theoretical framework within which the discussion was to be conducted, or without at least some 'truce' in the internecine theoretical warfare.

Such a claim is scarcely controversial, but its significance for this essay needs to be further clarified. If, in terms of the Buzan and Little tripartite scheme of systems transformations,[21] the last radical change—one resulting in the modern sovereign state system—occurred some five hundred years ago, then it seems clear that the end of the Cold War, narrowly conceived, scarcely registers on the radar for consideration as a change of this magnitude. Whatever the resultant polarity and/or degree of state co-operation, other essential systemic frameworks remain in place despite the passing of the Cold War. Accordingly, the argument that the end of the Cold War is worth thinking about at all as an historical landmark needs to be attached to a wider set of claims about the passing of the age of the modern sovereign state system. This, in turn, yields its own tripartite framework: we must assess the end of the Cold War within a frame of reference that links this to *modernity, sovereignty,* and the *state system.* It is in terms of its impact on such wider themes that the significance of the end of the Cold War deserves to be explored. Williams[22] indirectly makes the first connection, albeit in the negative:

---

[17] M. Cox, K. Booth, and T. Dunne, 'Introduction: The Interregnum: Controversies in World Politics, 1989–99', *Review of International Studies*, 25: Special Issue (December 1999), p. 4.

[18] H. Patomaki, 'What is it that Changed with the End of the Cold War? An Analysis of the Problem of Identifying and Explaining Change', in P. Allan and K. Goldmann (eds.), *The End of the Cold War: Evaluating Theories of InternationalRelations* (Dordrecht, Holland: Martinus Nijhoff, 1992), p. 180.

[19] C. Wight, 'Incommensurability and Cross-Paradigm Communication: "What's the Frequency Kenneth?"', *Millennium*, 25:2 (1996).

[20] Buzan and Little, *International Systems*, pp. 11–12.

[21] Ibid., p. 4.

[22] M. C. Williams, 'Modernity, Postmodernity and the New World Order', in Hansen and Heurlin, *New World Order*, p. 82.

From a postmodern position, thinking about the NWO cannot be limited solely to a consideration of the end of the Cold War. As important as this transformation is, it needs to be placed within the broader context of a shift from modern to increasingly postmodern intellectual, social and political forms. If we look to the end of the Cold War as a 'revolutionary' turning point, we will undoubtedly be disappointed.

Waever voices the second of these wider perspectives when he opines of the recent changes taking place in the international system that the 'strongest elements of systems change are elements of change in relation to sovereignty and not least the relationship between sovereignty and territory'.[23] This viewpoint might be taken as representative of the entire 'post-Westphalian' family of arguments that have gained wide currency in the past decade or so. In turn, this overlaps with the third perspective—the demise of a states system—because of the emergence of diverse actors, and its replacement by some alternative order, be it neo-medieval or globalized in form.

The point about each of these three positions is that, if the theoretical bar for measuring change is set too high, the end of the Cold War is unlikely to come anywhere close to clearing it, *unless* the end of the Cold War is understood to refer to wider sets of developments than the mere ending of the struggle between the two superpowers alone. Thus transmuted, that *ending* becomes but a shorthand device for encapsulating other seismic shifts in one or all of the three constituents of the pre-existing system. In other words, the end of the Cold War only registers on the Richter scale of systemic change at all if it can be demonstrated to be symbolic of, or associated with, one of these more profound changes. Otherwise, it must be demoted to one of history's rhythmic, and relatively frequent, punctuation points (1648, 1713, 1815 and so on). Whilst these are of some arcane interest to the historian of the modern sovereign state system, they give rise to no particular pause on the part of the grand theorist of system transformation.

Starting from this more modest position—that the end of the Cold War be viewed as something less than the end of the modern sovereign states system—there are many studies to suggest that we can still sensibly discuss significant degrees of change 'within' an existing system. Examples of this genre include the following. Osiander[24] traces the evolution of consensus principles within the state system from 1648 to the present. It is his argument that the degree of stability in the international system at any one point in time is related to the nature and extent of these principles. There have been many of these and they have evolved over time. They include principles of autonomy, custom, equilibrium, equality, great powerhood, and national self-determination. On this kind of basis, we can tell a compelling story of the evolution of the international system, crafted around the changes in the substance of these consensus principles.

Although differing in his organizational scheme, and working with a more refined set of conceptual categories, Reus-Smit[25] likewise tells a story of change predicated

---

[23] O. Waever, 'Power, Principles and Perspectivism: Understanding Peaceful Change in Post-Cold War Europe', in H. Patomaki (ed.), *Peaceful Changes in World Politics* (Tampere, Finland: Tampere Peace Research Institute, 1995), p. 259.

[24] A. Osiander, *The States System of Europe 1640–1990: Peacemaking and the Condition of International Stability* (Oxford: Oxford University Press, 1994).

[25] C. Reus-Smit, *The Moral Purpose of the State* (Princeton, NJ: Princeton University Press, 1999).

upon the 'constitutive structure' or 'moral purpose' of the state. His is a narrative of changing international societies, the change from one to another being traceable through the deeply embedded constitutional structures that lie at their base. What is so innovative about his argument is that, when this is done, sovereignty becomes less of a test in its own right for measuring the extent of change. A key part of his argument is the salient change during the nineteenth century when, for all the seeming continuities of the sovereignty game, the international system nonetheless underwent radical transformation in accord with shifts in that moral purpose. The age of revolution then takes centre stage in this transformative tale.[26] According to it, we move less confidently and directly from 1648 to the present. As a consequence of our obsessive preoccupation with sovereignty as the basic norm, we have been prepared to see evidence of dramatic change only towards the end of the twentieth century, on the grounds of the multiple threats to sovereignty that were believed to be emerging by that time. However, if we look beyond sovereignty, tell-tale signs of transformation can be found much earlier. The changing practice between the Vienna settlement and the Hague conferences becomes, for Reus-Smit, a landmark that has been unduly neglected by the historians of system transformation.

Similar in general concept, but differing in specific details, is Hall's narrative of shifts in the international system as reflections of changing national collective identities.[27] Hall depicts a tripartite scheme of development from the medieval to the dynastic-sovereign system (Augsburg, 1555), from thence to the territorial-sovereign system (Westphalia, 1648), and finally to the national-sovereign system (French Revolution, 1789).[28] Critically, in terms of the argument developed below, Hall contends that changes in 'individual and collective identity result in changes in the legitimating principles of global and domestic social order'.[29] While there is here a close family resemblance to the evolution mapped by Reus-Smit, Hall's account is formulated in terms of shifting sovereignty norms, and not on some moral purpose that is more fundamental than sovereignty. Significantly, however, his history once again undermines any notion of the 'timeless wisdom' of behaviour within a state system. The prime evidence of this flux is to be discovered in the system's evolving legitimating principles: these form the geological deposits by which the passing of distinct ages can be detected and mapped in time.

Finally, and from a quite different perspective, there is the engagingly robust position advanced by Krasner in this volume and elsewhere.[30] In his distinctive way, he also enjoins us to look beyond sovereignty for evidence of system change, because sovereignty has been honoured in the breach ever since Westphalia. The idea that we can measure change by pointing to the erosion of sovereignty is, for that reason, highly suspect.

But if not to sovereignty, to what is the historian of change to direct attention? A different framework for making such assessments has recently been deployed by

[26] Reus-Smit, *Moral Purpose*, pp. 152–3.
[27] R. B. Hall, *National Collective Identity: Social Constructs and International Systems* (New York: Columbia University Press, 1999).
[28] Hall, *National Collective Identity*, p. 6.
[29] Ibid., p. 29.
[30] S. D. Krasner, 'Compromising Westphalia', *International Security*, 20:3 (1995/6); *Sovereignty: Organized Hypocrisy* (Princeton, NJ: Princeton University Press, 1999).

John Ikenberry,[31] and by the present author.[32] Although there are substantial differences between these two approaches, they share a 'peace settlement' perspective, and within that frame both make similar arguments about the continuities and discontinuities embodied in the post-Cold War order. Both challenge the notion of a 'clear break' in 1989–91. Both approach the end of the Cold War by regarding it as equivalent to one of the great peace settlements that have come in the aftermath of major wars. The reason for doing so is that the style and content of peace settlements tend to be profoundly expressive of the norms of international society at any period of time.[33]

As with Osiander, the starting point for both these accounts is the assumption that attempts to reconstruct post-war international systems are likely to be revealing of fundamental norms and consensus principles. As with Reus-Smit, both go beyond Osiander's relatively narrowly defined 'structural' agenda. Osiander had claimed that there is a distinction to be found in peace settlements between 'structural principles' and 'procedural rules'. The former he specifies as the basic assumptions of the system about 'the identity of the international actors, their relative status, and the distribution of territories and populations between them'. The latter he sees as prescribing the 'way that relations between the actors are conducted'. He is of the opinion that the former is more important to the stability of the system than the latter[34] and, accordingly, most of his study is concentrated upon this aspect. In contrast, and reflecting the intent to broaden the constructivist agenda, both Reus-Smit and Hall encourage us to go beyond the structuralist aspect, and to seek out instead the rules of the game in the deeply embedded purposes of the state, and its shifting identity.

These changes are often clearly revealed in the kinds of peace settlements that the victors seek to establish in the aftermath of war. Ikenberry's important contribution to this debate is couched in his general survey of the strategy of 'institutionalization' pursued by victors since 1815. After victory, the winners may choose simply to take all, and to enforce the peace thereafter. But this is a costly strategy. Alternatively, they may choose to trade in some of the 'returns to power' by settling for less, and by creating instead the wider norms and institutions that provide incentives for others, including the lately defeated, to comply with the terms of peace:

> Beginning with the 1815 settlement and increasingly after 1919 and 1945, the leading state has resorted to institutional strategies as mechanisms to establish restraints on indiscriminate and arbitrary state power and 'lock in' a favorable and durable postwar order.[35]

According to this analysis, the kind of settlement sought at the end of the Cold War is powerfully reflective of the moral purposes of the key victor states, especially the United States. In my own overlapping interpretation, I have set out an alternative framework, but equally focusing upon the story of change that can be told on the basis of historical exercises in peacemaking.[36] As with Ikenberry, it leads to the

---

[31] G. John Ikenberry, *After Victory: Institutions, Strategic Restraint, and the Rebuilding of Order after Major Wars* (Princeton, NJ: Princeton University Press, 2000).
[32] Clark, *Post-Cold War Order*.
[33] See Krasner, 'Compromising Westphalia', p. 140; Osiander, *States System of Europe*, p. 14.
[34] Osiander, *States System of Europe*, p. 5.
[35] Ikenberry, *After Victory*, p. 4.
[36] Clark, *Post-Cold War Order*.

conclusion that the best way to think about the post-Cold War order is in terms of traditional notions of warmaking and peacemaking, and this places the legitimating principles of the settlement at the heart of our concerns.

As is by now clear, many studies of change in international systems have explored the issue in terms of changing norms, and indeed this is a substantial part of the existing investigation into the extent of change in the post-Cold War system.[37] However, much of this discussion has been narrowly framed by the norm of sovereignty, and what, if anything, might be happening to it. While there are obvious reasons for coming at the question from this angle, given the centrality of sovereignty within the 'Westphalian' system, this is open to the objection that Krasner[38] has raised, namely that if we use sovereignty as the test, we are likely to find substantial evidence of change all along the line since 1648. So is there an alternative route down which we might head?

What follows is an attempt to develop the argument that the norms of international society are a good place to locate the argument, but that we should focus on concepts of legitimacy, rather than upon sovereignty alone. How might this develop, and with what benefits to understanding system change? We need to begin with some analysis of international legitimacy.

Legitimacy, change, and the end of the Cold War

It may seem odd to begin any discussion of the significance of the end of the Cold War by reference to principles of legitimacy. Some commentators have gone so far as to cast doubt on the existence of a post-Cold War international society itself, let alone of its agreed rules of legitimation. 'The dilemma of these times', it has been remarked, 'is that there is no international society to make the rules of a post-Cold War world'.[39] As against this, others have insisted that the 'issue of legitimacy is likely to grow in significance as the twenty-first century unfolds', in part because of the 'growing call that the *world order itself* is not legitimate, especially at the economic level'.[40] This suggests that what is happening to legitimacy itself might tell us important things about the nature and significance of the changes underway as part of the end of the Cold War.

The role of legitimacy is one of the fundamental, but as yet inadequately theorized, components of international society. In that respect, this article responds to the challenge of a recent authoritative study that 'there are few works that explicitly interrogate the idea of legitimacy at the international level'.[41] It needs briefly to explore the functions that legitimacy performs in relation to international society.

---

[37] Wheeler, *Saving Strangers*; G. M. Lyons and M. Mastanduno (eds.), *Beyond Westphalia? State Sovereignty and International Intervention* (Baltimore, MD: John Hopkins University Press, 1995).

[38] Krasner, 'Compromising Westphalia', passim.

[39] R. Steel, 'Prologue: 1919–1945–1989', in M. F. Boemeke, G. D. Feldman and E. Glaser (eds.), *The Treaty of Versailles: A Reassessment after 75 Years* (Cambridge: Cambridge University Press, 1998), p. 34.

[40] P. Kennedy, 'Conclusions', in G. Lundestad (ed.), *The Fall of Great Powers: Peace, Stability, and Legitimacy* (Oslo and Oxford: Scandinavian and Oxford University Presses, 1994), p. 378.

[41] Wheeler, *Saving Strangers*, p. 4.

There is a substantial literature within political science as a whole, largely dealing with 'domestic' legitimacy. In contrast, while legitimacy in its international aspects is discussed in a number of works, these remain scattered rather than consolidated treatments. The idea is explored specifically in the likes of Armstrong, Butler, Barnett, Hurd, Kissinger, Watson Wheeler, Wight, Williams,[42] as well as in passing mentions in a host of more general texts, especially within the English School. It is also widely discussed from a distinctively international legal perspective.[43]

The common assumption that appears to run through many of these writings is that legitimacy is related to the stability of international society. Specifically, international society is thought to be more stable at certain historical periods to the extent that its norms and institutions enjoy reasonable levels of legitimacy. This assumption, and the reasoning underlying it, needs to be analysed more explicitly. Is legitimacy a factor that independently influences degrees of stability? Is there some kind of causal relationship between the two? If so, why, and how does it work? The worry is that in some existing accounts, there is a complex tautology at work: once decoded, legitimacy emerges less as an independent factor in its own right, and merely as a transcription of stability in other terms. Were this to be the case, legitimacy would not be a cause of stability, but simply another way of describing it.

The treatment of this in the existing literature does not build up to a single, coherent picture. At the level of definitions, approaches span from the very narrow (a criterion for membership of international society[44]), to the extremely wide (a value judgment about what is right[45]). All along the spectrum in between, a host of competing perspectives and organizational categories are to be found. Some attest to the importance of legitimacy, but limit its scope to the great powers alone.[46] Elsewhere, it remains unclear whether it is something objective or subjective, procedural or substantive. If there are pluralist and solidarist[47] accounts of international society, does this mean that there are pluralist and solidarist conceptions of international legitimacy, and must one preclude the other? Or might both operate simultaneously, but at different 'constitutive' levels? Is legitimacy

---

[42] J. D. Armstrong, *Revolution and World Order: The Revolutionary State in International Society* (Oxford: Oxford University Press, 1993); P. F. Butler, 'Legitimacy in a States-System: Vattel's *Law of Nations*', in M. Donelan (ed.), *The Reason of States* (London: Allen and Unwin, 1978); Barnett, 'Bringing in the New World Order'; Hurd, 'Legitimacy and Authority'; H. Kissinger, *A World Restored: The Politics of Conservatism in a Revolutionary Era* (Boston, MA: Houghton Mifflin, 1957) and *Diplomacy* (New York: Simon and Schuster, 1994); A. Watson, *The Evolution of International Society* (London: Routledge, 1992); Wheeler, *Saving Strangers*; M. Wight, 'International Legitimacy', in H. Bull (ed.), *Systems of States* (Leicester: Leicester University Press, 1977); and J. Williams, 'Nothing Succeeds Like Success? Legitimacy in International Relations', in B. Holden (ed.), *The Ethical Dimensions of Global Change* (Houndmills, UK: Macmillan, 1996).

[43] Principally in T. M. Franck, *The Power of Legitimacy Among Nations* (New York: Oxford University Press, 1990).

[44] Wight, 'International Legitimacy'.

[45] Williams, 'Nothing Succeeds like Success?'.

[46] For example, Kissinger, *A World Restored;* R. Gilpin, 'The Cycle of Great Powers: Has it Finally been Broken?', in Lundestad, *The Fall*.

[47] I use these terms in the sense developed by Hedley Bull. Pluralism refers to a view of international society within which shared norms extend only to procedural goals, whereas solidarism reflects an international society that shares 'substantive' or 'purposive' values. See Bull, 'The Grotian Conception of International Society', in H. Butterfield and M. Wight (eds.), *Diplomatic Investigations* (London: Allen and Unwin, 1966); and *The Anarchical Society: A Study of Order in World Politics* (London: Macmillan, 1977).

something that 'makes' international society, or something that international society, once made, attempts to enforce (in the same way that it has been claimed that Bull had a Grotian view of the very existence of international society, but additionally a distinctively Grotian view of the types of norms that society could sustain)?[48] In effect, this is an instance of the general distinction often made between constitutive and regulative types of rules.[49] This issue arises directly out of Wheeler's[50] formulation: 'The rules that this book is interested in are those that constitute international society and the focus is on how far the society of states recognizes the legitimacy of using force against states who grossly violate human rights'. Are the latter rules the same as the former, or might they be of different orders? Finally, is legitimacy an expression of universal beliefs, or merely a disguise and rationalization of interests, especially of those of the strongest? Watson himself advised that the major powers might need to 'cloak hegemonial decisions in the legitimist rhetoric of independence for every member of international society'.[51]

As an instance of this generic issue, what we need to explore now is the nature of legitimacy since the end of the Cold War. The thesis of *The Post-Cold War Order* was that the strength of the principles of legitimacy derived from the pre-existing 'successes' of the Western system during the Cold War itself. Given this, it is not at all surprising that, as Williams[52] has claimed, the 'end of the Cold War ... has seen the standard of legitimacy move towards the concerns of liberalism'.

Principles of international legitimacy after the Cold War have been notably attached to the global economy, a form of collective security, and a broadly liberal rights order. Each of these has played an instrumental part in legitimizing what I have called the 'regulative' aspects of the post-Cold War peace. In many respects, the Cold War—objectively speaking—was a war fought on behalf of the global economy, even if that was not the only issue at stake. The lessons about the need for an integrated and multilateral economy had been profoundly learned by 1944, and already formed an important element within the abortive peace of 1945, as a set of principles to which all states were invited to subscribe. The apparent victory of capitalism in 1989 served only to further entrench the appeal of this doctrine, especially in those many parts of the world that had hitherto been excluded from it. As an accompaniment to this multilateralism in the economic sphere, the end of the Cold War also saw obeisance paid to a more self-conscious adherence to multilateralism in the realm of security. Again this was not new, but sought to realize the potential of the system that had prematurely been set in place in 1945. This might now be thought capable of working in the absence of significant centres of power resistant to the wishes of the dominant 'coalitions of the willing'. Finally, the key principle of legitimacy was specified in terms of adherence to certain liberal forms, with due respect for human rights. Once more, this was scarcely a novel programmatic departure. What was potentially new about it was the seemingly heightened prospect of some measures towards its implementation.

---

[48] K. Alderson and A. Hurrell, 'Introduction', in Alderson and Hurrell (eds.), *Hedley Bull on International Society* (Houndmills, UK: Macmillan, 2000), p. 9.
[49] See J. G. Ruggie, *Constructing the World Polity* (London: Routledge, 1998), pp. 22–5.
[50] Wheeler, *Saving Strangers*, p. 6.
[51] Watson, *The Evolution*, p. 323.
[52] Williams, 'Nothing Succeeds like Success', pp. 60–1.

In that earlier work, I suggested the argument that what was unusual about the post-Cold War settlement was that these regulative provisions fashioned a legitimacy based on continuity rather than change. Traditionally, the legitimizing principles attached to peace settlements have fostered change, rather than continuity. Of course, peace settlements are not the only statements about legitimacy in international society and, given their peculiar nature, one can understand that they might normally be more concerned to facilitate change than preserve the past (since change is what hegemonic wars are supposed to be about). This does, nonetheless, invite the question why the aftermath of the Cold War should yield an outcome that was appreciably different. The plausible answer to this might be that the post-Cold War order privileged a degree of conservatism, since it resulted from a war of hegemonic reaffirmation, rather than from one of hegemonic change.

It is equally instructive to examine the role played by legitimacy at the end of the Cold War from the perspective of earlier moments of historical transition. Some counsel that legitimation itself becomes most important when 'the rules of the game are in flux'.[53] This echoes the similar point made much earlier by Inis Claude, who had identified 'the crucial periods in political history' as being those 'transitional years of conflict between old and new concepts of legitimacy, the historical interstices between the initial challenge to the established concept and the general acceptance of its replacement'.[54] Osiander himself had recognized that those principles that generally operate in the 'collective subconscious' would tend to be brought to the surface 'when they are challenged in some crisis'.[55] Accordingly, it is not at all surprising that a debate about legitimacy has become indicative of the uncertainties generated by the end of the Cold War.[56]

The obverse side of the assumption that legitimacy enhances stability is the notion that instability is increased when legitimizing principles and international practice become too far separated from each other. This was certainly Adam Watson's view. 'Legitimacy usually lags behind practice', he averred. 'But a conspicuous and growing gap between legitimacy and practice causes tension and the impression of disorder'.[57] This suggests a complication, but also an interesting avenue of exploration. If we are to apply a legitimacy test to detect the degree of change within the international system, what is it that is being measured by the test? Are we attempting to assess the gap between practice and principle, on the assumption that the content of the principles has not altered? Are the punctuation points of international history instances of this kind of disjunction? Alternatively, does the test imply that the great historical transformations in the international system are those where the actual principles of legitimacy have themselves undergone a radical shift? Which test it is that is being applied has important implications for our understanding of the significance of the end of the Cold War.

---

[53] Barnett, 'Bringing in the New World Order', p. 548.
[54] I. L. Claude, 'Collective Legitimization as a Political Function of the United Nations', *International Organization*, 20:3 (1966), p. 369.
[55] Osiander, *States System of Europe*, p. 14.
[56] Williams, 'Nothing Succeeds like Success', p. 40.
[57] Watson, *The Evolution*, pp. 323–4. On the 'crisis of legitimacy' caused by a gap between principle and practice, see also Hall, *National Collective Identity*; A. Claire Cutler, 'Critical Reflections on the Westphalian Assumptions of International Law and Organization: A Crisis of Legitimacy', *Review of International Studies*, 27:2 (2001).

For all its criticality, it would be naïve to imagine that we can make a simple and straightforward distinction between these two situations. This can be illustrated with reference to two interconnected developments in the historical evolution of international society. It might be thought, first of all, that there is a good example of 'crisis' in the disjunction between the legitimating principles of a European-based state system, and an actual practice of the increasingly globally-based international relationships, resulting from the transitions of the late nineteenth and early twentieth centuries. But even this distinction is itself more blurred than it might appear to be at first sight. Tellingly, two erudite commentators upon this very issue were led to reach the following circumspect conclusion:

> This European international society, it should be noted, did not first evolve its own rules and institutions and then export them to the rest of the world. The evolution of the European system of interstate relations and the expansion of Europe across the globe were simultaneous processes, which influenced and affected each other.[58]

For that very reason, the separation between principles and practices is by no means a straightforward one to make. In the same way, a second illustration can be found in one commentary upon the application of the 'standard of civilization' in late nineteenth-century international society. Referring to Gong's analysis of this, Roland Robertson points to the mutuality that was involved in these 'encounters between civilizations' and the extent to which, as Gong had suggested, there were resulting changes both in European international society *and* in those new non-European members of it.[59] In these circumstances, it is casuistic to assert a clear division between legitimating principles and international practices, since both were constantly interacting with each other.

And yet, if not precisely in terms of principles and practices, *some* kind of distinction seems appropriate between changes in the content of the legitimating principles themselves, as against a continuity of these principles which might nonetheless allow new practices to be observed. At some historical periods, the changes have been predominantly of the former kind, whereas at others a basic continuity in principles has been accompanied by significant innovations in the actual conduct of international relations. Into which of these two broad categories should we place the transitions associated with the end of the Cold War and, by doing so, what would have been clarified about the nature of this transition?

The point can be further developed by recalling earlier stages of the discussion. Changes to the existing frameworks of legitimacy have traditionally been those that have established new membership criteria for inclusion within international society. These have often been articulated as new principles of legitimacy, either at the end of the great wars of modern history, or at other equally revolutionary moments. Examples are the shifts towards sovereign absolutism, then towards popular sovereignty, and finally to nationalism and self-determination. These are the stereotypical landmarks in the changing substance of international legitimacy, viewed as a criterion of 'fit' membership of international society. As against these, and following on from Reus-Smit, there have been those shifts that do not derive from any pronounced shift in the framework of legitimacy, or at least not from any major

[58] Bull and Watson, *The Expansion,* pp. 6–7.
[59] R. Roberston, *Globalization: Social Theory and Global Culture* (London: Sage, 1992), p. 124.

reworking of the principle of sovereignty itself. Nonetheless, and although couched within a framework of continuity, those legitimizing principles may allow for a variety of innovative, and often radically transformative, state practices. Reus-Smit's revolution of the nineteenth century would be an example of this latter kind.

On this basis, the suggestion here is that the end of the Cold War is best understood as falling into this second category: a constancy of principle but with the potential for a revolution in practice. The content of its prime legitimizing principles did not change. On the contrary, what enhanced their authority was precisely the degree to which they embodied the sound principles already set in place in 1944 and 1945, and which appeared to have been even more thoroughly vindicated by the experiences of the 1980s. To be sure, those principles might now be appealed to in an attempt to legitimize new activities (as in the case of humanitarian intervention). They were also to be appealed to as part of the process by which the often radical adjustments wrought by the end of the Cold War were set in place.[60] But this was not because of any change in the fundamental content of the principles themselves. At this level, they stood for a basic continuity with the Cold-War past, even though they had now become more deeply entrenched and more extensive in their ambit. Accordingly, if we look at the end of the Cold War for a revolution in the basic principles of international legitimacy, the episode is bound to disappoint: it was much more conservative than it was radical. However, that by itself is no reason to minimize the profound changes that accompanied the end of the Cold War, as these were often legitimized in the name of these same conservative principles. It is this central paradox—and one that is explicable in the above terms—that has led to so much confusion about whether or not the end of the Cold War marks a point of radical departure, or one of marked continuity. In reality, it was both.

The end of the Cold War and the imperial project

It is at this point that the analysis of the principles of legitimacy in post-Cold War international society invites a deeper reflection upon the character of that society itself. While much of the rhetoric of that New World Order had been avowedly about self-determination, there comes a point when the 'solidarist' dimensions of an international society might also be regarded as a veiled form of hegemony or empire. In short, the question that needs to be addressed is the extent to which it is these very principles of international legitimacy that define the nature of the contemporary imperial project. Imperial rule, as Lundestad reminded us, may have lost its legitimacy,[61] but might legitimacy be the new form of imperial rule?

The discussion here reverts to the earlier theme of the relationship between legitimacy and power. Unless legitimacy adds value to our understanding of political behaviour, it is redundant. The general assumption is then that an order that enjoys legitimacy is one that is distinct from one that relies upon power alone. According to theorists like Kissinger, it is the very legitimacy of an order that is the key to its

---

[60]   Clark, *Post-Cold War Order*, Part 2.
[61]   'The Fall', in Lundestad, *The Fall*, p. 385.

stability, and hence to its durability, as after 1815. The same idea is very much present in Ikenberry's rendition of the 'institutionalized peace' after the Cold War. His strategy of institutionalization is clearly to be understood as one that is different from reliance upon coercive power alone. Even if he eschews the concept of legitimacy as such, it is fundamental to his understanding of the post-Cold War order that, however hegemonic American power might be, it resides in institutional bases that generate high levels of willing compliance on the part of other actors in the system. 'It is not the preponderance of American power that keeps the system intact', he suggests, 'but its unique ability to engage in strategic restraint'.[62] I have elsewhere questioned the tenability of this argument[63], on the grounds of Ikenberry's own admission that the ability to engage in strategic restraint is a 'type of power'.[64] This is assuredly so, but it calls into question the meaningful distinction between the returns to power and strategic restraint.

A good example of this tension can be provided by the post-Cold War treatment of the former Soviet Union. It is certainly arguable that the West pursued two types of policy towards Russia and that these became increasingly incompatible with each other. In the period until 1992–93, the United States continued to attach high priority to its Russian policy, and to the continuance of its residual partnership with it. However, after that period, the policy became much less mindful of Russian sensitivities, and less concerned to implement only those policies that met with some kind of consent from Russia. The sequence of policy squabbles that developed over the issue of NATO enlargement, and intensified with reference to the war over Kosovo, is illustrative of this degenerative trend. In the wider scheme of analysis, this picture might also be thought to confirm a drift away from a consensual—and hence legitimate—post-Cold War order, and towards one that was more expressly reliant upon the West's power. There was less strategic restraint as the decade of the 1990s unfolded, and the returns to power were more overtly garnered in.

In part, this reflected a deep-seated tension in policy objectives with regard to Russia. As in all post-war situations, the victors seek for a strategy that will remove the risk of a recurrence of threat from the vanquished. This can be done by punitive military, territorial, and economic measures designed to eliminate any resurgence on the late enemy's part. It can also be done by transforming the political complexion of the defeated state, so that it will willingly comply with the new order. In these terms, the West embarked initially on a policy of co-opting Russia as a reformed democratic and market system, thereby establishing the bases of a legitimate order for the post-Cold War world. However, by way of insurance, it also took measures (such as NATO enlargement) that had the unfortunate side effect of contributing to Russian disenchantment with its own accommodative policy, thereby undercutting its willing compliance. In this respect, we can again witness the succumbing of a policy of strategic restraint to the temptations of a more direct exaction of the returns to power. The more coercive the post-Cold War order has become, the less legitimate it is seen to be (not in the eyes of Russians alone), and the worse are its resulting prospects for stability.

---

[62] Ikenberry, *After Victory*, p. 270.
[63] Clark, *Post-Cold War Order*, p. 249.
[64] Ikenberry, *After Victory*, p. 259.

In a nutshell, is the stability of the present order to be derived from its legitimacy, or from the quasi-hegemony that underpins it? There is now a substantial literature that develops a range of concepts—security community, global or western state, and empire—all of which have substantial overtones of hegemony associated with them. So is the latest iteration of principles of legitimacy for international society to be construed as a set of norms for a genuinely pluralistic society of states, or is it taking on significant dimensions of a more imperial nature? Is the final irony of the end of the Cold War that the explicit rejection of one imperial vision (the Soviet one) has simply initiated the beginning of a new cycle that will push us back towards to the imperial end of the spectrum? If, as Watson insisted, the Westphalian settlement 'established a definitive anti-hegemonial legitimacy for the European society of states',[65] do contemporary developments suggest a weakening of this phase? While conceding that the 'collapse of imperial governance in our time is indeed impressive', William McNeill nonetheless cautioned against assuming that 'the forces that so persistently restored polyethnic empire after periods of disruption in the Eurasian past have lost their cogency'.[66] Is the paradox of contemporary principles of legitimacy that they underwrite a pluralistic conception of international society only as a means to its further centralization through an orthodoxy of values?

Such a suggestion has been around for some time, in embryonic form, in much of the liberal peace literature, and even more so in recent exegeses of the concept of 'security community'.[67] However, its most direct referent can be found in versions of the global or Western state, particularly as expounded in the work of Martin Shaw. He contends that 'the singularity of state is already partially realized in the dominance of a single set of new norms and institutions, which more or less governs the various state centres'.[68] This global layer 'simultaneously depends on and transforms the power of the West'.[69] Most interestingly of all, we are informed that the 'first and most important element of the global layer is the institutional framework of legitimate global political power and its enforcement'. The suggestion here is neither of any form of world government, nor of global governance as conventionally understood. Nor is it any replication of more traditional imperial structures. This is a new hybrid category that obfuscates the distinction between single global state and multiple pluralistic states. At its core is an articulation of values, emanating preponderantly from the West and ultimately reliant upon Western power, but attaching itself to and colonizing wider structures of global legitimacy.

It is precisely some such image that is to be found in other recent reformulations of the liberal peace argument. These reject any idea that the democratic peace prevails because of any inherently pacific quality within democratic states. They also chastise those liberal theorists for making a false initial assumption that the peace is produced by the character of these several and separate states at all. There is instead a more profound explanation for the condition of peace:

The use of force between these states is unlikely because they are embedded in geostrategic and political economic relations that buttress international state and capitalist power in

---

[65] Watson, *The Evolution*, p. 315

[66] In Lundestad, *The Fall*, p. 7.

[67] E. Adler and M. Barnett (eds.), *Security Communities* (Cambridge: Cambridge University Press, 1998).

[68] Martin Shaw, *Theory of the Global State* (Cambridge: Cambridge University Press, 2000), p. 214.

[69] Shaw, *Global State*, pp. 214–5.

hegemonic, i.e non-violent, ways. Beginning with a set of liberal democratic *states* rather than an emergent Western or transnational *state* means that the democratic peace debates remain caught in the territorial trap.[70]

What this highlights is the notion that peace is not a property of the individual democratic state, but of the larger collectivity within which the core states are increasingly submerged. While this should not be construed as an 'empire' in any strict historical sense, it operates nonetheless as an increasingly solidarist society in pursuit of certain common ends. Such peace as prevails within it is a function of these shared norms, not of common democratic practices. Moreover, the core states employ their privileged position both to make appeal to global legitimating institutions, and increasingly to define the content of those principles. Legitimacy is part of the imperial project to the extent that it cannot sensibly be understood in separation from the global distribution of power.

In combination, these various notions help make sense of one of the seeming developments of the past decade or so, and this is with regard to the legitimacy of the use of armed force. The trend towards increasingly 'collective' forms of legitimation of the use of force should not be understood, simplistically, as the effect of globalization in hollowing out the security functions of the state.[71] Instead, it should be approached through the more complex prism of shifting state-societal bargains. Whereas in the past, the state's use of force was legitimized by its being the provider of essential social goods to its citizens (who in turn owed the state a debt of military service), many of these services are now no longer provided on a 'national' basis. Accordingly, the state no longer enjoys exclusive legitimacy in this sphere. Simultaneously, it is the wider 'global state' that sanctions the resort to force, presumably in return for its now being the ultimate provider of many civic and economic goods to 'its' citizens. The unbundling of the state thus finds its natural counterpart in the accretion of legitimacy by the wider social group that does most to sustain and succour an increasingly transnational citizenship. Unsurprisingly, Shaw himself locates the military enterprise at the heart of his global state. He describes it as an 'integrated and authoritative organization of violence', and, above all, as functioning as a 'single centre of military state power'. Even more importantly, however, he is insistent that its 'authoritative deployment of violence' is reinforced by its attachment to global symbols of legitimacy, such as the United Nations.[72]

Conclusion

How deeply do the post-Cold War changes run, and how does legitimacy help us to comprehend them? Is legitimacy, in Watson's terminology, simply the oil that makes possible a change within the existing international society? Or do the shifts legitimize the wider changes betokened by a move outside the existing framework of the modern state system? To return to the opening reference to Buzan and Little,

[70] T. Barkawi and M. Laffey, 'The Imperial Peace: Democracy, Force and Globalization', *European Journal of International Relations*, 5:4 (1999), p. 419.
[71] Clark, *Globalization and International Relations Theory* (Oxford: Oxford University Press, 1999), ch. 6.
[72] Shaw, *Global State*, pp. 199–200.

what evidence does this provide that helps us think about whether or not we are 'on the brink of another transformation of the international system'?

The short answer is that the evidence at least points to the potential of, if not the explicit intention behind, the post-Cold War settlement—and its legitimizing principles —to contribute to a movement in this direction. This point can be made by drawing a contrast with Reus-Smit. Although his is by no means a narrowly 'state-centric' book, the very fact that a key element of the constitutional structure of the system should be depicted in terms of the 'moral purpose of the state' is itself revealing. As a legitimizing principle, this might be thought to be reproductive of a state system at some basic level. As against this, the legitimizing principles canvassed above, and which seem to have played a significant role in facilitating the end of the Cold War, all point in directions that are open-ended as regards the system's structure. They concentrate upon certain global economic principles, security orders and liberal values, but are neutral as to the structures within which these principles are to be implemented. To be sure, it is contrary to the above argument that these regulative aspects of the post-Cold War peace be understood as revolutionary principles, since their main intent was to be conservative, buttressing the prevailing order instead. But part of their ambiguity—and, indeed, the reason why they seemed relevant to such an apocalyptic moment—was that they were at the same time in keeping with the *potentiality* for such radical transformation. While they did not, in fact, inaugurate a new world order, they set out an agenda that could serve as the legitimizing rationale for one. Albeit that the purpose was fundamentally conservative, these principles, once unleashed, might in the end exceed the wishes of those who were their original sponsors. It would not be the first time that ideas about future international orders,[73] once set free into the public domain, have gone on to legitimize changes far in excess of the original intentions of their authors.

In the meantime, we are left with a double movement in the evolution of international society. In the first of these, there was an expansion of international society into a global state system. This was in the limited sense, captured by Bull and Watson, that 'it was the European dominated international society of the nineteenth and early twentieth centuries that first expressed its political unification'.[74] At that time, principles of legitimacy imposed a test for membership of international society by application of European standards of statehood, clothed in wider standards of civilization. This was at one and the same time an expression of European dominance, and an intimation of a future diminution of European control. Ever since, the rules of this global state system have diluted, if not eliminated, the traces of its specifically European origins. As a result, there has been a greater diffusion of power throughout the twentieth century, most obviously in the relative decline of Europe itself. However, in the second stage, the wider West—incorporating most of Europe but led by the United States—has struck back at the very pluralism that the global state system had generated, and of which the World Wars and Cold War were symptomatic. It has sought to reassert a greater central control of the international system. Its chosen instrument has been the forging of a new international society— adhering to a thicker set of legitimating principles embracing democracy, liberal

---

[73] A. Williams, *Failed Imagination? New World Orders of the Twentieth Century* (Manchester: Manchester University Press, 1998).

[74] 'Introduction', in Bull and Watson, *The Expansion*, p. 2.

values and capitalism—that has been progressively formed from within the original. The end of the Cold War has been a critical formative stage in this latter process whereby a second international society has emerged from within the confines of its Western Cold-War phase, and begun more self-consciously to articulate its legitimating values as being appropriate for the wider international system as a whole. It was thus a culminating point in that 'double movement' that is currently leading to the reinvention of international society.

That process of reinvention did not, however, begin with the end of the Cold War. It had been underway for much of the twentieth century, and 1945 was a more conspicuous landmark in its realization than was 1989. What the end of the Cold War represented was the fuller working out of this logic, and one which had been implicit all along in the problems created for the West by its own actions in expanding international society in the first place. While an international society of sovereign states was the outcome of the first stage of this movement, a more intense international society of semi-sovereign states of a particular *type* has been the goal of the second. The elaboration and implementation of principles of international legitimacy have been central to this latter endeavour.

Capitalism and world (dis)order

GIOVANNI ARRIGHI AND BEVERLY J. SILVER

A sea change of major proportions is taking place in the historical social system forming the modern world, creating a widespread sense of uncertainty about the present and foreseeable future. In the words of Eric Hobsbawm, as 'the citizens of the *fin de siècle* tapped their way through the global fog that surrounded them, into the third millennium, all they knew for certain was that an era of history had ended. They knew very little else'.[1]

Yet even the era of history that has ended is the subject of debate. For Hobsbawm the 1970s and 1980s were the closing phase of his Short Twentieth Century (1914–1991). In his view, the collapse of communist regimes 'destroyed the ... system that had stabilized international relations for some forty years. ... and revealed the precariousness of the domestic political systems that had essentially rested on that stability'. The result was 'an enormous zone of political uncertainty, instability, chaos and civil war. ... The future of politics was obscure, but its crisis at the end of the Short Twentieth Century was patent'.[2]

In Hobsbawm's view, the late-twentieth century also marks a crisis of the rationalist and humanist assumptions, shared by liberal capitalism and communism, 'on which modern society had been founded since the Moderns won their famous battle against the Ancients in the early eighteenth century'.[3] In a similar vein, Immanuel Wallerstein has claimed that the year 1989 marks the end of the particular politico-cultural era launched by the Enlightenment and the French Revolution. For Wallerstein, however, it also marks the beginnings of a terminal crisis of the modern world system that came into existence in the 'long sixteenth century'.[4] Starting from different premises, James Rosenau concurs with this assessment. In his view, the parameters that have framed action in the international system are being transformed so fundamentally today 'as to bring about the first turbulence in world politics since comparable shifts culminated in the Treaty of Westphalia in 1648'.[5]

Whatever era of history is thought to be ending—the Cold War era, or the longer era of 'liberalism' and the Enlightenment, or the even longer era of the system of

---

[1] Eric J. Hobsbawm, *The Age of Extremes: A History of the World, 1914–1991* (New York: Vintage, 1994), pp. 558–9.
[2] Hobsbawm, *The Age of Extremes*, pp. 9–11.
[3] Ibid., p. 11.
[4] Immanuel Wallerstein, *After Liberalism* (New York, The New Press, 1995), pp. 1, 268; Immanuel Wallerstein, 'Crisis as Transition', in S. Amin, G. Arrighi, A. G. Frank, and I. Wallerstein, *Dynamics of Global Crisis* (New York: Monthly Review Press, 1982), p. 11.
[5] James N. Rosenau, *Turbulence in World Politics: A Theory of Change and Continuity* (Princeton, NJ, Princeton University Press, 1990), p. 10.

national states—these authors argue that structures that had provided for some predictability are breaking down and that a trend towards uncertainty and unpredictability is likely to characterize the present and foreseeable future.

Systemic cycles of accumulation and hegemonic transitions

Our attempts to dissipate at least some of the 'global fog' that surrounds us as we enter the third millennium and to narrow the range of uncertainty and unpredictability about the present and foreseeable future[6] is premised on three closely related observations. The first observation is that the beginning and the end of the twentieth century are broadly comparable periods, with the centrality of 'finance capital' being one of the crucial common denominators between the two periods.[7] The second observation is derived from Fernand Braudel's argument that this financialization of capital has been a recurrent feature of historical capitalism since the sixteenth century. Our third observation is that periods of financial expansion are not just an expression of cyclical processes of historical capitalism—as emphasized by Braudel; rather they also have been periods of major reorganizations of the world capitalist system—what we call hegemonic transitions. We shall discuss each of these three observations in turn in the remainder of this section.[8]

The centrality of finance capital at the end of the nineteenth and beginning of the twentieth century gave rise to liberal and Marxist theories of 'finance capital' and 'imperialism', which saw this phenomenon as signalling a new, unprecedented or highest stage of capitalism.[9] At the end of the twentieth century, the renewed cen-

---

[6] Giovanni Arrighi, *The Long Twentieth Century: Money, Power, and the Origins of Our Time* (London: Verso, 1994); Giovanni Arrighi and Beverly J. Silver, et al., *Chaos and Governance in the Modern World System* (Minneapolis, MN: University of Minnesota Press, 1999); Giovanni Arrighi and Beverly J. Silver, 'Hegemonic Transitions: A Rejoinder', *Political Power and Social Theory*, 13 (1999), pp. 307–15.

[7] This is a fairly widely noted observation; see, among others, David Gordon, 'The Global Economy: New Edifice or Crumbling Foundations?' *New Left Review*, 168 (1988), pp. 24–65; Robert Zevin, 'Our World Financial Market is More Open? If So, Why and With What Effect?' in T. Banuri and J.B. Schor (eds.), *Financial Openness and National Autonomy: Opportunity and Constraints* (New York, Oxford University Press, 1992); David Harvey, 'Globalization in Question', *Rethinking Marxism*, 8: 4 (1995), pp. 1–17. Paul Hirst and Grahame Thompson, *Globalization in Question: The International Economy and the Possibilities of Governance* (Cambridge: Polity Press, 1996).

[8] One point of clarification about the scope of our analysis is in order. Most accounts of capitalist development have been based on observations and conceptual frameworks that refer implicitly or explicitly to national dynamics. This is a perfectly legitimate and useful way of analysing capitalist development, provided that we do not conflate the dynamic of capitalist development as it unfolds in specific national (or sub-national) locales with the dynamic of capitalist development as it unfolds in a 'world' consisting of a large number and variety of such locales. Although these two dynamics influence one another, each has a logic of its own and must be treated as an object of analysis in its own right. Our premise in this article is that the world dynamic of capitalist development is something more and different that the 'sum' of national dynamics. It is something that can be perceived only if we take as the unit of analysis, not individual states, but the *system* of states in which world capitalism has been embedded.

[9] John Hobson, *Imperialism: A Study* (London: George Allen & Unwin, 1938 [1902]). Rudolf Hilferding, *Finance Capital: A Study of the Latest Phase of Capitalist Development* (London: Routledge and Kegan Paul, 1981 [1910]). Nikolai Bukharin, *Imperialism and World Economy* (New York: Monthly Review Press, 1973 [1915]); V.I. Lenin, 'Imperialism: The Highest Stage of Capitalism', in *Selected Works*, vol. I (Moscow: Foreign Languages Publishing House, 1952. [1916]).

trality of finance capital has given rise to theories of 'globalization' and 'financializ-ation of capital', which likewise see the present as a new and unprecedented phase of capitalist development.[10] The language and concepts have changed but the idea that finance capital constitutes a new, latest, highest phase/stage in the development of capitalism is at least as widely held today as it was a century ago. This recurrence of a discourse in which finance capital is presented as a new, latest, highest stage of capitalist development, we would argue, is in part an outcome of methods of analysis whose time horizon is too short to detect a long-term cyclical dynamic within historical capitalism.

This brings us to our second observation. As Fernand Braudel underscored, early-twentieth-century characterizations that portrayed finance capital as a new phase of capitalist development were shortsighted. 'Finance capitalism', he noted, 'was no newborn child of the 1900s; I would even argue that in the past—in say Genoa or Amsterdam—*following a wave of growth in commercial capitalism and the accumulation of capital on a scale beyond the normal channels for investment*, finance capitalism was already in a position to take over and dominate, for a *while at least*, all the activities of the business world.[11]

The idea that long before the early twentieth century the accumulation of capital through the purchase and sale of commodities 'on a scale beyond the normal channels for investment' enabled finance capitalism 'to take over and dominate, for a while at least, all the activities of the business world', is a recurrent theme of the second and third volumes of Braudel's trilogy *Civilization and Capitalism*. It under-lies Braudel's contention that the essential feature of historical capitalism over its *longue durée*, that is, over its entire lifetime, has been the 'flexibility' and 'eclecticism' of capital rather than the concrete forms it assumed at different places and at different times. In certain periods, even long periods, capitalism did seem to 'specialize', as in the nineteenth century, when '[it] moved so spectacularly into the new world of industry'. This specialization led many 'to regard industry as the final flowering which gave capitalism its "true" identity'. But this is a short-term view. '[After] the initial boom of mechanization, the most advanced kind of capitalism reverted to eclecticism, to an indivisibility of interests so to speak, as if the charac-teristic advantage of standing at the commanding heights of the economy ... consisted precisely of *not* having to confine oneself to a single choice, of being eminently adaptable, hence non-specialized'.[12]

These passages can be read as a restatement of Karl Marx's general formula of capital, MCM'. Money capital (M) means liquidity, flexibility, freedom of choice. Commodity capital (C) means capital invested in a particular input-output combin-ation in view of a profit. Hence, it means concreteness, rigidity, and a narrowing down or closing of options. M' means *expanded* liquidity, flexibility and freedom of choice. Thus understood, Marx's formula tells us that capitalist agencies invest

---

[10] See among others, Andrew Walter, *World Power and World Money: The Role of Hegemony and International Monetary Order* (New York: St. Martin's Press, 1991). Erik R. Peterson, 'Surrendering to Markets', *The Washington Quarterly*, 17: 4 (1995), pp. 103–15. Manuel Castells, *The Rise of the Network Society*, 2nd edn. (Oxford: Blackwell, 2000).

[11] Fernand Braudel, *Civilization and Capitalism, 15th-18th Century*, vol. III: *The Perspective of the World* (New York, Harper & Row, 1984), p. 604; emphasis added.

[12] Fernand Braudel, *Civilization and Capitalism, 15th-18th Century*, vol. II: *The Wheels of Commerce* (New York: Harper & Row, 1982), p. 381; emphasis in the original; translation amended as indicated in Immanuel Wallerstein, *Unthinking Social Science* (Cambridge: Polity Press.1991) p. 213.

money in particular input-output combinations, with all the loss of flexibility and of freedom of choice that goes with it, not as an end in itself. Rather, they do so as a *means* towards the end of securing an even greater flexibility and freedom of choice at some future point in time. Marx's formula also tells us that, if there is no expectation on the part of capitalist agencies that their freedom of choice will increase, or if this expectation goes unfulfilled systematically, capital *tends* to revert to more flexible forms of investment, first and foremost to its money form. In other words, the 'preference' of capitalist agencies for liquidity increases and an unusually large share of their cash flows tends to remain in liquid form.

This second reading is implicit in Braudel's characterization of 'financial expansion' as a symptom of maturity of a particular phase of capitalist development. In discussing the withdrawal of the Dutch from commerce around 1740 to become 'the bankers of Europe', Braudel suggests that this withdrawal is a recurrent world-systemic tendency. The same tendency had already been in evidence in fifteenth-century Italy, and again around 1560, when the leading groups of the Genoese business diaspora gradually withdrew from commerce to exercise for about seventy years a rule over European finances comparable to that exercised in the twentieth century by the Bank of International Settlement at Basle—'a rule that was so discreet and sophisticated that historians for a long time failed to notice it'. After the Dutch, the English replicated the tendency during and after the Great Depression of 1873–96, when the end of 'the fantastic venture of the industrial revolution' created an overabundance of money capital.[13]

After the equally 'fantastic venture' of so-called Fordism-Keynesianism, US capital since the 1970's has followed a similar trajectory. We can easily recognize in this latest 'rebirth' of finance capital yet another instance of that recurrent reversal to 'eclecticism' which in the past has been associated with the maturity of a major capitalist development. '[Every] capitalist development of this order seems, by reaching the stage of financial expansion, to have in some sense announced its maturity: it [is] *a sign of autumn*'.[14]

In the light of these observations, we may interpret Marx's general formula of capital (MCM′) as depicting, not just the logic of individual capitalist investments, but also a recurrent pattern of historical capitalism as world system. The central aspect of this pattern is the alternation of epochs of material expansion (that is, MC phases of capital accumulation) with phases of financial rebirth and expansion (that is, CM′ phases). In phases of material expansion money capital 'sets in motion' an increasing mass of commodities (commoditized labour power and gifts of nature included); and in phases of financial expansion an increasing mass of money capital 'sets itself free' from its commodity form and accumulation proceeds through financial deals (as in Marx's abridged formula MM′). Taken together, the two epochs or phases constitute a full *systemic cycle of accumulation* (MCM′).

Starting from these premises, we can identify four systemic cycles of accumulation: a Genoese-Iberian cycle, stretching from the fifteenth through the early seventeenth centuries; a Dutch cycle, stretching from the late sixteenth through the late eighteenth centuries; a British cycle, stretching from the mid eighteenth through to the early twentieth centuries; and a US cycle, stretching from the late nineteenth

---

[13] Braudel, *Civilization and Capitalism*, vol. III, pp. 157, 164, 242–3, 246.
[14] Ibid., vol. III, p. 246, emphasis added.

through the current phase of financial expansion. Each cycle is named after (and defined by) the particular complex of governmental and business agencies that led the world capitalist *system*, first towards the material and then towards the financial expansions that jointly constitute the cycle. The strategies and structures through which these leading agencies have promoted, organized, and regulated the expansion or the restructuring of the world capitalist system is what we shall understand by 'regime of accumulation' on a world scale.

Our third observation is that the recurrence of system-wide financial expansions is not just the expression of 'a certain unity in capitalism, from thirteenth-century Italy to the present-day West', as Braudel claims.[15] It is also the expression of recurrent fundamental reorganizations of the world capitalist system. This is why, as the above periodization implies, consecutive systemic cycles of accumulation overlap with one another at their beginnings and ends. All phases of financial expansion have indeed been the 'autumn' of major developments of world capitalism. But they have also been periods of *hegemonic transition*, in the course of which a new leadership emerged interstitially and over time reorganized the system so as to make its further expansion possible.

Far from proceeding along a single track laid some four to five hundred years ago—as Wallerstein implies[16]—the formation and expansion of the world capitalist system has thus occurred through several switches to new tracks laid by specific complexes of governmental and business agencies. These leading complexes—the Dutch complex in the seventeenth century, the British complex in the nineteenth century, and the US complex in the twentieth century—have all acted as 'tracklaying vehicles' (to borrow an expression from Michael Mann).[17] In leading the system in a new direction, they also transformed it. Under Dutch leadership, the emergent system of European states was formally instituted by the Treaties of Westphalia. Under British leadership, the Eurocentric system of sovereign states moved to dominion globally. And under US leadership, the system lost its Eurocentricity to gain further in reach and penetration.

We have laid out in detail the historical underpinnings of these conceptualizations in two studies, one focused on the reconstruction of the four systemic cycles of accumulation[18] and one on a comparison of present transformations of world capitalism with those of two previous periods of hegemonic transition—the transition from Dutch to British hegemony in the eighteenth century and the transition from British to US hegemony in the late-nineteenth and early-twentieth centuries.[19] In what follows, we shall limit ourselves to elucidating the logic and mechanisms that underlie the dynamics of the cycles and the transitions. First we deal with the cycles and the evolutionary pattern that can be detected from their succession. Then we turn to the hegemonic transitions and to what they can tell us about the direction and possible outcomes of present transformations.

---

[15] Ibid., vol. II, p. 433.
[16] Immanuel Wallerstein, *The Politics of the World-Economy: The States, the Movements and the Civilizations* (Cambridge, Cambridge University Press, 1984), esp. ch. 4.
[17] Michael Mann, *The Sources of Social Power*, vol. I: *A History of Power from the Beginning to AD 1760* (Cambridge: Cambridge University Press, 1986), p. 28. Cf. Peter Taylor, 'Ten Years that Shook the World? The United Provinces as First Hegemonic State', *Sociological Perspectives*, 37: 1 (1994), p. 27.
[18] Arrighi, *The Long Twentieth Century*.
[19] Arrighi and Silver, et al., *Chaos and Governance*.

Financial expansions and the evolution of world capitalism

Material and financial expansions are both processes of the world capitalist system —a system that has increased in scale and scope over the centuries but has encompassed from its earliest beginnings a large number and variety of governmental and business agencies. Material expansions occur because of the emergence of a particular bloc of governmental and business agencies capable of leading the system towards wider or deeper divisions of labour that create conditions of increasing returns to capital invested in trade and production. Under these conditions profits tend to be ploughed back into the further expansion of trade and production more or less routinely, and knowingly or unknowingly, the system's main centres co-operate in sustaining one another's expansion. Over time, however, the investment of an ever-growing mass of profits in the further expansion of trade and production inevitably leads to the accumulation of capital 'on a scale beyond the normal channels for investment', as Braudel put it, or as we would say, over and above what can be reinvested in the purchase and sale of commodities without drastically reducing profit margins. Decreasing returns set in, competitive pressures intensify, and the stage is set for the change of phase from material to financial expansion.

In this progression from increasing to decreasing returns, from co-operation to competition, the relevant organizational structures are not those of the units of the system but those of the system itself. Thus, with specific reference to the latest, US cycle, the relevant organizational structures are not merely those of the vertically-integrated, bureaucratically-managed corporations, which were only one component of the bloc of governmental and business agencies that led world capitalism through the material expansion of the 1950s and 1960s. Rather, they are the organizational structures of the Cold War world order in which the expansion was embedded. As the expansion unfolded, it generated three closely related tendencies that progressively undermined the capacity of those structures to sustain the expansion: the tendency of competitive pressures on US corporations to intensify; the tendency of subordinate groups to claim a larger share of the pie; and the tendency of US corporations to hoard the profits of the material expansion in extra-territorial financial markets. Already in evidence in the late 1960s and early 1970s, these were the tendencies that triggered the change of phase from material to financial expansion.[20]

As Robert Pollin has pointed out, the idea of recurrent and protracted phases of financial expansion poses a basic question: 'Where do the profits come from if not from the production and exchange of commodities?' As he suggests, this question has three possible answers, each pointing to a different source of profits. First, some capitalists are making money at the expense of other capitalists so that there is a redistribution of profits within the capitalist class. Second, profits for the capitalist class as a whole expand because financial deals enable capitalists to force a redistribution of wealth and income in their favour. Finally, 'financial deals can be profitable on a sustained basis ... if [they enable] capitalists to move their funds out of less profitable and into more profitable areas of production and exchange'.[21]

---

[20] Arrighi, *The Long Twentieth Century*, ch. 4; Arrighi and Silver, et al., *Chaos and Governance*, pp. 211–16.

[21] Robert Pollin, 'Contemporary Economic Stagnation in World Historical Perspective,' *New Left Review*, 219 (1996), pp. 115–16.

In our conceptualization of financial expansions, each of these three sources of profitability plays a distinct role. The first source provides the link between the crises of over-accumulation that signal the end of material expansions and the financial expansions that follow. Thus, at the onset of each financial expansion 'an over-accumulation of capital leads capitalist organizations to invade one another's spheres of operation; the division of labour that previously defined the terms of their mutual co-operation breaks down; and, increasingly … competition turns from a positive-sum into a zero-sum (or even a negative-sum) game'.[22] In and by itself, this source of profits does not provide a plausible explanation of the long periods of financial expansion—longer, as a rule, than half a century—that have intervened between the end of every phase of material expansion and the beginnings of the next. Nevertheless, cut-throat competition among capitalist agencies consolidates what we may call the 'supply' conditions of sustained financial expansions. That is to say, by accentuating the overall tendency of profit margins in trade and production to fall, it strengthens the disposition of capitalist agencies to keep in liquid form a growing proportion of their incoming cash flows.

Sustained financial expansions materialize only when the enhanced liquidity preference of capitalist agencies is matched by adequate 'demand' conditions. Historically, the crucial factor in creating the demand conditions of all financial expansions has been an intensification of interstate competition for mobile capital—a competition that Max Weber called 'the world-historical distinctiveness of [the modern] era'.[23] The occurrence of financial expansions in periods of particularly intense interstate competition for mobile capital is no mere historical accident. Rather, it can be traced to the tendency of territorial organizations to respond to the tighter budget constraints that ensue from the slowdown in the expansion of trade and production by competing intensely with one another for the capital that accumulates in financial markets. This tendency brings about massive, system-wide redistributions of income and wealth from all kinds of communities to the agencies that control mobile capital, thereby inflating and sustaining the profitability of financial deals largely divorced from commodity trade and production (Pollin's second source of financial profits). All the *belle époques* of finance capitalism—from Renaissance Florence to the Reagan and Clinton eras—have been characterized by redistributions of this kind.[24]

Finally, Pollin's third source of financial profit—the reallocation of funds from less to more profitable areas of material production and exchange—comes into the picture, not as a critical factor in making financial deals profitable on a sustained basis, but as a factor in the *supersession* of financial expansions by a new phase of material expansion. Particularly illuminating in this connection is Marx's observation that the credit system has been a key instrument, both nationally and internationally, of the transfer of surplus capital from declining to rising centres of capitalist trade and production. Since Marx's core argument in *Capital* abstracts from the role of states in processes of capital accumulation, national debts and the

---

[22] Arrighi, *The Long Twentieth Century*, p. 227.
[23] Max Weber, *Economy and Society* (Berkeley, CA: California University Press, 1978), p. 354; see also Max Weber, *General Economic History* (New York, Collier, 1961), p. 249.
[24] Arrighi, *The Long Twentieth Century*; Arrighi and Silver, et al., *Chaos and Governance*, especially ch. 3.

alienation of the assets and future revenues of states are dealt with under the rubric of 'primitive accumulation', that is, 'an accumulation not the result of the capitalist mode of production, but its starting point'.[25] This conceptualization prevented Marx from appreciating, as Weber did, the continuing historical significance of national debts in a world capitalist system embedded in states continually competing with one another for mobile capital. Nevertheless, Marx did acknowledge the continuing significance of national debts, not as an expression of interstate competition, but as means of an 'invisible' inter-capitalist co-operation that 'started' capital accumulation over and over again across the space-time of the world capitalist system from its inception through his own days:

With the national debt arose an international credit system, which often conceals one of the sources of primitive accumulation in this or that people. Thus the villainies of the Venetian thieving system formed one of the secret bases of the capital-wealth of Holland to whom Venice in her decadence lent large sums of money. So was it with Holland and England. By the beginning of the 18th century. ... Holland had ceased to be the nation preponderant in commerce and industry. One of its main lines of business, therefore, [became] the lending out of enormous amounts of capital, especially to its great rival England. [And the] same thing is going on to-day between England and the United States.[26]

Marx never developed the theoretical implications of this historical observation. In spite of the considerable space dedicated to 'money-dealing capital' in the third volume of *Capital*, he never rescued national debts and the alienation of the state from their confinement to the mechanisms of an accumulation that is 'not the result of the capitalist mode of production but its starting point'. And yet, in his own historical observation, what appears as a 'starting point' in one centre (Holland, England, the United States) is at the same time the 'result' of long periods of capital accumulation in previously established centres (Venice, Holland, England). To use Braudel's imagery, each and every financial expansion is simultaneously the 'Autumn' of a capitalist development of world-historical significance that has reached its limits in one place and the 'Spring' of a development of even greater significance that is about to begin in another place.

The similar dynamic of systemic cycles of accumulation—each consisting of the emergence of a new regime in the course of the financial expansion of an old regime—makes the cycles comparable with one another. But as soon as we compare the agencies, strategies and structures of successive cycles, we discover, not only that they are different, but also that the sequence of these differences describes an evolutionary pattern towards regimes of increasing size, scope and complexity. The first column of Figure 1 sums up this evolutionary pattern, focusing on the 'containers of power'—as Anthony Giddens[27] has aptly characterized states—that have housed the 'headquarters' of the leading capitalist agencies of the successive regimes: the Republic of Genoa, the United Provinces, the United Kingdom, and the United States.

At the time of the rise and full expansion of the Genoese regime, the Republic of Genoa was a city-state small in size and simple in organization, which contained very little power indeed. Deeply divided socially, and rather defenceless militarily, it

[25] Karl Marx, *Capital*, vol. I (Moscow: Foreign Languages Publishing House, 1959), pp. 713, 754–5.
[26] Marx, *Capital*, vol. I, pp. 755–6.
[27] Anthony Giddens, *The Nation-State and Violence* (Berkeley, CA: University of California Press, 1987).

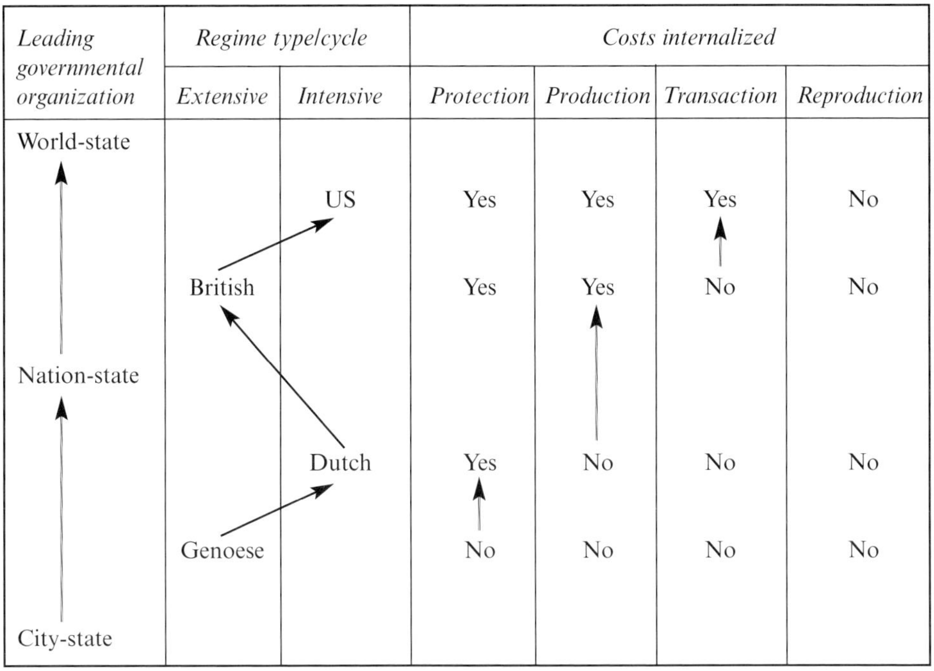

Leading governmental organization	Regime type/cycle		Costs internalized			
	Extensive	*Intensive*	*Protection*	*Production*	*Transaction*	*Reproduction*
World-state ↑		US	Yes	Yes	Yes	No
	British		Yes	Yes	No	No
Nation-state ↑		Dutch	Yes	No	No	No
	Genoese		No	No	No	No
City-state						

Figure 1. *Evolutionary patterns of world capitalism.*

was by most criteria a weak state in comparison with and in relation to all the great powers of the time, among which its old rival Venice still ranked fairly high. Yet, thanks to its far-flung commercial and financial networks the Genoese capitalist class, organized in a cosmopolitan diaspora, could deal on a par with the most powerful territorialist rulers of Europe, and turn the relentless competition for mobile capital among these rulers into a powerful engine for the self-expansion of its own capital.[28]

At the time of the rise and full expansion of the Dutch regime of accumulation, the United Provinces was a hybrid kind of organization that combined some of the features of the disappearing city-states with some of the features of the rising nation-states. A larger and far more complex organization than the Republic of Genoa, the United Provinces 'contained' sufficient power to win independence from Imperial Spain, to carve out of the latter's sea-borne and territorial empire a highly profitable empire of commercial outposts, and to keep at bay the military challenges of England by sea and France by land. This greater power of the Dutch state relative to the Genoese enabled the Dutch capitalist class to do what the Genoese had already been doing—turn interstate competition for mobile capital into an engine for the self-expansion of its own capital—but without having to 'buy' protection from territorialist states, as the Genoese had done through a relationship of political exchange with Iberian rulers. The Dutch regime, in other words,

---

[28] Arrighi, *The Long Twentieth Century*, pp. 109–32, 145–51.

'internalized' the protection costs that the Genoese had 'externalized' (see Figure 1, column 4).[29]

At the time of the rise and full expansion of the British regime of accumulation, the United Kingdom was not only a fully developed nation-state. It was also in the process of conquering a world-encompassing commercial and territorial empire that gave its ruling groups and its capitalist class a command over the world's human and natural resources without parallel or precedent. This command enabled the British capitalist class to do what the Dutch had already been able to do—turn to its own advantage interstate competition for mobile capital and 'produce' all the protection required by the self-expansion of its capital—but without having to rely on foreign and often hostile territorialist organizations for most of the agro-industrial production on which the profitability of its commercial activities rested. If the Dutch regime relative to the Genoese had internalized protection costs, the British regime relative to the Dutch internalized production costs as well (see Figure 1, column 5).[30]

Finally, at the time of the rise and full expansion of the US regime of accumulation, the US was already something more than a fully developed nation-state. It was a continental military-industrial complex with sufficient power to provide a wide range of subordinate and allied governments with effective protection and to make credible threats of economic strangulation or military annihilation towards unfriendly governments anywhere in the world. Combined with the size, insularity, and natural wealth of its domestic territory, this power enabled the US capitalist class to internalize not just protection and production costs—as the British capitalist class had already done—but transaction costs as well, that is to say, the markets on which the self-expansion of its capital depended (see Figure 1, column 6).[31]

This steady increase in the size, scope and complexity of successive regimes of capital accumulation on a world scale is somewhat obscured by another feature of the temporal sequence of such regimes. This feature is a double movement, forward and backward at the same time. For each step forward in the process of internalization of costs by a new regime of accumulation has involved a revival of governmental and business strategies and structures that had been superseded by the preceding regime.

Thus, the internalization of protection costs by the Dutch regime in comparison with the Genoese regime occurred through a revival of the strategies and structures of Venetian state monopoly capitalism that the Genoese regime had superseded. Similarly, the internalization of production costs by the British regime in comparison with the Dutch regime occurred through a revival in new and more complex forms of the strategies and structures of Genoese cosmopolitan capitalism and Iberian global territorialism. And the same pattern recurred once again with the rise and full expansion of the US regime, which internalized transaction costs by reviving in new and more complex forms the strategies and structures of Dutch corporate capitalism (see Figure 1, columns 1 & 2).[32]

This recurrent revival of previously superseded strategies and structures of accumulation generates a pendulum-like movement back and forth between 'cosmo-

---

[29] Ibid., pp. 36–47, 127–51.
[30] Ibid., pp.43–58; 174–238.
[31] Ibid., pp. 58–74 and ch. 4.
[32] Ibid., pp. 57–8; 70–2; 243ff.

politan-imperial' and 'corporate-national' organizational structures, the first being typical of 'extensive' regimes—as the Genoese-Iberian and the British were—and the second of 'intensive' regimes—as the Dutch and the US were. The Genoese-Iberian and British 'cosmopolitan-imperial' regimes were extensive in the sense that they have been responsible for most of the geographical expansion of the world capitalist system. Under the Genoese regime, the world was 'discovered', and under the British it was 'conquered'. The Dutch and the US 'corporate-national' regimes, in contrast, were intensive in the sense that they have been responsible for the geographical consolidation rather than expansion of the world capitalist system. Under the Dutch regime, the 'discovery' of the world realized primarily by the Iberian partners of the Genoese was consolidated into an Amsterdam-centred system of commercial *entrepôts* and joint-stock chartered companies. And under the US regime, the 'conquest' of the world realized primarily by the British themselves was consolidated into a US-centred system of national markets and transnational corporations.

This alternation of extensive and intensive regimes blurs our perception of the underlying, truly long-term, tendency towards the formation of regimes of increasing size, scope and complexity. When the pendulum swings in the direction of extensive regimes, the underlying trend is magnified, and when it swings in the direction of intensive regimes, the underlying trend appears to have been less significant than it really was. Nevertheless, once we control for these swings by comparing the two intensive and the two extensive regimes with one another—the Genoese-Iberian with the British, and the Dutch with the US—the underlying trend becomes unmistakable.

The development of historical capitalism as a world system has thus been based on the formation of ever more powerful cosmopolitan-imperial (or corporate-national) blocs of governmental and business organizations endowed with the capability of widening (or deepening) the functional and spatial scope of the world capitalist system. And yet, the more powerful these blocs have become, the shorter the life-cycle of the regimes of accumulation that they have brought into being—the shorter, that is, the time that it has taken for these regimes to emerge out of the crisis of the preceding dominant regime, to become themselves dominant, and to attain their limits as signalled by the beginning of a new financial expansion. Relying on Braudel's dating of the beginning of financial expansions, this time was less than half, both in the case of the British regime relative to the Genoese and in the case of the US regime relative to the Dutch.[33]

This pattern of capitalist development whereby an increase in the power of regimes of accumulation is associated with a decrease in their duration, calls to mind Marx's contention that '*the real barrier* of capitalist production is *capital itself*' and that capitalist production continually overcomes its immanent barriers 'only by means which again place these barriers in its way on a more formidable scale'.[34] But the contradiction between the self-expansion of capital on the one side, and the development of the material forces of production and of an appropriate world market on the other, can in fact be reformulated in even more general terms than Marx did. For historical capitalism as world system of accumulation became a

---

[33] Ibid., pp. 216–17.
[34] Karl Marx, *Capital*, vol. III (Moscow, Foreign Languages Publishing House, 1962), pp. 244–5, emphasis in the original.

'mode of production'—that is, it internalized production costs—only in its third (British) stage of development. And yet, the principle that the real barrier to capitalist development is capital itself, that the self-expansion of existing capital is in constant tension, and recurrently enters into open contradiction with the expansion of world trade and production and the creation of an appropriate world market—all this was clearly at work already in the Genoese and Dutch stages of development, notwithstanding the continuing externalization of agro-industrial production by their leading agencies.

In both the Genoese and Dutch stages the starting and closing point of the expansion of world trade and production was the pursuit of profit as an end in itself on the part of a particular capitalist agency. In the first stage, the 'Great Discoveries', the organization of long-distance trade within and across the boundaries of the far-flung Iberian empire(s), and the creation of an embryonic 'world market' in Antwerp, Lyons and Seville were to Genoese capital mere means of its own self-expansion. And when around 1560 these means no longer served this purpose, Genoese capital promptly pulled out of trade to specialize in high finance. Likewise, the undertaking of carrying trade among separate and often distant political juris-dictions, the centralization of *entrepôt* trade in Amsterdam and of high-value-added industries in Holland, the creation of a worldwide network of commercial outposts and exchanges, and the 'production' of whatever protection was required by all these activities, were to Dutch capital mere means of its own self-expansion. And again, when around 1740 these means no longer served this purpose, Dutch capital abandoned them in favour of a more thorough specialization in high finance.

From this angle of vision, in the nineteenth century British capital simply repeated a pattern that had been established long before historical capitalism as mode of accumulation had become also a mode of production. The only difference was that, in addition to carrying, *entrepôt*, and other kinds of long-distance and short-distance trade and related protection and production activities, in the British cycle extractive and manufacturing activities—that is, what we may call production in a narrow sense—had become critical means of the self-expansion of capital. But around 1870, when production and related trade activities no longer served this purpose, British capital moved fast towards specialization in financial speculation and intermediation, just as Dutch capital had done 130 years earlier and Genoese capital 310 years earlier, and US capital would do 100 years later.

In all instances the contradiction is that the expansion of world trade and production were mere means in endeavours aimed primarily at increasing the value of capital and yet, over time, it tended to drive down the rate of profit and thereby curtail the value of capital. Thanks to their continuing centrality in networks of high finance, the established organizing centres are best positioned to turn the intensifying competition for mobile capital to their advantage, and thereby reflate their profits and power at the expense of the rest of the system. From this point of view, the reflation of US profits and power in the 1990s follows a pattern that has been typical of world capitalism from its earliest beginnings.[35] The question that remains open is whether this long established pattern can be expected to result, in the future as it did in the past, in the replacement of the still dominant US regime by another regime.

[35] Arrighi and Silver, et al., 1999, *Chaos and Governance*, pp. 272–5.

Hegemonic transitions: past and present

Figure 1 sums up the patterns of recurrence and evolution that we have inferred from a comparison of successive systemic cycles of accumulation. Were the future of world capitalism fully inscribed in these patterns—something that is even less likely to be the case in the present than it was in past transitions, as we shall presently see—the task of forecasting what to expect over the next half century or so would be straightforward. Our expectations would be the following.

First, within ten or at most twenty years the US regime would experience its terminal crisis. Second, over time (let us say, in another twenty years or so) the crisis would be superseded by the formation of a new regime capable of sustaining a new material expansion of world capitalism. Third, the leading governmental organiz-ation of this new regime would approximate the features of a 'world-state' more closely than the United States already has. Fourth, unlike the US regime, the new regime would be of the extensive ('cosmopolitan-imperial') rather than of the intensive ('corporate-national') variety. Finally, and most important, the new regime would internalize reproduction costs, that is, the kind of costs that the US regime has tended to externalize ever more massively.

We cannot rule out that these expectations will actually be fulfilled. But their fulfilment is neither the only nor, indeed, the most likely of possible futures, because transitions from one regime to another are not fully inscribed in previously estab-lished patterns. Established patterns of recurrence and evolution show that the *succession* of emergent developmental paths that over the centuries has propelled the expansion of the world capitalist system to its present, all-encompassing global dimensions, has not been a purely random process. But the emergence of a newly successful developmental path in the course of each and every transition has been contingent upon, and thoroughly shaped by, a range of historical and geographical factors that were themselves transformed and recombined by the competition and struggles that underlie financial expansions.

The patterns that we observe *ex post*, in other words, are as much the outcome of geographical and historical contingencies as they are of historical necessity. In speculating *ex ante* about future outcomes of the present transition, therefore, we must pay equal attention to phenomena that fit into past patterns of recurrence and evolution and to phenomena that do not, that is, to significant anomalies that can be expected to make future outcomes deviate from past patterns. In an attempt to identify such anomalies, we have engaged in an in-depth analysis of the dynamic of the present transition in comparison with past hegemonic transitions.[36] While the analysis has found sufficient similarities between present and past transitions to make their comparison meaningful, it has also identified a number of anomalies that warn us against the pitfalls of any mechanical projection of past patterns into the future.

Figure 2 sums up the overall model of hegemonic transition that has emerged from the analysis.[37] The model describes systemic expansions as being embedded in

---

[36] Ibid.
[37] For more specific models of the hegemonic transitions as seen from different angles of vision, see Arrighi and Silver, et al., *Chaos and Governance*, pp. 65, 122, 180.

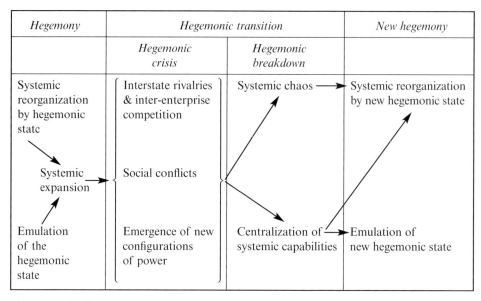

Figure 2. *The dynamics of hegemonic transitions.*

particular hegemonic structures that over time they tend to undermine. The expansions are the outcome of the two different kinds of leadership that jointly define hegemonic situations. On the one hand, leadership of the *system* in a new direction perceived to be in the general interest (systemic reorganization) promotes expansion by endowing the system with a wider or deeper division of labour and specialization of functions. On the other hand, leadership of other *states* onto the path of development of the dominant state (emulation) provides the separate states with the motivational drive needed to mobilize energies and resources in the expansion (see Figure 2, column 1).[38]

There is always a tension between these two tendencies because a wider and deeper division of labour and specialization of functions involves co-operation among the system's units, while emulation is based on and fosters their mutual competition. Initially, emulation operates in a context that is predominantly co-operative and thereby acts as an engine of expansion. But expansion increases what Emile Durkheim[39] has called the 'volume' and 'dynamic density' of the system, that is, the number of socially relevant units that interact within the system and the number, variety and velocity of transactions that link the units to one another. Over time, this increase in the volume and dynamic density of the system tends to intensify competition among the system's units beyond the regulatory capacities of existing institutions. When that happens, the tendency of separate states to pursue their national interest without regard for system-level problems that require system-

---

[38] On the distinction between these two kinds of leadership and their relationship to the concept of world hegemony, see Arrighi and Silver, et al., *Chaos and Governance*, pp. 26–28
[39] Emile Durkheim, *The Rules of Sociological Method* (New York, Free Press, 1964), p. 115 and *The Division of Labor in Society* (New York, Free Press, 1984), pp. 200–5.

level solutions—that is, what Kenneth Waltz[40] has called 'the tyranny of small decisions'—regains the upper hand, the power of the hegemonic state experiences a deflation, and a hegemonic crisis sets in.

Hegemonic crises have been characterized by three distinct but closely related processes: the intensification of interstate and inter-enterprise competition; the escalation of social conflicts; and the interstitial emergence of new configurations of power (see Figure 2, column 2). The form that these processes take and the way in which they relate to one another in space and time has varied from crisis to crisis. But some combination of the three processes can be detected in each of the two, so-far-completed hegemonic transitions—from Dutch to British and from British to US hegemony—as well as in the present transition from US hegemony to a yet unknown destination.

Moreover, in the past transitions (although not yet in the current one), hegemonic crises eventually led to a complete hegemonic breakdown and 'systemic chaos'. By systemic chaos we understand a situation of severe and seemingly irremediable systemic disorganization. As competition and conflicts escalate beyond the regulatory capacity of existing structures, new structures emerge interstitially and destabilize further the dominant configuration of power. Disorder tends to become self-reinforcing, threatening to provoke or actually provoking the complete breakdown in the system's organization (see Figure 2, column 3).

Financial expansions have been an integral aspect of hegemonic crises, both past and present, as well as of the eventual transformation of past hegemonic crises into hegemonic breakdowns. Their impact on the tendency of crises to turn into breakdowns is ambivalent. On the one hand, they hold it in check by temporarily inflating the power of the declining hegemonic state. As the 'autumn' of major capitalist developments, financial expansions are also the autumn of the hegemonic structures in which these developments are embedded. They are the time when the leader of a major expansion of world trade and production which is drawing to a close reaps the fruits of its leadership in the form of a privileged access to the overabundant liquidity that accumulates in world financial markets. Thanks to its continuing centrality in networks of high finance, the declining hegemon can turn the competition for mobile capital to its advantage and thereby experience a reflation of its waning power. This reflation enables the declining hegemonic state to contain, at least for a time, the forces that challenge its continuing dominance.

On the other hand, however, financial expansions strengthen these same forces by widening and deepening the scope of interstate and inter-enterprise competition and social conflict, and by reallocating capital to emergent structures that promise greater security or higher returns than the dominant structure. Declining hegemonic states are thus faced with the Sisyphean task of containing forces that keep rolling forth with ever renewed strength. Sooner or later, even a small disturbance can tilt the balance in favour of the forces that wittingly or unwittingly are undermining the already precarious stability of existing structures, thereby provoking a breakdown of systemic organization.

Hegemonic breakdowns are the decisive turning points of hegemonic transitions. They are the time when the systemic organization that had been put in place by the

---

[40] Kenneth Waltz, *Theory of International Politics* (Reading, MA: Addison-Wesley 1979), pp. 108–9.

declining hegemonic power disintegrates and systemic chaos sets in. But they are also the time when new hegemonies are forged.

For increasing systemic disorganization curtails the collective power of the system's dominant groups. And the greater the curtailment, the more widely and deeply felt the demand for system-level governance. Nevertheless, this demand can be satisfied and a new hegemony emerge only if increasing systemic disorganization is accompanied by the emergence of a new complex of governmental and business agencies endowed with greater system-level organizational capabilities than those of the preceding hegemonic complex. The breakdown of any given hegemonic order is ultimately due to the fact that the increase in the volume and dynamic density of the system outgrows the organizational capabilities of the particular hegemonic complex that had created the conditions of the systemic expansion. Ultimately, therefore, the ensuing self-reinforcing disorder can be overcome, and the conditions of a new systemic expansion can be created, only if a new complex emerges that is endowed with greater systemic capabilities than the old hegemonic complex.

Historically, the same processes that have generated systemic chaos have generated also the greater concentration of systemic capabilities that eventually resulted in the establishment of a new hegemony. As the rising hegemon leads the system in the direction of greater co-operation among the system's units, while drawing them onto its own path of development, systemic chaos subsides and a new hegemonic cycle begins (see Figure 2, column 4). But each cycle differs from the preceding one in two main respects: the greater concentration of organizational capabilities wielded by the hegemonic state in comparison with its predecessor, and the higher volume and dynamic density of the system that is being reorganized by the hegemonic state.

Our model thus describes a pattern of recurrence—hegemony leading to expansion, expansion to chaos and chaos to a new hegemony—which is also a pattern of evolution—each new hegemony reflecting a greater concentration of organizational capabilities and a higher volume and density of the system than the preceding hegemony. This double pattern concerns past hegemonic transitions. In the present transition there are few signs of an imminent breakdown of US hegemony. Nevertheless, we can detect some important similarities between present transformations of the global political economy and those typical of past transitions. The most important is the similarity between the present US-centred financial expansion, not just with the British-centred financial expansion of the late-nineteenth and early twentieth centuries as many observers have noted, but also with the Dutch-centred financial expansion of the mid-eighteenth century. As we shall see, there are good reasons for expecting the present financial expansion to end differently from earlier ones. But there are just as good reasons for interpreting the present expansion and the attendant reflation of US power as signs of a hegemonic crisis analogous to those of 100 and 250 years ago.

In the past, as in the present, the reflation of the power of the declining hegemons tended to blind them to the increasingly fragile nature of their dominance. The reflation came late and was minor in the case of the Dutch; it came early and was major in the case of the British. But in both cases these power revivals and the financial expansions that underlay them ended with the complete breakdown of the decaying hegemonic order some 30–40 years after they had begun. In both transitions, the financial expansions that reflated the power of the declining hegemonic state would have come to an end anyway under the weight of their own contradictions. But the blindness that led the ruling groups of these states to mistake the 'autumn' for a new 'spring' of their hegemonic power meant that the end came sooner and more catastrophically than it might otherwise have—mostly for itself in the case of the Dutch Republic, mostly for Europe and the world at large in the case of Britain.[41]

A similar blindness is evident today. The ease with which the United States has succeeded in mobilizing resources in global financial markets to defeat the USSR in what Fred Halliday[42] has called the Second Cold War, and then to sustain a long domestic economic expansion and a spectacular boom in the New York stock exchange, has led to the belief that 'America's back!' Even assuming that US global power has been reflated as much as this belief implies, it would be a very different *kind* of power than the one deployed at the height of US hegemony. That power rested on the capacity of the United States to rise and raise other states above 'the tyranny of small decisions' so as to solve the system-level problems that had plagued the world in the systemic chaos of the 1930s and 1940s. The new power that the United States has come to enjoy in the 1980s and 1990s, in contrast, rests on the capacity of the United States to outcompete most other states in global financial markets, thereby resurrecting a new tyranny of small decisions in the context of ever more pressing system-level problems that neither the United States nor any other state seems capable of solving.

Moreover, the *extent* to which US power itself has been reflated is not as great as generally assumed by US elites. For one thing, the financial expansion itself seems to rest on increasingly precarious grounds. Even the most enthusiastic supporters of interstate competition in globally integrated financial markets have begun to fear that financial globalization is turning into 'a brakeless train wreaking havoc'. They worry about a 'mounting backlash' against the effects of such a destructive force, first and foremost 'the rise of a new brand of populist politicians' fostered by the 'mood … of helplessness and anxiety' that is taking hold even of wealthy countries.[43] A backlash of this kind has been a typical feature of past financial expansions.[44] It announces that the massive redistribution of income and wealth on which the expansion rests has reached, or is about to reach, its limits. And once the re-distribution can no longer be sustained economically, socially and politically, the financial expansion is bound to end. The only question that remains open in this respect is not whether but how soon and how catastrophically the present global dominance of finance capital will draw to a close. Indeed, the bursting of the 'New Economy' bubble in 2000–01 may well be an early sign that the financial expansion and concomitant reflation of US power have already reached their limits.

Finally and equally important, the US-centred financial expansion has been accompanied by a major shift of the global economy's centre of gravity from North America to East Asia. In 1960, at the height of US hegemony, East Asia's Gross National Product (GNP) was only 35 per cent of the North American GNP. By 1990, in contrast, it was almost as large (91 per cent). In the 1990s, the combination of US resurgence and Japanese collapse slowed down but did not reverse the shift—

---

[41] Arrighi and Silver, et al., *Chaos and Governance,* chapters 1, 3 and conclusions.
[42] Fred Halliday, *The Making of the Second Cold War* (London: Verso, 1986).
[43] Quoted in Harvey, 'Globalization in Question', pp. 8, 12.
[44] Arrighi and Silver, *Chaos and Governance*, ch. 3.

the East Asian GNP relative to the North American rose further, to 92 per cent by 1998, thanks primarily to continuing rapid growth in the 'China Circle' (Mainland China, Singapore, Hong Kong and Taiwan).[45] The shift, however, is even more significant than these figures imply. As Eamonn Fingleton has recently noted, focusing exclusively on US–Japanese relations, Japan's continuing advance in manufacturing activities relative to the United States in the 1990s generated large and persistent surpluses in the Japanese balance of trade and deficits in the US balance, thereby deepening the reversal of positions between the two countries in the international credit system.

Japan is now exporting more capital in real terms than any nation since America's days of global economic dominance in the 1950s. ... [As a result,] in the first nine years of the 1990s Japan's net external assets jumped from \$294 billion to \$1,153 bn. Meanwhile, US net external liabilities rocketed from \$49 bn to \$1,537 bn. In the long run this changing balance of financial power will be about the only thing that historians will remember about US–Japanese economic rivalry in the last decade. Yet it was the one thing that Western observers generally overlooked.[46]

It is hard to tell what future historians will actually remember about the 1990s. Nevertheless, the ongoing reversal of the East Asian and North American fortunes in the international credit system[47] bears a close resemblance to the reversal of the US and British fortunes during the hegemonic transition of the first half of the twentieth century. To be sure, reversals of this order bring problems of their own, as witnessed by the turbulence that has characterized the East Asian economies from the 1990–92 Crash of the Tokyo stock exchange through the East Asian crisis of 1997–98. Problems of this kind, however, have been typical of all newly emergent centres of world capitalism. In past hegemonic transitions, as Braudel himself noted, the crises that ushered in the demise of the old financial centre were felt earliest and most severely in the *rising* financial centres, London in 1772 and New York in 1929.[48] It follows that the Asian financial crises of the 1990s are not in themselves signs of a long-term regional weakness, nor of a reversal of recent trends towards the rotation of the global economy's centre of gravity back to East Asia, where it was in pre-modern and early-modern times.

In sum, the global financial expansion of the last 25 years or so is neither a new stage of world capitalism nor the harbinger of a 'coming hegemony of global markets'. Rather, it is the clearest sign that we are in the midst of a hegemonic transition analogous to the Dutch-to-British and British-to-US transitions. The analogy makes us sceptical about the long-term stability of the present global dominance of finance capital and associated reflation of US power. But it also

---

[45] Calculated from World Bank, *World Development Indicators*, CD ROM (Washington, DC: World Bank, 2000) and Republic of China, *National Income in Taiwan Area of the Republic of China* (Taipei: Bureau of Statistics, DGBAS, Executive Yuan, various years). 'North America' consists of the United States and Canada. 'East Asia' consists of China, Hong Kong, Indonesia, Japan, Malaysia, Philippines, Singapore, South Korea, Taiwan and Thailand.

[46] Eamonn Fingleton, 'Quibble All You Like, Japan Still Looks Like a Strong Winner'. *International Herald Tribune*, 2 January (2001), p.6.; cf. Eamonn Fingleton, *Blindside: Why Japan Is Still on Track to Overtake the US by the Year 2000* (Boston: Houghton Mifflin, 1995).

[47] The reversal is even greater than indicated by Fingleton once we take into account the rapid increase in the external assets of the 'China Circle', since all of its members had sizeable and growing current account surpluses in the 1990s.

[48] Arrighi and Silver, et al., *Chaos and Governance*, pp. 74–5, 95–6, 274–5.

enables us to identify the true novelties of the present transition in comparison with previous ones. By way of conclusion, let us review the most important among these novelties, as well as their implications for the ongoing transformations.

Possible futures

Geopolitically, the most important novelty of present transformations is a bifurcation of military and financial capabilities that has no precedent in earlier hegemonic transitions. In all past transitions, financial expansions were characterized by the interstitial emergence of governmental-business complexes that were (or could be plausibly expected to become) more powerful both militarily and financially than the still dominant governmental-business complex—as the US complex was relative to the British in the early twentieth century, the British complex relative to the Dutch in the early eighteenth century, and the Dutch relative to the Genoese in the late sixteenth century. In the present transition, in contrast, no such emergence can be detected.

As in past transitions, the declining but still dominant (US) complex has been transformed from the world's leading creditor into the world's leading debtor nation. Unlike in past transitions, however, military resources (of any global significance) have become more than ever concentrated in the hands of the still dominant complex. The declining hegemon is thus left in the anomalous situation that it faces no credible military challenge—a circumstance that makes war among the system's great powers less likely than in past transitions—but it does not have the financial means needed to solve system-level problems that require system-level solutions—a circumstance that may very well lead to a hegemonic breakdown even in the absence of world wars among the system's great powers.

The obverse side of this anomalous situation is the re-emergence of city-states (Hong Kong and Singapore) and semi-sovereign states (Japan and Taiwan) as the 'cash-boxes' of the world capitalist system.[49] Not since the elimination of the Dutch Republic from the high politics of Europe, have cash-boxes of this kind exercised as much influence on the politics of the modern world as they do now. Also in this respect—as in the rotation of the centre of gravity of the global economy back to East Asia—the present transition seems to be reviving features of early and pre-modern times. Since all these cash-boxes owe their fortunes to a strict specialization in the pursuit of wealth rather than the pursuit of power, none of them—the biggest one (Japan) included—can be expected to change course by either trying to become a military power of more than regional significance or by trying to provide system-level solutions for system-level problems. This is a further reason for expecting that the present crisis has no inherent tendency to escalate into a war among the system's most powerful units, but has no inherent tendency towards the avoidance of a hegemonic breakdown either.[50]

---

[49] On Japan as semi-sovereign state, see Bruce Cumings, 'Japan and Northeast Asia into the Twenty-first Century', in P. J. Katzenstein and T. Shiraishi (eds.), *Network Power: Japan and Asia* (Ithaca, NY: Cornell University Press, 1997), p. 155.

[50] Arrighi and Silver, et al., *Chaos and Governance*, pp. 88–96, 263–70, 275–8, 286–9; Arrighi and Silver, 'Hegemonic Transitions', pp. 310–11.

Just as important as the geopolitical novelty is the social novelty of present transformations. In past hegemonic transitions, systemwide financial expansions contributed to an escalation of social conflict. The massive redistribution of rewards and social dislocations entailed by financial expansions provoked movements of resistance and rebellion by subordinate groups and strata whose established ways of life were coming under attack. Interacting with the interstate power struggle, these movements eventually forced the dominant groups to form a new hegemonic social bloc that selectively included previously excluded groups and strata.

In the transition from Dutch to British hegemony, the aspirations of the European propertied classes for greater political representation and the aspirations of the settler bourgeoisies of the Americas for self-determination were accommodated in a new dominant social bloc. But the aspirations of the European non-propertied classes and of the African slaves in the Americas were not, in spite of their respective contributions to the upheavals that transformed the dominant social bloc. Under British hegemony, slavery was slowly but surely eliminated, but the attendant gains towards racial equality were blunted by European expansion in Asia and Africa, and by new means of effectively subordinating the freed slaves in the Americas.[51]

With the transition from British to US hegemony—under the joint impact of the revolt against the West and working-class rebellions—the hegemonic social bloc was further expanded through the promise of a global New Deal. The working classes of the wealthier countries of the West were promised security of employment and high mass consumption. The elites of the non-Western world were promised the right to national self-determination and development (that is, assistance in catching up with the standards of wealth and welfare established by Western states). It soon became clear, however, that this package of promises could not be delivered. Moreover, it engendered expectations in the world's subordinate strata that seriously threatened the stability and eventually precipitated the crisis of US hegemony.[52]

Here lies the peculiar social character of this crisis in comparison with earlier hegemonic crises. The crisis of Dutch hegemony was a long drawn out process in which a systemwide financial expansion came late and systemwide social conflict later still. The crisis of British hegemony unfolded more rapidly but the systemwide financial expansion still preceded systemwide social conflict. In the crisis of US hegemony, in contrast, the systemwide explosion of social conflict of the late 1960s and early 1970s preceded and thoroughly shaped the subsequent financial expansion.

Indeed, in a very real sense the present financial expansion has been primarily an instrument—to paraphrase Wallerstein[53]—of the containment of the combined demands of the peoples of the non-Western world (for relatively little per person but for a lot of people) and of the Western working classes (for relatively few people but for quite a lot per person). The financial expansion and associated restructuring of the global political economy have undoubtedly succeeded in disorganizing the social forces that were the bearers of these demands in the upheavals of the late 1960s and 1970s. At the same time, however, the underlying contradiction of a world capitalist

[51] Arrighi and Silver, et al., *Chaos and Governance*, pp. 153–76.
[52] Ibid., pp. 176–216.
[53] Immanuel Wallerstein, 'Response: Declining States, Declining Rights?' *International Labor and Working-Class History*, 47 (1995), p. 25.

system that promotes the formation of a world proletariat but cannot accommodate a generalized living wage (that is, the most basic of reproduction costs), far from being solved, has become more acute than ever.[54]

The combination of the geopolitical and social anomalies of present transformations points to the pitfalls involved in any simple extrapolation into the future of the long-term tendencies depicted in Figure 1. Social pressures for the internalization of reproduction costs within the structures of world capitalism have not been eliminated. And yet, the bifurcation of military and financial power and the decentralization of financial power in otherwise politically weak states do not augur well for an easy or imminent accommodation of those pressures. This does not mean that there are no solutions to the crisis of over-accumulation that underlies the ongoing financial expansion. Rather, it means that the crisis has more than one possible solution—some involving a continuation of past patterns, others their reversal, and still others the emergence of new patterns. Which particular solution will eventually materialize depends on an ongoing process of struggle that for the most part still lies in front of us.

To complicate things further, this process of struggle can be expected to be shaped by a third major novelty of present transformations. This is the previously noted shift of the epicentre of the global economy to East Asia—a region that unlike all previous organizing centres of world capitalism lies outside the historical boundaries of Western civilization. It is this shift above all else that has led Samuel Huntington to advance his highly influential and controversial thesis of a coming 'clash of civilizations'.[55]

In reality, a clash between Western and non-Western civilizations has been a constant of the historical process whereby the world capitalist system was transformed from a European to a global system. The transition from Dutch to British hegemony was marked by the violent conquest or destabilization of the indigenous world systems of Asia. The transition from British to US hegemony was marked, first, by a further extension of Western territorial empires in Asia and Africa, and then by a general revolt against Western domination.[56]

Under US hegemony, the map of the world was redrawn to accommodate demands for national self-determination. By and large this new map reflected the legacy of Western colonialism and imperialism, including the cultural hegemony that led non-Western elites to claim for themselves more or less viable 'nation-states' in the image of the metropolitan political organizations of their former imperial masters. There was nonetheless one major exception to the rule: East Asia. Except for some states on its southern fringes (most notably, Indonesia, Malaysia, the Philippines and the city-states of Hong Kong and Singapore), the region's map reflected primarily the legacy of the China-centred world system, which the Western intrusion had destabilized and transformed at the margins but never managed to destroy and recreate in the Western image. All the region's most important nations

---

[54] Arrighi and Silver, et al., *Chaos and Governance*, pp. 282–6.
[55] Samuel Huntington, 'The Clash of Civilizations?' *Foreign Affairs*, 73: 3 (1993), pp. 22–49. For early responses, see Samuel Huntington, et al., *The Clash of Civilizations? The Debate* (New York: Council on Foreign Relations, 1993). For a critical assessment of the debate, see Hayward Alker, 'If Not Huntington's "Civilizations", Then Whose?' *Review* (Fernand Braudel Center), 18: 4 (1995), pp. 33–62.
[56] Arrighi and Silver, et al., *Chaos and Governance*, pp. 219–63.

that were formally incorporated in the expanded Westphalia system—from Japan, Korea, and China to Vietnam, Laos, Kampuchea, and Thailand—had all been nations long before the European arrival. What's more, they had all been nations linked to one another, directly or through the Chinese centre, by diplomatic and trade relations and held together by a shared understanding of the principles, norms, and rules that regulated their mutual interactions as a world among other worlds.[57]

This geopolitical relict was as difficult to integrate into the US Cold War world order as into the British world order. The fault-lines between the US and Soviet spheres of influence in the East Asian region started breaking down soon after they were established—first by the Chinese rebellion against Soviet domination, and then by the US failure to split the Vietnamese nation along the Cold War divide. Then, while the two superpowers escalated their competition in the final embrace of the Second Cold War, the various pieces of the East Asian puzzle reassembled themselves into the world's most dynamic regional economy.[58]

The astonishing speed with which this regional economy has become the new workshop and cash-box of the world has contributed to a widespread 'fear of falling' in the Western world. A more or less imminent fall of the West from the commanding heights of world capitalism is certainly possible. But what should be feared about it is not at all clear.

The fall is likely because the leading states of the West are prisoners of the developmental paths that have made their fortunes, both political and economic. The paths are yielding decreasing returns in terms of rates of accumulation relative to the East Asian regional path, but they cannot be abandoned in favour of the more dynamic path without causing social strains so unbearable that they would result in chaos rather than 'competitiveness'. A similar situation arose in past hegemonic transitions. At the time of their respective hegemonic crises, both the Dutch and the British got themselves ever more deeply into the particular path of development that had made their fortunes, despite the fact that more dynamic paths were being opened up at the margins of their radius of action. And neither got out of the established path until the world system centred on them broke down.

As David Calleo[59] has suggested, the 'international system breaks down not only because unbalanced and aggressive new powers seek to dominate their neighbours, but also because declining powers, rather than adjusting and accommodating, try to cement their slipping pre-eminence into an exploitative hegemony'. Our comparison of past transitions shows that the role of aggressive new powers in precipitating systemic breakdowns has decreased from transition to transition, while the role of exploitative domination by the declining hegemon has increased. Dutch world power was already so diminished in the declining decades of its hegemony that Dutch resistance played only a marginal role in the systemic breakdown in comparison with the role played by the emerging, aggressive empire-building nation-states, first and

---

[57] On the China-centred regional world system, see especially Takeshi Hamashita, 'The Intra-Regional System in East Asia in Modern Times', in Peter J. Katzenstein and T. Shiraishi (eds.), *Network Power: Japan and Asia* (Ithaca, NY: Cornell University Press, 1997), pp.113–35; and Sato Ikeda 'The History of the Capitalist World-System vs. The History of East-Southeast Asia', *Review* (Fernand Braudel Center), 19: 1 (1996), pp. 49–76.

[58] Arrighi and Silver, et al., *Chaos and Governance*, pp. 263–70.

[59] David Calleo, *Beyond American Hegemony: The Future of the Western Alliance* (New York: Basic Books, 1987), p. 142.

foremost Britain and France. By the time of its own hegemonic decline, in contrast, Britain remained powerful enough to transform its hegemony into exploitative domination. Although the emergence of aggressive new powers—first and foremost Germany—still played a major role in the breakdown of the British-centred world system, Britain's resistance to adjustment and accommodation was also crucial.

Today we have reached the other end of the spectrum. There are no credible aggressive new powers that can provoke the breakdown of the US-centred world system but the United States has even greater capabilities than Britain did a century ago to convert its declining hegemony into an exploitative domination. If the system eventually breaks down, it will be primarily because of US resistance to adjustment and accommodation. And conversely, US adjustment and accommodation to the rising economic power of the East Asian region is an essential condition for a non-catastrophic transition to a new world order.

An equally essential condition is the emergence of a new global leadership from the main centres of the East Asian economic expansion. This leadership must be willing and able to rise up to the task of providing system-level solutions to the system-level problems left behind by US hegemony. The most severe among these problems is the seemingly unbridgeable gulf between the life-chances of a small minority of the world population (between 10 and 20 per cent) and the vast majority. In order to provide a viable and sustainable solution to this problem, the 'tracklaying vehicles' of East Asia must open up a new path of development for themselves and for the world that departs radically from the one that is now at a dead-end.

This is an imposing task that the dominant groups of East Asian states have hardly begun to undertake. In past hegemonic transitions, dominant groups successfully took on the task of fashioning a new world order only after coming under intense pressure from movements of protest and self-protection. This pressure from below has widened and deepened from transition to transition, leading to enlarged social blocs with each new hegemony. Thus, we can expect social contradictions to play a far more decisive role than ever before in shaping both the unfolding transition and whatever new world order eventually emerges out of the impending systemic chaos. But whether the movements will largely follow and be shaped by the escalation of violence (as in past transitions) or precede and effectively work toward containing the systemic chaos is a question that is open. Its answer is ultimately in the hands of the movements.

Variation, change, and transitions in international politics

ROBERT JERVIS

Abstract. Policymakers and scholars have to deal with the difficult problems of variation, change, and transitions in world politics. Practitioners have to estimate the capabilities and intentions of those with whom they are interacting and need to determine the kind and extent of variety in their environments. Detecting, diagnosing, and dealing with change also is particular difficult. Scholars have shown the wide range of units and systems that human beings have created, but need to also examine the extent to which they are characterized by common processes and dynamics. The balance of power generally operates through un-intended consequences and can characterize systems even when no one seeks balance. Change may be more common than scholars often appreciate. Nuclear weapons undermine much traditional international politics and even greater changes will flow from the fact that the leading powers in the world no longer contemplate war with each other.

Variation, change, and transition are among the most vexing problems of inter-national politics for theorists and practitioners alike. Since we are the former, the implications for scholarly understanding receives most of our attention. But the problems for national leaders are worth more thought than we have given them, both because they constitute an important topic and because national behaviour is a great part of what we seek to explain. So I start with this topic.

Variation, change, and transitions: problems for practitioners

The essays in this issue make clear that international politics varies in important dimensions from one geographical area and historical era to another. While this gives scholars important analytical leverage by allowing them to examine a range—if not the entire range—of possible arrangements, it is not directly relevant to most practitioners, who live in one period of time and one area. But the question of variety can arise for them in three ways. First, there is significant variation even within a narrow setting. Much day-to-day international politics is taken up by the problem of assessment—that is, the attempts by diplomats and leaders to discern the contours of their environments, which are largely the actual and potential behaviours of other actors. Most obviously, states[1] vary in their capabilities and intentions in ways that are difficult to determine at the time (not that it is easy even in retrospect).

---

[1] In some systems the relevant actors are not states, but the same analysis could apply to them and for linguistic simplicity I will simply use the term states.

This is a crucial problem for statecraft because a policy that is appropriate for dealing with one type of state is likely to fail badly when dealing with another. If all states were the same, one important source of uncertainty and choice would be removed. In such a world, actors could predict others' behaviour by introspection, by the actor asking herself what she would do in the others' circumstances.[2]

In fact, introspection is inadequate because states are not all alike and foreign policy often turns on an estimate of how others will react to alternative courses of action that the state could follow. To oversimplify, the question is whether the other side is basically satisfied with the *status quo* or whether it is an expansionist that is willing to run high risks to change it in ways that would do great damage to what the state values. In the former case co-operation and conciliation is generally the best policy and armaments and threats are likely to set off a spiral of tensions and hostility; in the latter case arms and alliances are likely to be necessary (although perhaps not sufficient) and conciliation will be useless at best and harmful at worst. The fact that states' intentions can vary in ways that are not easy to detect makes the task of estimating as difficult as it is crucial, and much of international history is determined by the accuracy or errors that result. Even in retrospect, there is often disagreement on what the 'correct' estimate was and, indeed, the scholarly consensus is likely to shift over time, as can be seen by changing views about the nature of Wilhelmine foreign policy and whether the images held by British diplomats were accurate.

The two World Wars and the Cold War were strongly influenced by each side's estimates of the other's intentions and capabilities. Diplomats and national leaders have theories, often implicit, about how others stand on these dimensions, but, as these cases indicate, they are probabilistic and deeply flawed. Leaders then cope with this variability as best that they can, and the results of their estimates often produce important changes in world politics.

One way to cope with uncertainty is to deny it, or to act as though it did not exist. In particular cases, national leaders often claim to be certain about other's intentions. Sometimes they do so in order to rally domestic support and bolster domestic confidence; sometimes they are fooling themselves in order to banish debilitating doubts from their own minds. In still other cases, they may decide to act on 'worst

---

[2] This would not remove all sources of uncertainty and all grounds for choice because the circumstances themselves grow out of the interaction of multiple actors, each of which is trying to predict what the others will do. Even if you and I are alike, my prediction of what you will do depends on my estimate of your prediction of my behaviour. As an aside, I should note that our common and often implicit assumption that states and individuals know their own capabilities and likely responses is not correct. Just as individuals may not be able to judge their own strength or stamina, so national leaders often misjudge what their own countries are capable of. One reason why the British appeased Germany in the 1930s was the widespread fear that the country could not survive major bombing attacks, largely because working class morale and loyalty was believed to be low. More recently, Gorbachev's reform policies were premised on a great overestimate of the strength and resilience of central authority and its ability to manage fundamental transitions at home and in Eastern Europe. Individuals and states may misjudge not only their capabilities, but also how they will respond to various situations. For example, although before June 1950 US government officials had thought that they would not respond with force to a North Korean attack on the South, in the event they decided to do so. During the Cold War there was much speculation about whether the US would use nuclear weapons in response to a conventional Soviet attack in Europe, but it is a mistake to think that declassified records will provide a definitive answer: while the relevant discussions are interesting, it is far from clear that they provide much guidance about how the US would have reacted to such an unprecedented and existential situation.

case' assumptions—that is, premise their behaviour on the chance that the other side is hostile, in part because of their awareness that even if the other is satisfied with the *status quo* today, it may develop expansionist appetites later. Of course the danger is that such a policy will become a self-fulfilling prophecy; that it will lead the other side to become hostile and bring on the war it was designed to avoid. If everyone adopts this model, variability will indeed decrease, although few people are likely to be happy with the results.

Variability enters in a more dramatic way when actors of very different types first come into contact with each other. The obvious example is when civilizations meet, as when adventurers, soldiers, traders, settlers, and missionaries from Europe first ventured into Africa and the Western Hemisphere. These situations are much less well structured than those discussed in the previous section. The problem was not to figure out which of several fairly well understood models the other actor represented, but to understand people, units, and civilizations of a type never before encountered. It is not surprising that people did not do these tasks very well. A different civilization poses dramatic intellectual, psychological, and political challenges. Even if there were no other difficulties, the purely intellectual task of understanding people who operate in an unknown mental and cultural world is enormously difficult. Indeed, it is not even clear what 'understanding' means here. Recreating how the 'natives' see the world and what they value? Predicting how they will react? Explaining how it is that they have come to their worldviews and social structures? Of course, the challenges are more than intellectual. Realizing that others can hold very different views about the world can be profoundly psychologically threatening. For those who believe that capitalism is the main generator of cruelty in the world, for example, seeing pre-capitalist societies as warlike and brutal can be deeply disturbing. Thus many anthropologists have resisted the evidence that prehistoric war was endemic and that some societies engaged in cannibalism, which is ironic because our revulsion against the latter practice is merely a reflection of modern Western values. Furthermore, political as well as psychological needs influence people's attempts to come to grips with variety. It is convenient for people who want to conquer another society to see it as primitive and unworthy. The intellectual, psychological, and political dimensions often coincide and reinforce each other, leading to a denigration of diversity or a failure to appreciate it.[3]

A third kind of variety faced by decision-makers occurs when conditions rapidly shift, when they may be facing a transition from one era to another. The problem confronting diplomats here is whether they need a drastically changed intellectual map of the world and, if they do, how to develop it. It is often argued that, like most people, national leaders are too slow to perceive and adapt to new circumstances. Just as studies of scientists cite numerous cases in which they were too slow to abandon old paradigms or to recognize the significance of experiments and data that were incompatible with well-established theories, so critics can easily find cases of policymakers who stubbornly maintain that the world has not changed. But these analyses suffer from a sampling bias. If one examines only cases in which hindsight indicates that the world has fundamentally changed, it will be easy to find people

---

[3] Richard Cottam, *Foreign Policy Motivation* (Pittsburgh: University of Pittsburgh Press, 1977). Humanists have recently discovered and made much of these kinds of perceptual and intellectual biases.

who incorrectly saw continuity. This does not prove that this error is more common or costly than the opposite one, however. Just as scientists sometimes incorrectly claim to have found fundamental discoveries that violate standard scientific beliefs, such as the existence of 'cold fusion', so leaders and scholars often say that the world has changed fundamentally when it has not. But I suspect that the hold of our established concepts and perceptual frameworks is so strong that people are much more likely to fail to perceive drastic change than to detect it when it is not present. Even political radicals are cognitively conservative and almost all of us are prone to see evidence and events as consistent with what we already believe, and even as providing independent confirmation of it.[4]

Nevertheless, there may be reason for leaders to perceive more change than is occurring. It is only natural for them to believe that they are at an historic moment where both the challenges and their achievements are enormous. Even if Secretary of State Dean Acheson was not justified to entitle his memoirs *Present at the Creation*, it would have been less satisfactory to have written 'present at the maintenance' and to have argued that he and his colleagues simply applied long-standing principles of international politics to a situation that differed only marginally from those in the past. Most leaders and people feel that their own eras are particularly difficult and represent a sharp break from the past. One wit said that an era of transition is a period between two eras of transition. Perhaps the stereo-typical peasant living in a pre-industrial society believed that she was living in an unchanged and unchanging universe; leaders rarely do.

Actors have their own theories of change. Records of diplomatic deliberations are full of analyses of instabilities, pressures for and against change, feedbacks, and other dynamics. This is true even—or perhaps especially—of leaders who are later perceived as hidebound and fearful of change. Metternich and John Foster Dulles, for example, thought long and deeply about how their worlds were changing and could change. Although much of the analysis in Kissinger's *A World Restored* is quite good, the title is wildly misguided. Metternich and his colleagues realized full well that the world that existed before the French Revolution could not be restored, and, if it was, would produce renewed destruction. They saw their task as building a new world that would fulfil many of the older values, while taming the forces that had caused so much devastating warfare not only in the proceeding generation, but in the eighteenth century as well. They came to a radically different view of state-society relations and the way to conduct world politics.[5] Dulles thought that world politics was characterized by constant dynamism, especially in his own era, and that it was crucial for the US to mobilize the forces of change in a constructive fashion. To try to stand still or construct bulwarks against change was foolish; rather the task of the leader was to see how forces for change could be generated, mobilized, and channelled to increase freedom and individual rights.[6] One of the main challenges for American foreign relations was to convince others that the West represented the legitimate aspirations of people throughout the globe and that Soviet and Chinese

[4] Robert Jervis, *Perception and Misperception in International Politics* (Princeton, NJ: Princeton University Press, 1976), ch. 4.
[5] Paul Schroeder, *The Transformation of European Politics, 1763–1848* (New York: Cambridge University Press, 1994).
[6] Richard Immerman, *John Foster Dulles: Piety, Pragmatism, and Power in US Foreign Policy* (Wilmington, DE: SR Books, 1999).

Communism, far from being forward-looking and dynamic, actually suppressed change, could not adapt, and eventually would collapse.

More broadly, many policies are premised on the expectation of either positive or negative feedback. When diplomats counsel against over-reaching, they are implicitly flagging the importance of the latter. That is, the attempt to gain excessive territory or undue advantage can lead others to react in a way that counteracts these policies. Positive feedback can also be anticipated, feared, and perhaps manipulated. The most obvious example of the fear of positive feedback driving policy is the domino theory. Although the term is only 50 years old, the concept, like so much else, can be found in Thucydides. The essential point is that victories and defeats feed on each other. Accretions of strength allow an actor to expand further; prestige leads to greater prestige; defeats reduce resources and, as was stressed in the nuclear era, lead to perceptions of weak resolve. The latter argument brings up a general pheno-menon that makes the social world different from the physical one: people's behaviour is influenced not only by the theories they hold but by their theories of the theories that others believe. This can produce strange results, as the case of the domino theory illustrates. Leaders who believe the domino theory and are forced to retreat in one encounter will have strong incentives to stop the positive feedback that they fear. They will then feel the need to stand firm in the next confrontation in order to show that their resolve is not weak. If the other side understands this, it will realize that the very fact that the first state believes that domino dynamics often operate will lead it to maintain a particularly hard bargaining position and so will avoid another challenge. Belief in the theory will then lead to outcomes that are contrary to it.[7] The general point is that actors hold theories about international politics and about others' theories of international politics, and the resulting complexities can effect many aspects of international politics, including the nature of change.

Variety, transitions, and change: implications for theory

As the other essays in this issue show, the nature of the units in international politics have varied greatly from one area and era to another. Our familiar language of states and diplomats is not universal; neither are the incentives and ideologies that have characterized Western international politics in the last two centuries. This means, of course, that the sources of power were different as well because of material differences (control over oil was of no value before the internal combustion engine, for example) and differences in worldviews and sources of legitimacy. Although it is extraordinarily difficult to capture the ways in which people far removed from us in time and culture saw their world, it is not so clear that current understandings of politics cannot help us grasp some of the patterns of the politics that resulted. Realists have long argued that Thucydides' analysis applies very closely to many modern situations, most obviously the Cold War, and symmetrically have implied that our current intellectual tools shed light on the Peloponnesian Wars.

---

[7] For further discussion, see Robert Jervis, *System Dynamics: Complexity in Political and Social Life* (Princeton, NJ: Princeton University Press, 1997), pp. 263–71.

While Constructivists read Thucydides very differently, the fact that they can use their current understandings to interpret him and the events that he described similarly implies that great differences in era need not render current understandings irrelevant.[8] Without suggesting that politics in general or international politics in particular is invariant across time and culture, it is worth asking whether some key characteristics might be consistent. This would not necessarily mean that the resulting patterns would be similar, however. Because of interaction effects, a factor that is constant might have very different influences depending on the status of other variables. To take the deeply contested question of anarchy, the fact—if it is a fact—that international systems are always anarchic in the sense of lacking an ultimate authority and arbiter does not necessarily mean that all international systems closely resemble each other. Although it might simplify our lives as social scientists if this were the case, anarchy might always be important, but lead to quite different patterns depending on, for example, the nature of the units in the system and the prevailing values and beliefs (including beliefs about anarchy).

The essays in the rest of this volume are fascinating partly because they are written to reveal variety across systems. It would be an interesting test to see what would be said by experts on these systems who shared a common perspective that led them to expect common patterns. Thus Bruce Bueno de Mesquita has analysed the interaction between twelfth century Popes and kings through a rational choice approach and finds that the bargaining fits theories derived from modern experience.[9] My guess is that had Andreas Osiander written an essay on this topic, it would have come out very differently. Similarly, it is not surprising that the only essay in this issue that finds patterns generally consistent with Realism is produced by William Wohlforth: Wohlforth is a Realist.

Although the variety that the essays here display cannot be fitted into any simple pattern, a number of the processes and characteristics would not surprise a Realist. They are quite general and point more toward problems that actors face than towards solutions, but they do indicate that the great variety in the nature of the units and the political cultures do not make these worlds entirely foreign to us.

In all the worlds described, each unit faces competition from others. The competition varies on such crucial dimensions as severity, forms of power, and beliefs about appropriate behaviour. But just as there are significant similarities in the writings of Thucydides and Machiavelli, so the actors discussed in these essays all have to be deeply concerned about what others are doing lest these behaviours threaten their values, power, and very existence. Actors, especially those who succeed, often must either emulate the successful behaviour of others or seek ways of offsetting it. Internal impulses can be very strong; the 'imperatives' of the system do not completely determine behaviour (a point stressed by Waltz but sometimes missed by his critics).[10] But only in unusual conditions can the units be entirely shielded from the actions of others and, even in systems very different from modern

---

[8] Daniel Garst, 'Thucydides and Neo-Realism', *International Studies Quarterly*, 33:1 (March 1989), pp. 3–28; Richard Ned Lebow, 'Thucydides the Constructivist', *American Political Science Review*, 95:3 (September 2001), pp. 547–60.

[9] Bruce Bueno de Mesquita, 'Popes, Kings, and Endogenous Institutions: The Concordat of Worms and the Origins of Sovereignty', *International Studies Review*, 2:2 (2000), pp. 93–118.

[10] Kenneth Waltz, *Theory of International Politics* (Reading, MA: Addison-Wesley, 1979), pp. 76–7.

Western ones, ineffective responses are usually dangerous. Much about the units' internal arrangements is also likely to be influenced by the environments in which they operate.[11] The essays make clear that in many eras and places one cannot sharply distinguish what is inside the unit and what is external to it (indeed, it is not clear that this distinction can be clearly drawn now or in earlier periods of Western history). Nevertheless, even in systems where sovereignty is overlapping, vague, and ambiguous, one can still detect units that are acting for particular sets of questions and ask how they are affected by competition from others.

The interaction of units is prone to produce unanticipated consequences. This is central to Waltz's analysis of international politics and the phenomenon is broader and characterizes interactions among units throughout our political and social world.[12] Sofka stresses this in his essay and while I will indicate a disagreement with him below, I think he is clearly correct to argue that the outcomes of eighteenth century international politics were not desired or intended by any of the participants. Indeed, I suspect that the other essay writers could have made similar points about the politics they were studying. This is not surprising: when individuals seek independent goals and react to what others are doing, the outcomes will rarely be intended by any of them and cannot be intended by all of them. Even in hierarchical systems in which orders can be given, the way that incentives play out rarely conforms to the wishes or expectations of those who gave the orders, as is clearly illustrated by the fate of centrally planned economies.

Where I disagree with Sofka is not in his description, but in his definition of the balance of power as a system in which the individual actors seek balance. As he clearly shows, this was not true in the eighteenth century. It rarely is. But this is not what most theorists of balance of power expect. Rather, they see the balance as the outcome of behaviour, not its motivation.[13] When units want to survive, are willing to ally with one another on the basis of short-run self interest, and can resort to armed force if need be, they will band together in moments of great danger to defeat the efforts of any one of them to dominate the entire system. The units that form this grand blocking coalition may not desire balance; each may instead want to dominate. But they all share an interest in seeing that no one else seizes control. This theory says very little about day-to-day international politics, but explains a fact we usually take for granted—that international politics continues to exist and that no one unit has established itself as the seat of world government. Thus from the balance of power perspective it is striking—although expected –that despite the variety of systems and units discussed in this issue, in no case did one unit come to absorb or control all of the others.

Such a 'roll up' of the system did occur in ancient China in which the state of Qin swallowed up a series of competitors of roughly equal size to establish a massive state filling the approximate contours of modern China. Victoria Tin-bor Hui, who has provided the most analytical study of this process, argues that the internal

---

[11] Peter Gourevitch, 'The Second Image Reversed: The International Sources of Domestic Politics', *International Organization*, 32:4 (1978), pp. 881–911; Brian Downing, *The Military Revolution and Political Change: Origins of Democracy and Autocracy in Early Modern Europe* (Princeton, NJ: Princeton University Press, 1992).

[12] Waltz, *Theory of International Politics*; Jervis, *System Effects*.

[13] See, for example, Inis Claude, *Power and International Relations* (New York: Random House, 1962); Waltz, *Theory of International Politics*; Jervis, *System Effects*.

strength of the Chinese states enabled the leaders to draw extensive resources from their societies and enact 'self-strengthening reforms' that yielded war-making potential without mortgaging the power of the state to other powerful domestic actors. They then faced few restraints and so generated and lived in a more competitive and Hobbesian world than did their European counterparts.[14] Of course alternative explanations are possible, but the main point here is simply that the balance of power can fail. In light of this, it is particularly interesting that it did not do so even in systems of very different types, including ones in which the concept of the balance of power does not seem to have existed.

All rulers face the problem of resource extraction. The nature of the resources varies widely, as do the ends to which they are put, but in almost all cases the former includes forms of money so that rulers can provide material incentives for others to undertake difficult and painful tasks, the most obvious of which is engaging in armed combat. Rulers in different eras and places extracted resources differently, but the trajectory of politics always has as one of its key components how this is to be done and the arrangements that result.[15] As Hui and several of the essays in this issue show, what units can do to help and (especially) hurt each other depends heavily upon the resources they can extract and deploy. Conquest and internal consolidation are very difficult when only minimal resources can be extracted, or when the modes of extraction decentralize power. Conversely, many of the forms of modern international politics assume that a high level of resources can be extracted and centrally controlled. Not only an efficient system of taxation, but also a high degree of legitimacy and voluntary support is required. As the essays in this issue show, when this is not forthcoming the nature and scale of warfare and many other aspects of international politics will be quite different from the model of modern Western Europe.

Change and transitions

It is often argued that international politics lacks an adequate theory of change. I would not disagree, but would deny the implication that we have excellent theories of stasis. When we find forms of stability we often point to factors that do not seem to change and attribute causal significance to them, but I am not sure that a systematic survey would reveal many well developed and verified theories of why things do not change. Theoretically, stability should not be any easier to explain than its absence, especially when we take account of the prevalence of unintended consequences. The fact—if it is a fact—that many people seek stability does not explain why or how it occurs.

[14] Victoria Tin-bor Hui, 'Rethinking War, State Formation, and System Formation: A Historical Comparison of Ancient China (659–221 BC) and Early Modern Europe (1485–1585 AD)', Ph.D. thesis, Department of Political Science, Columbia University, 2000.

[15] Margaret Levi, *Of Rule and Revenue* (Berkeley, CA: University of California Press, 1988); Carolyn Webber and Aaron Wildavsky, *A History of Taxation and Expenditure in the Western World* (New York: Simon and Schuster, 1986).

One set of arguments seeks to explain both change and stability in the form of cycles of the rise and fall of major units.[16] The basic claim is that over time one unit is likely to grow stronger than most of its neighbours and expand past the point at which growth can be maintained. Excessive commitments are undertaken and excessive enemies are created. Simultaneously, as the unit gets richer its citizens get accustomed to living well and lose their willingness to make the sacrifices necessary to maintain the empire. Expansion then both creates challenges and undermines the unit's ability to cope with them. The unit then eventually declines, a process accompanied and accelerated by large-scale war, and another one takes its place. The cycle itself is repeated; change occurs as it moves through phases, as different units rise and fall, and as technology, the scope and intensity of economic activities, and beliefs about the world change.[17] In this view, what does not change is the constant struggle for survival and dominance, although its form and outcome varies with stages of the cycle, and, in its details, with many other factors. This perspective stands in stark contrast to portrayals of international progress.[18]

Theories of change in general and progress in particular can be rooted in material factors or ideas (or, of course, in some combination of the two). Marxist and Liberal theories share the basic functionalist argument that economic change and growth inevitably produces progressive changes in politics, including international politics. Economic incentives and logic eventually triumph, although not without extensive bloodshed. At the end of the very long day, the interests of the working class (in Marxism) or of populations in general (in Liberalism) produce a peaceful order that allows individuals and populations to enjoy prosperity, realize their individual and collective desires, and co-operate with each other on the basis of equality. The logic of international politics is not given by anarchy and competition, important as these are at some stages, but stems from the prevailing economic interests and arrangements. Perhaps one reason for the attractiveness of Marxism and Liberalism is their portrayal of inevitable progress. By contrast, conservative or reactionary theories are deeply pessimistic, seeing flaws in human nature if not original sin as making us strive to elevate ourselves over others and expecting the forces of change that are generated by economic growth to produce decadence, lack of discipline, and wanton violence. Although this perspective is out of favour now, especially in academia, we should not forget that change does not necessarily mean change for the better. It would not take many instances of biological warfare to drive this point home.

---

[16] The best known recent examples are Robert Gilpin, *War and Change in World Politics* (New York: Cambridge University Press, 1981); Paul Kennedy, *The Rise and Fall of Great Powers: Economic Change and Military Conflict from 1500–2000* (New York: Random House, 1987). Narrower theories of cycles can also be developed and I have argued that with a bit of twisting of the relevant history, one can develop a quite simple theory of cycles of the alternation of balance of power and concerts: 'From Balance to Concert', in Kenneth Oye (ed.), *Cooperation Under Anarchy* (Princeton, NJ: Princeton University Press, 1986), pp. 58–79.

[17] For theories of geology that portray cycles, steady change, or combinations, see Stephen Jay Gould, *Time's Cycle, Time's Arrow* (Cambridge, MA: Harvard University Press, 1987).

[18] Emanuel Adler and Beverly Crawford (eds.), *Progress in Postwar International Relations* (New York: Columbia University Press, 1991); Paul Schroeder, 'Historical Reality vs. Neo-Realist Theory', *International Security*, 19: 1 (Summer 1994), pp. 108–148. It seems hard to imagine theories of progress in face of the horrifying international bloodshed of the first half of the twentieth century and the continuing incidence of genocide, but this terrifying history precludes only progress of a simple and linear kind. For the argument that, while progress is not inevitable, certain (beneficial) changes in world politics are irreversible, see Alexander Wendt, *Social Theory of International Politics* (Cambridge: Cambridge University Press, 1999), pp. 311–12.

It is usually argued that because Realism stresses the central role of anarchy, it believes that international politics does not change, or at most follows the kind of cycles discussed earlier. I do not think that this is entirely correct: Realism in at least some of its variants both has room for extensive co-operation and expects the behaviour of actors to change as the incentives they face do, especially because of the changing opportunities and dangers. Thus I join many other scholars in believing that the development of nuclear weapons has led to revolutionary changes in international politics. The relevant arguments are well known, if disputed, and need only be briefly and crudely summarized here.[19] The essential point was made by Bernard Brodie at the dawn of the nuclear age: 'Thus far the chief purpose of our military establishment has been to win wars. From now on its chief purpose must be to avert them. It can have almost no other useful purpose'.[20] Throughout much of the Cold War, many if not most observers thought that a war was inevitable. After all, the existence of such powerful weapons seemed to provide the temptation for their use, especially in the hands of what was seen as the rash and inexperienced hands of the Soviet Union and United States. Great powers had always fought each other every generation or two, at least in the Western world, and so there were good historical reasons for expecting this propensity to continue even if the rivalry had not been compounded by deep ideological hostilities. We can of course debate the reasons why the rivalry did not escalate to direct warfare and why the Soviet Union declined and dissolved peacefully rather than striking out in desperation, but this is just what the theory of nuclear revolution would lead one to expect. When both sides have nuclear weapons deployed in large numbers and in relatively invulnerable places (creating what is known as mutual second-strike capability), then military victory is impossible. As Reagan and Gorbachev agreed at their first meeting, 'A nuclear war cannot be won and must never be fought'. In the past, even wars that were enormously destructive generally had a winner in the sense that even while both sides might be worse off at the end of the war than they had been at its start, one of them preferred having fought to the outcome expected in the absence of fighting. But mutual second-strike capability meant that this sense of victory would no longer even apply: the levels of destruction on both sides would have been so overwhelming that both would have been better off conceding—and even being conquered—than fighting an all-out war.

Although mutual second-strike capability does not rule out war, it does make it much less likely.[21] Mechanical or human accidents could have led to war[22] and escalation might have run out of control through a variety of mechanisms. But the former process was quite improbable and the latter operated in earlier eras as well. Most wars in the past may have been errors, but they were not inadvertent; rather they were chosen as the most likely way to reach national or personal goals or to avoid disaster. Mutual second-strike capability foreclosed these common paths to

---

[19] For a general discussion and extensive bibliography, see Robert Jervis, *The Meaning of the Nuclear Revolution* (Ithaca, NY: Cornell University Press, 1989).

[20] Bernard Brodie, et al., *The Absolute Weapon* (New York: Harcourt Brace, 1946), p. 76.

[21] Note, however, that this cannot explain why the US did not go to war before the Soviets acquired second-strike capability in the mid-1960s. For a provocative discussion, see George Quester, *Nuclear Monopoly* (New Brunswick, NJ: Transaction Publishers, 2000).

[22] The best account is Scott Sagan, *The Limits of Safety: Organizations, Accidents, and Nuclear Safety* (Princeton, NJ: Princeton University Press, 1993).

war and brought about major alterations in many bargaining tactics and aspects of diplomacy.[23]

Variation, change, and transitions: the current era

It is always hard to discern the magnitude of a change at the time it occurs, but I would argue that the triple and closely related developments of the end of bipolarity, the end of the Cold War, and the dissolving of the Soviet empire bring us into a new era. The obvious questions are what caused these changes and what will be the characteristics of the period we are entering. Lack of ideas even more than lack of space requires me to offer only sketchy answers.

The willingness of Gorbachev to peacefully end the Cold War with few concessions from the West is generally seen as a refutation of Realism and other theories based on material sources of power and interest.[24] It is certainly true that Gorbachev's personality and the ideas he espoused were very different from those of his predecessors and led to very different policies. But his approach was not a purely intellectual creation: it was the product of his understanding that the Soviet system was bankrupt, that it could not produce welfare at home or good relations abroad. It was clear to him that the USSR had lost the competition with the West, and this perception was grounded in reality. Although alternative courses of action were open to him, the starting point for his behaviour was the fact that the West was lengthening its lead over the USSR in all dimensions. Furthermore, the Soviet empire had become badly over-extended and its maintenance was exacting a political and economic price far greater than the return, just as we would have expected from reading Gilpin, Kennedy, and Waltz. This is certainly not the entire story, but just as certainly it is the first chapter of it.

Nuclear weapons played a role here as well. Mutual second-strike capability meant that large conventional forces and a protective glacis in Eastern Europe were not necessary to provide military security (although the latter may have been necessary for ideological security). Furthermore, nuclear weapons meant that it made no sense to follow the path of previous declining empires and strike out in a gamble that victory could reverse its fortunes and a belief that defeat would be no worse than continued decline. Nuclear weapons did not determine the end of the Cold War; indeed, as John Gaddis has argued, the fact that the USSR gained status as a nuclear superpower despite its failure on so many other dimensions may have prolonged the conflict,[25] but they contributed to ending it peacefully.

---

[23] A detailed discussion can be found in Jervis, *Meaning of the Nuclear Revolution.*

[24] See, for example, Richard Ned Lebow and Thomas Risse-Kappen (eds.), *International Relations Theory and the End of the Cold War* (New York: Columbia University Press, 1995); for good rebuttals see William Wohlforth, 'Realism and the End of the Cold War', *International Security*, 19:3 (Winter 19991/92), pp. 91–129; Randall Schweller and William Wolforth, 'Power Test: Updating Realism in Response to the End of the Cold War', *Security Studies*, 9:2 (Winter 2000), pp. 60–108; Stephen Brooks and William Wohlforth, 'Power, Globalization, and the End of the Cold War', *International Security*, 25:3 (Winter 2000/01), pp. 5–53.

[25] John Lewis Gaddis, *We Now Know: Rethinking Cold War History* (New York : Oxford University Press, 1997).

The nature of the transition and the new world we are entering remain even more difficult to discern than the causes of where we have been. Ten years after the end of War World II, the foundations for the remainder of the era had been quite firmly set. I do not think that it is only the difference in historical perspective that leads most people to see much more flux and less certainty ten years after the end of the Cold War.

One question is the degree to which there will be great variety in the units acting in future international politics. Some argue that globalization will produce uniformity. Not only the supposed dictates of efficiency, but also sociological and psychological pressures for emulation may lead actors to adopt the most common forms.[26] One reason for the triumph of the nation-state was that units of this type preferred to deal with units that resembled themselves.[27] A few countries and groups may wall themselves off from the world, as Myanmar has done, but by doing so will doom their populations to poverty and their political leaders to irrelevance beyond their own borders. For the rest of the world, high levels of interaction will produce much greater uniformity than has been true in the past. Thus while many African states do not resemble those in the West in detail, the resemblance is much greater than when they had much less contact. Corporate forms may also vary somewhat from one country to another, but national styles and methods of organizing and conducting business will be less salient. Transnational groups may play a larger role than they did previously, but for them also the need to operate in a globalized environment will reduce their diversity.

This line of argument may exaggerate the extent and potency of globalization, however.[28] States have retained enormous powers which may increase as the tasks they are asked to accomplish and the tools at their disposal grow. With this comes continued if not increased room for choice and diversity. Even in the tightly interconnected economies of Western Europe, state goals, values, and policies are not uniform and states that seek to guide their future rather than following the supposed dictates of the market do not suffer greatly.[29] In parts of the world where states are weaker, the very norms that establish them as the only legitimate form of authoritative political organization provide the freedom for those that are failures to continue in existence, thus providing for more diversity than would be the case if the competition were played by rougher rules.[30] Furthermore, evolutionary game theory shows that uniformity is unlikely. As one kind of unit or kind of strategy grows more prevalent, ecological niches often open for those who would be different.[31]

---

[26] John Meyer and Michael Hannan (eds.), *National Development and the World-System* (Chicago, IL: University of Chicago Press, 1979); Martha Finnemore, *National Interests in International Society* (Ithaca, NY: Cornell University Press, 1996).

[27] Hendrik Spryut, *The Sovereign State and Its Competitors* (Princeton, NJ: Princeton University Press, 1994).

[28] The best critic continues to be Kenneth Waltz: see, for example, his 'Globalization and Governance', *PS: Politics and Society*, 32:4 (December 1999), pp. 693–700.

[29] Geoffrey Garrett, *Partisan Politics in the Global Economy* (New York : Cambridge University Press, 1998).

[30] Robert Jackson, *Quasi-States: Sovereignty, International Relations, and the Third World* (New York: Cambridge University Press, 1990).

[31] John Maynard Smith, *Evolution and the Theory of Games* (New York: Cambridge University Press, 1982). For a discussion of variety from a very different perspective, see Hans-Henrik Holm and George Sørensen, 'International Relations Theory in a World of Variation', in Holm and Sørensen (eds.), *Whose World Order? Uneven Globalization and the End of the Cold War* (Boulder, CO: Westview Press, 1995), pp. 187–206.

Thus the spread of chain stores has indeed destroyed many local businesses, but far from all. Indeed, it has created a number of specialty markets catering to those who dislike chains, who want to differentiate themselves from those who patronize the more common stores, or whose tastes, once developed by the chains, have been transformed. In much the same way, even if globalization were to lead many units to emulate each other, this very tendency would be likely to generate strands of diversity.

Most obviously, a world in which nation-states lose economic and security functions (see below) could permit the development of all sorts of new forms, some territorial and others not. Corporations could take on more governance tasks and powers; transportation and information technologies could allow individuals dispersed throughout the globe to form self-regulating communities; regions could develop into semi-autonomous units spanning national lines; authority might become removed from territorial jurisdictions, loosely following the Medieval pattern.[32]

The final question I want to address is whether and how international politics is likely to be transformed. John Mearsheimer and others expect the end of the Cold War to herald the return of traditional multipolar politics.[33] I think this is unlikely and while much remains uncertain, believe that politics among the most developed countries of the world—the US, West Europe, and Japan—will be very different from what it was in the past. These countries form what Karl Deutsch called a security community—that is, a group of countries among whom war is literally unthinkable in the sense that neither the publics nor the political elites nor the military establishments think about fighting each other.[34] This development challenges many of our theories and raises many questions about future world politics. Security communities are not unprecedented, but what is unprecedented is for one to be formed by the leading members of the international system who are natural rivals and who in the past were central to the violent struggle for security, power, and contested values. Social Constructivists, Liberals, Realists, and Marxists have provided complementary and competing explanations for the development of the Community, and one can try to tease from them alternative expectations for the future.[35] But here what is essential is the 'mere' fact that the Community exists and is likely to continue. I do not think it is an exaggeration to say that war and the

---

[32] See, for example, Ronnie Lipschutz, *After Authority: War, Peace, and Global Politics in the 21st Century* (Albany, NY: SUNY Press, 2000); James N. Rosenau, *Turbulence in World Politics: A Theory of Change and Continuity* (Princeton, NJ: Princeton University Press, 1990); Martin Van Creveld, *The Rise and Decline of the State* (New York: Cambridge University Press, 1999); Joachim Blatter, 'Debordering the World of States: Towards a Multi-Level System in Europe and a Multi-Polity System in North America? Insights from Border Regions', *European Journal of International Relations*, 7:2 (2001), pp. 175–210.

[33] John Mearsheimer, 'Back to the Future: Instability in Europe After the Cold War', *International Security*, 15: 1 (Summer 1990), pp. 5–56; Christopher Layne, 'US Hegemony and the Perpetuation of NATO', *Journal of Strategic Studies*, 23:3 (September 2000), pp. 59–91.

[34] Karl Deutsch, et al., *Political Community and the North Atlantic Area: International Organizations in the Light of Historical Experience* (Princeton, NJ: Princeton University Press, 1957); also see Emanuel Adler and Michael Barnett (eds.), *Security Communities* (Cambridge: Cambridge University Press, 1998). A fuller account of my own thinking along these lines can be found in 'The Future of World Politics: Will it Resemble the Past?' *International Security*, 16:3 (1991/92), pp. 39–73, and 'Theories of War in an Era of Leading Power Peace,' *American Political Science Review*, 96:1 (forthcoming, March 2002).

[35] They are discussed in Jervis, 'Theories of War'.

possibility of war among the leading states has been the motor of international politics. Now that it has been turned off, much will change.

This is not to deny the possibility of war elsewhere or between one or more members of this Community and others outside it. A great deal has been written about the dangers posed by terrorism, 'rogue' states, and changes in our physical and social environment. A full treatment of the future of international politics would of course encompass them, but all I want to do here is note that even if these dangers have not been exaggerated, they do not diminish the point that the absence of the fear of war among the leading states is an enormously consequential change. Similarly, a war with Russia or China is possible but would not be a struggle for dominance of the international system the way previous Great Power wars were, but rather would grow out of Russian or Chinese desire for a traditional sphere of influence and the American belief that such arrangements are inappropriate in today's world—at least for others.

To claim that there is a security Community is not to argue that all of its members are equal. The US clearly is dominant (indeed its dominance provides one explanation for the Community's maintenance), and one central question is how it will relate to the other members of the Community. Ikenberry believes that it has institutionalized mechanisms for sharing its power.[36] If this is correct, the Community should function relatively harmoniously. But it is far from clear that the US is as constrained as this view implies. Indeed, under President Bush if not before, the US has become a rogue state in the eyes of many Community members, although they are careful not to put it quite this bluntly. Strong states are prone to act on their own, or at least to insist on getting their own way, and there is a particularly strong strand of unilateralism in American history and political culture. One can readily imagine three results if this path is followed. First, others could accept the American 'leadership', which probably would be about as benign as any hegemony can be. The difficulties of overcoming the collective action problem and the costs of becoming a competing power centre (for example, the need to increase military spending) might seem excessive. Second, the Europeans might unite and work closely with Japan and others outside the Community to contain or counteract the US. But we should not see this as typical balance of power politics, because the balance involves the potential if not actual resort to force. A third possibility is that a combination of European assertiveness and American objections to European 'free riding' would lead the US to withdraw its forces from Europe. In the absence of complete European unity, this could awaken European fears of each other, and especially of Germany—the British and French opposition to German unification could be a harbinger of things to come. I do not think that even the last two paths would lead to the destruction of the Community, however. What they would do would be to bring us to a new place in which, while conflicts of interests and rivalries would be familiar, world politics would be very different because force would no longer be the final arbiter.

---

[36] John Ikenberry, 'American Power and the Empire of Capitalist Democracy', this issue; *After Victory: Institutions, Strategic Restraint, and the Rebuilding of Order After Major Wars* (Princeton, NJ : Princeton University Press, 2001). Also see Thomas Risse-Kappen, *Cooperation Among Democracies: The European Influence on US Foreign Policy* (Princeton, NJ: Princeton University Press, 1995).

In a sense, the argument that the most developed countries form a security Community merely states the obvious. I doubt that many readers expect a war among these states in their lifetimes. But this will be an enormous change in international politics with great and not entirely foreseeable consequences. Throughout history the most powerful states have fought and prepared to fight each other. It would be as though the law of gravity had been repealed—a great many things will become unstuck. Winston Churchill exaggerated only a bit when he declared that 'people talked a lot of nonsense when they said nothing was ever settled by war. Nothing in history was ever settled *except* by wars'.[37] That this is no longer true for the leading powers in the system provides perhaps the single most striking discontinuity in the history of international politics.[38]

*   *   *

This article was completed in August and an obvious question is whether the fight against terrorism will transform the international system.

While the attacks show the power of non-state actors and the perverse effects of technology and globalization, states hardly are taking a back seat. If all reports are to be believed, Al Qaeda gained much of its power because it was able to harness the Afghan state, weak as it was. Even more strikingly, the responses affirmed state power: the US is employing military instruments to try to replace the govenment in Afghanistan; it forged coalition of states; at home everyone turned to the government and granted it increased powers, much to the displeasure of civil libertarians and conservative Republicans.

This leaves open the question of whether all or most states will now make the suppression of terrorism their prime concern. While this would leave many generalizations about world politics intact, it would create new norms, further change the practice of sovereignty, and drastically alter prevailing alignments. Despite rhetoric to the contrary, however, I believe that there is little chance that the world will unite to combat terrorism. Not only are the forms and sources of this scourge varied and some are useful tools for leaders, but states have many other competing interests. Indeed, by calling for a war against terrorism with a worldwide reach (that is, able to kill Americans), the US has indicated both that its narrow interests are primary and that it is hopeless if not undesirable to seek the end of all terror. The US asks other countries to put aside their individual goals, calls on India and Pakistan to 'stand down' to facilitate the campaign against Al Qaeda, and asks Israel and the PLO to stop shooting so that Muslim opinion will not be further inflamed. But these and other countries have concerns that are more important to them than combating terrorism. I think it unlikely that others will change their outlooks, but rather will use the new American stance to further the interests that they had before 11 September.

---

[37] Quoted in Martin Gilbert, *Winston S. Churchill*, vol. VI: *The Finest Hour 1939–1941* (London: Heinemann, 1983), pp. 860–61.

[38] I have adapted this statement from Evan Luard, *War in International Society* (London: I. B. Tauris, 1986), p. 77.

Index